Real World OCaml: Functional Programming for the Masses

This fast-moving tutorial introduces you to OCaml, an industrial-strength programming language designed for expressiveness, safety, and speed. Through the book's many examples, you'll quickly learn how OCaml stands out as a tool for writing fast, succinct, and readable systems code using functional programming.

Real World OCaml takes you through the concepts of the language at a brisk pace, and then helps you explore the tools and techniques that make OCaml an effective and practical tool. You'll also delve deep into the details of the compiler toolchain and OCaml's simple and efficient runtime system.

This second edition brings the book up to date with almost a decade of improvements in the OCaml language and ecosystem, with new chapters covering testing, GADTs, and platform tooling. All of the example code is available online at realworldocaml.org.

This title is also available as open access on Cambridge Core, thanks to the support of Tarides. Their generous contribution will bring more people to OCaml.

Anil Madhavapeddy is an associate professor in the Department of Computer Science and Technology at the University of Cambridge. He has used OCaml professionally for over two decades in numerous ventures, such as XenSource/Citrix and Unikernel Systems/Docker, and co-founded the MirageOS unikernel project. He is a member of the OCaml development team.

Yaron Minsky is Co-head of Technology at Jane Street, a major quantitative trading firm, where he introduced OCaml, and helped it become the firm's primary development platform. He is also the host of Jane Street's tech podcast, *Signals & Threads*, and has worked on everything from developer tools to trading strategies.

Real World OCaml: Functional Programming for the Masses

ANIL MADHAVAPEDDY
University of Cambridge

YARON MINSKY
Jane Street Group

CAMBRIDGE
UNIVERSITY PRESS

CAMBRIDGE
UNIVERSITY PRESS

University Printing House, Cambridge CB2 8BS, United Kingdom

One Liberty Plaza, 20th Floor, New York, NY 10006, USA

477 Williamstown Road, Port Melbourne, VIC 3207, Australia

314–321, 3rd Floor, Plot 3, Splendor Forum, Jasola District Centre,
New Delhi – 110025, India

103 Penang Road, #05–06/07, Visioncrest Commercial, Singapore 238467

Cambridge University Press is part of the University of Cambridge.

It furthers the University's mission by disseminating knowledge in the pursuit of
education, learning, and research at the highest international levels of excellence.

www.cambridge.org
Information on this title: www.cambridge.org/9781009125802
DOI: 10.1017/9781009129220

First edition published in 2014 by O'Reilly Media, Inc.
Second edition 2022

A catalogue record for this publication is available from the British Library.

ISBN 978-1-009-12580-2 Paperback

Cambridge University Press has no responsibility for the persistence or accuracy of
URLs for external or third-party internet websites referred to in this publication
and does not guarantee that any content on such websites is, or will remain,
accurate or appropriate.

For Lisa, a believer in the power of words,
who helps me find mine. –Yaron

For Mum and Dad, who took me to the library
and unlocked my imagination. –Anil

Contents

1   Prologue

1.1   Why OCaml?

Programming languages matter. They affect the reliability, security, and efficiency of the code you write, as well as how easy it is to read, refactor, and extend. The languages you know can also change how you think, influencing the way you design software even when you're not using them.

We wrote this book because we believe in the importance of programming languages, and that OCaml in particular is an important language to learn. Both of us have been using OCaml in our academic and professional lives for over 20 years, and in that time we've come to see it as a powerful tool for building complex software systems. This book aims to make this tool available to a wider audience, by providing a clear guide to what you need to know to use OCaml effectively in the real world.

What makes OCaml special is that it occupies a sweet spot in the space of programming language designs. It provides a combination of efficiency, expressiveness and practicality that is matched by no other language. That is in large part because OCaml is an elegant combination of a set of language features that have been developed over the last 60 years. These include:

- *Garbage collection* for automatic memory management, now a common feature of modern, high-level languages.
- *First-class functions* that can be passed around like ordinary values, as seen in JavaScript, Common Lisp, and C#.
- *Static type-checking* to increase performance and reduce the number of runtime errors, as found in Java and C#.
- *Parametric polymorphism*, which enables the construction of abstractions that work across different data types, similar to generics in Java, Rust, and C# and templates in C++.
- Good support for *immutable programming*, *i.e.*, programming without making destructive updates to data structures. This is present in traditional functional languages like Scheme, and is also commonly found in everything from distributed, big-data frameworks to user-interface toolkits.
- *Type inference*, so you don't need to annotate every variable in your program with its type. Instead, types are inferred based on how a value is used. Available in a

limited form in C# with implicitly typed local variables, and in C++11 with its
auto keyword.

- *Algebraic data types* and *pattern matching* to define and manipulate complex data
structures. Available in Scala, Rust, and F#.

Some of you will know and love all of these features, and for others they'll be
largely new, but most of you will have seen some of them in other languages that
you've used. As we'll demonstrate over the course of this book, there is something
transformative about having all these features together and able to interact in a single
language. Despite their importance, these ideas have made only limited inroads into
mainstream languages, and when they do arrive there, like first-class functions in C#
or parametric polymorphism in Java, it's typically in a limited and awkward form. The
only languages that completely embody these ideas are *statically typed, functional
programming languages* like OCaml, F#, Haskell, Scala, Rust, and Standard ML.

Among this worthy set of languages, OCaml stands apart because it manages to
provide a great deal of power while remaining highly pragmatic. The compiler has a
straightforward compilation strategy that produces performant code without requiring
heavy optimization and without the complexities of dynamic just-in-time (JIT) compilation. This, along with OCaml's strict evaluation model, makes runtime behavior
easy to predict. The garbage collector is *incremental*, letting you avoid large garbage
collection (GC)-related pauses, and *precise*, meaning it will collect all unreferenced
data (unlike many reference-counting collectors), and the runtime is simple and highly
portable.

All of this makes OCaml a great choice for programmers who want to step up to a
better programming language, and at the same time get practical work done.

1.1.1   A Brief History

OCaml was written in 1996 by Xavier Leroy, Jérôme Vouillon, Damien Doligez, and
Didier Rémy at INRIA in France. It was inspired by a long line of research into ML
starting in the 1960s, and continues to have deep links to the academic community.

ML was originally the *meta language* of the LCF (Logic for Computable Functions)
proof assistant released by Robin Milner in 1972 (at Stanford, and later at Cambridge).
ML was turned into a compiler in order to make it easier to use LCF on different
machines, and it was gradually turned into a full-fledged system of its own by the
1980s.

The first implementation of Caml appeared in 1987. It was created by Ascánder
Suárez (as part of the Formel project at INRIA headed by Gérard Huet) and later
continued by Pierre Weis and Michel Mauny. In 1990, Xavier Leroy and Damien
Doligez built a new implementation called Caml Light that was based on a bytecode
interpreter with a fast, sequential garbage collector. Over the next few years useful
libraries appeared, such as Michel Mauny's syntax manipulation tools, and this helped
promote the use of Caml in education and research teams.

Xavier Leroy continued extending Caml Light with new features, which resulted in the 1995 release of Caml Special Light. This improved the executable efficiency significantly by adding a fast native code compiler that made Caml's performance competitive with mainstream languages such as C++. A module system inspired by Standard ML also provided powerful facilities for abstraction and made larger-scale programs easier to construct.

The modern OCaml emerged in 1996, when a powerful and elegant object system was implemented by Didier Rémy and Jérôme Vouillon. This object system was notable for supporting many common object-oriented idioms in a statically type-safe way, whereas the same idioms required runtime checks in languages such as C++ or Java. In 2000, Jacques Garrigue extended OCaml with several new features such as polymorphic methods, variants, and labeled and optional arguments.

The last two decades has seen OCaml attract a significant user base, and language improvements have been steadily added to support the growing commercial and academic codebases. By 2012, the OCaml 4.0 release had added Generalized Algebraic Data Types (GADTs) and first-class modules to increase the flexibility of the language. Since then, OCaml has had a steady yearly release cadence, and OCaml 5.0 with multi-core support is around the corner in 2022. There is also fast native code support for the latest CPU architectures such as x86_64, ARM, RISC-V and PowerPC, making OCaml a good choice for systems where resource usage, predictability, and performance all matter.

1.1.2 The Base Standard Library

However good it is, a language on its own isn't enough. You also need a set of libraries to build your applications on. A common source of frustration for those learning OCaml is that the standard library that ships with the compiler is limited, covering only a subset of the functionality you would expect from a general-purpose standard library. That's because the standard library isn't really a general-purpose tool; its fundamental role is in bootstrapping the compiler, and has been purposefully kept small and portable.

Happily, in the world of open source software, nothing stops alternative libraries from being written to supplement the compiler-supplied standard library. Base is an example of such a library, and it's the standard library we'll use through most of this book.

Jane Street, a company that has been using OCaml for more than 20 years, developed the code in Base for its own internal use, but from the start designed it with an eye toward being a general-purpose standard library. Like the OCaml language itself, Base is engineered with correctness, reliability, and performance in mind. It's also designed to be easy to install and highly portable. As such, it works on every platform OCaml does, including UNIX, macOS, Windows, and JavaScript.

Base is distributed with a set of syntax extensions that provide useful new functionality to OCaml, and there are additional libraries that are designed to work well with it, including Core, an extension to Base that includes a wealth of new data structures and tools; and Async, a library for concurrent programming of the kind that often comes up when building user interfaces or networked applications. All of these libraries are distributed under a liberal Apache 2 license to permit free use in hobby, academic, and commercial settings.

1.1.3   The OCaml Platform

Base is a comprehensive and effective standard library, but there's much more OCaml software out there. A large community of programmers has been using OCaml since its first release in 1996, and has generated many useful libraries and tools. We'll introduce some of these libraries in the course of the examples presented in the book.

The installation and management of these third-party libraries is made much easier via a package management tool known as opam[1]. We'll explain more about opam as the book unfolds, but it forms the basis of the OCaml Platform, which is a set of tools and libraries that, along with the OCaml compiler, lets you build real-world applications quickly and effectively. Constituent tools of the OCaml Platform include the dune[2] build system and a language server to integrate with popular editors such as Visual Studio Code (or Emacs or Vim).

We'll also use opam for installing the utop command-line interface. This is a modern interactive tool that supports command history, macro expansion, module completion, and other niceties that make it much more pleasant to work with the language. We'll be using utop throughout the book to let you step through the examples interactively.

1.2   About This Book

Real World OCaml is aimed at programmers who have some experience with conventional programming languages, but not specifically with statically typed functional programming. Depending on your background, many of the concepts we cover will be new, including traditional functional-programming techniques like higher-order functions and immutable data types, as well as aspects of OCaml's powerful type and module systems.

If you already know OCaml, this book may surprise you. Base redefines most of the standard namespace to make better use of the OCaml module system and expose a number of powerful, reusable data structures by default. Older OCaml code will still interoperate with Base, but you may need to adapt it for maximal benefit. All the new code that we write uses Base, and we believe the Base model is worth learning; it's been successfully used on large, multimillion-line codebases and removes a big barrier to building sophisticated applications in OCaml.

Code that uses only the traditional compiler standard library will always exist, but there are other online resources for learning how that works. *Real World OCaml* focuses on the techniques the authors have used in their personal experience to construct scalable, robust software systems.

---

[1] https://opam.ocaml.org/
[2] https://dune.build

1.2.1   What to Expect

Real World OCaml is split into three parts:

- Part I covers the language itself, opening with a guided tour designed to provide a quick sketch of the language. Don't expect to understand everything in the tour; it's meant to give you a taste of many different aspects of the language, but the ideas covered there will be explained in more depth in the chapters that follow.

  After covering the core language, Part I then moves onto more advanced features like modules, functors, and objects, which may take some time to digest. Understanding these concepts is important, though. These ideas will put you in good stead even beyond OCaml when switching to other modern languages, many of which have drawn inspiration from ML.
- Part II builds on the basics by working through useful tools and techniques for addressing common practical applications, from command-line parsing to asynchronous network programming. Along the way, you'll see how some of the concepts from Part I are glued together into real libraries and tools that combine different features of the language to good effect.
- Part III discusses OCaml's runtime system and compiler toolchain. It is remarkably simple when compared to some other language implementations (such as Java's or .NET's CLR). Reading this part will enable you to build very-high-performance systems, or to interface with C libraries. This is also where we talk about profiling and debugging techniques using tools such as GNU gdb.

1.2.2   Installation Instructions

Real World OCaml uses some tools that we've developed while writing this book. Some of these resulted in improvements to the OCaml compiler, which means that you will need to ensure that you have an up-to-date development environment (using the 4.13.1 version of the compiler). The installation process is largely automated through the opam package manager. Instructions on how to set it up and what packages to install can be found at the installation page[3].

Some of the libraries we use, notably Base, work anywhere OCaml does, and in particular work on Windows and JavaScript. The examples in Part I of the book will for the most part stick to such highly portable libraries. Some of the libraries used, however, require a UNIX based operating system, and so only work on systems like macOS, Linux, FreeBSD, OpenBSD, and the Windows Subsystem for Linux (WSL). Core and Async are notable examples here.

This book is not intended as a reference manual. We aim to teach you about the language as well as the libraries, tools, and techniques that will help you be a more effective OCaml programmer. But it's no replacement for API documentation or the OCaml manual and man pages. You can find documentation for all of the libraries and tools referenced in the book online[4].

---

[3] http://dev.realworldocaml.org/install.html
[4] https://v3.ocaml.org/packages

1.2.3   Code Examples

All of the code examples in this book are available freely online under a public-domain-like license. You are welcome to copy and use any of the snippets as you see fit in your own code, without any attribution or other restrictions on their use.

The full text of the book, along with all of the example code is available online at https://github.com/realworldocaml/book[5].

1.3   Contributors

We would especially like to thank the following individuals for improving *Real World OCaml*:

- Jason Hickey was our co-author on the first edition of this book, and is instrumental to the structure and content that formed the basis of this revised edition.
- Leo White and Jason Hickey contributed greatly to the content and examples in Chapter 13 (Objects) and Chapter 14 (Classes).
- Jeremy Yallop authored and documented the Ctypes library described in Chapter 23 (Foreign Function Interface).
- Stephen Weeks is responsible for much of the modular architecture behind Base and Core, and his extensive notes formed the basis of Chapter 24 (Memory Representation of Values) and Chapter 25 (Understanding the Garbage Collector). Sadiq Jaffer subsequently refreshed the garbage collector chapter to reflect the latest changes in OCaml 4.13.
- Jérémie Dimino, the author of `utop`, the interactive command-line interface that is used throughout this book. We're particularly grateful for the changes that he pushed through to make `utop` work better in the context of the book.
- Thomas Gazagnaire, Thibaut Mattio, David Allsopp and Jonathan Ludlam contributed to the OCaml Platform chapter, including fixes to core tools to better aid new user installation.
- Ashish Agarwal, Christoph Troestler, Thomas Gazagnaire, Etienne Millon, Nathan Rebours, Charles-Edouard Lecat, Jules Aguillon, Rudi Grinberg, Sonja Heinze and Frederic Bour worked on improving the book's toolchain. This allowed us to update the book to track changes to OCaml and various libraries and tools. Ashish also developed a new and improved version of the book's website.
- David Tranah, Clare Dennison, Anna Scriven and Suresh Kumar from Cambridge University Press for input into the layout of the print edition. Airlie Anderson drew the cover art, and Christy Nyberg advised on the design and layout.
- The many people who collectively submitted over 4000 comments to online drafts of this book, through whose efforts countless errors were found and fixed.

---

[5] https://github.com/realworldocaml/book

Part I

Language Concepts

Part I covers the language itself, opening with a guided tour designed to provide a quick sketch of the language. Don't expect to understand everything in the tour; it's meant to give you a taste of many different aspects of the language, but the ideas covered there will be explained in more depth in the chapters that follow.

After covering the core language, Part I then moves onto more advanced features like modules, functors, and objects, which may take some time to digest. Understanding these concepts is important, though. These ideas will put you in good stead even beyond OCaml when switching to other modern languages, many of which have drawn inspiration from ML.

2   A Guided Tour

This chapter gives an overview of OCaml by walking through a series of small examples that cover most of the major features of the language. This should provide a sense of what OCaml can do, without getting too deep into any one topic.

Throughout the book we're going to use `Base`, a more full-featured and capable replacement for OCaml's standard library. We'll also use `utop`, a shell that lets you type in expressions and evaluate them interactively. `utop` is an easier-to-use version of OCaml's standard toplevel (which you can start by typing *ocaml* at the command line). These instructions will assume you're using `utop`, but the ordinary toplevel should mostly work fine.

Before going any further, make sure you've followed the steps in the installation page[1].

Base and Core

`Base` comes along with another, yet more extensive standard library replacement, called `Core`. We're going to mostly stick to `Base`, but it's worth understanding the differences between these libraries.

- *Base* is designed to be lightweight, portable, and stable, while providing all of the fundamentals you need from a standard library. It comes with a minimum of external dependencies, so `Base` just takes seconds to build and install.
- *Core* extends `Base` in a number of ways: it adds new data structures, like heaps, hash-sets, and functional queues; it provides types to represent times and time-zones; well-integrated support for efficient binary serializers; and much more. At the same time, it has many more dependencies, and so takes longer to build, and will add more to the size of your executables.

As of the version of `Base` and `Core` used in this book (version v0.14), `Core` is less portable than `Base`, running only on UNIX-like systems. For that reason, there is another package, `Core_kernel`, which is the portable subset of `Core`. That said, in the latest stable release, v0.15 (which was released too late to be adopted for this edition of the book) `Core` is portable, and `Core_kernel` has been deprecated. Given that, we don't use `Core_kernel` in this text.

---

[1] http://dev.realworldocaml.org/install.html

Before getting started, make sure you have a working OCaml installation so you can try out the examples as you read through the chapter.

2.1   OCaml as a Calculator

Our first step is to open `Base`:

```
# open Base;;
```

By opening `Base`, we make the definitions it contains available without having to reference `Base` explicitly. This is required for many of the examples in the tour and in the remainder of the book.

Now let's try a few simple numerical calculations:

```
# 3 + 4;;
- : int = 7
# 8 / 3;;
- : int = 2
# 3.5 +. 6.;;
- : float = 9.5
# 30_000_000 / 300_000;;
- : int = 100
# 3 * 5 > 14;;
- : bool = true
```

By and large, this is pretty similar to what you'd find in any programming language, but a few things jump right out at you:

- We needed to type ;; in order to tell the toplevel that it should evaluate an expression. This is a peculiarity of the toplevel that is not required in standalone programs (though it is sometimes helpful to include ;; to improve OCaml's error reporting, by making it more explicit where a given top-level declaration was intended to end).
- After evaluating an expression, the toplevel first prints the type of the result, and then prints the result itself.
- OCaml allows you to place underscores in the middle of numeric literals to improve readability. Note that underscores can be placed anywhere within a number, not just every three digits.
- OCaml carefully distinguishes between `float`, the type for floating-point numbers, and `int`, the type for integers. The types have different literals (6. instead of 6) and different infix operators (+. instead of +), and OCaml doesn't automatically cast between these types. This can be a bit of a nuisance, but it has its benefits, since it prevents some kinds of bugs that arise in other languages due to unexpected differences between the behavior of `int` and `float`. For example, in many languages, 1 / 3 is zero, but 1.0 /. 3.0 is a third. OCaml requires you to be explicit about which operation you're using.

We can also create a variable to name the value of a given expression, using the `let` keyword. This is known as a *let binding*:

```
# let x = 3 + 4;;
val x : int = 7
# let y = x + x;;
val y : int = 14
```

After a new variable is created, the toplevel tells us the name of the variable (x or y), in addition to its type (int) and value (7 or 14).

Note that there are some constraints on what identifiers can be used for variable names. Punctuation is excluded, except for _ and ', and variables must start with a lowercase letter or an underscore. Thus, these are legal:

```
# let x7 = 3 + 4;;
val x7 : int = 7
# let x_plus_y = x + y;;
val x_plus_y : int = 21
# let x' = x + 1;;
val x' : int = 8
```

The following examples, however, are not legal:

```
# let Seven = 3 + 4;;
Line 1, characters 5-10:
Error: Unbound constructor Seven
# let 7x = 7;;
Line 1, characters 5-7:
Error: Unknown modifier 'x' for literal 7x
# let x-plus-y = x + y;;
Line 1, characters 7-11:
Error: Syntax error
```

This highlights that variables can't be capitalized, can't begin with numbers, and can't contain dashes.

2.2   Functions and Type Inference

The let syntax can also be used to define a function:

```
# let square x = x * x;;
val square : int -> int = <fun>
# square 2;;
- : int = 4
# square (square 2);;
- : int = 16
```

Functions in OCaml are values like any other, which is why we use the let keyword to bind a function to a variable name, just as we use let to bind a simple value like an integer to a variable name. When using let to define a function, the first identifier after the let is the function name, and each subsequent identifier is a different argument to the function. Thus, square is a function with a single argument.

Now that we're creating more interesting values like functions, the types have gotten more interesting too. int -> int is a function type, in this case indicating a function that takes an int and returns an int. We can also write functions that take multiple arguments. (Reminder: Don't forget open Base, or these examples won't work!)

```
# let ratio x y =
    Float.of_int x /. Float.of_int y;;
val ratio : int -> int -> float = <fun>
# ratio 4 7;;
- : float = 0.571428571428571397
```

Note that in OCaml, function arguments are separated by spaces instead of by parentheses and commas, which is more like the UNIX shell than it is like traditional programming languages such as Python or Java.

The preceding example also happens to be our first use of modules. Here, `Float.of_int` refers to the `of_int` function contained in the `Float` module. This is different from what you might expect from an object-oriented language, where dot-notation is typically used for accessing a method of an object. Note that module names always start with a capital letter.

Modules can also be opened to make their contents available without explicitly qualifying by the module name. We did that once already, when we opened `Base` earlier. We can use that to make this code a little easier to read, both avoiding the repetition of `Float` above, and avoiding use of the slightly awkward `/.` operator. In the following example, we open the `Float.O` module, which has a bunch of useful operators and functions that are designed to be used in this kind of context. Note that this causes the standard int-only arithmetic operators to be shadowed locally.

```
# let ratio x y =
    let open Float.O in
    of_int x / of_int y;;
val ratio : int -> int -> float = <fun>
```

We used a slightly different syntax for opening the module, since we were only opening it in the local scope inside the definition of `ratio`. There's also a more concise syntax for local opens, as you can see here.

```
# let ratio x y =
    Float.O.(of_int x / of_int y);;
val ratio : int -> int -> float = <fun>
```

The notation for the type-signature of a multiargument function may be a little surprising at first, but we'll explain where it comes from when we get to function currying in Chapter 3.2.2 (Multiargument Functions). For the moment, think of the arrows as separating different arguments of the function, with the type after the final arrow being the return value. Thus, `int -> int -> float` describes a function that takes two int arguments and returns a `float`.

We can also write functions that take other functions as arguments. Here's an example of a function that takes three arguments: a test function and two integer arguments. The function returns the sum of the integers that pass the test:

```
# let sum_if_true test first second =
    (if test first then first else 0)
    + (if test second then second else 0);;
val sum_if_true : (int -> bool) -> int -> int -> int = <fun>
```

If we look at the inferred type signature in detail, we see that the first argument is a function that takes an integer and returns a boolean, and that the remaining two arguments are integers. Here's an example of this function in action:

```
# let even x =
    x % 2 = 0;;
val even : int -> bool = <fun>
# sum_if_true even 3 4;;
- : int = 4
# sum_if_true even 2 4;;
- : int = 6
```

Note that in the definition of even, we used = in two different ways: once as part of the let binding that separates the thing being defined from its definition; and once as an equality test, when comparing x % 2 to 0. These are very different operations despite the fact that they share some syntax.

2.2.1   Type Inference

As the types we encounter get more complicated, you might ask yourself how OCaml is able to figure them out, given that we didn't write down any explicit type information.

OCaml determines the type of an expression using a technique called *type inference*, by which the type of an expression is inferred from the available type information about the components of that expression.

As an example, let's walk through the process of inferring the type of sum_if_true:

1.. OCaml requires that both branches of an if expression have the same type, so the expression

        if test first then first else 0

   requires that first must be the same type as 0, and so first must be of type int. Similarly, from

        if test second then second else 0

   we can infer that second has type int.
2.. test is passed first as an argument. Since first has type int, the input type of test must be int.
3.. test first is used as the condition in an if expression, so the return type of test must be bool.
4.. The fact that + returns int implies that the return value of sum_if_true must be int.

Together, that nails down the types of all the variables, which determines the overall type of sum_if_true.

Over time, you'll build a rough intuition for how the OCaml inference engine works, which makes it easier to reason through your programs. You can also make it easier to understand the types of a given expression by adding explicit type annotations. These annotations don't change the behavior of an OCaml program, but they can serve as useful documentation, as well as catch unintended type changes. They can also be helpful in figuring out why a given piece of code fails to compile.

Here's an annotated version of sum_if_true:

```
# let sum_if_true (test : int -> bool) (x : int) (y : int) : int =
    (if test x then x else 0)
    + (if test y then y else 0);;
val sum_if_true : (int -> bool) -> int -> int -> int = <fun>
```

In the above, we've marked every argument to the function with its type, with the final annotation indicating the type of the return value. Such type annotations can be placed on any expression in an OCaml program.

2.2.2   Inferring Generic Types

Sometimes, there isn't enough information to fully determine the concrete type of a given value. Consider this function..

```
# let first_if_true test x y =
    if test x then x else y;;
val first_if_true : ('a -> bool) -> 'a -> 'a -> 'a = <fun>
```

first_if_true takes as its arguments a function test, and two values, x and y, where x is to be returned if test x evaluates to true, and y otherwise. So what's the type of the x argument to first_if_true? There are no obvious clues such as arithmetic operators or literals to narrow it down. That makes it seem like first_if_true would work on values of any type.

Indeed, if we look at the type returned by the toplevel, we see that rather than choose a single concrete type, OCaml has introduced a *type variable* 'a to express that the type is generic. (You can tell it's a type variable by the leading single quote mark.) In particular, the type of the test argument is ('a -> bool), which means that test is a one-argument function whose return value is bool and whose argument could be of any type 'a. But, whatever type 'a is, it has to be the same as the type of the other two arguments, x and y, and of the return value of first_if_true. This kind of genericity is called *parametric polymorphism* because it works by parameterizing the type in question with a type variable. It is very similar to generics in C# and Java.

Because the type of first_if_true is generic, we can write this:

```
# let long_string s = String.length s > 6;;
val long_string : string -> bool = <fun>
# first_if_true long_string "short" "loooooong";;
- : string = "loooooong"
```

As well as this:

```
# let big_number x = x > 3;;
val big_number : int -> bool = <fun>
# first_if_true big_number 4 3;;
- : int = 4
```

Both long_string and big_number are functions, and each is passed to first_if_true with two other arguments of the appropriate type (strings in the first example, and integers in the second). But we can't mix and match two different concrete types for 'a in the same use of first_if_true:

```
# first_if_true big_number "short" "loooooong";;
Line 1, characters 26-33:
Error: This expression has type string but an expression was expected
    of type
        int
```

In this example, `big_number` requires that `'a` be instantiated as `int`, whereas `"short"` and `"loooooong"` require that `'a` be instantiated as `string`, and they can't both be right at the same time.

Type Errors Versus Exceptions

There's a big difference in OCaml between errors that are caught at compile time and those that are caught at runtime. It's better to catch errors as early as possible in the development process, and compilation time is best of all.

Working in the toplevel somewhat obscures the difference between runtime and compile-time errors, but that difference is still there. Generally, type errors like this one:

```
# let add_potato x =
    x + "potato";;
Line 2, characters 9-17:
Error: This expression has type string but an expression was expected
    of type
        int
```

are compile-time errors (because + requires that both its arguments be of type `int`), whereas errors that can't be caught by the type system, like division by zero, lead to runtime exceptions:

```
# let is_a_multiple x y =
    x % y = 0;;
val is_a_multiple : int -> int -> bool = <fun>
# is_a_multiple 8 2;;
- : bool = true
# is_a_multiple 8 0;;
Exception:
(Invalid_argument "8 % 0 in core_int.ml: modulus should be positive")
```

The distinction here is that type errors will stop you whether or not the offending code is ever actually executed. Merely defining `add_potato` is an error, whereas `is_a_multiple` only fails when it's called, and then, only when it's called with an input that triggers the exception.

2.3   Tuples, Lists, Options, and Pattern Matching

2.3.1   Tuples

So far we've encountered a handful of basic types like `int`, `float`, and `string`, as well as function types like `string -> int`. But we haven't yet talked about any data structures. We'll start by looking at a particularly simple data structure, the tuple. A tuple is an ordered collection of values that can each be of a different type. You can create a tuple by joining values together with a comma.

```
# let a_tuple = (3,"three");;
val a_tuple : int * string = (3, "three")
# let another_tuple = (3,"four",5.);;
val another_tuple : int * string * float = (3, "four", 5.)
```

For the mathematically inclined, * is used in the type t * s because that type corresponds to the set of all pairs containing one value of type t and one of type s. In other words, it's the *Cartesian product* of the two types, which is why we use *, the symbol for product.

You can extract the components of a tuple using OCaml's pattern-matching syntax, as shown below:

```
# let (x,y) = a_tuple;;
val x : int = 3
val y : string = "three"
```

Here, the (x,y) on the left-hand side of the let binding is the pattern. This pattern lets us mint the new variables x and y, each bound to different components of the value being matched. These can now be used in subsequent expressions:

```
# x + String.length y;;
- : int = 8
```

Note that the same syntax is used both for constructing and for pattern matching on tuples.

Pattern matching can also show up in function arguments. Here's a function for computing the distance between two points on the plane, where each point is represented as a pair of floats. The pattern-matching syntax lets us get at the values we need with a minimum of fuss:

```
# let distance (x1,y1) (x2,y2) =
    Float.sqrt ((x1 -. x2) **. 2. +. (y1 -. y2) **. 2.);;
val distance : float * float -> float * float -> float = <fun>
```

The **. operator used above is for raising a floating-point number to a power.

This is just a first taste of pattern matching. Pattern matching is a pervasive tool in OCaml, and as you'll see, it has surprising power.

Operators in Base and the Stdlib

OCaml's standard library and Base mostly use the same operators for the same things, but there are some differences. For example, in Base, **. is float exponentiation, and ** is integer exponentiation, whereas in the standard library, ** is float exponentiation, and integer exponentiation isn't exposed as an operator.

Base does what it does to be consistent with other numerical operators like *. and *, where the period at the end is used to mark the floating-point versions.

In general, Base is not shy about presenting different APIs than OCaml's standard library when it's done in the service of consistency and clarity.

2.3.2   Lists

Where tuples let you combine a fixed number of items, potentially of different types, lists let you hold any number of items of the same type. Consider the following example:

```
# let languages = ["OCaml";"Perl";"C"];;
val languages : string list = ["OCaml"; "Perl"; "C"]
```

Note that you can't mix elements of different types in the same list, unlike tuples:

```
# let numbers = [3;"four";5];;
Line 1, characters 18-24:
Error: This expression has type string but an expression was expected
    of type
        int
```

The List Module

Base comes with a `List` module that has a rich collection of functions for working with lists. We can access values from within a module by using dot notation. For example, this is how we compute the length of a list:

```
# List.length languages;;
- : int = 3
```

Here's something a little more complicated. We can compute the list of the lengths of each language as follows:

```
# List.map languages ~f:String.length;;
- : int list = [5; 4; 1]
```

`List.map` takes two arguments: a list and a function for transforming the elements of that list. It returns a new list with the transformed elements and does not modify the original list.

Notably, the function passed to `List.map` is passed under a *labeled argument* ~f. Labeled arguments are specified by name rather than by position, and thus allow you to change the order in which arguments are presented to a function without changing its behavior, as you can see here:

```
# List.map ~f:String.length languages;;
- : int list = [5; 4; 1]
```

We'll learn more about labeled arguments and why they're important in Chapter 3 (Variables and Functions).

Constructing Lists with ::

In addition to constructing lists using brackets, we can use the list constructor `::` for adding elements to the front of a list:

```
# "French" :: "Spanish" :: languages;;
- : string list = ["French"; "Spanish"; "OCaml"; "Perl"; "C"]
```

Here, we're creating a new and extended list, not changing the list we started with, as you can see below:

```
# languages;;
- : string list = ["OCaml"; "Perl"; "C"]
```

Semicolons Versus Commas

Unlike many other languages, OCaml uses semicolons to separate list elements in lists rather than commas. Commas, instead, are used for separating elements in a tuple. If you try to use commas in a list, you'll see that your code compiles but doesn't do quite what you might expect:

```
# ["OCaml", "Perl", "C"];;
- : (string * string * string) list = [("OCaml", "Perl", "C")]
```

In particular, rather than a list of three strings, what we have is a singleton list containing a three-tuple of strings.

This example uncovers the fact that commas create a tuple, even if there are no surrounding parens. So, we can write:

```
# 1,2,3;;
- : int * int * int = (1, 2, 3)
```

to allocate a tuple of integers. This is generally considered poor style and should be avoided.

The bracket notation for lists is really just syntactic sugar for ::. Thus, the following declarations are all equivalent. Note that [] is used to represent the empty list and that :: is right-associative:

```
# [1; 2; 3];;
- : int list = [1; 2; 3]
# 1 :: (2 :: (3 :: []));;
- : int list = [1; 2; 3]
# 1 :: 2 :: 3 :: [];;
- : int list = [1; 2; 3]
```

The :: constructor can only be used for adding one element to the front of the list, with the list terminating at [], the empty list. There's also a list concatenation operator, @, which can concatenate two lists:

```
# [1;2;3] @ [4;5;6];;
- : int list = [1; 2; 3; 4; 5; 6]
```

It's important to remember that, unlike ::, this is not a constant-time operation. Concatenating two lists takes time proportional to the length of the first list.

List Patterns Using Match

The elements of a list can be accessed through pattern matching. List patterns are based on the two list constructors, [] and ::. Here's a simple example:

```
# let my_favorite_language (my_favorite :: the_rest) =
    my_favorite;;
Lines 1-2, characters 26-16:
Warning 8 [partial-match]: this pattern-matching is not exhaustive.
Here is an example of a case that is not matched:
[]
val my_favorite_language : 'a list -> 'a = <fun>
```

By pattern matching using `::`, we've isolated and named the first element of the list (`my_favorite`) and the remainder of the list (`the_rest`). If you know Lisp or Scheme, what we've done is the equivalent of using the functions `car` and `cdr` to isolate the first element of a list and the remainder of that list.

As you can see, however, the toplevel did not like this definition and spit out a warning indicating that the pattern is not exhaustive. This means that there are values of the type in question that won't be captured by the pattern. The warning even gives an example of a value that doesn't match the provided pattern, in particular, `[]`, the empty list. If we try to run `my_favorite_language`, we'll see that it works on nonempty lists and fails on empty ones:

```
# my_favorite_language ["English";"Spanish";"French"];;
- : string = "English"
# my_favorite_language [];;
Exception: "Match_failure //toplevel//:1:26"
```

You can avoid these warnings, and more importantly make sure that your code actually handles all of the possible cases, by using a `match` expression instead.

A `match` expression is a kind of juiced-up version of the `switch` statement found in C and Java. It essentially lets you list a sequence of patterns, separated by pipe characters. (The one before the first case is optional.) The compiler then dispatches to the code following the first matching pattern. As we've already seen, the pattern can mint new variables that correspond to parts of the value being matched.

Here's a new version of `my_favorite_language` that uses `match` and doesn't trigger a compiler warning:

```
# let my_favorite_language languages =
    match languages with
    | first :: the_rest -> first
    | [] -> "OCaml" (* A good default! *);;
val my_favorite_language : string list -> string = <fun>
# my_favorite_language ["English";"Spanish";"French"];;
- : string = "English"
# my_favorite_language [];;
- : string = "OCaml"
```

The preceding code also includes our first comment. OCaml comments are bounded by `(*` and `*)` and can be nested arbitrarily and cover multiple lines. There's no equivalent of C++-style single-line comments that are prefixed by `//`.

The first pattern, `first :: the_rest`, covers the case where `languages` has at least one element, since every list except for the empty list can be written down with one or more `::`'s. The second pattern, `[]`, matches only the empty list. These cases are exhaustive, since every list is either empty or has at least one element, a fact that is verified by the compiler.

Recursive List Functions

Recursive functions, or functions that call themselves, are an important part of working in OCaml or really any functional language. The typical approach to designing a recursive function is to separate the logic into a set of *base cases* that can be solved directly and a set of *inductive cases*, where the function breaks the problem down into smaller pieces and then calls itself to solve those smaller problems.

When writing recursive list functions, this separation between the base cases and the inductive cases is often done using pattern matching. Here's a simple example of a function that sums the elements of a list:

```
# let rec sum l =
    match l with
    | [] -> 0                        (* base case *)
    | hd :: tl -> hd + sum tl    (* inductive case *);;
val sum : int list -> int = <fun>
# sum [1;2;3];;
- : int = 6
```

Following the common OCaml idiom, we use hd to refer to the head of the list and tl to refer to the tail. Note that we had to use the rec keyword to allow sum to refer to itself. As you might imagine, the base case and inductive case are different arms of the match.

Logically, you can think of the evaluation of a simple recursive function like sum almost as if it were a mathematical equation whose meaning you were unfolding step by step:

```
sum [1;2;3]
= 1 + sum [2;3]
= 1 + (2 + sum [3])
= 1 + (2 + (3 + sum []))
= 1 + (2 + (3 + 0))
= 1 + (2 + 3)
= 1 + 5
= 6
```

This suggests a reasonable if not entirely accurate mental model for what OCaml is actually doing to evaluate a recursive function.

We can introduce more complicated list patterns as well. Here's a function for removing sequential duplicates:

```
# let rec remove_sequential_duplicates list =
    match list with
    | [] -> []
    | first :: second :: tl ->
      if first = second then
        remove_sequential_duplicates (second :: tl)
      else
        first :: remove_sequential_duplicates (second :: tl);;
Lines 2-8, characters 5-61:
Warning 8 [partial-match]: this pattern-matching is not exhaustive.
Here is an example of a case that is not matched:
_::[]
val remove_sequential_duplicates : int list -> int list = <fun>
```

Again, the first arm of the match is the base case, and the second is the inductive case. Unfortunately, this code has a problem, as indicated by the warning message. In particular, it doesn't handle one-element lists. We can fix this warning by adding another case to the match:

```
# let rec remove_sequential_duplicates list =
    match list with
    | [] -> []
    | [x] -> [x]
    | first :: second :: tl ->
      if first = second then
        remove_sequential_duplicates (second :: tl)
      else
        first :: remove_sequential_duplicates (second :: tl);;
val remove_sequential_duplicates : int list -> int list = <fun>
# remove_sequential_duplicates [1;1;2;3;3;4;4;1;1;1];;
- : int list = [1; 2; 3; 4; 1]
```

Note that this code used another variant of the list pattern, [hd], to match a list with a single element. We can do this to match a list with any fixed number of elements; for example, [x;y;z] will match any list with exactly three elements and will bind those elements to the variables x, y, and z.

In the last few examples, our list processing code involved a lot of recursive functions. In practice, this isn't usually necessary. Most of the time, you'll find yourself happy to use the iteration functions found in the List module. But it's good to know how to use recursion for when you need to iterate in a new way.

2.3.3   Options

Another common data structure in OCaml is the *option*. An option is used to express that a value might or might not be present. For example:

```
# let divide x y =
    if y = 0 then None else Some (x / y);;
val divide : int -> int -> int option = <fun>
```

The function divide either returns None if the divisor is zero, or Some of the result of the division otherwise. Some and None are constructors that let you build optional values, just as :: and [] let you build lists. You can think of an option as a specialized list that can only have zero or one elements.

To examine the contents of an option, we use pattern matching, as we did with tuples and lists. Let's see how this plays out in a small example. We'll write a function that takes a filename, and returns a version of that filename with the file extension (the part after the dot) downcased. We'll base this on the function String.rsplit2 to split the string based on the rightmost period found in the string. Note that String.rsplit2 has return type (string * string) option, returning None when no character was found to split on.

```
# let downcase_extension filename =
    match String.rsplit2 filename ~on:'.' with
    | None -> filename
    | Some (base,ext) ->
      base ^ "." ^ String.lowercase ext;;
val downcase_extension : string -> string = <fun>
# List.map ~f:downcase_extension
    [ "Hello_World.TXT"; "Hello_World.txt"; "Hello_World" ];;
```

```
- : string list = ["Hello_World.txt"; "Hello_World.txt";
    "Hello_World"]
```

Note that we used the ^ operator for concatenating strings. The concatenation operator is provided as part of the Stdlib module, which is automatically opened in every OCaml program.

Options are important because they are the standard way in OCaml to encode a value that might not be there; there's no such thing as a NullPointerException in OCaml. This is different from most other languages, including Java and C#, where most if not all data types are *nullable*, meaning that, whatever their type is, any given value also contains the possibility of being a null value. In such languages, null is lurking everywhere.

In OCaml, however, missing values are explicit. A value of type string * string always contains two well-defined values of type string. If you want to allow, say, the first of those to be absent, then you need to change the type to string option * string. As we'll see in Chapter 8 (Error Handling), this explicitness allows the compiler to provide a great deal of help in making sure you're correctly handling the possibility of missing data.

2.4   Records and Variants

So far, we've only looked at data structures that were predefined in the language, like lists and tuples. But OCaml also allows us to define new data types. Here's a toy example of a data type representing a point in two-dimensional space:

```
type point2d = { x : float; y : float }
```

point2d is a *record* type, which you can think of as a tuple where the individual fields are named, rather than being defined positionally. Record types are easy enough to construct:

```
# let p = { x = 3.; y = -4. };;
val p : point2d = {x = 3.; y = -4.}
```

And we can get access to the contents of these types using pattern matching:

```
# let magnitude { x = x_pos; y = y_pos } =
    Float.sqrt (x_pos **. 2. +. y_pos **. 2.);;
val magnitude : point2d -> float = <fun>
```

The pattern match here binds the variable x_pos to the value contained in the x field, and the variable y_pos to the value in the y field.

We can write this more tersely using what's called *field punning*. In particular, when the name of the field and the name of the variable it is bound to coincide, we don't have to write them both down. Using this, our magnitude function can be rewritten as follows:

```
# let magnitude { x; y } = Float.sqrt (x **. 2. +. y **. 2.);;
val magnitude : point2d -> float = <fun>
```

Alternatively, we can use dot notation for accessing record fields:

```
# let distance v1 v2 =
    magnitude { x = v1.x -. v2.x; y = v1.y -. v2.y };;
val distance : point2d -> point2d -> float = <fun>
```

And we can of course include our newly defined types as components in larger types. Here, for example, are some types for modeling different geometric objects that contain values of type point2d:

```
type circle_desc  = { center: point2d; radius: float }
type rect_desc    = { lower_left: point2d; width: float; height:
    float }
type segment_desc = { endpoint1: point2d; endpoint2: point2d }
```

Now, imagine that you want to combine multiple objects of these types together as a description of a multi-object scene. You need some unified way of representing these objects together in a single type. *Variant* types let you do just that:

```
type scene_element =
  | Circle  of circle_desc
  | Rect    of rect_desc
  | Segment of segment_desc
```

The | character separates the different cases of the variant (the first | is optional), and each case has a capitalized tag, like Circle, Rect or Segment, to distinguish that case from the others.

Here's how we might write a function for testing whether a point is in the interior of some element of a list of scene_elements. Note that there are two let bindings in a row without a double semicolon between them. That's because the double semicolon is required only to tell *utop* to process the input, not to separate two declarations

```
# let is_inside_scene_element point scene_element =
    let open Float.O in
    match scene_element with
    | Circle { center; radius } ->
      distance center point < radius
    | Rect { lower_left; width; height } ->
      point.x   > lower_left.x && point.x < lower_left.x + width
      && point.y > lower_left.y && point.y < lower_left.y + height
    | Segment _ -> false

  let is_inside_scene point scene =
    List.exists scene
      ~f:(fun el -> is_inside_scene_element point el);;
val is_inside_scene_element : point2d -> scene_element -> bool = <fun>
val is_inside_scene : point2d -> scene_element list -> bool = <fun>
# is_inside_scene {x=3.;y=7.}
  [ Circle {center = {x=4.;y= 4.}; radius = 0.5 } ];;
- : bool = false
# is_inside_scene {x=3.;y=7.}
  [ Circle {center = {x=4.;y= 4.}; radius = 5.0 } ];;
- : bool = true
```

You might at this point notice that the use of match here is reminiscent of how we used match with option and list. This is no accident: option and list are just examples of variant types that are important enough to be defined in the standard library (and in the case of lists, to have some special syntax).

We also made our first use of an *anonymous function* in the call to `List.exists`. Anonymous functions are declared using the `fun` keyword, and don't need to be explicitly named. Such functions are common in OCaml, particularly when using iteration functions like `List.exists`.

The purpose of `List.exists` is to check if there are any elements of the list in question for which the provided function evaluates to `true`. In this case, we're using `List.exists` to check if there is a scene element within which our point resides.

Base and Polymorphic Comparison

One other thing to notice was the fact that we opened `Float.O` in the definition of `is_inside_scene_element`. That allowed us to use the simple, un-dotted infix operators, but more importantly it brought the float comparison operators into scope. When using `Base`, the default comparison operators work only on integers, and you need to explicitly choose other comparison operators when you want them. OCaml also offers a special set of *polymorphic comparison operators* that can work on almost any type, but those are considered to be problematic, and so are hidden by default by `Base`. We'll learn more about polymorphic compare in Chapter 4.6 (Terser and Faster Patterns).

2.5   Imperative Programming

The code we've written so far has been almost entirely *pure* or *functional*, which roughly speaking means that the code in question doesn't modify variables or values as part of its execution. Indeed, almost all of the data structures we've encountered are *immutable*, meaning there's no way in the language to modify them at all. This is a quite different style from *imperative* programming, where computations are structured as sequences of instructions that operate by making modifications to the state of the program.

Functional code is the default in OCaml, with variable bindings and most data structures being immutable. But OCaml also has excellent support for imperative programming, including mutable data structures like arrays and hash tables, and control-flow constructs like `for` and `while` loops.

2.5.1   Arrays

Perhaps the simplest mutable data structure in OCaml is the array. Arrays in OCaml are very similar to arrays in other languages like C: indexing starts at 0, and accessing or modifying an array element is a constant-time operation. Arrays are more compact in terms of memory utilization than most other data structures in OCaml, including lists. Here's an example:

```
# let numbers = [| 1; 2; 3; 4 |];;
val numbers : int array = [|1; 2; 3; 4|]
# numbers.(2) <- 4;;
- : unit = ()
# numbers;;
- : int array = [|1; 2; 4; 4|]
```

The .(i) syntax is used to refer to an element of an array, and the <- syntax is for modification. Because the elements of the array are counted starting at zero, element numbers.(2) is the third element.

The unit type that we see in the preceding code is interesting in that it has only one possible value, written (). This means that a value of type unit doesn't convey any information, and so is generally used as a placeholder. Thus, we use unit for the return value of an operation like setting a mutable field that communicates by side effect rather than by returning a value. It's also used as the argument to functions that don't require an input value. This is similar to the role that void plays in languages like C and Java.

2.5.2 Mutable Record Fields

The array is an important mutable data structure, but it's not the only one. Records, which are immutable by default, can have some of their fields explicitly declared as mutable. Here's an example of a mutable data structure for storing a running statistical summary of a collection of numbers.

```
type running_sum =
  { mutable sum: float;
    mutable sum_sq: float; (* sum of squares *)
    mutable samples: int;
  }
```

The fields in running_sum are designed to be easy to extend incrementally, and sufficient to compute means and standard deviations, as shown in the following example.

```
# let mean rsum = rsum.sum /. Float.of_int rsum.samples;;
val mean : running_sum -> float = <fun>
# let stdev rsum =
    Float.sqrt
       (rsum.sum_sq /. Float.of_int rsum.samples -. mean rsum **. 2.);;
val stdev : running_sum -> float = <fun>
```

We also need functions to create and update running_sums:

```
# let create () = { sum = 0.; sum_sq = 0.; samples = 0 };;
val create : unit -> running_sum = <fun>
# let update rsum x =
    rsum.samples <- rsum.samples + 1;
    rsum.sum     <- rsum.sum     +. x;
    rsum.sum_sq  <- rsum.sum_sq  +. x *. x;;
val update : running_sum -> float -> unit = <fun>
```

create returns a running_sum corresponding to the empty set, and update rsum x changes rsum to reflect the addition of x to its set of samples by updating the number of samples, the sum, and the sum of squares.

Note the use of single semicolons to sequence operations. When we were working purely functionally, this wasn't necessary, but you start needing it when you're writing imperative code.

Here's an example of create and update in action. Note that this code uses List.iter, which calls the function ~f on each element of the provided list:

```
# let rsum = create ();;
val rsum : running_sum = {sum = 0.; sum_sq = 0.; samples = 0}
# List.iter [1.;3.;2.;-7.;4.;5.] ~f:(fun x -> update rsum x);;
- : unit = ()
# mean rsum;;
- : float = 1.33333333333333326
# stdev rsum;;
- : float = 3.94405318873307698
```

Warning: the preceding algorithm is numerically naive and has poor precision in the presence of many values that cancel each other out. This Wikipedia article on algorithms for calculating variance[2] provides more details.

2.5.3 Refs

We can create a single mutable value by using a ref. The ref type comes predefined in the standard library, but there's nothing really special about it. It's just a record type with a single mutable field called contents:

```
# let x = { contents = 0 };;
val x : int ref = {contents = 0}
# x.contents <- x.contents + 1;;
- : unit = ()
# x;;
- : int ref = {contents = 1}
```

There are a handful of useful functions and operators defined for refs to make them more convenient to work with:

```
# let x = ref 0   (* create a ref, i.e., { contents = 0 } *);;
val x : int ref = {Base.Ref.contents = 0}
# !x              (* get the contents of a ref, i.e., x.contents *);;
- : int = 0
# x := !x + 1     (* assignment, i.e., x.contents <- ... *);;
- : unit = ()
# !x;;
- : int = 1
```

There's nothing magical with these operators either. You can completely reimplement the ref type and all of these operators in just a few lines of code:

```
# type 'a ref = { mutable contents : 'a };;
type 'a ref = { mutable contents : 'a; }
# let ref x = { contents = x };;
```

---

[2] http://en.wikipedia.org/wiki/Algorithms_for_calculating_variance

```
val ref : 'a -> 'a ref = <fun>
# let (!) r = r.contents;;
val ( ! ) : 'a ref -> 'a = <fun>
# let (:=) r x = r.contents <- x;;
val ( := ) : 'a ref -> 'a -> unit = <fun>
```

The 'a before the ref indicates that the ref type is polymorphic, in the same way that lists are polymorphic, meaning it can contain values of any type. The parentheses around ! and := are needed because these are operators, rather than ordinary functions.

Even though a ref is just another record type, it's important because it is the standard way of simulating the traditional mutable variables you'll find in most languages. For example, we can sum over the elements of a list imperatively by calling List.iter to call a simple function on every element of a list, using a ref to accumulate the results:

```
# let sum list =
    let sum = ref 0 in
    List.iter list ~f:(fun x -> sum := !sum + x);
    !sum;;
val sum : int list -> int = <fun>
```

This isn't the most idiomatic way to sum up a list, but it shows how you can use a ref in place of a mutable variable.

Nesting lets with `let` and `in`

The definition of sum in the above examples was our first use of let to define a new variable within the body of a function. A let paired with an in can be used to introduce a new binding within any local scope, including a function body. The in marks the beginning of the scope within which the new variable can be used. Thus, we could write:

```
# let z = 7 in
  z + z;;
- : int = 14
```

Note that the scope of the let binding is terminated by the double-semicolon, so the value of z is no longer available:

```
# z;;
Line 1, characters 1-2:
Error: Unbound value z
```

We can also have multiple let bindings in a row, each one adding a new variable binding to what came before:

```
# let x = 7 in
  let y = x * x in
  x + y;;
- : int = 56
```

This kind of nested let binding is a common way of building up a complex expression, with each let naming some component, before combining them in one final expression.

2.5.4   For and While Loops

OCaml also supports traditional imperative control-flow constructs like `for` and `while` loops. Here, for example, is some code for permuting an array that uses a `for` loop:

```
# let permute array =
    let length = Array.length array in
    for i = 0 to length - 2 do
      (* pick a j to swap with *)
      let j = i + Random.int (length - i) in
      (* Swap i and j *)
      let tmp = array.(i) in
      array.(i) <- array.(j);
      array.(j) <- tmp
    done;;
val permute : 'a array -> unit = <fun>
```

This is our first use of the `Random` module. Note that `Random` starts with a fixed seed, but you can call `Random.self_init` to choose a new seed at random.

From a syntactic perspective, you should note the keywords that distinguish a `for` loop: for, to, do, and done.

Here's an example run of this code:

```
# let ar = Array.init 20 ~f:(fun i -> i);;
val ar : int array =
  [|0; 1; 2; 3; 4; 5; 6; 7; 8; 9; 10; 11; 12; 13; 14; 15; 16; 17; 18;
    19|]
# permute ar;;
- : unit = ()
# ar;;
- : int array =
[|12; 16; 5; 13; 1; 6; 0; 7; 15; 19; 14; 4; 2; 11; 3; 8; 17; 9; 10;
  18|]
```

OCaml also supports `while` loops, as shown in the following function for finding the position of the first negative entry in an array. Note that `while` (like `for`) is also a keyword:

```
# let find_first_negative_entry array =
    let pos = ref 0 in
    while !pos < Array.length array && array.(!pos) >= 0 do
      pos := !pos + 1
    done;
    if !pos = Array.length array then None else Some !pos;;
val find_first_negative_entry : int array -> int option = <fun>
# find_first_negative_entry [|1;2;0;3|];;
- : int option = None
# find_first_negative_entry [|1;-2;0;3|];;
- : int option = Some 1
```

As a side note, the preceding code takes advantage of the fact that &&, OCaml's "and" operator, short-circuits. In particular, in an expression of the form *expr1&&expr2*, *expr2* will only be evaluated if *expr1* evaluated to true. Were it not for that, then the preceding function would result in an out-of-bounds error. Indeed, we can trigger that out-of-bounds error by rewriting the function to avoid the short-circuiting:

```
# let find_first_negative_entry array =
    let pos = ref 0 in
    while
      let pos_is_good = !pos < Array.length array in
      let element_is_non_negative = array.(!pos) >= 0 in
      pos_is_good && element_is_non_negative
    do
      pos := !pos + 1
    done;
    if !pos = Array.length array then None else Some !pos;;
val find_first_negative_entry : int array -> int option = <fun>
# find_first_negative_entry [|1;2;0;3|];;
Exception: (Invalid_argument "index out of bounds")
```

The or operator, ||, short-circuits in a similar way to &&.

2.6   A Complete Program

So far, we've played with the basic features of the language via utop. Now we'll show
how to create a simple standalone program. In particular, we'll create a program that
sums up a list of numbers read in from the standard input.

Here's the code, which you can save in a file called sum.ml. Note that we don't
terminate expressions with ;; here, since it's not required outside the toplevel.

```
open Base
open Stdio

let rec read_and_accumulate accum =
  let line = In_channel.input_line In_channel.stdin in
  match line with
  | None -> accum
  | Some x -> read_and_accumulate (accum +. Float.of_string x)

let () =
  printf "Total: %F\n" (read_and_accumulate 0.)
```

This is our first use of OCaml's input and output routines, and we needed to open
another library, Stdio, to get access to them. The function read_and_accumulate is a
recursive function that uses In_channel.input_line to read in lines one by one from
the standard input, invoking itself at each iteration with its updated accumulated sum.
Note that input_line returns an optional value, with None indicating the end of the
input stream.

After read_and_accumulate returns, the total needs to be printed. This is done
using the printf command, which provides support for type-safe format strings. The
format string is parsed by the compiler and used to determine the number and type
of the remaining arguments that are required. In this case, there is a single formatting
directive, %F, so printf expects one additional argument of type float.

2.6.1   Compiling and Running

We'll compile our program using dune, a build system that's designed for use with OCaml projects. First, we need to write a dune-project file to specify the project's root directory.

```
(lang dune 2.9)
(name rwo-example)
```

Then, we need to write a dune file to specify the specific thing being built. Note that a single project will have just one dune-project file, but potentially many sub-directories with different dune files.

In this case, however, we just have one:

```
(executable
 (name      sum)
 (libraries base stdio))
```

All we need to specify is the fact that we're building an executable (rather than a library), the name of the executable, and the name of the libraries we depend on.

We can now invoke dune to build the executable.

```
$ dune build sum.exe
```

The .exe suffix indicates that we're building a native-code executable, which we'll discuss more in Chapter 5 (Files, Modules, and Programs). Once the build completes, we can use the resulting program like any command-line utility. We can feed input to sum.exe by typing in a sequence of numbers, one per line, hitting **Ctrl-D** when we're done:

```
$ ./_build/default/sum.exe
1
2
3
94.5
Total: 100.5
```

More work is needed to make a really usable command-line program, including a proper command-line parsing interface and better error handling, all of which is covered in Chapter 16 (Command-Line Parsing).

2.7   Where to Go from Here

That's it for the guided tour! There are plenty of features left and lots of details to explain, but we hope that you now have a sense of what to expect from OCaml, and that you'll be more comfortable reading the rest of the book as a result.

3 Variables and Functions

Variables and functions are fundamental ideas that show up in virtually all programming languages. OCaml has a different take on these concepts than most languages you're likely to have encountered, so this chapter will cover OCaml's approach to variables and functions in some detail, starting with the basics of how to define a variable, and ending with the intricacies of functions with labeled and optional arguments.

Don't be discouraged if you find yourself overwhelmed by some of the details, especially toward the end of the chapter. The concepts here are important, but if they don't connect for you on your first read, you should return to this chapter after you've gotten a better sense of the rest of the language.

3.1   Variables

At its simplest, a variable is an identifier whose meaning is bound to a particular value. In OCaml these bindings are often introduced using the `let` keyword. We can type a so-called *top-level* `let` binding with the following syntax. Note that variable names must start with a lowercase letter or an underscore.

```
let <variable> = <expr>
```

As we'll see when we get to the module system in Chapter 5 (Files, Modules, and Programs), this same syntax is used for `let` bindings at the top level of a module.

Every variable binding has a *scope*, which is the portion of the code that can refer to that binding. When using utop, the scope of a top-level `let` binding is everything that follows it in the session. When it shows up in a module, the scope is the remainder of that module.

Here's a simple example.

```
# open Base;;
# let x = 3;;
val x : int = 3
# let y = 4;;
val y : int = 4
# let z = x + y;;
val z : int = 7
```

`let` can also be used to create a variable binding whose scope is limited to a particular expression, using the following syntax.

```
let <variable> = <expr1> in <expr2>
```

This first evaluates *expr1* and then evaluates *expr2* with `variable` bound to whatever value was produced by the evaluation of *expr1*. Here's how it looks in practice.

```
# let languages = "OCaml,Perl,C++,C";;
val languages : string = "OCaml,Perl,C++,C"
# let dashed_languages =
    let language_list = String.split languages ~on:',' in
    String.concat ~sep:"-" language_list;;
val dashed_languages : string = "OCaml-Perl-C++-C"
```

Note that the scope of `language_list` is just the expression `String.concat ~sep:"-" language_list` and is not available at the toplevel, as we can see if we try to access it now. [let bindings/local]

```
# language_list;;
Line 1, characters 1-14:
Error: Unbound value language_list
```

A `let` binding in an inner scope can *shadow*, or hide, the definition from an outer scope. So, for example, we could have written the `dashed_languages` example as follows.

```
# let languages = "OCaml,Perl,C++,C";;
val languages : string = "OCaml,Perl,C++,C"
# let dashed_languages =
    let languages = String.split languages ~on:',' in
    String.concat ~sep:"-" languages;;
val dashed_languages : string = "OCaml-Perl-C++-C"
```

This time, in the inner scope we called the list of strings `languages` instead of `language_list`, thus hiding the original definition of `languages`. But once the definition of `dashed_languages` is complete, the inner scope has closed and the original definition of languages is still available.

```
# languages;;
- : string = "OCaml,Perl,C++,C"
```

One common idiom is to use a series of nested `let`/`in` expressions to build up the components of a larger computation. Thus, we might write.

```
# let area_of_ring inner_radius outer_radius =
    let pi = Float.pi in
    let area_of_circle r = pi *. r *. r in
    area_of_circle outer_radius -. area_of_circle inner_radius;;
val area_of_ring : float -> float -> float = <fun>
# area_of_ring 1. 3.;;
- : float = 25.132741228718345
```

It's important not to confuse a sequence of `let` bindings with the modification of a mutable variable. For example, consider how `area_of_ring` would work if we had instead written this purposefully confusing bit of code:

```
# let area_of_ring inner_radius outer_radius =
    let pi = Float.pi in
    let area_of_circle r = pi *. r *. r in
```

```
    let pi = 0. in
    area_of_circle outer_radius -. area_of_circle inner_radius;;
Line 4, characters 9-11:
Warning 26 [unused-var]: unused variable pi.
val area_of_ring : float -> float -> float = <fun>
```

Here, we redefined `pi` to be zero after the definition of `area_of_circle`. You might think that this would mean that the result of the computation would now be zero, but in fact, the behavior of the function is unchanged. That's because the original definition of `pi` wasn't changed; it was just shadowed, which means that any subsequent reference to `pi` would see the new definition of `pi` as `0`, but earlier references would still see the old one. But there is no later use of `pi`, so the binding of `pi` to `0.` made no difference at all. This explains the warning produced by the toplevel telling us that there is an unused variable.

In OCaml, `let` bindings are immutable. There are many kinds of mutable values in OCaml, which we'll discuss in Chapter 9 (Imperative Programming), but there are no mutable variables.

Why Don't Variables Vary?

One source of confusion for people new to OCaml is the fact that variables are immutable. This seems pretty surprising even on linguistic terms. Isn't the whole point of a variable that it can vary?

The answer to this is that variables in OCaml (and generally in functional languages) are really more like variables in an equation than a variable in an imperative language. If you think about the mathematical identity $x(y + z) = xy + xz$, there's no notion of mutating the variables x, y, and z. They vary in the sense that you can instantiate this equation with different numbers for those variables, and it still holds.

The same is true in a functional language. A function can be applied to different inputs, and thus its variables will take on different values, even without mutation.

3.1.1   Pattern Matching and Let

Another useful feature of `let` bindings is that they support the use of *patterns* on the left-hand side. Consider the following code, which uses `List.unzip`, a function for converting a list of pairs into a pair of lists.

```
# let (ints,strings) = List.unzip [(1,"one"); (2,"two");
    (3,"three")];;
val ints : int list = [1; 2; 3]
val strings : string list = ["one"; "two"; "three"]
```

Here, `(ints,strings)` is a pattern, and the `let` binding assigns values to both of the identifiers that show up in that pattern. A pattern is essentially a description of the shape of a data structure, where some components are names to be bound to values. As we saw in Chapter 2.3 (Tuples, Lists, Options, and Pattern Matching), OCaml has patterns for a variety of different data types.

Using a pattern in a `let` binding makes the most sense for a pattern that is *irrefutable*, *i.e.*, where any value of the type in question is guaranteed to match the pattern. Tuple and record patterns are irrefutable, but list patterns are not. Consider the following code that implements a function for upper casing the first element of a comma-separated list.

```
# let upcase_first_entry line =
    let (first :: rest) = String.split ~on:',' line in
    String.concat ~sep:"," (String.uppercase first :: rest);;
Lines 2-3, characters 5-60:
Warning 8 [partial-match]: this pattern-matching is not exhaustive.
Here is an example of a case that is not matched:
[]
val upcase_first_entry : string -> string = <fun>
```

This case can't really come up in practice, because `String.split` always returns a list with at least one element, even when given the empty string.

```
# upcase_first_entry "one,two,three";;
- : string = "ONE,two,three"
# upcase_first_entry "";;
- : string = ""
```

But the compiler doesn't know this, and so it emits the warning. It's generally better to use a `match` expression to handle such cases explicitly:

```
# let upcase_first_entry line =
    match String.split ~on:',' line with
    | [] -> assert false (* String.split returns at least one element
      *)
    | first :: rest -> String.concat ~sep:"," (String.uppercase first
      :: rest);;
val upcase_first_entry : string -> string = <fun>
```

Note that this is our first use of `assert`, which is useful for marking cases that should be impossible. We'll discuss `assert` in more detail in Chapter 8 (Error Handling).

3.2   Functions

Given that OCaml is a functional language, it's no surprise that functions are important and pervasive. Indeed, functions have come up in almost every example we've looked at so far. This section will go into more depth, explaining the details of how OCaml's functions work. As you'll see, functions in OCaml differ in a variety of ways from what you'll find in most mainstream languages.

3.2.1   Anonymous Functions

We'll start by looking at the most basic style of function declaration in OCaml: the *anonymous function*. An anonymous function is a function that is declared without being named. These can be declared using the `fun` keyword, as shown here.

```
# (fun x -> x + 1);;
- : int -> int = <fun>
```

Anonymous functions operate in much the same way as named functions. For example, we can apply an anonymous function to an argument:

```
# (fun x -> x + 1) 7;;
- : int = 8
```

or pass it to another function. Passing functions to iteration functions like List.map is probably the most common use case for anonymous functions.

```
# List.map ~f:(fun x -> x + 1) [1;2;3];;
- : int list = [2; 3; 4]
```

You can even stuff a function into a data structure, like a list:

```
# let transforms = [ String.uppercase; String.lowercase ];;
val transforms : (string -> string) list = [<fun>; <fun>]
# List.map ~f:(fun g -> g "Hello World") transforms;;
- : string list = ["HELLO WORLD"; "hello world"]
```

It's worth stopping for a moment to puzzle this example out. Notice that (fun g -> g "Hello World") is a function that takes a function as an argument, and then applies that function to the string "Hello World". The invocation of List.map applies (fun g -> g "Hello World") to the elements of transforms, which are themselves functions. The returned list contains the results of these function applications.

The key thing to understand is that functions are ordinary values in OCaml, and you can do everything with them that you'd do with an ordinary value, including passing them to and returning them from other functions and storing them in data structures. We even name functions in the same way that we name other values, by using a let binding.

```
# let plusone = (fun x -> x + 1);;
val plusone : int -> int = <fun>
# plusone 3;;
- : int = 4
```

Defining named functions is so common that there is some syntactic sugar for it. Thus, the following definition of plusone is equivalent to the previous definition.

```
# let plusone x = x + 1;;
val plusone : int -> int = <fun>
```

This is the most common and convenient way to declare a function, but syntactic niceties aside, the two styles of function definition are equivalent.

let and fun

Functions and let bindings have a lot to do with each other. In some sense, you can think of the parameter of a function as a variable being bound to the value passed by the caller. Indeed, the following two expressions are nearly equivalent.

```
# (fun x -> x + 1) 7;;
- : int = 8
# let x = 7 in x + 1;;
- : int = 8
```

This connection is important, and will come up more when programming in a monadic style, as we'll see in Chapter 17 (Concurrent Programming with Async).

3.2.2   Multiargument Functions

OCaml of course also supports multiargument functions, such as:

```
# let abs_diff x y = abs (x - y);;
val abs_diff : int -> int -> int = <fun>
# abs_diff 3 4;;
- : int = 1
```

You may find the type signature of `abs_diff` with all of its arrows a little hard to parse. To understand what's going on, let's rewrite `abs_diff` in an equivalent form, using the `fun` keyword.

```
# let abs_diff =
    (fun x -> (fun y -> abs (x - y)));;
val abs_diff : int -> int -> int = <fun>
```

This rewrite makes it explicit that `abs_diff` is actually a function of one argument that returns another function of one argument, which itself returns the final result. Because the functions are nested, the inner expression `abs (x - y)` has access to both `x`, which was bound by the outer function application, and `y`, which was bound by the inner one.

This style of function is called a *curried* function. (Currying is named after Haskell Curry, a logician who had a significant impact on the design and theory of programming languages.) The key to interpreting the type signature of a curried function is the observation that `->` is right-associative. The type signature of `abs_diff` can therefore be parenthesized as follows.

```
val abs_diff : int -> (int -> int)
```

The parentheses don't change the meaning of the signature, but they make it easier to see the currying.

Currying is more than just a theoretical curiosity. You can make use of currying to specialize a function by feeding in some of the arguments. Here's an example where we create a specialized version of `abs_diff` that measures the distance of a given number from 3.

```
# let dist_from_3 = abs_diff 3;;
val dist_from_3 : int -> int = <fun>
# dist_from_3 8;;
- : int = 5
# dist_from_3 (-1);;
- : int = 4
```

The practice of applying some of the arguments of a curried function to get a new function is called *partial application*.

Note that the `fun` keyword supports its own syntax for currying, so the following definition of `abs_diff` is equivalent to the previous one.

```
# let abs_diff = (fun x y -> abs (x - y));;
val abs_diff : int -> int -> int = <fun>
```

You might worry that curried functions are terribly expensive, but this is not the case. In OCaml, there is no penalty for calling a curried function with all of its arguments. (Partial application, unsurprisingly, does have a small extra cost.)

Currying is not the only way of writing a multiargument function in OCaml. It's also possible to use the different parts of a tuple as different arguments. So, we could write.

```
# let abs_diff (x,y) = abs (x - y);;
val abs_diff : int * int -> int = <fun>
# abs_diff (3,4);;
- : int = 1
```

OCaml handles this calling convention efficiently as well. In particular it does not generally have to allocate a tuple just for the purpose of sending arguments to a tuple-style function. You can't, however, use partial application for this style of function.

There are small trade-offs between these two approaches, but most of the time, one should stick to currying, since it's the default style in the OCaml world.

3.2.3   Recursive Functions

A function is *recursive* if it refers to itself in its definition. Recursion is important in any programming language, but is particularly important in functional languages, because it is the way that you build looping constructs. (As will be discussed in more detail in Chapter 9 (Imperative Programming), OCaml also supports imperative looping constructs like for and while, but these are only useful when using OCaml's imperative features.)

In order to define a recursive function, you need to mark the let binding as recursive with the rec keyword, as shown in this function for finding the first sequentially repeated element in a list.

```
# let rec find_first_repeat list =
    match list with
    | [] | [_] ->
      (* only zero or one elements, so no repeats *)
      None
    | x :: y :: tl ->
      if x = y then Some x else find_first_repeat (y::tl);;
val find_first_repeat : int list -> int option = <fun>
```

The pattern [] | [_] is itself a disjunction of multiple patterns, otherwise known as an *or-pattern*. An or-pattern matches if any of the sub-patterns match. In this case, [] matches the empty list, and [_] matches any single element list. The _ is there so we don't have to put an explicit name on that single element.

We can also define multiple mutually recursive values by using let rec combined with the and keyword. Here's a (gratuitously inefficient) example.

```
# let rec is_even x =
```

```
      if x = 0 then true else is_odd (x - 1)
    and is_odd x =
      if x = 0 then false else is_even (x - 1);;
val is_even : int -> bool = <fun>
val is_odd : int -> bool = <fun>
# List.map ~f:is_even [0;1;2;3;4;5];;
- : bool list = [true; false; true; false; true; false]
# List.map ~f:is_odd [0;1;2;3;4;5];;
- : bool list = [false; true; false; true; false; true]
```

OCaml distinguishes between nonrecursive definitions (using `let`) and recursive definitions (using `let rec`) largely for technical reasons: the type-inference algorithm needs to know when a set of function definitions are mutually recursive, and these have to be marked explicitly by the programmer.

But this decision has some good effects. For one thing, recursive (and especially mutually recursive) definitions are harder to reason about than nonrecursive ones. It's therefore useful that, in the absence of an explicit `rec`, you can assume that a `let` binding is nonrecursive, and so can only build upon previous definitions.

In addition, having a nonrecursive form makes it easier to create a new definition that extends and supersedes an existing one by shadowing it.

3.2.4   Prefix and Infix Operators

So far, we've seen examples of functions used in both prefix and infix style.

```
# Int.max 3 4    (* prefix *);;
- : int = 4
# 3 + 4          (* infix  *);;
- : int = 7
```

You might not have thought of the second example as an ordinary function, but it very much is. Infix operators like + really only differ syntactically from other functions. In fact, if we put parentheses around an infix operator, you can use it as an ordinary prefix function.

```
# (+) 3 4;;
- : int = 7
# List.map ~f:((+) 3) [4;5;6];;
- : int list = [7; 8; 9]
```

In the second expression, we've partially applied (+) to create a function that increments its single argument by 3.

A function is treated syntactically as an operator if the name of that function is chosen from one of a specialized set of identifiers. This set includes identifiers that are sequences of characters from the following set:

```
~ ! $ % & * + - . / : < = > ? @ ^ |
```

as long as the first character is not ~, !, or $.

There are also a handful of predetermined strings that count as infix operators, including `mod`, the modulus operator, and `lsl`, for "logical shift left," a bit-shifting operation.

We can define (or redefine) the meaning of an operator. Here's an example of a simple vector-addition operator on `int` pairs.

```
# let (+!) (x1,y1) (x2,y2) = (x1 + x2, y1 + y2);;
val ( +! ) : int * int -> int * int -> int * int = <fun>
# (3,2) +! (-2,4);;
- : int * int = (1, 6)
```

You have to be careful when dealing with operators containing *. Consider the following example.

```
# let (***) x y = (x **. y) **. y;;
Line 1, characters 18-19:
Error: This expression has type int but an expression was expected of
       type
           float
```

What's going on is that `(***)` isn't interpreted as an operator at all; it's read as a comment! To get this to work properly, we need to put spaces around any operator that begins or ends with *.

```
# let ( *** ) x y = (x **. y) **. y;;
val ( *** ) : float -> float -> float = <fun>
```

The syntactic role of an operator is typically determined by its first character or two, though there are a few exceptions. The OCaml manual has an explicit table of each class of operator[1] and its associated precedence.

We won't go through the full list here, but there's one important special case worth mentioning: `-` and `-.`, which are the integer and floating-point subtraction operators, and can act as both prefix operators (for negation) and infix operators (for subtraction). So, both `-x` and `x - y` are meaningful expressions. Another thing to remember about negation is that it has lower precedence than function application, which means that if you want to pass a negative value, you need to wrap it in parentheses, as you can see in this code.

```
# Int.max 3 (-4);;
- : int = 3
# Int.max 3 -4;;
Line 1, characters 1-10:
Warning 5 [ignored-partial-application]: this function application is
    partial,
maybe some arguments are missing.
Line 1, characters 1-10:
Error: This expression has type int -> int
       but an expression was expected of type int
```

Here, OCaml is interpreting the second expression as equivalent to.

```
# (Int.max 3) - 4;;
Line 1, characters 1-12:
Warning 5 [ignored-partial-application]: this function application is
    partial,
maybe some arguments are missing.
```

[1] https://ocaml.org/manual/expr.html#ss:precedence-and-associativity

```
Line 1, characters 1-12:
Error: This expression has type int -> int
       but an expression was expected of type int
```

which obviously doesn't make sense.

Here's an example of a very useful operator from the standard library whose behavior depends critically on the precedence rules described previously.

```
# let (|>) x f = f x;;
val ( |> ) : 'a -> ('a -> 'b) -> 'b = <fun>
```

This is called the *reverse application operator*, and it's not quite obvious at first what its purpose is: it just takes a value and a function and applies the function to the value. Despite that bland-sounding description, it has the useful role of sequencing operations, similar in spirit to using the pipe character in the UNIX shell. Consider, for example, the following code for printing out the unique elements of your PATH.

```
# open Stdio;;
# let path = "/usr/bin:/usr/local/bin:/bin:/sbin:/usr/bin";;
val path : string = "/usr/bin:/usr/local/bin:/bin:/sbin:/usr/bin"
# String.split ~on:':' path
  |> List.dedup_and_sort ~compare:String.compare
  |> List.iter ~f:print_endline;;
/bin
/sbin
/usr/bin
/usr/local/bin
- : unit = ()
```

We can do this without |> by naming the intermediate values, but the result is a bit more verbose.

```
# let split_path = String.split ~on:':' path in
  let deduped_path = List.dedup_and_sort ~compare:String.compare
     split_path in
  List.iter ~f:print_endline deduped_path;;
/bin
/sbin
/usr/bin
/usr/local/bin
- : unit = ()
```

An important part of what's happening here is partial application. For example, List.iter takes two arguments: a function to be called on each element of the list, and the list to iterate over. We can call List.iter with all its arguments:

```
# List.iter ~f:print_endline ["Two"; "lines"];;
Two
lines
- : unit = ()
```

or, we can pass it just the function argument, leaving us with a function for printing out a list of strings.

```
# List.iter ~f:print_endline;;
- : string list -> unit = <fun>
```

It is this later form that we're using in the preceding |> pipeline.

But |> only works in the intended way because it is left-associative. Let's see what happens if we try using a right-associative operator, like (^>).

```
# let (^>) x f = f x;;
val ( ^> ) : 'a -> ('a -> 'b) -> 'b = <fun>
# String.split ~on:':' path
  ^> List.dedup_and_sort ~compare:String.compare
  ^> List.iter ~f:print_endline;;
Line 3, characters 6-32:
Error: This expression has type string list -> unit
       but an expression was expected of type
         (string list -> string list) -> 'a
       Type string list is not compatible with type
         string list -> string list
```

The type error is a little bewildering at first glance. What's going on is that, because ^> is right associative, the operator is trying to feed the value `List.dedup_and_sort ~compare:String.compare` to the function `List.iter ~f:print_endline`. But `List.iter ~f:print_endline` expects a list of strings as its input, not a function.

The type error aside, this example highlights the importance of choosing the operator you use with care, particularly with respect to associativity.

The Application Operator

|> is known as the *reverse application operator*. You might be unsurprised to learn that there's also an *application operator*:

```
# (@@);;
- : ('a -> 'b) -> 'a -> 'b = <fun>
```

This one is useful for cases where you want to avoid many layers of parentheses when applying functions to complex expressions. In particular, you can replace `f (g (h x))` with `f @@ g @@ h x`. Note that, just as we needed |> to be left associative, we need @@ to be right associative.

3.2.5 Declaring Functions with `function`

Another way to define a function is using the `function` keyword. Instead of having syntactic support for declaring multiargument (curried) functions, `function` has built-in pattern matching. Here's an example.

```
# let some_or_zero = function
    | Some x -> x
    | None -> 0;;
val some_or_zero : int option -> int = <fun>
# List.map ~f:some_or_zero [Some 3; None; Some 4];;
- : int list = [3; 0; 4]
```

This is equivalent to combining an ordinary function definition with a `match`.

```
# let some_or_zero num_opt =
```

```
    match num_opt with
    | Some x -> x
    | None -> 0;;
val some_or_zero : int option -> int = <fun>
```

We can also combine the different styles of function declaration together, as in the following example, where we declare a two-argument (curried) function with a pattern match on the second argument.

```
# let some_or_default default = function
    | Some x -> x
    | None -> default;;
val some_or_default : 'a -> 'a option -> 'a = <fun>
# some_or_default 3 (Some 5);;
- : int = 5
# List.map ~f:(some_or_default 100) [Some 3; None; Some 4];;
- : int list = [3; 100; 4]
```

Also, note the use of partial application to generate the function passed to List.map. In other words, some_or_default 100 is a function that was created by feeding just the first argument to some_or_default.

3.2.6   Labeled Arguments

Up until now, the functions we've defined have specified their arguments positionally, *i.e.*, by the order in which the arguments are passed to the function. OCaml also supports labeled arguments, which let you identify a function argument by name. Indeed, we've already encountered functions from Base like List.map that use labeled arguments. Labeled arguments are marked by a leading tilde, and a label (followed by a colon) is put in front of the variable to be labeled. Here's an example.

```
# let ratio ~num ~denom = Float.of_int num /. Float.of_int denom;;
val ratio : num:int -> denom:int -> float = <fun>
```

We can then provide a labeled argument using a similar convention. As you can see, the arguments can be provided in any order.

```
# ratio ~num:3 ~denom:10;;
- : float = 0.3
# ratio ~denom:10 ~num:3;;
- : float = 0.3
```

OCaml also supports *label punning*, meaning that you get to drop the text after the colon if the name of the label and the name of the variable being used are the same. We were actually already using label punning when defining ratio. The following shows how punning can be used when invoking a function.

```
# let num = 3 in
  let denom = 4 in
  ratio ~num ~denom;;
- : float = 0.75
```

Where Are Labels Useful?

Labeled arguments are a surprisingly useful feature, and it's worth walking through some of the cases where they come up.

Explicating Long Argument Lists

Beyond a certain number, arguments are easier to remember by name than by position. Letting the names be used at the call-site (and used in any order) makes client code easier to read and to write.

```
val create_hashtable : int -> bool -> ('a,'b) Hashtable.t
```

The signature makes it hard to divine the meaning of those two arguments. but with labeled arguments, we can make the intent immediately clear.

```
val create_hashtable :
   init_size:int -> allow_shrinking:bool -> ('a,'b) Hashtable.t
```

Choosing label names well is especially important for Boolean values, since it's often easy to get confused about whether a value being true is meant to enable or disable a given feature.

Adding Information to Uninformative Argument Types

Consider a function for creating a hash table whose first argument is the initial size of the array backing the hash table, and the second is a Boolean flag, which indicates whether that array will ever shrink when elements are removed.

Disambiguating Similar Arguments

This issue comes up most often when a function has multiple arguments of the same type. Consider this signature for a function that extracts a substring.

```
val substring: string -> int -> int -> string
```

Here, the two ints are the starting position and length of the substring to extract, respectively, but you wouldn't know that from the type signature. We can make the signature more informative by adding labels.

```
val substring: string -> pos:int -> len:int -> string
```

This improves the readability of both the signature and of client code, and makes it harder to accidentally swap the position and the length.

Flexible Argument Ordering and Partial Application

Consider a function like `List.iter` which takes two arguments: a function and a list of elements to call that function on. A common pattern is to partially apply `List.iter` by giving it just the function, as in the following example from earlier in the chapter.

```
# String.split ~on:':' path
  |> List.dedup_and_sort ~compare:String.compare
  |> List.iter ~f:print_endline;;
/bin
/sbin
```

```
/usr/bin
/usr/local/bin
- : unit = ()
```

This requires that we put the function argument first.

Other orderings can be useful either for partial application, or for simple reasons of readability. For example, when using `List.iter` with a complex, multi-line iteration function, it's generally easier to read if the function comes second, after the statement of what list is being iterated over. On the other hand, when calling `List.iter` with a small function, but a large, explicitly written list of values, it's generally easier if the values come last.

Higher-Order Functions and Labels

One surprising gotcha with labeled arguments is that while order doesn't matter when calling a function with labeled arguments, it does matter in a higher-order context, *e.g.*, when passing a function with labeled arguments to another function. Here's an example.

```
# let apply_to_tuple f (first,second) = f ~first ~second;;
val apply_to_tuple : (first:'a -> second:'b -> 'c) -> 'a * 'b -> 'c =
    <fun>
```

Here, the definition of `apply_to_tuple` sets up the expectation that its first argument is a function with two labeled arguments, `first` and `second`, listed in that order. We could have defined `apply_to_tuple` differently to change the order in which the labeled arguments were listed.

```
# let apply_to_tuple_2 f (first,second) = f ~second ~first;;
val apply_to_tuple_2 : (second:'a -> first:'b -> 'c) -> 'b * 'a -> 'c =
    <fun>
```

It turns out this order matters. In particular, if we define a function that has a different order:

```
# let divide ~first ~second = first / second;;
val divide : first:int -> second:int -> int = <fun>
```

we'll find that it can't be passed in to `apply_to_tuple_2`.

```
# apply_to_tuple_2 divide (3,4);;
Line 1, characters 18-24:
Error: This expression has type first:int -> second:int -> int
       but an expression was expected of type second:'a -> first:'b ->
    'c
```

But, it works smoothly with the original `apply_to_tuple`.

```
# let apply_to_tuple f (first,second) = f ~first ~second;;
val apply_to_tuple : (first:'a -> second:'b -> 'c) -> 'a * 'b -> 'c =
    <fun>
# apply_to_tuple divide (3,4);;
- : int = 0
```

As a result, when passing labeled functions as arguments, you need to take care to be consistent in your ordering of labeled arguments.

3.2.7   Optional Arguments

An optional argument is like a labeled argument that the caller can choose whether or not to provide. Optional arguments are passed in using the same syntax as labeled arguments, and, like labeled arguments, can be provided in any order.

Here's an example of a string concatenation function with an optional separator. This function uses the ^ operator for pairwise string concatenation.

```
# let concat ?sep x y =
    let sep = match sep with None -> "" | Some s -> s in
    x ^ sep ^ y;;
val concat : ?sep:string -> string -> string -> string = <fun>
# concat "foo" "bar"             (* without the optional argument *);;
- : string = "foobar"
# concat ~sep:":" "foo" "bar"    (* with the optional argument    *);;
- : string = "foo:bar"
```

Here, ? is used in the definition of the function to mark sep as optional. And while the caller can pass a value of type string for sep, internally to the function, sep is seen as a string option, with None appearing when sep is not provided by the caller.

The preceding example needed a bit of boilerplate to choose a default separator when none was provided. This is a common enough pattern that there's an explicit syntax for providing a default value, which allows us to write concat more concisely.

```
# let concat ?(sep="") x y = x ^ sep ^ y;;
val concat : ?sep:string -> string -> string -> string = <fun>
```

Optional arguments are very useful, but they're also easy to abuse. The key advantage of optional arguments is that they let you write functions with multiple arguments that users can ignore most of the time, only worrying about them when they specifically want to invoke those options. They also allow you to extend an API with new functionality without changing existing code.

The downside is that the caller may be unaware that there is a choice to be made, and so may unknowingly (and wrongly) pick the default behavior. Optional arguments really only make sense when the extra concision of omitting the argument outweighs the corresponding loss of explicitness.

This means that rarely used functions should not have optional arguments. A good rule of thumb is to avoid optional arguments for functions internal to a module, *i.e.*, functions that are not included in the module's interface, or mli file. We'll learn more about mlis in Chapter 5 (Files, Modules, and Programs).

Explicit Passing of an Optional Argument

Under the covers, a function with an optional argument receives None when the caller doesn't provide the argument, and Some when it does. But the Some and None are normally not explicitly passed in by the caller.

But sometimes, passing in Some or None explicitly is exactly what you want. OCaml lets you do this by using ? instead of ~ to mark the argument. Thus, the following two lines are equivalent ways of specifying the sep argument to concat:

```
# concat ~sep:":" "foo" "bar" (* provide the optional argument *);;
- : string = "foo:bar"
# concat ?sep:(Some ":") "foo" "bar" (* pass an explicit [Some] *);;
- : string = "foo:bar"
```

and the following two lines are equivalent ways of calling concat without specifying sep.

```
# concat "foo" "bar" (* don't provide the optional argument *);;
- : string = "foobar"
# concat ?sep:None "foo" "bar" (* explicitly pass `None` *);;
- : string = "foobar"
```

One use case for this is when you want to define a wrapper function that mimics the optional arguments of the function it's wrapping. For example, imagine we wanted to create a function called uppercase_concat, which is the same as concat except that it converts the first string that it's passed to uppercase. We could write the function as follows.

```
# let uppercase_concat ?(sep="") a b = concat ~sep (String.uppercase
    a) b;;
val uppercase_concat : ?sep:string -> string -> string -> string =
    <fun>
# uppercase_concat "foo" "bar";;
- : string = "FOObar"
# uppercase_concat "foo" "bar" ~sep:":";;
- : string = "FOO:bar"
```

In the way we've written it, we've been forced to separately make the decision as to what the default separator is. Thus, if we later change concat's default behavior, we'll need to remember to change uppercase_concat to match it.

Instead, we can have uppercase_concat simply pass through the optional argument to concat using the ? syntax.

```
# let uppercase_concat ?sep a b = concat ?sep (String.uppercase a) b;;
val uppercase_concat : ?sep:string -> string -> string -> string =
    <fun>
```

Now, if someone calls uppercase_concat without an argument, an explicit None will be passed to concat, leaving concat to decide what the default behavior should be.

Inference of Labeled and Optional Arguments

One subtle aspect of labeled and optional arguments is how they are inferred by the type system. Consider the following example for computing numerical derivatives of a function of two real variables. The function takes an argument delta, which determines the scale at which to compute the derivative; values x and y, which determine at which point to compute the derivative; and the function f, whose derivative is being computed. The function f itself takes two labeled arguments, x and y. Note that you can use an apostrophe as part of a variable name, so x' and y' are just ordinary variables.

```
# let numeric_deriv ~delta ~x ~y ~f =
    let x' = x +. delta in
    let y' = y +. delta in
```

```
      let base = f ~x ~y in
      let dx = (f ~x:x' ~y -. base) /. delta in
      let dy = (f ~x ~y:y' -. base) /. delta in
      (dx,dy);;
val numeric_deriv :
  delta:float ->
  x:float -> y:float -> f:(x:float -> y:float -> float) -> float *
    float =
  <fun>
```

In principle, it's not obvious how the order of the arguments to f should be chosen. Since labeled arguments can be passed in arbitrary order, it seems like it could as well be `y:float -> x:float -> float` as it is `x:float -> y:float -> float`.

Even worse, it would be perfectly consistent for f to take an optional argument instead of a labeled one, which could lead to this type signature for `numeric_deriv`.

```
val numeric_deriv :
  delta:float ->
  x:float -> y:float -> f:(?x:float -> y:float -> float) -> float *
    float
```

Since there are multiple plausible types to choose from, OCaml needs some heuristic for choosing between them. The heuristic the compiler uses is to prefer labels to options and to choose the order of arguments that shows up in the source code.

Note that these heuristics might at different points in the source suggest different types. Here's a version of `numeric_deriv` where different invocations of f list the arguments in different orders.

```
# let numeric_deriv ~delta ~x ~y ~f =
    let x' = x +. delta in
    let y' = y +. delta in
    let base = f ~x ~y in
    let dx = (f ~y ~x:x' -. base) /. delta in
    let dy = (f ~x ~y:y' -. base) /. delta in
    (dx,dy);;
Line 5, characters 15-16:
Error: This function is applied to arguments
          in an order different from other calls.
          This is only allowed when the real type is known.
```

As suggested by the error message, we can get OCaml to accept the fact that f is used with different argument orders if we provide explicit type information. Thus, the following code compiles without error, due to the type annotation on f.

```
# let numeric_deriv ~delta ~x ~y ~(f: x:float -> y:float -> float) =
    let x' = x +. delta in
    let y' = y +. delta in
    let base = f ~x ~y in
    let dx = (f ~y ~x:x' -. base) /. delta in
    let dy = (f ~x ~y:y' -. base) /. delta in
    (dx,dy);;
val numeric_deriv :
  delta:float ->
  x:float -> y:float -> f:(x:float -> y:float -> float) -> float *
    float =
  <fun>
```

Optional Arguments and Partial Application

Optional arguments can be tricky to think about in the presence of partial application. We can of course partially apply the optional argument itself.

```
# let colon_concat = concat ~sep:":";;
val colon_concat : string -> string -> string = <fun>
# colon_concat "a" "b";;
- : string = "a:b"
```

But what happens if we partially apply just the first argument?

```
# let prepend_pound = concat "# ";;
val prepend_pound : string -> string = <fun>
# prepend_pound "a BASH comment";;
- : string = "# a BASH comment"
```

The optional argument ?sep has now disappeared, or been *erased*. Indeed, if we try to pass in that optional argument now, it will be rejected.

```
# prepend_pound "a BASH comment" ~sep:":";;
Line 1, characters 1-14:
Error: This function has type Base.String.t -> Base.String.t
       It is applied to too many arguments; maybe you forgot a `;'.
```

So when does OCaml decide to erase an optional argument?

The rule is: an optional argument is erased as soon as the first positional (i.e., neither labeled nor optional) argument defined *after* the optional argument is passed in. That explains the behavior of prepend_pound. But if we had instead defined concat with the optional argument in the second position:

```
# let concat x ?(sep="") y = x ^ sep ^ y;;
val concat : string -> ?sep:string -> string -> string = <fun>
```

then application of the first argument would not cause the optional argument to be erased.

```
# let prepend_pound = concat "# ";;
val prepend_pound : ?sep:string -> string -> string = <fun>
# prepend_pound "a BASH comment";;
- : string = "# a BASH comment"
# prepend_pound "a BASH comment" ~sep:"--- ";;
- : string = "# --- a BASH comment"
```

However, if all arguments to a function are presented at once, then erasure of optional arguments isn't applied until all of the arguments are passed in. This preserves our ability to pass in optional arguments anywhere on the argument list. Thus, we can write.

```
# concat "a" "b" ~sep:"=";;
- : string = "a=b"
```

An optional argument that doesn't have any following positional arguments can't be erased at all, which leads to a compiler warning.

```
# let concat x y ?(sep="") = x ^ sep ^ y;;
Line 1, characters 18-24:
```

```
Warning 16 [unerasable-optional-argument]: this optional argument
    cannot be erased.
val concat : string -> string -> ?sep:string -> string = <fun>
```

And indeed, when we provide the two positional arguments, the `sep` argument is not erased, instead returning a function that expects the `sep` argument to be provided.

```
# concat "a" "b";;
- : ?sep:string -> string = <fun>
```

As you can see, OCaml's support for labeled and optional arguments is not without its complexities. But don't let these complexities obscure the usefulness of these features. Labels and optional arguments are very effective tools for making your APIs both more convenient and safer, and it's worth the effort of learning how to use them effectively.

4   Lists and Patterns

This chapter will focus on two common elements of programming in OCaml: lists and pattern matching. Both of these were discussed in Chapter 2 (A Guided Tour), but we'll go into more depth here, presenting the two topics together and using one to help illustrate the other.

4.1   List Basics

An OCaml list is an immutable, finite sequence of elements of the same type. As we've seen, OCaml lists can be generated using a bracket-and-semicolon notation:

```
# open Base;;
# [1;2;3];;
- : int list = [1; 2; 3]
```

And they can also be generated using the equivalent :: notation:

```
# 1 :: (2 :: (3 :: []));;
- : int list = [1; 2; 3]
# 1 :: 2 :: 3 :: [];;
- : int list = [1; 2; 3]
```

As you can see, the :: operator is right-associative, which means that we can build up lists without parentheses. The empty list [] is used to terminate a list. Note that the empty list is polymorphic, meaning it can be used with elements of any type, as you can see here:

```
# let empty = [];;
val empty : 'a list = []
# 3 :: empty;;
- : int list = [3]
# "three" :: empty;;
- : string list = ["three"]
```

The way in which the :: operator attaches elements to the front of a list reflects the fact that OCaml's lists are in fact singly linked lists. The figure below is a rough graphical representation of how the list 1 :: 2 :: 3 :: [] is laid out as a data structure. The final arrow (from the box containing 3) points to the empty list.

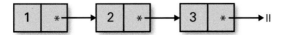

Each :: essentially adds a new block to the preceding picture. Such a block contains two things: a reference to the data in that list element, and a reference to the remainder of the list. This is why :: can extend a list without modifying it; extension allocates a new list element but does not change any of the existing ones, as you can see:

```
# let l = 1 :: 2 :: 3 :: [];;
val l : int list = [1; 2; 3]
# let m = 0 :: l;;
val m : int list = [0; 1; 2; 3]
# l;;
- : int list = [1; 2; 3]
```

4.2   Using Patterns to Extract Data from a List

We can read data out of a list using a match expression. Here's a simple example of a recursive function that computes the sum of all elements of a list:

```
# let rec sum l =
    match l with
    | [] -> 0
    | hd :: tl -> hd + sum tl;;
val sum : int list -> int = <fun>
# sum [1;2;3];;
- : int = 6
# sum [];;
- : int = 0
```

This code follows the convention of using hd to represent the first element (or head) of the list, and tl to represent the remainder (or tail).

The match expression in sum is really doing two things: first, it's acting as a case-analysis tool, breaking down the possibilities into a pattern-indexed list of cases. Second, it lets you name substructures within the data structure being matched. In this case, the variables hd and tl are bound by the pattern that defines the second case of the match expression. Variables that are bound in this way can be used in the expression to the right of the arrow for the pattern in question.

The fact that match expressions can be used to bind new variables can be a source of confusion. To see how, imagine we wanted to write a function that filtered out from a list all elements equal to a particular value. You might be tempted to write that code as follows, but when you do, the compiler will immediately warn you that something is wrong:

```
# let rec drop_value l to_drop =
    match l with
    | [] -> []
    | to_drop :: tl -> drop_value tl to_drop
    | hd :: tl -> hd :: drop_value tl to_drop;;
```

```
Line 5, characters 7-15:
Warning 11 [redundant-case]: this match case is unused.
val drop_value : 'a list -> 'a -> 'a list = <fun>
```

Moreover, the function clearly does the wrong thing, filtering out all elements of the list rather than just those equal to the provided value, as you can see here:

```
# drop_value [1;2;3] 2;;
- : int list = []
```

So, what's going on?

The key observation is that the appearance of to_drop in the second case doesn't imply a check that the first element is equal to the value to_drop that was passed in as an argument to drop_value. Instead, it just causes a new variable to_drop to be bound to whatever happens to be in the first element of the list, shadowing the earlier definition of to_drop. The third case is unused because it is essentially the same pattern as we had in the second case.

A better way to write this code is not to use pattern matching for determining whether the first element is equal to to_drop, but to instead use an ordinary if expression:

```
# let rec drop_value l to_drop =
    match l with
    | [] -> []
    | hd :: tl ->
      let new_tl = drop_value tl to_drop in
      if hd = to_drop then new_tl else hd :: new_tl;;
val drop_value : int list -> int -> int list = <fun>
# drop_value [1;2;3] 2;;
- : int list = [1; 3]
```

If we wanted to drop a particular literal value, rather than a value that was passed in, we could do this using something like our original implementation of drop_value:

```
# let rec drop_zero l =
    match l with
    | [] -> []
    | 0  :: tl -> drop_zero tl
    | hd :: tl -> hd :: drop_zero tl;;
val drop_zero : int list -> int list = <fun>
# drop_zero [1;2;0;3];;
- : int list = [1; 2; 3]
```

4.3   Limitations (and Blessings) of Pattern Matching

The preceding example highlights an important fact about patterns, which is that they can't be used to express arbitrary conditions. Patterns can characterize the layout of a data structure and can even include literals, as in the drop_zero example, but that's where they stop. A pattern can check if a list has two elements, but it can't check if the first two elements are equal to each other.

You can think of patterns as a specialized sublanguage that can express a limited (though still quite rich) set of conditions. The fact that the pattern language is limited turns out to be a good thing, making it possible to build better support for patterns in the compiler. In particular, both the efficiency of match expressions and the ability of the compiler to detect errors in matches depend on the constrained nature of patterns.

4.3.1 Performance

Naively, you might think that it would be necessary to check each case in a match in sequence to figure out which one fires. If the cases of a match were guarded by arbitrary code, that would be the case. But OCaml is often able to generate machine code that jumps directly to the matched case based on an efficiently chosen set of runtime checks.

As an example, consider the following rather silly functions for incrementing an integer by one. The first is implemented with a match expression, and the second with a sequence of if expressions:

```
# let plus_one_match x =
    match x with
    | 0 -> 1
    | 1 -> 2
    | 2 -> 3
    | 3 -> 4
    | 4 -> 5
    | 5 -> 6
    | _ -> x + 1;;
val plus_one_match : int -> int = <fun>
# let plus_one_if x =
    if       x = 0 then 1
    else if x = 1 then 2
    else if x = 2 then 3
    else if x = 3 then 4
    else if x = 4 then 5
    else if x = 5 then 6
    else x + 1;;
val plus_one_if : int -> int = <fun>
```

Note the use of _ in the above match. This is a wildcard pattern that matches any value, but without binding a variable name to the value in question.

If you benchmark these functions, you'll see that plus_one_if is considerably slower than plus_one_match, and the advantage gets larger as the number of cases increases. Here, we'll benchmark these functions using the core_bench library, which can be installed by running opam install core_bench from the command line.

```
# #require "core_bench";;
# open Core_bench;;
# [ Bench.Test.create ~name:"plus_one_match" (fun () ->
        plus_one_match 10)
  ; Bench.Test.create ~name:"plus_one_if" (fun () ->
        plus_one_if 10) ]
  |> Bench.bench;;
Estimated testing time 20s (2 benchmarks x 10s). Change using -quota
    SECS.

  Name                    Time/Run
```

```
plus_one_match    34.86ns
plus_one_if       54.89ns
```

```
- : unit = ()
```

Here's another, less artificial example. We can rewrite the `sum` function we described earlier in the chapter using an `if` expression rather than a match. We can then use the functions `is_empty`, `hd_exn`, and `tl_exn` from the `List` module to deconstruct the list, allowing us to implement the entire function without pattern matching:

```
# let rec sum_if l =
    if List.is_empty l then 0
    else List.hd_exn l + sum_if (List.tl_exn l);;
val sum_if : int list -> int = <fun>
```

Again, we can benchmark these to see the difference:

```
# let numbers = List.range 0 1000 in
  [ Bench.Test.create ~name:"sum_if" (fun () -> sum_if numbers)
  ; Bench.Test.create ~name:"sum"    (fun () -> sum numbers) ]
  |> Bench.bench;;
Estimated testing time 20s (2 benchmarks x 10s). Change using -quota
    SECS.
```

```
Name      Time/Run

sum_if    62.00us
sum       17.99us
```

```
- : unit = ()
```

In this case, the `match`-based implementation is many times faster than the `if`-based implementation. The difference comes because we need to effectively do the same work multiple times, since each function we call has to reexamine the first element of the list to determine whether or not it's the empty cell. With a `match` expression, this work happens exactly once per list element.

This is a more general phenomenon: pattern matching is very efficient, and is usually faster than what you might write yourself.

4.3.2   Detecting Errors

The error-detecting capabilities of `match` expressions are if anything more important than their performance. We've already seen one example of OCaml's ability to find problems in a pattern match: in our broken implementation of `drop_value`, OCaml warned us that the final case was redundant. There are no algorithms for determining if a predicate written in a general-purpose language is redundant, but it can be solved reliably in the context of patterns.

OCaml also checks `match` expressions for exhaustiveness. Consider what happens if we modify `drop_zero` by deleting the handler for one of the cases. As you can see, the compiler will produce a warning that we've missed a case, along with an example of an unmatched pattern:

```
# let rec drop_zero l =
    match l with
    | [] -> []
    | 0  :: tl -> drop_zero tl;;
Lines 2-4, characters 5-31:
Warning 8 [partial-match]: this pattern-matching is not exhaustive.
Here is an example of a case that is not matched:
1::_
val drop_zero : int list -> 'a list = <fun>
```

Even for simple examples like this, exhaustiveness checks are pretty useful. But as we'll see in Chapter 7 (Variants), they become yet more valuable as you get to more complicated examples, especially those involving user-defined types. In addition to catching outright errors, they act as a sort of refactoring tool, guiding you to the locations where you need to adapt your code to deal with changing types.

4.4   Using the List Module Effectively

We've so far written a fair amount of list-munging code using pattern matching and recursive functions. In real life, you're usually better off using the List module, which is full of reusable functions that abstract out common patterns for computing with lists.

Let's work through a concrete example. We'll write a function render_table that, given a list of column headers and a list of rows, prints them out in a well-formatted text table. When we're done, here's how the resulting function should work:

```
# Stdio.print_endline
    (render_table
       ["language";"architect";"first release"]
       [ ["Lisp" ;"John McCarthy" ;"1958"] ;
         ["C"    ;"Dennis Ritchie";"1969"] ;
         ["ML"   ;"Robin Milner"  ;"1973"] ;
         ["OCaml";"Xavier Leroy"  ;"1996"] ;
       ]);;
| language | architect       | first release |
|----------+-----------------+---------------|
| Lisp     | John McCarthy   | 1958          |
| C        | Dennis Ritchie  | 1969          |
| ML       | Robin Milner    | 1973          |
| OCaml    | Xavier Leroy    | 1996          |
- : unit = ()
```

The first step is to write a function to compute the maximum width of each column of data. We can do this by converting the header and each row into a list of integer lengths, and then taking the element-wise max of those lists of lengths. Writing the code for all of this directly would be a bit of a chore, but we can do it quite concisely by making use of three functions from the List module: map, map2_exn, and fold.

List.map is the simplest to explain. It takes a list and a function for transforming elements of that list, and returns a new list with the transformed elements. Thus, we can write:

```
# List.map ~f:String.length ["Hello"; "World!"];;
```

```
- : int list = [5; 6]
```

List.map2_exn is similar to List.map, except that it takes two lists and a function for combining them. Thus, we might write:

```
# List.map2_exn ~f:Int.max [1;2;3] [3;2;1];;
- : int list = [3; 2; 3]
```

The _exn is there because the function throws an exception if the lists are of mismatched length:

```
# List.map2_exn ~f:Int.max [1;2;3] [3;2;1;0];;
Exception: (Invalid_argument "length mismatch in map2_exn: 3 <> 4")
```

List.fold is the most complicated of the three, taking three arguments: a list to process, an initial accumulator value, and a function for updating the accumulator. List.fold walks over the list from left to right, updating the accumulator at each step and returning the final value of the accumulator when it's done. You can see some of this by looking at the type-signature for fold:

```
# List.fold;;
- : 'a list -> init:'accum -> f:('accum -> 'a -> 'accum) -> 'accum = <fun>
```

We can use List.fold for something as simple as summing up a list:

```
# List.fold ~init:0 ~f:(+) [1;2;3;4];;
- : int = 10
```

This example is particularly simple because the accumulator and the list elements are of the same type. But fold is not limited to such cases. We can for example use fold to reverse a list, in which case the accumulator is itself a list:

```
# List.fold ~init:[] ~f:(fun acc hd -> hd :: acc) [1;2;3;4];;
- : int list = [4; 3; 2; 1]
```

Let's bring our three functions together to compute the maximum column widths:

```
# let max_widths header rows =
    let lengths l = List.map ~f:String.length l in
    List.fold rows
      ~init:(lengths header)
      ~f:(fun acc row ->
          List.map2_exn ~f:Int.max acc (lengths row));;
val max_widths : string list -> string list list -> int list = <fun>
```

Using List.map we define the function lengths, which converts a list of strings to a list of integer lengths. List.fold is then used to iterate over the rows, using map2_exn to take the max of the accumulator with the lengths of the strings in each row of the table, with the accumulator initialized to the lengths of the header row.

Now that we know how to compute column widths, we can write the code to generate the line that separates the header from the rest of the text table. We'll do this in part by mapping String.make over the lengths of the columns to generate a string of dashes of the appropriate length. We'll then join these sequences of dashes together using String.concat, which concatenates a list of strings with an optional separator string, and ^, which is a pairwise string concatenation function, to add the delimiters on the outside:

```
# let render_separator widths =
    let pieces = List.map widths
        ~f:(fun w -> String.make w '-')
    in
    "|-" ^ String.concat ~sep:"-+-" pieces ^ "-|";;
val render_separator : int list -> string = <fun>
# render_separator [3;6;2];;
- : string = "|-----+--------+----|"
```

Note that we make the line of dashes two larger than the provided width to provide some whitespace around each entry in the table.

Performance of `String.concat` and `^`

In the preceding code we've concatenated strings two different ways: `String.concat`, which operates on lists of strings; and `^`, which is a pairwise operator. You should avoid `^` for joining large numbers of strings, since it allocates a new string every time it runs. Thus, the following code

```
# let s = "." ^ "." ^ "." ^ "." ^ "." ^ "." ^ ".";;
val s : string = "......."
```

will allocate strings of length 2, 3, 4, 5, 6 and 7, whereas this code

```
# let s = String.concat [".";".";".";".";".";".";"."];;
val s : string = "......."
```

allocates one string of size 7, as well as a list of length 7. At these small sizes, the differences don't amount to much, but for assembling large strings, it can be a serious performance issue.

Now we need code for rendering a row with data in it. We'll first write a function called pad, for padding out a string to a specified length:

```
# let pad s length =
    s ^ String.make (length - String.length s) ' ';;
val pad : string -> int -> string = <fun>
# pad "hello" 10;;
- : string = "hello     "
```

We can render a row of data by merging together the padded strings. Again, we'll use `List.map2_exn` for combining the list of data in the row with the list of widths:

```
# let render_row row widths =
    let padded = List.map2_exn row widths ~f:pad in
    "| " ^ String.concat ~sep:" | " padded ^ " |";;
val render_row : string list -> int list -> string = <fun>
# render_row ["Hello";"World"] [10;15];;
- : string = "| Hello      | World           |"
```

Finally, we can bring this all together to build the `render_table` function we wanted at the start!

```
# let render_table header rows =
    let widths = max_widths header rows in
    String.concat ~sep:"\n"
```

```
        (render_row header widths
        :: render_separator widths
        :: List.map rows ~f:(fun row -> render_row row widths)
        );;
val render_table : string list -> string list list -> string = <fun>
```

4.4.1   More Useful List Functions

The previous example touched on only three of the functions in `List`. We won't cover the entire interface (for that you should look at the online docs[1]), but a few more functions are useful enough to mention here.

Combining List Elements with `List.reduce`

`List.fold`, which we described earlier, is a very general and powerful function. Sometimes, however, you want something simpler and easier to use. One such function is `List.reduce`, which is essentially a specialized version of `List.fold` that doesn't require an explicit starting value, and whose accumulator has to consume and produce values of the same type as the elements of the list it applies to.

Here's the type signature:

```
# List.reduce;;
- : 'a list -> f:('a -> 'a -> 'a) -> 'a option = <fun>
```

reduce returns an optional result, returning `None` when the input list is empty.

Now we can see reduce in action:

```
# List.reduce ~f:(+) [1;2;3;4;5];;
- : int option = Some 15
# List.reduce ~f:(+) [];;
- : int option = None
```

Filtering with `List.filter` and `List.filter_map`

Very often when processing lists, you want to restrict your attention to a subset of the values on your list. The `List.filter` function is one way of doing that:

```
# List.filter ~f:(fun x -> x % 2 = 0) [1;2;3;4;5];;
- : int list = [2; 4]
```

Sometimes, you want to both transform and filter as part of the same computation. In that case, `List.filter_map` is what you need. The function passed to `List.filter_map` returns an optional value, and `List.filter_map` drops all elements for which `None` is returned.

Here's an example. The following function computes a list of file extensions from a list of files, piping the results through `List.dedup_and_sort` to return the list with duplicates removed and in sorted order. Note that this example uses `String.rsplit2` from the String module to split a string on the rightmost appearance of a given character:

---

[1] https://v3.ocaml.org/p/base/v0.14.3/doc/Base/List/index.html

```
# let extensions filenames =
    List.filter_map filenames ~f:(fun fname ->
        match String.rsplit2 ~on:'.' fname with
        | None  | Some ("",_) -> None
        | Some (_,ext) ->
            Some ext)
    |> List.dedup_and_sort ~compare:String.compare;;
val extensions : string list -> string list = <fun>
# extensions ["foo.c"; "foo.ml"; "bar.ml"; "bar.mli"];;
- : string list = ["c"; "ml"; "mli"]
```

The preceding code is also an example of an or-pattern, which allows you to have multiple subpatterns within a larger pattern. In this case, `None | Some ("",_)` is an or-pattern. As we'll see later, or-patterns can be nested anywhere within larger patterns.

Partitioning with `List.partition_tf`

Another useful operation that's closely related to filtering is partitioning. The function `List.partition_tf` takes a list and a function for computing a Boolean condition on the list elements, and returns two lists. The `tf` in the name is a mnemonic to remind the user that `true` elements go to the first list and `false` ones go to the second. Here's an example:

```
# let is_ocaml_source s =
    match String.rsplit2 s ~on:'.' with
    | Some (_,("ml"|"mli")) -> true
    | _ -> false;;
val is_ocaml_source : string -> bool = <fun>
# let (ml_files,other_files) =
    List.partition_tf ["foo.c"; "foo.ml"; "bar.ml"; "bar.mli"]
        ~f:is_ocaml_source;;
val ml_files : string list = ["foo.ml"; "bar.ml"; "bar.mli"]
val other_files : string list = ["foo.c"]
```

Combining lists

Another very common operation on lists is concatenation. The `List` module actually comes with a few different ways of doing this. There's `List.append`, for concatenating a pair of lists.

```
# List.append [1;2;3] [4;5;6];;
- : int list = [1; 2; 3; 4; 5; 6]
```

There's also @, an operator equivalent of `List.append`.

```
# [1;2;3] @ [4;5;6];;
- : int list = [1; 2; 3; 4; 5; 6]
```

In addition, there is `List.concat`, for concatenating a list of lists:

```
# List.concat [[1;2];[3;4;5];[6];[]];;
- : int list = [1; 2; 3; 4; 5; 6]
```

Here's an example of using `List.concat` along with `List.map` to compute a recursive listing of a directory tree.

```
# module Sys = Core.Sys
  module Filename = Core.Filename;;
module Sys = Core.Sys
module Filename = Core.Filename
# let rec ls_rec s =
    if Sys.is_file_exn ~follow_symlinks:true s
    then [s]
    else
      Sys.ls_dir s
      |> List.map ~f:(fun sub -> ls_rec (Filename.concat s sub))
      |> List.concat;;
val ls_rec : string -> string list = <fun>
```

Note that this example uses some functions from the Sys and Filename modules from Core for accessing the filesystem and dealing with filenames.

The preceding combination of List.map and List.concat is common enough that there is a function List.concat_map that combines these into one, more efficient operation:

```
# let rec ls_rec s =
    if Sys.is_file_exn ~follow_symlinks:true s
    then [s]
    else
      Sys.ls_dir s
      |> List.concat_map ~f:(fun sub -> ls_rec (Filename.concat s
    sub));;
val ls_rec : string -> string list = <fun>
```

4.5   Tail Recursion

The only way to compute the length of an OCaml list is to walk the list from beginning to end. As a result, computing the length of a list takes time linear in the size of the list. Here's a simple function for doing so:

```
# let rec length = function
    | [] -> 0
    | _ :: tl -> 1 + length tl;;
val length : 'a list -> int = <fun>
# length [1;2;3];;
- : int = 3
```

This looks simple enough, but you'll discover that this implementation runs into problems on very large lists, as we'll show in the following code:

```
# let make_list n = List.init n ~f:(fun x -> x);;
val make_list : int -> int list = <fun>
# length (make_list 10);;
- : int = 10
# length (make_list 10_000_000);;
Stack overflow during evaluation (looping recursion?).
```

The preceding example creates lists using List.init, which takes an integer n and a function f and creates a list of length n, where the data for each element is created by calling f on the index of that element.

To understand where the error in the above example comes from, you need to learn a bit more about how function calls work. Typically, a function call needs some space to keep track of information associated with the call, such as the arguments passed to the function, or the location of the code that needs to start executing when the function call is complete. To allow for nested function calls, this information is typically organized in a stack, where a new *stack frame* is allocated for each nested function call, and then deallocated when the function call is complete.

And that's the problem with our call to length: it tried to allocate 10 million stack frames, which exhausted the available stack space. Happily, there's a way around this problem. Consider the following alternative implementation:

```
# let rec length_plus_n l n =
    match l with
    | [] -> n
    | _ :: tl -> length_plus_n tl (n + 1);;
val length_plus_n : 'a list -> int -> int = <fun>
# let length l = length_plus_n l 0;;
val length : 'a list -> int = <fun>
# length [1;2;3;4];;
- : int = 4
```

This implementation depends on a helper function, length_plus_n, that computes the length of a given list plus a given n. In practice, n acts as an accumulator in which the answer is built up, step by step. As a result, we can do the additions along the way rather than doing them as we unwind the nested sequence of function calls, as we did in our first implementation of length.

The advantage of this approach is that the recursive call in length_plus_n is a *tail call*. We'll explain more precisely what it means to be a tail call shortly, but the reason it's important is that tail calls don't require the allocation of a new stack frame, due to what is called the *tail-call optimization*. A recursive function is said to be *tail recursive* if all of its recursive calls are tail calls. length_plus_n is indeed tail recursive, and as a result, length can take a long list as input without blowing the stack:

```
# length (make_list 10_000_000);;
- : int = 10000000
```

So when is a call a tail call? Let's think about the situation where one function (the *caller*) invokes another (the *callee*). The invocation is considered a tail call when the caller doesn't do anything with the value returned by the callee except to return it. The tail-call optimization makes sense because, when a caller makes a tail call, the caller's stack frame need never be used again, and so you don't need to keep it around. Thus, instead of allocating a new stack frame for the callee, the compiler is free to reuse the caller's stack frame.

Tail recursion is important for more than just lists. Ordinary non-tail recursive calls are reasonable when dealing with data structures like binary trees, where the depth of the tree is logarithmic in the size of your data. But when dealing with situations where the depth of the sequence of nested calls is on the order of the size of your data, tail recursion is usually the right approach.

4.6   Terser and Faster Patterns

Now that we know more about how lists and patterns work, let's consider how we can improve on an example from Chapter 2.3.2 (Recursive List Functions): the function `remove_sequential_duplicates`. Here's the implementation that was described earlier:

```
# let rec remove_sequential_duplicates list =
    match list with
    | [] -> []
    | [x] -> [x]
    | first :: second :: tl ->
      if first = second then
        remove_sequential_duplicates (second :: tl)
      else
        first :: remove_sequential_duplicates (second :: tl);;
val remove_sequential_duplicates : int list -> int list = <fun>
```

We'll consider some ways of making this code more concise and more efficient.

First, let's consider efficiency. One problem with the above code is that it in some cases re-creates on the right-hand side of the arrow a value that already existed on the left-hand side. Thus, the pattern `[hd] -> [hd]` actually allocates a new list element, when really, it should be able to just return the list being matched. We can reduce allocation here by using an as pattern, which allows us to declare a name for the thing matched by a pattern or subpattern. While we're at it, we'll use the `function` keyword to eliminate the need for an explicit match:

```
# let rec remove_sequential_duplicates = function
    | [] as l -> l
    | [_] as l -> l
    | first :: (second :: _ as tl) ->
      if first = second then
        remove_sequential_duplicates tl
      else
        first :: remove_sequential_duplicates tl;;
val remove_sequential_duplicates : int list -> int list = <fun>
```

We can further collapse this by combining the first two cases into one, using an *or-pattern*:

```
# let rec remove_sequential_duplicates list =
    match list with
    | [] | [_] as l -> l
    | first :: (second :: _ as tl) ->
      if first = second then
        remove_sequential_duplicates tl
      else
        first :: remove_sequential_duplicates tl;;
val remove_sequential_duplicates : int list -> int list = <fun>
```

We can make the code slightly terser now by using a when clause. A when clause allows us to add an extra precondition to a pattern in the form of an arbitrary OCaml expression. In this case, we can use it to include the check on whether the first two elements are equal:

```
# let rec remove_sequential_duplicates list =
    match list with
    | [] | [_] as l -> l
    | first :: (second :: _ as tl) when first = second ->
      remove_sequential_duplicates tl
    | first :: tl -> first :: remove_sequential_duplicates tl;;
val remove_sequential_duplicates : int list -> int list = <fun>
```

Polymorphic Compare

You might have noticed that remove_sequential_duplicates is specialized to lists of integers. That's because Base's default equality operator is specialized to integers, as you can see if you try to apply it to values of a different type.

```
# open Base;;
# "foo" = "bar";;
Line 1, characters 1-6:
Error: This expression has type string but an expression was expected
    of type
          int
```

OCaml also has a collection of polymorphic equality and comparison operators, which we can make available by opening the module Base.Poly.

```
# open Base.Poly;;
# "foo" = "bar";;
- : bool = false
# 3 = 4;;
- : bool = false
# [1;2;3] = [1;2;3];;
- : bool = true
```

Indeed, if we look at the type of the equality operator, we'll see that it is polymorphic.

```
# (=);;
- : 'a -> 'a -> bool = <fun>
```

If we rewrite remove_sequential_duplicates with Base.Poly open, we'll see that it gets a polymorphic type, and can now be used on inputs of different types.

```
# let rec remove_sequential_duplicates list =
    match list with
    | [] | [_] as l -> l
    | first :: (second :: _ as tl) when first = second ->
      remove_sequential_duplicates tl
    | first :: tl -> first :: remove_sequential_duplicates tl;;
val remove_sequential_duplicates : 'a list -> 'a list = <fun>
# remove_sequential_duplicates [1;2;2;3;4;3;3];;
- : int list = [1; 2; 3; 4; 3]
# remove_sequential_duplicates ["one";"two";"two";"two";"three"];;
- : string list = ["one"; "two"; "three"]
```

OCaml comes with a whole family of polymorphic comparison operators, including the standard infix comparators, <, >=, etc., as well as the function `compare` that returns -1, 0, or 1 to flag whether the first operand is smaller than, equal to, or greater than the second, respectively.

You might wonder how you could build functions like these yourself if OCaml didn't come with them built in. It turns out that you *can't* build these functions on your own. OCaml's polymorphic comparison functions are built into the runtime to a low level. These comparisons are polymorphic on the basis of ignoring almost everything about the types of the values that are being compared, paying attention only to the structure of the values as they're laid out in memory. (You can learn more about this structure in Chapter 24 (Memory Representation of Values).)

Polymorphic compare does have some limitations. For example, it will fail at runtime if it encounters a function value.

```
# (fun x -> x + 1) = (fun x -> x + 1);;
Exception: (Invalid_argument "compare: functional value")
```

Similarly, it will fail on values that come from outside the OCaml heap, like values from C bindings. But it will work in a reasonable way for most other kinds of values.

For simple atomic types, polymorphic compare has the semantics you would expect: for floating-point numbers and integers, polymorphic compare corresponds to the expected numerical comparison functions. For strings, it's a lexicographic comparison.

That said, experienced OCaml developers typically avoid polymorphic comparison. That's surprising, given how obviously useful it is, but there's a good reason. While it's very convenient, in some cases, the type oblivious nature of polymorphic compare means that it does something that doesn't make sense for the particular type of values you're dealing with. This can lead to surprising and hard to resolve bugs in your code. It's for this reason that `Base` discourages the use of polymorphic compare by hiding it by default.

We'll discuss the downsides of polymorphic compare in more detail in Chapter 15 (Maps and Hash Tables).

Note that when clauses have some downsides. As we noted earlier, the static checks associated with pattern matches rely on the fact that patterns are restricted in what they can express. Once we add the ability to add an arbitrary condition to a pattern, something is lost. In particular, the ability of the compiler to determine if a match is exhaustive, or if some case is redundant, is compromised.

Consider the following function, which takes a list of optional values, and returns the number of those values that are `Some`. Because this implementation uses when clauses, the compiler can't tell that the code is exhaustive:

```
# let rec count_some list =
    match list with
    | [] -> 0
    | x :: tl when Option.is_none x -> count_some tl
    | x :: tl when Option.is_some x -> 1 + count_some tl;;
Lines 2-5, characters 5-57:
```

```
Warning 8 [partial-match]: this pattern-matching is not exhaustive.
Here is an example of a case that is not matched:
_::_
(However, some guarded clause may match this value.)
val count_some : 'a option list -> int = <fun>
```

Despite the warning, the function does work fine:

```
# count_some [Some 3; None; Some 4];;
- : int = 2
```

If we add another redundant case without a when clause, the compiler will stop complaining about exhaustiveness and won't produce a warning about the redundancy.

```
# let rec count_some list =
    match list with
    | [] -> 0
    | x :: tl when Option.is_none x -> count_some tl
    | x :: tl when Option.is_some x -> 1 + count_some tl
    | x :: tl -> -1 (* unreachable *);;
val count_some : 'a option list -> int = <fun>
```

Probably a better approach is to simply drop the second when clause:

```
# let rec count_some list =
    match list with
    | [] -> 0
    | x :: tl when Option.is_none x -> count_some tl
    | _ :: tl -> 1 + count_some tl;;
val count_some : 'a option list -> int = <fun>
```

This is a little less clear, however, than the direct pattern-matching solution, where the meaning of each pattern is clearer on its own:

```
# let rec count_some list =
    match list with
    | [] -> 0
    | None   :: tl -> count_some tl
    | Some _ :: tl -> 1 + count_some tl;;
val count_some : 'a option list -> int = <fun>
```

The takeaway from all of this is although when clauses can be useful, we should prefer patterns wherever they are sufficient.

As a side note, the above implementation of count_some is longer than necessary; even worse, it is not tail recursive. In real life, you would probably just use the List.count function:

```
# let count_some l = List.count ~f:Option.is_some l;;
val count_some : 'a option list -> int = <fun>
```

5 Files, Modules, and Programs

We've so far experienced OCaml largely through the toplevel. As you move from exercises to real-world programs, you'll need to leave the toplevel behind and start building programs from files. Files are more than just a convenient way to store and manage your code; in OCaml, they also correspond to modules, which act as boundaries that divide your program into conceptual units.

In this chapter, we'll show you how to build an OCaml program from a collection of files, as well as the basics of working with modules and module signatures.

5.1 Single-File Programs

We'll start with an example: a utility that reads lines from `stdin`, computes a frequency count of the lines, and prints out the ten most frequent lines. We'll start with a simple implementation, which we'll save as the file *freq.ml*.

This implementation will use two functions from the `List.Assoc` module, which provides utility functions for interacting with *association lists*, *i.e.*, lists of key/value pairs. In particular, we use the function `List.Assoc.find`, which looks up a key in an association list; and `List.Assoc.add`, which adds a new binding to an association list, as shown here:

```
# open Base;;
# let assoc = [("one", 1); ("two",2); ("three",3)];;
val assoc : (string * int) list = [("one", 1); ("two", 2); ("three",
  3)]
# List.Assoc.find ~equal:String.equal assoc "two";;
- : int option = Some 2
# List.Assoc.add ~equal:String.equal assoc "four" 4;;
- : (string, int) Base.List.Assoc.t =
[("four", 4); ("one", 1); ("two", 2); ("three", 3)]
# List.Assoc.add ~equal:String.equal assoc "two"  4;;
- : (string, int) Base.List.Assoc.t = [("two", 4); ("one", 1);
  ("three", 3)]
```

Note that `List.Assoc.add` doesn't modify the original list, but instead allocates a new list with the requisite key/value pair added.

Now we can write `freq.ml`.

```
open Base
open Stdio
```

```
let build_counts () =
  In_channel.fold_lines In_channel.stdin ~init:[] ~f:(fun counts line
    ->
      let count =
        match List.Assoc.find ~equal:String.equal counts line with
        | None -> 0
        | Some x -> x
      in
      List.Assoc.add ~equal:String.equal counts line (count + 1))

let () =
  build_counts ()
  |> List.sort ~compare:(fun (_, x) (_, y) -> Int.descending x y)
  |> (fun l -> List.take l 10)
  |> List.iter ~f:(fun (line, count) -> printf "%3d: %s\n" count line)
```

The function build_counts reads in lines from stdin, constructing from those lines an association list with the frequencies of each line. It does this by invoking In_channel.fold_lines (similar to the function List.fold described in Chapter 4 (Lists and Patterns)), which reads through the lines one by one, calling the provided fold function for each line to update the accumulator. That accumulator is initialized to the empty list.

With build_counts defined, we then call the function to build the association list, sort that list by frequency in descending order, grab the first 10 elements off the list, and then iterate over those 10 elements and print them to the screen. These operations are tied together using the |> operator described in Chapter 3.2.4 (Prefix and Infix Operators).

Where Is main?

Unlike programs in C, Java or C#, programs in OCaml don't have a unique main function. When an OCaml program is evaluated, all the statements in the implementation files are evaluated in the order in which they were linked together. These implementation files can contain arbitrary expressions, not just function definitions. In this example, the declaration starting with let () = plays the role of the main function, kicking off the processing. But really the entire file is evaluated at startup, and so in some sense the full codebase is one big main function.

The idiom of writing let () = may seem a bit odd, but it has a purpose. The let binding here is a pattern-match to a value of type unit, which is there to ensure that the expression on the right-hand side returns unit, as is common for functions that operate primarily by side effect.

If we weren't using Base or any other external libraries, we could build the executable like this:

```
$ ocamlopt freq.ml -o freq
File "freq.ml", line 1, characters 5-9:
1 | open Base
         ^^^^
Error: Unbound module Base
```

[2]

But as you can see, it fails because it can't find `Base` and `Stdio`. We need a somewhat more complex invocation to get them linked in:

```
$ ocamlfind ocamlopt -linkpkg -package base -package stdio freq.ml -o
     freq
```

This uses `ocamlfind`, a tool which itself invokes other parts of the OCaml toolchain (in this case, `ocamlopt`) with the appropriate flags to link in particular libraries and packages. Here, `-package base` is asking `ocamlfind` to link in the `Base` library; `-linkpkg` asks ocamlfind to link in the packages as is necessary for building an executable.

While this works well enough for a one-file project, more complicated projects require a tool to orchestrate the build. One good tool for this task is dune. To invoke dune, you need to have two files: a `dune-project` file for the overall project, and a dune file that configures the particular directory. This is a single-directory project, so we'll just have one of each, but more realistic projects will have one `dune-project` and many dune files.

At its simplest, the `dune-project` just specifies the version of the dune configuration-language in use.

```
(lang dune 3.0)
```

We also need a dune file to declare the executable we want to build, along with the libraries it depends on.

```
(executable
  (name      freq)
  (libraries base stdio))
```

With that in place, we can invoke dune as follows.

```
$ dune build freq.exe
```

We can run the resulting executable, `freq.exe`, from the command line. Executables built with dune will be left in the `_build/default` directory, from which they can be invoked. The specific invocation below will count the words that come up in the file `freq.ml` itself.

```
$ grep -Eo '[[:alpha:]]+' freq.ml | ./_build/default/freq.exe
  5: line
  5: List
  5: counts
  4: count
  4: fun
  4: x
  4: equal
  3: let
  2: f
  2: l
```

Conveniently, dune allows us to combine the building and running an executable into a single operation, which we can do using dune `exec`.

```
$ grep -Eo '[[:alpha:]]+' freq.ml | dune exec ./freq.exe
  5: line
  5: List
  5: counts
  4: count
  4: fun
  4: x
  4: equal
  3: let
  2: f
  2: l
```

We've really just scratched the surface of what can be done with dune. We'll discuss dune in more detail in Chapter 1.1.3 (The OCaml Platform).

Bytecode Versus Native Code

OCaml ships with two compilers: the ocamlopt native code compiler and the ocamlc bytecode compiler. Programs compiled with ocamlc are interpreted by a virtual machine, while programs compiled with ocamlopt are compiled to machine code to be run on a specific operating system and processor architecture. With dune, targets ending with .bc are built as bytecode executables, and those ending with .exe are built as native code.

Aside from performance, executables generated by the two compilers have nearly identical behavior. There are a few things to be aware of. First, the bytecode compiler can be used on more architectures, and has some tools that are not available for native code. For example, the OCaml debugger only works with bytecode (although gdb, the GNU Debugger, works with some limitations on OCaml native-code applications). The bytecode compiler is also quicker than the native-code compiler. In addition, in order to run a bytecode executable, you typically need to have OCaml installed on the system in question. That's not strictly required, though, since you can build a bytecode executable with an embedded runtime, using the -custom compiler flag.

As a general matter, production executables should usually be built using the native-code compiler, but it sometimes makes sense to use bytecode for development builds. And, of course, bytecode makes sense when targeting a platform not supported by the native-code compiler. We'll cover both compilers in more detail in Chapter 27 (The Compiler Backend: Bytecode and Native code).

5.2   Multifile Programs and Modules

Source files in OCaml are tied into the module system, with each file compiling down into a module whose name is derived from the name of the file. We've encountered modules before, such as when we used functions like find and add from the List.Assoc module. At its simplest, you can think of a module as a collection of definitions that are stored within a namespace.

Let's consider how we can use modules to refactor the implementation of freq.ml.

Remember that the variable counts contains an association list representing the counts of the lines seen so far. But updating an association list takes time linear in the length of the list, meaning that the time complexity of processing a file is quadratic in the number of distinct lines in the file.

We can fix this problem by replacing association lists with a more efficient data structure. To do that, we'll first factor out the key functionality into a separate module with an explicit interface. We can consider alternative (and more efficient) implementations once we have a clear interface to program against.

We'll start by creating a file, counter.ml, that contains the logic for maintaining the association list used to represent the frequency counts. The key function, called touch, bumps the frequency count of a given line by one.

```
open Base

let touch counts line =
  let count =
    match List.Assoc.find ~equal:String.equal counts line with
    | None -> 0
    | Some x -> x
  in
  List.Assoc.add ~equal:String.equal counts line (count + 1)
```

The file *counter.ml* will be compiled into a module named Counter, where the name of the module is derived automatically from the filename. The module name is capitalized even if the file is not. Indeed, module names are always capitalized.

We can now rewrite freq.ml to use Counter.

```
open Base
open Stdio

let build_counts () =
  In_channel.fold_lines In_channel.stdin ~init:[] ~f:Counter.touch

let () =
  build_counts ()
  |> List.sort ~compare:(fun (_, x) (_, y) -> Int.descending x y)
  |> (fun l -> List.take l 10)
  |> List.iter ~f:(fun (line, count) -> printf "%3d: %s\n" count line)
```

The resulting code can still be built with dune, which will discover dependencies and realize that counter.ml needs to be compiled.

```
$ dune build freq.exe
```

5.3   Signatures and Abstract Types

While we've pushed some of the logic to the Counter module, the code in freq.ml can still depend on the details of the implementation of Counter. Indeed, if you look at the definition of build_counts, you'll see that it depends on the fact that the empty set of frequency counts is represented as an empty list. We'd like to prevent this kind of dependency, so we can change the implementation of `Counter` without needing to change client code like that in `freq.ml`.

The implementation details of a module can be hidden by attaching an *interface*. (Note that in the context of OCaml, the terms *interface*, *signature*, and *module type* are all used interchangeably.) A module defined by a file `filename.ml` can be constrained by a signature placed in a file called `filename.mli`.

For `counter.mli`, we'll start by writing down an interface that describes what's currently available in `counter.ml`, without hiding anything. `val` declarations are used to specify values in a signature. The syntax of a `val` declaration is as follows:

```
val <identifier> : <type>
```

Using this syntax, we can write the signature of `counter.ml` as follows.

```
open Base

(** Bump the frequency count for the given string. *)
val touch : (string * int) list -> string -> (string * int) list
```

Note that dune will detect the presence of the `mli` file automatically and include it in the build.

To hide the fact that frequency counts are represented as association lists, we'll need to make the type of frequency counts *abstract*. A type is abstract if its name is exposed in the interface, but its definition is not. Here's an abstract interface for `Counter`:

```
open Base

(** A collection of string frequency counts *)
type t

(** The empty set of frequency counts *)
val empty : t

(** Bump the frequency count for the given string. *)
val touch : t -> string -> t

(** Converts the set of frequency counts to an association list. A
    string shows up at most once, and the counts are >= 1. *)
val to_list : t -> (string * int) list
```

We added `empty` and `to_list` to `Counter`, since without them there would be no way to create a `Counter.t` or get data out of one.

We also used this opportunity to document the module. The `mli` file is the place where you specify your module's interface, and as such is a natural place to put documentation. We started our comments with a double asterisk to cause them to be picked up by the odoc tool when generating API documentation. We'll discuss odoc more in Chapter 22.2.2 (Browsing Interface Documentation).

Here's a rewrite of `counter.ml` to match the new `counter.mli`:

```
open Base

type t = (string * int) list
```

```
let empty = []
let to_list x = x

let touch counts line =
  let count =
    match List.Assoc.find ~equal:String.equal counts line with
    | None -> 0
    | Some x -> x
  in
  List.Assoc.add ~equal:String.equal counts line (count + 1)
```

If we now try to compile freq.ml, we'll get the following error:

```
$ dune build freq.exe
File "freq.ml", line 5, characters 53-66:
5 |     In_channel.fold_lines In_channel.stdin ~init:[] ~f:Counter.touch
                                                         ^^^^^^^^^^^^^
Error: This expression has type Counter.t -> Export.string ->
    Counter.t
        but an expression was expected of type
          'a list -> Export.string -> 'a list
        Type Counter.t is not compatible with type 'a list
[1]
```

This is because freq.ml depends on the fact that frequency counts are represented as association lists, a fact that we've just hidden. We just need to fix build_counts to use Counter.empty instead of [] and to use Counter.to_list to convert the completed counts to an association list. The resulting implementation is shown below.

```
open Base
open Stdio

let build_counts () =
  In_channel.fold_lines
    In_channel.stdin
    ~init:Counter.empty
    ~f:Counter.touch

let () =
  build_counts ()
  |> Counter.to_list
  |> List.sort ~compare:(fun (_, x) (_, y) -> Int.descending x y)
  |> (fun counts -> List.take counts 10)
  |> List.iter ~f:(fun (line, count) -> printf "%3d: %s\n" count line)
```

With this implementation, the build now succeeds!

```
$ dune build freq.exe
```

Now we can turn to optimizing the implementation of Counter. Here's an alternate and far more efficient implementation, based on Base's Map data structure.

```
open Base

type t = int Map.M(String).t

let empty = Map.empty (module String)
let to_list t = Map.to_alist t
```

```
let touch t s =
  let count =
    match Map.find t s with
    | None -> 0
    | Some x -> x
  in
  Map.set t ~key:s ~data:(count + 1)
```

There's some unfamiliar syntax in the above example, in particular the use of `int Map.M(String).t` to indicate the type of a map, and `Map.empty (module String)` to generate an empty map. Here, we're making use of a more advanced feature of the language (specifically, functors and first-class modules, which we'll get to in later chapters). The use of these features for the Map data-structure in particular is covered in Chapter 15 (Maps and Hash Tables).

5.4   Concrete Types in Signatures

In our frequency-count example, the module `Counter` had an abstract type `Counter.t` for representing a collection of frequency counts. Sometimes, you'll want to make a type in your interface *concrete*, by including the type definition in the interface.

For example, imagine we wanted to add a function to `Counter` for returning the line with the median frequency count. If the number of lines is even, then there is no single median, and the function would return the lines before and after the median instead. We'll use a custom type to represent the fact that there are two possible return values. Here's a possible implementation:

```
type median =
  | Median of string
  | Before_and_after of string * string

let median t =
  let sorted_strings =
    List.sort (Map.to_alist t) ~compare:(fun (_, x) (_, y) ->
        Int.descending x y)
  in
  let len = List.length sorted_strings in
  if len = 0 then failwith "median: empty frequency count";
  let nth n = fst (List.nth_exn sorted_strings n) in
  if len % 2 = 1
  then Median (nth (len / 2))
  else Before_and_after (nth ((len / 2) - 1), nth (len / 2))
```

In the above, we use `failwith` to throw an exception for the case of the empty list. We'll discuss exceptions more in Chapter 8 (Error Handling). Note also that the function `fst` simply returns the first element of any two-tuple.

Now, to expose this usefully in the interface, we need to expose both the function and the type `median` with its definition. Note that values (of which functions are an example) and types have distinct namespaces, so there's no name clash here. Adding the following two lines to `counter.mli` does the trick.

```
(** Represents the median computed from a set of strings. In the case
    where there is an even number of choices, the one before and after
    the median is returned. *)
type median =
  | Median of string
  | Before_and_after of string * string

val median : t -> median
```

The decision of whether a given type should be abstract or concrete is an important one. Abstract types give you more control over how values are created and accessed, and make it easier to enforce invariants beyond what is enforced by the type itself; concrete types let you expose more detail and structure to client code in a lightweight way. The right choice depends very much on the context.

5.5   Nested Modules

Up until now, we've only considered modules that correspond to files, like counter.ml. But modules (and module signatures) can be nested inside other modules. As a simple example, consider a program that needs to deal with multiple identifiers like usernames and hostnames. If you just represent these as strings, then it becomes easy to confuse one with the other.

A better approach is to mint new abstract types for each identifier, where those types are under the covers just implemented as strings. That way, the type system will prevent you from confusing a username with a hostname, and if you do need to convert, you can do so using explicit conversions to and from the string type.

Here's how you might create such an abstract type, within a submodule:

```
open Base

module Username : sig
  type t

  val of_string : string -> t
  val to_string : t -> string
  val ( = ) : t -> t -> bool
end = struct
  type t = string

  let of_string x = x
  let to_string x = x
  let ( = ) = String.( = )
end
```

Note that the to_string and of_string functions above are implemented simply as the identity function, which means they have no runtime effect. They are there purely as part of the discipline that they enforce on the code through the type system. We also chose to put in an equality function, so you can check if two usernames match. In a real application, we might want more functionality, like the ability to hash and compare usernames, but we've kept this example purposefully simple.

The basic structure of a module declaration like this is:

```
module <name> : <signature> = <implementation>
```

We could have written this slightly differently, by giving the signature its own top-level module type declaration, making it possible to create multiple distinct types with the same underlying implementation in a lightweight way:

```
open Base
module Time = Core.Time

module type ID = sig
  type t

  val of_string : string -> t
  val to_string : t -> string
  val ( = ) : t -> t -> bool
end

module String_id = struct
  type t = string

  let of_string x = x
  let to_string x = x
  let ( = ) = String.( = )
end

module Username : ID = String_id
module Hostname : ID = String_id

type session_info =
  { user : Username.t
  ; host : Hostname.t
  ; when_started : Time.t
  }

let sessions_have_same_user s1 s2 = Username.( = ) s1.user s2.host
```

The preceding code has a bug: it compares the username in one session to the host in the other session, when it should be comparing the usernames in both cases. Because of how we defined our types, however, the compiler will flag this bug for us.

```
$ dune build session_info.exe
File "session_info.ml", line 29, characters 59-66:
29 | let sessions_have_same_user s1 s2 = Username.( = ) s1.user
        s2.host

        ^^^^^^^
Error: This expression has type Hostname.t
       but an expression was expected of type Username.t
[1]
```

This is a trivial example, but confusing different kinds of identifiers is a very real source of bugs, and the approach of minting abstract types for different classes of identifiers is an effective way of avoiding such issues.

5.6   Opening Modules

Most of the time, you refer to values and types within a module by using the module name as an explicit qualifier. For example, you write List.map to refer to the map function in the List module. Sometimes, though, you want to be able to refer to the contents of a module without this explicit qualification. That's what the open statement is for.

We've encountered open already, specifically where we've written open Base to get access to the standard definitions in the Base library. In general, opening a module adds the contents of that module to the environment that the compiler looks at to find the definition of various identifiers. Here's an example:

```
# module M = struct let foo = 3 end;;
module M : sig val foo : int end
# foo;;
Line 1, characters 1-4:
Error: Unbound value foo
# open M;;
# foo;;
- : int = 3
```

Here's some general advice on how to use open effectively.

5.6.1   Open Modules Rarely

open is essential when you're using an alternative standard library like Base, but it's generally good style to keep the opening of modules to a minimum. Opening a module is basically a trade-off between terseness and explicitness—the more modules you open, the fewer module qualifications you need, and the harder it is to look at an identifier and figure out where it comes from.

When you do use open, it should mostly be with modules that were designed to be opened, like Base itself, or Option.Monad_infix or Float.O within Base..

5.6.2   Prefer Local Opens

It's generally better to keep down the amount of code affected by an open. One great tool for this is *local opens*, which let you restrict the scope of an open to an arbitrary expression. There are two syntaxes for local opens. The following example shows the let open syntax;

```
# let average x y =
    let open Int64 in
    (x + y) / of_int 2;;
val average : int64 -> int64 -> int64 = <fun>
```

Here, of_int and the infix operators are the ones from the Int64 module.

The following shows off a more lightweight syntax which is particularly useful for small expressions.

```
# let average x y =
    Int64.((x + y) / of_int 2);;
val average : int64 -> int64 -> int64 = <fun>
```

5.6.3   Using Module Shortcuts Instead

An alternative to local opens that makes your code terser without giving up on explicitness is to locally rebind the name of a module. So, when using the `Counter.median` type, instead of writing:

```
let print_median m =
  match m with
  | Counter.Median string -> printf "True median:\n   %s\n" string
  | Counter.Before_and_after (before, after) ->
    printf "Before and after median:\n   %s\n   %s\n" before after
```

you could write:

```
let print_median m =
  let module C = Counter in
  match m with
  | C.Median string -> printf "True median:\n   %s\n" string
  | C.Before_and_after (before, after) ->
    printf "Before and after median:\n   %s\n   %s\n" before after
```

Because the module name `C` only exists for a short scope, it's easy to read and remember what `C` stands for. Rebinding modules to very short names at the top level of your module is usually a mistake.

5.7   Including Modules

While opening a module affects the environment used to search for identifiers, *including* a module is a way of adding new identifiers to a module proper. Consider the following simple module for representing a range of integer values:

```
# module Interval = struct
    type t = | Interval of int * int
             | Empty

    let create low high =
      if high < low then Empty else Interval (low,high)
  end;;
module Interval :
  sig type t = Interval of int * int | Empty val create : int -> int
    -> t end
```

We can use the `include` directive to create a new, extended version of the `Interval` module:

```
# module Extended_interval = struct
    include Interval
```

```
    let contains t x =
      match t with
      | Empty -> false
      | Interval (low,high) -> x >= low && x <= high
  end;;
module Extended_interval :
  sig
    type t = Interval.t = Interval of int * int | Empty
    val create : int -> int -> t
    val contains : t -> int -> bool
  end
# Extended_interval.contains (Extended_interval.create 3 10) 4;;
- : bool = true
```

The difference between `include` and `open` is that we've done more than change how identifiers are searched for: we've changed what's in the module. If we'd used `open`, we'd have gotten a quite different result:

```
# module Extended_interval = struct
    open Interval

    let contains t x =
      match t with
      | Empty -> false
      | Interval (low,high) -> x >= low && x <= high
  end;;
module Extended_interval :
  sig val contains : Extended_interval.t -> int -> bool end
# Extended_interval.contains (Extended_interval.create 3 10) 4;;
Line 1, characters 29-53:
Error: Unbound value Extended_interval.create
```

To consider a more realistic example, imagine you wanted to build an extended version of the `Option` module, where you've added some functionality not present in the module as distributed in `Base`. That's a job for `include`.

```
open Base

(* The new function we're going to add *)
let apply f_opt x =
  match f_opt with
  | None -> None
  | Some f -> Some (f x)

(* The remainder of the option module *)
include Option
```

Now, how do we write an interface for this new module? It turns out that `include` works on signatures as well, so we can pull essentially the same trick to write our `mli`. The only issue is that we need to get our hands on the signature for the `Option` module. This can be done using `module type of`, which computes a signature from a module:

```
open Base

(* Include the interface of the option module from Base *)
include module type of Option
```

```
(* Signature of function we're adding *)
val apply : ('a -> 'b) t -> 'a -> 'b t
```

Note that the order of declarations in the `mli` does not need to match the order of declarations in the `ml`. The order of declarations in the `ml` mostly matters insofar as it affects which values are shadowed. If we wanted to replace a function in `Option` with a new function of the same name, the declaration of that function in the `ml` would have to come after the `include Option` declaration.

We can now use `Ext_option` as a replacement for `Option`. If we want to use `Ext_option` in preference to `Option` in our project, we can create a file of common definitions, which in this case we'll call `import.ml`.

```
module Option = Ext_option
```

Then, by opening `Import`, we can shadow `Base`'s `Option` module with our extension.

```
open Base
open Import

let lookup_and_apply map key x = Option.apply (Map.find map key) x
```

5.8 Common Errors with Modules

When OCaml compiles a program with an `ml` and an `mli`, it will complain if it detects a mismatch between the two. Here are some of the common errors you'll run into.

5.8.1 Type Mismatches

The simplest kind of error is where the type specified in the signature does not match the type in the implementation of the module. As an example, if we replace the `val` declaration in `counter.mli` by swapping the types of the first two arguments:

```
(** Bump the frequency count for the given string. *)
val touch : string -> t -> t
```

and we try to compile, we'll get the following error.

```
$ dune build freq.exe
File "counter.ml", line 1:
Error: The implementation counter.ml
       does not match the interface
    .freq.eobjs/byte/dune__exe__Counter.cmi:
       Values do not match:
         val touch :
           ('a, int, 'b) Base.Map.t -> 'a -> ('a, int, 'b) Base.Map.t
       is not included in
         val touch : string -> t -> t
       File "counter.mli", line 16, characters 0-28: Expected
    declaration
       File "counter.ml", line 8, characters 4-9: Actual declaration
[1]
```

5.8.2   Missing Definitions

We might decide that we want a new function in `Counter` for pulling out the frequency count of a given string. We could add that to the `mli` by adding the following line.

```
(** Returns the frequency count for the given string *)
val count : t -> string -> int
```

Now if we try to compile without actually adding the implementation, we'll get this error.

```
$ dune build freq.exe
File "counter.ml", line 1:
Error: The implementation counter.ml
       does not match the interface
    .freq.eobjs/byte/dune__exe__Counter.cmi:
       The value `count' is required but not provided
       File "counter.mli", line 15, characters 0-30: Expected
    declaration
[1]
```

A missing type definition will lead to a similar error.

5.8.3   Type Definition Mismatches

Type definitions that show up in an `mli` need to match up with corresponding definitions in the `ml`. Consider again the example of the type `median`. The order of the declaration of variants matters to the OCaml compiler, so the definition of `median` in the implementation listing those options in a different order:

```
(** Represents the median computed from a set of strings. In the case
    where there is an even number of choices, the one before and after
    the median is returned. *)
type median =
  | Before_and_after of string * string
  | Median of string

val median : t -> median
```

will lead to a compilation error.

```
$ dune build freq.exe
File "counter.ml", line 1:
Error: The implementation counter.ml
       does not match the interface
    .freq.eobjs/byte/dune__exe__Counter.cmi:
       Type declarations do not match:
         type median = Median of string | Before_and_after of string
    * string
       is not included in
         type median = Before_and_after of string * string | Median
    of string
       Constructors number 1 have different names, Median and
    Before_and_after.
       File "counter.mli", lines 21-23, characters 0-20: Expected
    declaration
```

```
      File "counter.ml", lines 17-19, characters 0-39: Actual
   declaration
[1]
```

Order is similarly important to other type declarations, including the order in which record fields are declared and the order of arguments (including labeled and optional arguments) to a function.

5.8.4   Cyclic Dependencies

In most cases, OCaml doesn't allow cyclic dependencies, i.e., a collection of definitions that all refer to one another. If you want to create such definitions, you typically have to mark them specially. For example, when defining a set of mutually recursive values (like the definition of is_even and is_odd in Chapter 3.2.3 (Recursive Functions)), you need to define them using let rec rather than ordinary let.

The same is true at the module level. By default, cyclic dependencies between modules are not allowed, and cyclic dependencies among files are never allowed. Recursive modules are possible but are a rare case, and we won't discuss them further here.

The simplest example of a forbidden circular reference is a module referring to its own module name. So, if we tried to add a reference to Counter from within counter.ml.

```
let singleton l = Counter.touch Counter.empty
```

we'll see this error when we try to build:

```
$ dune build freq.exe
File "counter.ml", line 18, characters 18-31:
18 | let singleton l = Counter.touch Counter.empty
                       ^^^^^^^^^^^^^
Error: The module Counter is an alias for module Dune__exe__Counter,
    which is the current compilation unit
[1]
```

The problem manifests in a different way if we create cyclic references between files. We could create such a situation by adding a reference to Freq from counter.ml, e.g., by adding the following line.

```
let _build_counts = Freq.build_counts
```

In this case, dune will notice the error and complain explicitly about the cycle:

```
$ dune build freq.exe
Error: Dependency cycle between the following files:
    _build/default/.freq.eobjs/freq.impl.all-deps
-> _build/default/.freq.eobjs/counter.impl.all-deps
-> _build/default/.freq.eobjs/freq.impl.all-deps
[1]
```

5.9   Designing with Modules

The module system is a key part of how an OCaml program is structured. As such, we'll close this chapter with some advice on how to think about designing that structure effectively.

5.9.1   Expose Concrete Types Rarely

When designing an `mli`, one choice that you need to make is whether to expose the concrete definition of your types or leave them abstract. Most of the time, abstraction is the right choice, for two reasons: it enhances the flexibility of your design, and it makes it possible to enforce invariants on the use of your module.

Abstraction enhances flexibility by restricting how users can interact with your types, thus reducing the ways in which users can depend on the details of your implementation. If you expose types explicitly, then users can depend on any and every detail of the types you choose. If they're abstract, then only the specific operations you want to expose are available. This means that you can freely change the implementation without affecting clients, as long as you preserve the semantics of those operations.

In a similar way, abstraction allows you to enforce invariants on your types. If your types are exposed, then users of the module can create new instances of that type (or if mutable, modify existing instances) in any way allowed by the underlying type. That may violate a desired invariant *i.e.*, a property about your type that is always supposed to be true. Abstract types allow you to protect invariants by making sure that you only expose functions that preserve your invariants.

Despite these benefits, there is a trade-off here. In particular, exposing types concretely makes it possible to use pattern-matching with those types, which as we saw in Chapter 4 (Lists and Patterns) is a powerful and important tool. You should generally only expose the concrete implementation of your types when there's significant value in the ability to pattern match, and when the invariants that you care about are already enforced by the data type itself.

5.9.2   Design for the Call Site

When writing an interface, you should think not just about how easy it is to understand the interface for someone who reads your carefully documented `mli` file, but more importantly, you want the call to be as obvious as possible for someone who is reading it at the call site.

The reason for this is that most of the time, people interacting with your API will be doing so by reading and modifying code that uses the API, not by reading the interface definition. By making your API as obvious as possible from that perspective, you simplify the lives of your users.

There are many ways of improving readability of client code. One example is labeled arguments (discussed in Chapter 3.2.6 (Labeled Arguments)), which act as documentation that is available at the call site.

You can also improve readability simply by choosing good names for your functions, variant tags and record fields. Good names aren't always long, to be clear. If you wanted to write an anonymous function for doubling a number: (fun x -> x * 2), a short variable name like x is best. A good rule of thumb is that names that have a small scope should be short, whereas names that have a large scope, like the name of a function in a module interface, should be longer and more descriptive.

There is of course a tradeoff here, in that making your APIs more explicit tends to make them more verbose as well. Another useful rule of thumb is that more rarely used names should be longer and more explicit, since the cost of verbosity goes down and the benefit of explicitness goes up the less often a name is used.

5.9.3 Create Uniform Interfaces

Designing the interface of a module is a task that should not be thought of in isolation. The interfaces that appear in your codebase should play together harmoniously. Part of achieving that is standardizing aspects of those interfaces.

Base, Core and related libraries have been designed with a uniform set of standards in mind around the design of module interfaces. Here are some of the guidelines that they use.

- *A module for (almost) every type.* You should mint a module for almost every type in your program, and the primary type of a given module should be called t.
- *Put t first.* If you have a module M whose primary type is M.t, the functions in M that take a value of type M.t should take it as their first argument.
- Functions that routinely throw an exception should end in _exn. Otherwise, errors should be signaled by returning an option or an Or_error.t (both of which are discussed in Chapter 8 (Error Handling)).

There are also standards in Base about what the type signature for specific functions should be. For example, the signature for map is always essentially the same, no matter what the underlying type it is applied to. This kind of function-by-function API uniformity is achieved through the use of *signature includes*, which allow for different modules to share components of their interface. This approach is described in Chapter 11.2.4 (Using Multiple Interfaces).

Base's standards may or may not fit your projects, but you can improve the usability of your codebase by finding some consistent set of standards to apply.

5.9.4 Interfaces Before Implementations

OCaml's concise and flexible type language enables a type-oriented approach to software design. Such an approach involves thinking through and writing out the types you're going to use before embarking on the implementation itself.

This is a good approach both when working in the core language, where you would write your type definitions before writing the logic of your computations, as well as at the module level, where you would write a first draft of your `mli` before working on the `ml`.

Of course, the design process goes in both directions. You'll often find yourself going back and modifying your types in response to things you learn by working on the implementation. But types and signatures provide a lightweight tool for constructing a skeleton of your design in a way that helps clarify your goals and intent, before you spend a lot of time and effort fleshing it out.

6 Records

One of OCaml's best features is its concise and expressive system for declaring new data types. *Records* are a key element of that system. We discussed records briefly in Chapter 2 (A Guided Tour), but this chapter will go into more depth, covering more of the technical details, as well as providing advice on how to use records effectively in your software designs.

A record represents a collection of values stored together as one, where each component is identified by a different field name. The basic syntax for a record type declaration is as follows:

```
type <record-name> =
    { <field> : <type>;
      <field> : <type>;
      ...
    }
```

Note that record field names must start with a lowercase letter.

Here's a simple example: a `service_info` record that represents an entry from the `/etc/services` file on a typical Unix system. That file is used for keeping track of the well-known port and protocol name for protocols such as FTP or SSH. Note that we're going to open `Core` in this example rather than `Base`, since we're using the Unix API, which you need `Core` for.

```
open Core
type service_info =
  { service_name : string;
    port         : int;
    protocol     : string;
  }
```

We can construct a `service_info` just as easily as we declared its type. The following function tries to construct such a record given as input a line from `/etc/services` file. To do this, we'll use `Re`, a regular expression engine for OCaml. If you don't know how regular expressions work, you can just think of them as a simple pattern language you can use for parsing a string. (You may need to install it first by running `opam install re`.)

```
# #require "re";;
# let service_info_of_string line =
    let matches =
      let pat = "([a-zA-Z]+)[ \t]+([0-9]+)/([a-zA-Z]+)" in
```

```
    Re.exec (Re.Posix.compile_pat pat) line
  in
  { service_name = Re.Group.get matches 1;
    port = Int.of_string (Re.Group.get matches 2);
    protocol = Re.Group.get matches 3;
  }
;;
val service_info_of_string : string -> service_info = <fun>
```

We can now construct a concrete record by calling the function on a line from the file.

```
# let ssh = service_info_of_string "ssh 22/udp # SSH Remote Login
    Protocol";;
val ssh : service_info = {service_name = "ssh"; port = 22; protocol =
    "udp"}
```

You might wonder how the compiler inferred that our function returns a value of type service_info. In this case, the compiler bases its inference on the field names used in constructing the record. That inference is most straightforward when each field name belongs to only one record type. We'll discuss later in the chapter what happens when field names are shared across different record types.

Once we have a record value in hand, we can extract elements from the record field using dot notation:

```
# ssh.port;;
- : int = 22
```

When declaring an OCaml type, you always have the option of parameterizing it by a polymorphic type. Records are no different in this regard. As an example, here's a type that represents an arbitrary item tagged with a line number.

```
type 'a with_line_num = { item: 'a; line_num: int }
```

We can then write polymorphic functions that operate over this parameterized type. For example, this function takes a file and parses it as a series of lines, using the provided function for parsing each individual line.

```
# let parse_lines parse file_contents =
    let lines = String.split ~on:'\n' file_contents in
    List.mapi lines ~f:(fun line_num line ->
      { item = parse line;
        line_num = line_num + 1;
      })
;;
val parse_lines : (string -> 'a) -> string -> 'a with_line_num list =
    <fun>
```

We can then use this function for parsing a snippet of a real /etc/services file.

```
# parse_lines service_info_of_string
    "rtmp              1/ddp     # Routing Table Maintenance Protocol
     tcpmux            1/udp     # TCP Port Service Multiplexer
     tcpmux            1/tcp     # TCP Port Service Multiplexer";;
- : service_info with_line_num list =
[{item = {service_name = "rtmp"; port = 1; protocol = "ddp"};
    line_num = 1};
```

```
{item = {service_name = "tcpmux"; port = 1; protocol = "udp"};
    line_num = 2};
{item = {service_name = "tcpmux"; port = 1; protocol = "tcp"};
    line_num = 3}]
```

The polymorphism lets us use the same function when parsing a different format, like this function for parsing a file containing an integer on every line.

```
# parse_lines Int.of_string "1\n10\n100\n1000";;
- : int with_line_num list =
[{item = 1; line_num = 1}; {item = 10; line_num = 2};
 {item = 100; line_num = 3}; {item = 1000; line_num = 4}]
```

6.1   Patterns and Exhaustiveness

Another way of getting information out of a record is by using a pattern match, as shown in the following function.

```
# let service_info_to_string
    { service_name = name; port = port; protocol = prot  }
    =
    sprintf "%s %i/%s" name port prot
  ;;
val service_info_to_string : service_info -> string = <fun>
# service_info_to_string ssh;;
- : string = "ssh 22/udp"
```

Note that the pattern we used had only a single case, rather than using several cases separated by |'s. We needed only one pattern because record patterns are *irrefutable*, meaning that a record pattern match will never fail at runtime. That's because the set of fields available in a record is always the same. In general, patterns for types with a fixed structure, like records and tuples, are irrefutable, unlike types with variable structures like lists and variants.

Another important characteristic of record patterns is that they don't need to be complete; a pattern can mention only a subset of the fields in the record. This can be convenient, but it can also be error prone. In particular, this means that when new fields are added to the record, code that should be updated to react to the presence of those new fields will not be flagged by the compiler.

As an example, imagine that we wanted to change our service_info record so that it preserves comments. We can do this by providing a new definition of service_info that includes a comment field:

```
type service_info =
  { service_name : string;
    port         : int;
    protocol     : string;
    comment      : string option;
  }
```

The code for service_info_to_string would continue to compile without change. But in this case, we should probably update the code so that the generated string includes the comment if it's there. It would be nice if the type system would warn us that we should consider updating the function.

Happily, OCaml offers an optional warning for missing fields in record patterns. With that warning turned on (which you can do in the toplevel by typing `#warnings "+9"`), the compiler will indeed warn us.

```
# #warnings "+9";;
# let service_info_to_string
    { service_name = name; port = port; protocol = prot  }
    =
    sprintf "%s %i/%s" name port prot
  ;;
Line 2, characters 5-59:
Warning 9 [missing-record-field-pattern]: the following labels are
    not bound in this record pattern:
comment
Either bind these labels explicitly or add '; _' to the pattern.
val service_info_to_string : service_info -> string = <fun>
```

We can disable the warning for a given pattern by explicitly acknowledging that we are ignoring extra fields. This is done by adding an underscore to the pattern:

```
# let service_info_to_string
    { service_name = name; port = port; protocol = prot; _ }
    =
    sprintf "%s %i/%s" name port prot
  ;;
val service_info_to_string : service_info -> string = <fun>
```

It's a good idea to enable the warning for incomplete record matches and to explicitly disable it with an _ where necessary.

Compiler Warnings

The OCaml compiler is packed full of useful warnings that can be enabled and disabled separately. These are documented in the compiler itself, so we could have found out about warning 9 as follows:

```
$ ocaml -warn-help | egrep '\b9\b'
  9 [missing-record-field-pattern] Missing fields in a record pattern.
  R Alias for warning 9.
```

You can think of OCaml's warnings as a powerful set of optional static analysis tools. They're enormously helpful in catching all sorts of bugs, and you should enable them in your build environment. You don't typically enable all warnings, but the defaults that ship with the compiler are pretty good.

The warnings used for building the examples in this book are specified with the following flag: `-w @A-4-33-40-41-42-43-34-44`.

The syntax of `-w` can be found by running `ocaml -help`, but this particular invocation turns on all warnings as errors, disabling only the numbers listed explicitly after the A.

Treating warnings as errors (i.e., making OCaml fail to compile any code that triggers a warning) is good practice, since without it, warnings are too often ignored during development. When preparing a package for distribution, however, this is a bad idea, since the list of warnings may grow from one release of the compiler to another, and so this may lead your package to fail to compile on newer compiler releases.

6.2 Field Punning

When the name of a variable coincides with the name of a record field, OCaml provides some handy syntactic shortcuts. For example, the pattern in the following function binds all of the fields in question to variables of the same name. This is called *field punning*:

```
# let service_info_to_string { service_name; port; protocol; comment
    } =
    let base = sprintf "%s %i/%s" service_name port protocol in
    match comment with
    | None -> base
    | Some text -> base ^ " #" ^ text;;
val service_info_to_string : service_info -> string = <fun>
```

Field punning can also be used to construct a record. Consider the following updated version of `service_info_of_string`.

```
# let service_info_of_string line =
    (* first, split off any comment *)
    let (line,comment) =
      match String.rsplit2 line ~on:'#' with
      | None -> (line,None)
      | Some (ordinary,comment) -> (ordinary, Some comment)
    in
    (* now, use a regular expression to break up the
       service definition *)
    let matches =
      Re.exec
        (Re.Posix.compile_pat
          "([a-zA-Z]+)[ \t]+([0-9]+)/([a-zA-Z]+)")
        line
    in
    let service_name = Re.Group.get matches 1 in
    let port = Int.of_string (Re.Group.get matches 2) in
    let protocol = Re.Group.get matches 3 in
    { service_name; port; protocol; comment };;
val service_info_of_string : string -> service_info = <fun>
```

In the preceding code, we defined variables corresponding to the record fields first, and then the record declaration itself simply listed the fields that needed to be included. You can take advantage of both field punning and label punning when writing a function for constructing a record from labeled arguments:

```
# let create_service_info ~service_name ~port ~protocol ~comment =
    { service_name; port; protocol; comment };;
val create_service_info :
  service_name:string ->
  port:int -> protocol:string -> comment:string option ->
    service_info =
  <fun>
```

This is considerably more concise than what you would get without punning:

```
# let create_service_info
        ~service_name:service_name ~port:port
        ~protocol:protocol ~comment:comment =
    { service_name = service_name;
      port = port;
      protocol = protocol;
      comment = comment;
    };;
val create_service_info :
  service_name:string ->
  port:int -> protocol:string -> comment:string option ->
    service_info =
  <fun>
```

Together, field and label punning encourage a style where you propagate the same names throughout your codebase. This is generally good practice, since it encourages consistent naming, which makes it easier to navigate the source.

6.3   Reusing Field Names

Defining records with the same field names can be problematic. As a simple example, let's consider a collection of types representing the protocol of a logging server.

We'll describe three message types: `log_entry`, `heartbeat`, and `logon`. The `log_entry` message is used to deliver a log entry to the server; the `logon` message is sent when initiating a connection and includes the identity of the user connecting and credentials used for authentication; and the `heartbeat` message is periodically sent by the client to demonstrate to the server that the client is alive and connected. All of these messages include a session ID and the time the message was generated.

```
type log_entry =
  { session_id: string;
    time: Time_ns.t;
    important: bool;
    message: string;
  }
type heartbeat =
  { session_id: string;
    time: Time_ns.t;
    status_message: string;
  }
type logon =
  { session_id: string;
    time: Time_ns.t;
    user: string;
    credentials: string;
  }
```

Reusing field names can lead to some ambiguity. For example, if we want to write a function to grab the `session_id` from a record, what type will it have?

```
# let get_session_id t = t.session_id;;
```

```
val get_session_id : logon -> string = <fun>
```

In this case, OCaml just picks the most recent definition of that record field. We can force OCaml to assume we're dealing with a different type (say, a `heartbeat`) using a type annotation:

```
# let get_heartbeat_session_id (t:heartbeat) = t.session_id;;
val get_heartbeat_session_id : heartbeat -> string = <fun>
```

While it's possible to resolve ambiguous field names using type annotations, the ambiguity can be a bit confusing. Consider the following functions for grabbing the session ID and status from a heartbeat:

```
# let status_and_session t = (t.status_message, t.session_id);;
val status_and_session : heartbeat -> string * string = <fun>
# let session_and_status t = (t.session_id, t.status_message);;
Line 1, characters 45-59:
Error: This expression has type logon
       There is no field status_message within type logon
```

Why did the first definition succeed without a type annotation and the second one fail? The difference is that in the first case, the type-checker considered the `status_message` field first and thus concluded that the record was a `heartbeat`. When the order was switched, the `session_id` field was considered first, and so that drove the type to be considered to be a `logon`, at which point `t.status_message` no longer made sense.

Adding a type annotation resolves the ambiguity, no matter what order the fields are considered in.

```
# let session_and_status (t:heartbeat) = (t.session_id,
    t.status_message);;
val session_and_status : heartbeat -> string * string = <fun>
```

We can avoid the ambiguity altogether, either by using nonoverlapping field names or by putting different record types in different modules. Indeed, packing types into modules is a broadly useful idiom (and one used quite extensively by `Base`), providing for each type a namespace within which to put related values. When using this style, it is standard practice to name the type associated with the module `t`. So, we would write:

```
module Log_entry = struct
  type t =
    { session_id: string;
      time: Time_ns.t;
      important: bool;
      message: string;
    }
end
module Heartbeat = struct
  type t =
    { session_id: string;
      time: Time_ns.t;
      status_message: string;
    }
```

```
    end
module Logon = struct
   type t =
      { session_id: string;
        time: Time_ns.t;
        user: string;
        credentials: string;
      }
end
```

Now, our log-entry-creation function can be rendered as follows:

```
# let create_log_entry ~session_id ~important message =
    { Log_entry.time = Time_ns.now ();
      Log_entry.session_id;
      Log_entry.important;
      Log_entry.message
    };;
val create_log_entry :
  session_id:string -> important:bool -> string -> Log_entry.t = <fun>
```

The module name `Log_entry` is required to qualify the fields, because this function is outside of the `Log_entry` module where the record was defined. OCaml only requires the module qualification for one record field, however, so we can write this more concisely. Note that we are allowed to insert whitespace between the module path and the field name:

```
# let create_log_entry ~session_id ~important message =
    { Log_entry.
      time = Time_ns.now (); session_id; important; message };;
val create_log_entry :
  session_id:string -> important:bool -> string -> Log_entry.t = <fun>
```

Earlier, we saw that you could help OCaml understand which record field was intended by adding a type annotation. We can use that here to make the example even more concise.

```
# let create_log_entry ~session_id ~important message : Log_entry.t =
    { time = Time_ns.now (); session_id; important; message };;
val create_log_entry :
  session_id:string -> important:bool -> string -> Log_entry.t = <fun>
```

This is not restricted to constructing a record; we can use the same approaches when pattern matching:

```
# let message_to_string { Log_entry.important; message; _ } =
    if important then String.uppercase message else message;;
val message_to_string : Log_entry.t -> string = <fun>
```

When using dot notation for accessing record fields, we can qualify the field by the module as well.

```
# let is_important t = t.Log_entry.important;;
val is_important : Log_entry.t -> bool = <fun>
```

The syntax here is a little surprising when you first encounter it. The thing to keep in mind is that the dot is being used in two ways: the first dot is a record field access, with everything to the right of the dot being interpreted as a field name; the second dot is accessing the contents of a module, referring to the record field `important` from within the module `Log_entry`. The fact that `Log_entry` is capitalized and so can't be a field name is what disambiguates the two uses.

Qualifying a record field by the module it comes from can be awkward. Happily, OCaml doesn't require that the record field be qualified if it can otherwise infer the type of the record in question. In particular, we can rewrite the above declarations by adding type annotations and removing the module qualifications.

```
# let message_to_string ({ important; message; _ } : Log_entry.t) =
    if important then String.uppercase message else message;;
val message_to_string : Log_entry.t -> string = <fun>
# let is_important (t:Log_entry.t) = t.important;;
val is_important : Log_entry.t -> bool = <fun>
```

This feature of the language, known by the somewhat imposing name of *type-directed constructor disambiguation*, applies to variant tags as well as record fields, as we'll see in Chapter 7 (Variants).

6.4   Functional Updates

Fairly often, you will find yourself wanting to create a new record that differs from an existing record in only a subset of the fields. For example, imagine our logging server had a record type for representing the state of a given client, including when the last heartbeat was received from that client.

```
type client_info =
  { addr: Unix.Inet_addr.t;
    port: int;
    user: string;
    credentials: string;
    last_heartbeat_time: Time_ns.t;
  }
```

We could define a function for updating the client information when a new heartbeat arrives as follows.

```
# let register_heartbeat t hb =
    { addr = t.addr;
      port = t.port;
      user = t.user;
      credentials = t.credentials;
      last_heartbeat_time = hb.Heartbeat.time;
    };;
val register_heartbeat : client_info -> Heartbeat.t -> client_info =
    <fun>
```

This is fairly verbose, given that there's only one field that we actually want to change, and all the others are just being copied over from `t`. We can use OCaml's *functional update* syntax to do this more tersely.

The following shows how we can use functional updates to rewrite `register_heartbeat` more concisely.

```
# let register_heartbeat t hb =
    { t with last_heartbeat_time = hb.Heartbeat.time };;
val register_heartbeat : client_info -> Heartbeat.t -> client_info =
    <fun>
```

The with keyword marks that this is a functional update, and the value assignments on the right-hand side indicate the changes to be made to the record on the left-hand side of the with.

Functional updates make your code independent of the identity of the fields in the record that are not changing. This is often what you want, but it has downsides as well. In particular, if you change the definition of your record to have more fields, the type system will not prompt you to reconsider whether your code needs to change to accommodate the new fields. Consider what happens if we decided to add a field for the status message received on the last heartbeat:

```
type client_info =
  { addr: Unix.Inet_addr.t;
    port: int;
    user: string;
    credentials: string;
    last_heartbeat_time: Time_ns.t;
    last_heartbeat_status: string;
  }
```

The original implementation of register_heartbeat would now be invalid, and thus the compiler would effectively warn us to think about how to handle this new field. But the version using a functional update continues to compile as is, even though it incorrectly ignores the new field. The correct thing to do would be to update the code as follows:

```
# let register_heartbeat t hb =
    { t with last_heartbeat_time   = hb.Heartbeat.time;
             last_heartbeat_status = hb.Heartbeat.status_message;
    };;
val register_heartbeat : client_info -> Heartbeat.t -> client_info =
    <fun>
```

These downsides notwithstanding, functional updates are very useful, and a good choice for cases where it's not important that you consider every field of the record when making a change.

6.5   Mutable Fields

Like most OCaml values, records are immutable by default. You can, however, declare individual record fields as mutable. In the following code, we've made the last two fields of client_info mutable:

```
type client_info =
  { addr: Unix.Inet_addr.t;
    port: int;
    user: string;
```

```
        credentials: string;
        mutable last_heartbeat_time: Time_ns.t;
        mutable last_heartbeat_status: string;
      }
```

The `<-` operator is used for setting a mutable field. The side-effecting version of `register_heartbeat` would be written as follows:

```
# let register_heartbeat t (hb:Heartbeat.t) =
    t.last_heartbeat_time   <- hb.time;
    t.last_heartbeat_status <- hb.status_message;;
val register_heartbeat : client_info -> Heartbeat.t -> unit = <fun>
```

Note that mutable assignment, and thus the `<-` operator, is not needed for initialization because all fields of a record, including mutable ones, are specified when the record is created.

OCaml's policy of immutable-by-default is a good one, but imperative programming is an important part of programming in OCaml. We go into more depth about how (and when) to use OCaml's imperative features in Chapter 9 (Imperative Programming).

6.6   First-Class Fields

Consider the following function for extracting the usernames from a list of `Logon` messages:

```
# let get_users logons =
    List.dedup_and_sort ~compare:String.compare
      (List.map logons ~f:(fun x -> x.Logon.user));;
val get_users : Logon.t list -> string list = <fun>
```

Here, we wrote a small function (`fun x -> x.Logon.user`) to access the user field. This kind of accessor function is a common enough pattern that it would be convenient to generate it automatically. The `ppx_fields_conv` syntax extension that ships with Core does just that.

The `[@@deriving fields]` annotation at the end of the declaration of a record type will cause the extension to be applied to a given type declaration. We need to enable the extension explicitly,

```
# #require "ppx_jane";;
```

at which point, we can define `Logon` as follows:

```
# module Logon = struct
    type t =
      { session_id: string;
        time: Time_ns.t;
        user: string;
        credentials: string;
      }
    [@@deriving fields]
  end;;
module Logon :
```

```
sig
  type t = {
    session_id : string;
    time : Time_ns.t;
    user : string;
    credentials : string;
  }
  val credentials : t -> string
  val user : t -> string
  val time : t -> Time_ns.t
  val session_id : t -> string
  module Fields :
    sig
      val names : string list
      val credentials :
        ([< `Read | `Set_and_create ], t, string) Field.t_with_perm
      val user :
        ([< `Read | `Set_and_create ], t, string) Field.t_with_perm
      val time :
        ([< `Read | `Set_and_create ], t, Time_ns.t)
      Field.t_with_perm
...
    end
end
```

Note that this will generate *a lot* of output because `fieldslib` generates a large collection of helper functions for working with record fields. We'll only discuss a few of these; you can learn about the remainder from the documentation that comes with `fieldslib`.

One of the functions we obtain is `Logon.user`, which we can use to extract the user field from a logon message:

```
# let get_users logons =
    List.dedup_and_sort ~compare:String.compare
  (List.map logons ~f:Logon.user);;
val get_users : Logon.t list -> string list = <fun>
```

In addition to generating field accessor functions, `fieldslib` also creates a submodule called `Fields` that contains a first-class representative of each field, in the form of a value of type `Field.t`. The `Field` module provides the following functions:

Field.name Returns the name of a field
Field.get Returns the content of a field
Field.fset Does a functional update of a field
Field.setter Returns `None` if the field is not mutable or `Some` f if it is, where f is a function for mutating that field

A `Field.t` has two type parameters: the first for the type of the record, and the second for the type of the field in question. Thus, the type of `Logon.Fields.session_id` is `(Logon.t, string) Field.t`, whereas the type of `Logon.Fields.time` is `(Logon.t, Time.t) Field.t`. Thus, if you call `Field.get` on `Logon.Fields.user`, you'll get a function for extracting the user field from a `Logon.t`:

```
# Field.get Logon.Fields.user;;
- : Logon.t -> string = <fun>
```

Thus, the first parameter of the `Field.t` corresponds to the record you pass to `get`, and the second parameter corresponds to the value contained in the field, which is also the return type of `get`.

The type of `Field.get` is a little more complicated than you might naively expect from the preceding one:

```
# Field.get;;
- : ('b, 'r, 'a) Field.t_with_perm -> 'r -> 'a = <fun>
```

The type is `Field.t_with_perm` rather than `Field.t` because fields have a notion of access control that comes up in some special cases where we expose the ability to read a field from a record, but not the ability to create new records, and so we can't expose functional updates.

We can use first-class fields to do things like write a generic function for displaying a record field:

```
# let show_field field to_string record =
    let name = Field.name field in
    let field_string = to_string (Field.get field record) in
    name ^ ": " ^ field_string;;
val show_field :
  ('a, 'b, 'c) Field.t_with_perm -> ('c -> string) -> 'b -> string =
    <fun>
```

This takes three arguments: the `Field.t`, a function for converting the contents of the field in question to a string, and a record from which the field can be grabbed.

Here's an example of `show_field` in action:

```
# let logon = { Logon.
               session_id = "26685";
               time = Time_ns.of_string "2017-07-21 10:11:45 EST";
               user = "yminsky";
               credentials = "Xy2d9W"; };;
val logon : Logon.t =
  {Logon.session_id = "26685"; time = 2017-07-21 15:11:45.000000000Z;
   user = "yminsky"; credentials = "Xy2d9W"}
# show_field Logon.Fields.user Fn.id logon;;
- : string = "user: yminsky"
# show_field Logon.Fields.time Time_ns.to_string logon;;
- : string = "time: 2017-07-21 15:11:45.000000000Z"
```

As a side note, the preceding example is our first use of the `Fn` module (short for "function"), which provides a collection of useful primitives for dealing with functions. `Fn.id` is the identity function.

`fieldslib` also provides higher-level operators, like `Fields.fold` and `Fields.iter`, which let you walk over the fields of a record. So, for example, in the case of `Logon.t`, the field iterator has the following type:

```
# Logon.Fields.iter;;
- : session_id:(([< `Read | `Set_and_create ], Logon.t, string)
               Field.t_with_perm -> unit) ->
```

```
time:(([< `Read | `Set_and_create ], Logon.t, Time_ns.t)
       Field.t_with_perm -> unit) ->
user:(([< `Read | `Set_and_create ], Logon.t, string)
Field.t_with_perm ->
       unit) ->
credentials:(([< `Read | `Set_and_create ], Logon.t, string)
             Field.t_with_perm -> unit) ->
 unit
= <fun>
```

This is a bit daunting to look at, largely because of the access control markers, but the structure is actually pretty simple. Each labeled argument is a function that takes a first-class field of the necessary type as an argument. Note that `iter` passes each of these callbacks the `Field.t`, not the contents of the specific record field. The contents of the field, though, can be looked up using the combination of the record and the `Field.t`.

Now, let's use `Logon.Fields.iter` and `show_field` to print out all the fields of a Logon record:

```
# let print_logon logon =
    let print to_string field =
      printf "%s\n" (show_field field to_string logon)
    in
    Logon.Fields.iter
      ~session_id:(print Fn.id)
      ~time:(print Time_ns.to_string)
      ~user:(print Fn.id)
      ~credentials:(print Fn.id);;
val print_logon : Logon.t -> unit = <fun>
# print_logon logon;;
session_id: 26685
time: 2017-07-21 15:11:45.000000000Z
user: yminsky
credentials: Xy2d9W
- : unit = ()
```

One nice side effect of this approach is that it helps you adapt your code when the fields of a record change. If you were to add a field to `Logon.t`, the type of `Logon.Fields.iter` would change along with it, acquiring a new argument. Any code using `Logon.Fields.iter` won't compile until it's fixed to take this new argument into account.

Field iterators are useful for a variety of record-related tasks, from building record-validation functions to scaffolding the definition of a web form from a record type. Such applications can benefit from the guarantee that all fields of the record type in question have been considered.

7 Variants

Variant types are one of the most useful features of OCaml and also one of the most unusual. They let you represent data that may take on multiple different forms, where each form is marked by an explicit tag. As we'll see, when combined with pattern matching, variants give you a powerful way of representing complex data and of organizing the case-analysis on that information.

The basic syntax of a variant type declaration is as follows:

```
type <variant> =
  | <Tag> [ of <type> [* <type>]... ]
  | <Tag> [ of <type> [* <type>]... ]
  | ...
```

Each row essentially represents a case of the variant. Each case has an associated tag (also called a *constructor*, since you use it to construct a value) and may optionally have a sequence of fields, where each field has a specified type.

Let's consider a concrete example of how variants can be useful. Most UNIX-like operating systems support terminals as a fundamental, text-based user interface. Almost all of these terminals support a set of eight basic colors.

Those colors can be naturally represented as a variant. Each color is declared as a simple tag, with pipes used to separate the different cases. Note that variant tags must be capitalized.

```
open Base
open Stdio
type basic_color =
  | Black | Red | Green | Yellow | Blue | Magenta | Cyan | White
```

As we show below, the variant tags introduced by the definition of basic_color can be used for constructing values of that type.

```
# Cyan;;
- : basic_color = Cyan
# [Blue; Magenta; Red];;
- : basic_color list = [Blue; Magenta; Red]
```

The following function uses pattern matching to convert each of these to the corresponding integer code that is used for communicating these colors to the terminal.

```
# let basic_color_to_int = function
    | Black -> 0 | Red     -> 1 | Green -> 2 | Yellow -> 3
    | Blue  -> 4 | Magenta -> 5 | Cyan  -> 6 | White  -> 7;;
```

```
val basic_color_to_int : basic_color -> int = <fun>
# List.map ~f:basic_color_to_int [Blue;Red];;
- : int list = [4; 1]
```

We know that the above function handles every color in `basic_color` because the compiler would have warned us if we'd missed one:

```
# let incomplete_color_to_int = function
    | Black -> 0 | Red -> 1 | White -> 7;;
Lines 1-2, characters 31-41:
Warning 8 [partial-match]: this pattern-matching is not exhaustive.
Here is an example of a case that is not matched:
(Green|Yellow|Blue|Magenta|Cyan)
val incomplete_color_to_int : basic_color -> int = <fun>
```

In any case, using the correct function, we can generate escape codes to change the color of a given string displayed in a terminal.

```
# let color_by_number number text =
    Printf.sprintf "\027[38;5;%dm%s\027[0m" number text;;
val color_by_number : int -> string -> string = <fun>
# let blue = color_by_number (basic_color_to_int Blue) "Blue";;
val blue : string = "\027[38;5;4mBlue\027[0m"
# printf "Hello %s World!\n" blue;;
Hello Blue World!
- : unit = ()
```

On most terminals, that word "Blue" will be rendered in blue.

In this example, the cases of the variant are simple tags with no associated data. This is substantively the same as the enumerations found in languages like C and Java. But as we'll see, variants can do considerably more than represent simple enumerations.

As it happens, an enumeration isn't enough to effectively describe the full set of colors that a modern terminal can display. Many terminals, including the venerable `xterm`, support 256 different colors, broken up into the following groups:

• The eight basic colors, in regular and bold versions
• A $6 \times 6 \times 6$ RGB color cube
• A 24-level grayscale ramp

We'll also represent this more complicated color space as a variant, but this time, the different tags will have arguments that describe the data available in each case. Note that variants can have multiple arguments, which are separated by *s.

```
type weight = Regular | Bold
type color =
  | Basic of basic_color * weight (* basic colors, regular and bold *)
  | RGB   of int * int * int      (* 6x6x6 color cube *)
  | Gray  of int                  (* 24 grayscale levels *)
```

As before, we can use these introduced tags to construct values of our newly defined type.

```
# [RGB (250,70,70); Basic (Green, Regular)];;
- : color list = [RGB (250, 70, 70); Basic (Green, Regular)]
```

And again, we'll use pattern matching to convert a color to a corresponding integer. In this case, the pattern matching does more than separate out the different cases; it also allows us to extract the data associated with each tag:

```
# let color_to_int = function
    | Basic (basic_color,weight) ->
       let base = match weight with Bold -> 8 | Regular -> 0 in
       base + basic_color_to_int basic_color
    | RGB (r,g,b) -> 16 + b + g * 6 + r * 36
    | Gray i -> 232 + i;;
val color_to_int : color -> int = <fun>
```

Now, we can print text using the full set of available colors:

```
# let color_print color s =
   printf "%s\n" (color_by_number (color_to_int color) s);;
val color_print : color -> string -> unit = <fun>
# color_print (Basic (Red,Bold)) "A bold red!";;
A bold red!
- : unit = ()
# color_print (Gray 4) "A muted gray...";;
A muted gray...
- : unit = ()
```

Variants, Tuples and Parens

Variants with multiple arguments look an awful lot like tuples. Consider the following example of a value of the type `color` we defined earlier.

```
# RGB (200,0,200);;
- : color = RGB (200, 0, 200)
```

It really looks like we've created a 3-tuple and wrapped it with the RGB constructor. But that's not what's really going on, as you can see if we create a tuple first and then place it inside the RGB constructor.

```
# let purple = (200,0,200);;
val purple : int * int * int = (200, 0, 200)
# RGB purple;;
Line 1, characters 1-11:
Error: The constructor RGB expects 3 argument(s),
       but is applied here to 1 argument(s)
```

We can also create variants that explicitly contain tuples, like this one.

```
# type tupled = Tupled of (int * int);;
type tupled = Tupled of (int * int)
```

The syntactic difference is unfortunately quite subtle, coming down to the extra set of parens around the arguments. But having defined it this way, we can now take the tuple in and out freely.

```
# let of_tuple x = Tupled x;;
val of_tuple : int * int -> tupled = <fun>
# let to_tuple (Tupled x) = x;;
val to_tuple : tupled -> int * int = <fun>
```

If, on the other hand, we define a variant without the parens, then we get the same behavior we got with the RGB constructor.

```
# type untupled = Untupled of int * int;;
type untupled = Untupled of int * int
# let of_tuple x = Untupled x;;
Line 1, characters 18-28:
Error: The constructor Untupled expects 2 argument(s),
       but is applied here to 1 argument(s)
# let to_tuple (Untupled x) = x;;
Line 1, characters 14-26:
Error: The constructor Untupled expects 2 argument(s),
       but is applied here to 1 argument(s)
```

Note that, while we can't just grab the tuple as a whole from this type, we can achieve more or less the same ends by explicitly deconstructing and reconstructing the data we need.

```
# let of_tuple (x,y) = Untupled (x,y);;
val of_tuple : int * int -> untupled = <fun>
# let to_tuple (Untupled (x,y)) = (x,y);;
val to_tuple : untupled -> int * int = <fun>
```

The differences between a multi-argument variant and a variant containing a tuple are mostly about performance. A multi-argument variant is a single allocated block in memory, while a variant containing a tuple requires an extra heap-allocated block for the tuple. You can learn more about OCaml's memory representation in Chapter 24 (Memory Representation of Values).

7.1   Catch-All Cases and Refactoring

OCaml's type system can act as a refactoring tool, warning you of places where your code needs to be updated to match an interface change. This is particularly valuable in the context of variants.

Consider what would happen if we were to change the definition of color to the following:

```
type color =
  | Basic of basic_color      (* basic colors *)
  | Bold  of basic_color      (* bold basic colors *)
  | RGB   of int * int * int (* 6x6x6 color cube *)
  | Gray  of int              (* 24 grayscale levels *)
```

We've essentially broken out the Basic case into two cases, Basic and Bold, and Basic has changed from having two arguments to one. color_to_int as we wrote it still expects the old structure of the variant, and if we try to compile that same code again, the compiler will notice the discrepancy:

```
# let color_to_int = function
    | Basic (basic_color,weight) ->
        let base = match weight with Bold -> 8 | Regular -> 0 in
```

```
        base + basic_color_to_int basic_color
    | RGB (r,g,b) -> 16 + b + g * 6 + r * 36
    | Gray i -> 232 + i;;
Line 2, characters 13-33:
Error: This pattern matches values of type 'a * 'b
       but a pattern was expected which matches values of type
    basic_color
```

Here, the compiler is complaining that the `Basic` tag is used with the wrong number of arguments. If we fix that, however, the compiler will flag a second problem, which is that we haven't handled the new `Bold` tag:

```
# let color_to_int = function
    | Basic basic_color -> basic_color_to_int basic_color
    | RGB (r,g,b) -> 16 + b + g * 6 + r * 36
    | Gray i -> 232 + i;;
Lines 1-4, characters 20-24:
Warning 8 [partial-match]: this pattern-matching is not exhaustive.
Here is an example of a case that is not matched:
Bold _
val color_to_int : color -> int = <fun>
```

Fixing this now leads us to the correct implementation:

```
# let color_to_int = function
    | Basic basic_color -> basic_color_to_int basic_color
    | Bold  basic_color -> 8 + basic_color_to_int basic_color
    | RGB (r,g,b) -> 16 + b + g * 6 + r * 36
    | Gray i -> 232 + i;;
val color_to_int : color -> int = <fun>
```

As we've seen, the type errors identified the things that needed to be fixed to complete the refactoring of the code. This is fantastically useful, but for it to work well and reliably, you need to write your code in a way that maximizes the compiler's chances of helping you find the bugs. To this end, a useful rule of thumb is to avoid catch-all cases in pattern matches.

Here's an example that illustrates how catch-all cases interact with exhaustion checks. Imagine we wanted a version of `color_to_int` that works on older terminals by rendering the first 16 colors (the eight `basic_color`s in regular and bold) in the normal way, but renders everything else as white. We might have written the function as follows.

```
# let oldschool_color_to_int = function
    | Basic (basic_color,weight) ->
      let base = match weight with Bold -> 8 | Regular -> 0 in
      base + basic_color_to_int basic_color
    | _ -> basic_color_to_int White;;
val oldschool_color_to_int : color -> int = <fun>
```

If we then applied the same fix we did above, we would have ended up with this.

```
# let oldschool_color_to_int = function
    | Basic basic_color -> basic_color_to_int basic_color
    | _ -> basic_color_to_int White;;
val oldschool_color_to_int : color -> int = <fun>
```

Because of the catch-all case, we'll no longer be warned about missing the Bold case. That's why you should beware of catch-all cases: they suppress exhaustiveness checking.

7.2   Combining Records and Variants

The term *algebraic data types* is often used to describe a collection of types that includes variants, records, and tuples. Algebraic data types act as a peculiarly useful and powerful language for describing data. At the heart of their utility is the fact that they combine two different kinds of types: *product types*, like tuples and records, which combine multiple different types together and are mathematically similar to Cartesian products; and *sum types*, like variants, which let you combine multiple different possibilities into one type, and are mathematically similar to disjoint unions.

Algebraic data types gain much of their power from the ability to construct layered combinations of sums and products. Let's see what we can achieve with this by reiterating the Log_entry message type that was described in Chapter 6 (Records).

```
module Time_ns = Core.Time_ns
module Log_entry = struct
  type t =
    { session_id: string;
      time: Time_ns.t;
      important: bool;
      message: string;
    }
end
```

This record type combines multiple pieces of data into a single value. In particular, a single Log_entry.t has a session_id *and* a time *and* an important flag *and* a message. More generally, you can think of record types as conjunctions. Variants, on the other hand, are disjunctions, letting you represent multiple possibilities. To construct an example of where this is useful, we'll first write out the other message types that came along-side Log_entry.

```
module Heartbeat = struct
  type t =
    { session_id: string;
      time: Time_ns.t;
      status_message: string;
    }
end
module Logon = struct
  type t =
    { session_id: string;
      time: Time_ns.t;
      user: string;
      credentials: string;
    }
end
```

A variant comes in handy when we want to represent values that could be any of these three types. The `client_message` type below lets you do just that.

```
type client_message = | Logon of Logon.t
                      | Heartbeat of Heartbeat.t
                      | Log_entry of Log_entry.t
```

In particular, a `client_message` is a Logon *or* a Heartbeat *or* a Log_entry. If we want to write code that processes messages generically, rather than code specialized to a fixed message type, we need something like `client_message` to act as one overarching type for the different possible messages. We can then match on the `client_message` to determine the type of the particular message being handled.

You can increase the precision of your types by using variants to represent differences between different cases, and records to represent shared structure. Consider the following function that takes a list of `client_messages` and returns all messages generated by a given user. The code in question is implemented by folding over the list of messages, where the accumulator is a pair of:

• The set of session identifiers for the user that have been seen thus far
• The set of messages so far that are associated with the user

Here's the concrete code:

```
# let messages_for_user user messages =
    let (user_messages,_) =
      List.fold messages ~init:([], Set.empty (module String))
        ~f:(fun ((messages,user_sessions) as acc) message ->
          match message with
          | Logon m ->
            if String.(m.user = user) then
              (message::messages, Set.add user_sessions m.session_id)
            else acc
          | Heartbeat _ | Log_entry _ ->
            let session_id = match message with
              | Logon     m -> m.session_id
              | Heartbeat m -> m.session_id
              | Log_entry m -> m.session_id
            in
            if Set.mem user_sessions session_id then
              (message::messages,user_sessions)
            else acc
        )
    in
    List.rev user_messages;;
val messages_for_user : string -> client_message list ->
    client_message list =
  <fun>
```

We take advantage of the fact that the type of the record m is known in the above code, so we don't have to qualify the record fields by the module they come from. *e.g.*, we write `m.user` instead of `m.Logon.user`.

One annoyance of the above code is that the logic for determining the session ID is somewhat repetitive, contemplating each of the possible message types (including the

Logon case, which isn't actually possible at that point in the code) and extracting the session ID in each case. This per-message-type handling seems unnecessary, since the session ID works the same way for all message types.

We can improve the code by refactoring our types to explicitly reflect the information that's shared between the different messages. The first step is to cut down the definitions of each per-message record to contain just the information unique to that record:

```
module Log_entry = struct
  type t = { important: bool;
             message: string;
           }
end
module Heartbeat = struct
  type t = { status_message: string; }
end
module Logon = struct
  type t = { user: string;
             credentials: string;
           }
end
```

We can then define a variant type that combines these types:

```
type details =
  | Logon of Logon.t
  | Heartbeat of Heartbeat.t
  | Log_entry of Log_entry.t
```

Separately, we need a record that contains the fields that are common across all messages:

```
module Common = struct
  type t = { session_id: string;
             time: Time_ns.t;
           }
end
```

A full message can then be represented as a pair of a `Common.t` and a `details`. Using this, we can rewrite our preceding example as follows. Note that we add extra type annotations so that OCaml recognizes the record fields correctly. Otherwise, we'd need to qualify them explicitly.

```
# let messages_for_user user (messages : (Common.t * details) list) =
    let (user_messages,_) =
      List.fold messages ~init:([],Set.empty (module String))
        ~f:(fun ((messages,user_sessions) as acc) ((common,details)
    as message) ->
          match details with
          | Logon m ->
            if String.(=) m.user user then
              (message::messages, Set.add user_sessions
  common.session_id)
            else acc
          | Heartbeat _ | Log_entry _ ->
            if Set.mem user_sessions common.session_id then
              (message::messages, user_sessions)
```

```
              else acc
          )
      in
      List.rev user_messages;;
val messages_for_user :
  string -> (Common.t * details) list -> (Common.t * details) list =
      <fun>
```

As you can see, the code for extracting the session ID has been replaced with the simple expression common.session_id.

In addition, this design allows us to grab the specific message and dispatch code to handle just that message type. In particular, while we use the type Common.t * details to represent an arbitrary message, we can use Common.t * Logon.t to represent a logon message. Thus, if we had functions for handling individual message types, we could write a dispatch function as follows:

```
# let handle_message server_state ((common:Common.t), details) =
    match details with
    | Log_entry m -> handle_log_entry server_state (common,m)
    | Logon     m -> handle_logon      server_state (common,m)
    | Heartbeat m -> handle_heartbeat server_state (common,m);;
val handle_message : server_state -> Common.t * details -> unit =
    <fun>
```

And it's explicit at the type level that handle_log_entry sees only Log_entry messages, handle_logon sees only Logon messages, etc.

7.2.1 Embedded Records

If we don't need to be able to pass the record types separately from the variant, then OCaml allows us to embed the records directly into the variant.

```
type details =
   | Logon     of { user: string; credentials: string; }
   | Heartbeat of { status_message: string; }
   | Log_entry of { important: bool; message: string; }
```

Even though the type is different, we can write messages_for_user in essentially the same way we did before.

```
# let messages_for_user user (messages : (Common.t * details) list) =
    let (user_messages,_) =
      List.fold messages ~init:([],Set.empty (module String))
        ~f:(fun ((messages,user_sessions) as acc) ((common,details)
    as message) ->
          match details with
          | Logon m ->
            if String.(=) m.user user then
              (message::messages, Set.add user_sessions
    common.session_id)
            else acc
          | Heartbeat _ | Log_entry _ ->
            if Set.mem user_sessions common.session_id then
              (message::messages, user_sessions)
```

```
            else acc
       )
    in
    List.rev user_messages;;
val messages_for_user :
  string -> (Common.t * details) list -> (Common.t * details) list =
    <fun>
```

Variants with inline records are both more concise and more efficient than having variants containing references to free-standing record types, because they don't require a separate allocated object for the contents of the variant.

The main downside is the obvious one, which is that an inline record can't be treated as its own free-standing object. And, as you can see below, OCaml will reject code that tries to do so.

```
# let get_logon_contents = function
    | Logon m -> Some m
    | _ -> None;;
Line 2, characters 23-24:
Error: This form is not allowed as the type of the inlined record
       could escape.
```

7.3   Variants and Recursive Data Structures

Another common application of variants is to represent tree-like recursive data structures. We'll show how this can be done by walking through the design of a simple Boolean expression language. Such a language can be useful anywhere you need to specify filters, which are used in everything from packet analyzers to mail clients.

An expression in this language will be defined by the variant expr, with one tag for each kind of expression we want to support:

```
type 'a expr =
  | Base  of 'a
  | Const of bool
  | And   of 'a expr list
  | Or    of 'a expr list
  | Not   of 'a expr
```

Note that the definition of the type expr is recursive, meaning that an expr may contain other exprs. Also, expr is parameterized by a polymorphic type 'a which is used for specifying the type of the value that goes under the Base tag.

The purpose of each tag is pretty straightforward. And, Or, and Not are the basic operators for building up Boolean expressions, and Const lets you enter the constants true and false.

The Base tag is what allows you to tie the expr to your application, by letting you specify an element of some base predicate type, whose truth or falsehood is determined by your application. If you were writing a filter language for an email processor, your base predicates might specify the tests you would run against an email, as in the following example:

```
type mail_field = To | From | CC | Date | Subject
type mail_predicate = { field: mail_field;
                        contains: string }
```

Using the preceding code, we can construct a simple expression with `mail_predicate` as its base predicate:

```
# let test field contains = Base { field; contains };;
val test : mail_field -> string -> mail_predicate expr = <fun>
# And [ Or [ test To "doligez"; test CC "doligez" ];
        test Subject "runtime";
      ];;
- : mail_predicate expr =
And
 [Or
    [Base {field = To; contains = "doligez"};
     Base {field = CC; contains = "doligez"}];
  Base {field = Subject; contains = "runtime"}]
```

Being able to construct such expressions isn't enough; we also need to be able to evaluate them. Here's a function for doing just that:

```
# let rec eval expr base_eval =
    (* a shortcut, so we don't need to repeatedly pass [base_eval]
       explicitly to [eval] *)
    let eval' expr = eval expr base_eval in
    match expr with
    | Base  base  -> base_eval base
    | Const bool  -> bool
    | And   exprs -> List.for_all exprs ~f:eval'
    | Or    exprs -> List.exists   exprs ~f:eval'
    | Not   expr  -> not (eval' expr);;
val eval : 'a expr -> ('a -> bool) -> bool = <fun>
```

The structure of the code is pretty straightforward—we're just pattern matching over the structure of the data, doing the appropriate calculation based on which tag we see. To use this evaluator on a concrete example, we just need to write the `base_eval` function, which is capable of evaluating a base predicate.

Another useful operation on expressions is *simplification*, which is the process of taking a boolean expression and reducing it to an equivalent one that is smaller. First, we'll build a few simplifying construction functions that mirror the tags of an `expr`.

The `and_` function below does a few things:

- Reduces the entire expression to the constant `false` if any of the arms of the `And` are themselves `false`.
- Drops any arms of the `And` that there the constant `true`.
- Drops the `And` if it only has one arm.
- If the `And` has no arms, then reduces it to `Const true`.

The code is below.

```
# let and_ l =
    if List.exists l ~f:(function Const false -> true | _ -> false)
    then Const false
```

```
    else
      match List.filter l ~f:(function Const true -> false | _ ->
    true) with
      | [] -> Const true
      | [ x ] -> x
      | l -> And l;;
val and_ : 'a expr list -> 'a expr = <fun>
```

Or is the dual of And, and as you can see, the code for or_ follows a similar pattern as that for and_, mostly reversing the role of true and false.

```
# let or_ l =
    if List.exists l ~f:(function Const true -> true | _ -> false)
    then Const true
    else
      match List.filter l ~f:(function Const false -> false | _ ->
    true) with
      | [] -> Const false
      | [x] -> x
      | l -> Or l;;
val or_ : 'a expr list -> 'a expr = <fun>
```

Finally, not_ just has special handling for constants, applying the ordinary boolean negation function to them.

```
# let not_ = function
    | Const b -> Const (not b)
    | e -> Not e;;
val not_ : 'a expr -> 'a expr = <fun>
```

We can now write a simplification routine that is based on the preceding functions. Note that this function is recursive, in that it applies all of these simplifications in a bottom-up way across the entire expression.

```
# let rec simplify = function
    | Base _ | Const _ as x -> x
    | And l -> and_ (List.map ~f:simplify l)
    | Or l  -> or_  (List.map ~f:simplify l)
    | Not e -> not_ (simplify e);;
val simplify : 'a expr -> 'a expr = <fun>
```

We can now apply this to a Boolean expression and see how good a job it does at simplifying it.

```
# simplify (Not (And [ Or [Base "it's snowing"; Const true];
  Base "it's raining"]));;
- : string expr = Not (Base "it's raining")
```

Here, it correctly converted the Or branch to Const true and then eliminated the And entirely, since the And then had only one nontrivial component.

There are some simplifications it misses, however. In particular, see what happens if we add a double negation in.

```
# simplify (Not (And [ Or [Base "it's snowing"; Const true];
  Not (Not (Base "it's raining"))]));;
- : string expr = Not (Not (Not (Base "it's raining")))
```

It fails to remove the double negation, and it's easy to see why. The `not_` function has a catch-all case, so it ignores everything but the one case it explicitly considers, that of the negation of a constant. Catch-all cases are generally a bad idea, and if we make the code more explicit, we see that the missing of the double negation is more obvious:

```
# let not_ = function
    | Const b -> Const (not b)
    | (Base _ | And _ | Or _ | Not _) as e -> Not e;;
val not_ : 'a expr -> 'a expr = <fun>
```

We can of course fix this by simply adding an explicit case for double negation:

```
# let not_ = function
    | Const b -> Const (not b)
    | Not e -> e
    | (Base _ | And _ | Or _ ) as e -> Not e;;
val not_ : 'a expr -> 'a expr = <fun>
```

The example of a Boolean expression language is more than a toy. There's a module very much in this spirit in `Core` called `Blang` (short for "Boolean language"), and it gets a lot of practical use in a variety of applications. The simplification algorithm in particular is useful when you want to use it to specialize the evaluation of expressions for which the evaluation of some of the base predicates is already known.

More generally, using variants to build recursive data structures is a common technique, and shows up everywhere from designing little languages to building complex data structures.

7.4 Polymorphic Variants

In addition to the ordinary variants we've seen so far, OCaml also supports so-called *polymorphic variants*. As we'll see, polymorphic variants are more flexible and syntactically more lightweight than ordinary variants, but that extra power comes at a cost.

Syntactically, polymorphic variants are distinguished from ordinary variants by the leading backtick. And unlike ordinary variants, polymorphic variants can be used without an explicit type declaration:

```
# let three = `Int 3;;
val three : [> `Int of int ] = `Int 3
# let four = `Float 4.;;
val four : [> `Float of float ] = `Float 4.
# let nan = `Not_a_number;;
val nan : [> `Not_a_number ] = `Not_a_number
# [three; four; nan];;
- : [> `Float of float | `Int of int | `Not_a_number ] list =
[`Int 3; `Float 4.; `Not_a_number]
```

As you can see, polymorphic variant types are inferred automatically, and when we combine variants with different tags, the compiler infers a new type that knows about all of those tags. Note that in the preceding example, the tag name (e.g., `Int) matches the type name (int). This is a common convention in OCaml.

The type system will complain if it sees incompatible uses of the same tag:

```
# let five = `Int "five";;
val five : [> `Int of string ] = `Int "five"
# [three; four; five];;
Line 1, characters 15-19:
Error: This expression has type [> `Int of string ]
       but an expression was expected of type
         [> `Float of float | `Int of int ]
       Types for tag `Int are incompatible
```

The > at the beginning of the variant types above is critical because it marks the types as being open to combination with other variant types. We can read the type [> `Float of float | `Int of int] as describing a variant whose tags include `Float of float and `Int of int, but may include more tags as well. In other words, you can roughly translate > to mean: "these tags or more."

OCaml will in some cases infer a variant type with <, to indicate "these tags or less," as in the following example:

```
# let is_positive = function
    | `Int   x -> x > 0
    | `Float x -> Float.(x > 0.);;
val is_positive : [< `Float of float | `Int of int ] -> bool = <fun>
```

The < is there because is_positive has no way of dealing with values that have tags other than `Float of float or `Int of int, but can handle types that have either or both of those two tags.

We can think of these < and > markers as indications of upper and lower bounds on the tags involved. If the same set of tags are both an upper and a lower bound, we end up with an *exact* polymorphic variant type, which has neither marker. For example:

```
# let exact = List.filter ~f:is_positive [three;four];;
val exact : [ `Float of float | `Int of int ] list = [`Int 3; `Float
    4.]
```

Perhaps surprisingly, we can also create polymorphic variant types that have distinct upper and lower bounds. Note that Ok and Error in the following example come from the Result.t type from Base.

```
# let is_positive = function
    | `Int   x -> Ok (x > 0)
    | `Float x -> Ok Float.0.(x > 0.)
    | `Not_a_number -> Error "not a number";;
val is_positive :
  [< `Float of float | `Int of int | `Not_a_number ] -> (bool, string)
    result =
  <fun>
# List.filter [three; four] ~f:(fun x ->
  match is_positive x with Error _ -> false | Ok b -> b);;
- : [< `Float of float | `Int of int | `Not_a_number > `Float `Int ]
    list =
[`Int 3; `Float 4.]
```

Here, the inferred type states that the tags can be no more than `` `Float ``, `` `Int ``, and `` `Not_a_number ``, and must contain at least `` `Float `` and `` `Int ``. As you can already start to see, polymorphic variants can lead to fairly complex inferred types.

Polymorphic Variants and Catch-All Cases

As we saw with the definition of `is_positive`, a `match` expression can lead to the inference of an upper bound on a variant type, limiting the possible tags to those that can be handled by the match. If we add a catch-all case to our `match` expression, we end up with a type with a lower bound.

```
# let is_positive_permissive = function
    | `Int   x -> Ok Int.(x > 0)
    | `Float x -> Ok Float.(x > 0.)
    | _ -> Error "Unknown number type";;
val is_positive_permissive :
    [> `Float of float | `Int of int ] -> (bool, string) result = <fun>
# is_positive_permissive (`Int 0);;
- : (bool, string) result = Ok false
# is_positive_permissive (`Ratio (3,4));;
- : (bool, string) result = Error "Unknown number type"
```

Catch-all cases are error-prone even with ordinary variants, but they are especially so with polymorphic variants. That's because you have no way of bounding what tags your function might have to deal with. Such code is particularly vulnerable to typos. For instance, if code that uses `is_positive_permissive` passes in `Float` misspelled as `Floot`, the erroneous code will compile without complaint.

```
# is_positive_permissive (`Floot 3.5);;
- : (bool, string) result = Error "Unknown number type"
```

With ordinary variants, such a typo would have been caught as an unknown tag. As a general matter, one should be wary about mixing catch-all cases and polymorphic variants.

7.4.1   Example: Terminal Colors Redux

To see how to use polymorphic variants in practice, we'll return to terminal colors. Imagine that we have a new terminal type that adds yet more colors, say, by adding an alpha channel so you can specify translucent colors. We could model this extended set of colors as follows, using an ordinary variant:

```
type extended_color =
    | Basic of basic_color * weight  (* basic colors, regular and bold
      *)
    | RGB   of int * int * int       (* 6x6x6 color space *)
    | Gray  of int                   (* 24 grayscale levels *)
    | RGBA  of int * int * int * int (* 6x6x6x6 color space *)
```

We want to write a function `extended_color_to_int` that works like `color_to_int` for all of the old kinds of colors, with new logic only for handling colors that include an alpha channel. One might try to write such a function as follows.

```
# let extended_color_to_int = function
    | RGBA (r,g,b,a) -> 256 + a + b * 6 + g * 36 + r * 216
    | (Basic _ | RGB _ | Gray _) as color -> color_to_int color;;
Line 3, characters 59-64:
Error: This expression has type extended_color
       but an expression was expected of type color
```

The code looks reasonable enough, but it leads to a type error because extended_color and color are in the compiler's view distinct and unrelated types. The compiler doesn't, for example, recognize any equality between the Basic tag in the two types.

What we want to do is to share tags between two different variant types, and polymorphic variants let us do this in a natural way. First, let's rewrite basic_color_to_int and color_to_int using polymorphic variants. The translation here is pretty straightforward:

```
# let basic_color_to_int = function
    | `Black -> 0 | `Red     -> 1 | `Green -> 2 | `Yellow -> 3
    | `Blue  -> 4 | `Magenta -> 5 | `Cyan  -> 6 | `White  -> 7;;
val basic_color_to_int :
  [< `Black | `Blue | `Cyan | `Green | `Magenta | `Red | `White |
   `Yellow ] ->
  int = <fun>
# let color_to_int = function
    | `Basic (basic_color,weight) ->
      let base = match weight with `Bold -> 8 | `Regular -> 0 in
      base + basic_color_to_int basic_color
    | `RGB (r,g,b) -> 16 + b + g * 6 + r * 36
    | `Gray i -> 232 + i;;
val color_to_int :
  [< `Basic of
       [< `Black
        | `Blue
        | `Cyan
        | `Green
        | `Magenta
        | `Red
        | `White
        | `Yellow ] *
       [< `Bold | `Regular ]
   | `Gray of int
   | `RGB of int * int * int ] ->
  int = <fun>
```

Now we can try writing extended_color_to_int. The key issue with this code is that extended_color_to_int needs to invoke color_to_int with a narrower type, i.e., one that includes fewer tags. Written properly, this narrowing can be done via a pattern match. In particular, in the following code, the type of the variable color includes only the tags `Basic, `RGB, and `Gray, and not `RGBA:

```
# let extended_color_to_int = function
    | `RGBA (r,g,b,a) -> 256 + a + b * 6 + g * 36 + r * 216
    | (`Basic _ | `RGB _ | `Gray _) as color -> color_to_int color;;
val extended_color_to_int :
  [< `Basic of
```

```
       [< `Black
         | `Blue
         | `Cyan
         | `Green
         | `Magenta
         | `Red
         | `White
         | `Yellow ] *
      [< `Bold | `Regular ]
   | `Gray of int
   | `RGB of int * int * int
   | `RGBA of int * int * int * int ] ->
   int = <fun>
```

The preceding code is more delicately balanced than one might imagine. In particular, if we use a catch-all case instead of an explicit enumeration of the cases, the type is no longer narrowed, and so compilation fails:

```
# let extended_color_to_int = function
    | `RGBA (r,g,b,a) -> 256 + a + b * 6 + g * 36 + r * 216
    | color -> color_to_int color;;
Line 3, characters 29-34:
Error: This expression has type [> `RGBA of int * int * int * int ]
       but an expression was expected of type
          [< `Basic of
               [< `Black
                | `Blue
                | `Cyan
                | `Green
                | `Magenta
                | `Red
                | `White
                | `Yellow ] *
               [< `Bold | `Regular ]
           | `Gray of int
           | `RGB of int * int * int ]
          The second variant type does not allow tag(s) `RGBA
```

Let's consider how we might turn our code into a proper library with an implementation in an `ml` file and an interface in a separate `mli`, as we saw in Chapter 5 (Files, Modules, and Programs). Let's start with the `mli`.

```
open Base

type basic_color =
   [ `Black   | `Blue | `Cyan  | `Green
   | `Magenta | `Red  | `White | `Yellow ]

type color =
   [ `Basic of basic_color * [ `Bold | `Regular ]
   | `Gray of int
   | `RGB  of int * int * int ]

type extended_color =
   [ color
   | `RGBA of int * int * int * int ]
```

```
val color_to_int              : color -> int
val extended_color_to_int : extended_color -> int
```

Here, extended_color is defined as an explicit extension of color. Also, notice
that we defined all of these types as exact variants. We can implement this library as
follows.

```
open Base

type basic_color =
    [ `Black   | `Blue | `Cyan  | `Green
    | `Magenta | `Red  | `White | `Yellow ]

type color =
    [ `Basic of basic_color * [ `Bold | `Regular ]
    | `Gray of int
    | `RGB  of int * int * int ]

type extended_color =
    [ color
    | `RGBA of int * int * int * int ]

let basic_color_to_int = function
    | `Black -> 0 | `Red      -> 1 | `Green -> 2 | `Yellow -> 3
    | `Blue  -> 4 | `Magenta -> 5 | `Cyan   -> 6 | `White  -> 7

let color_to_int = function
    | `Basic (basic_color,weight) ->
      let base = match weight with `Bold -> 8 | `Regular -> 0 in
      base + basic_color_to_int basic_color
    | `RGB (r,g,b) -> 16 + b + g * 6 + r * 36
    | `Gray i -> 232 + i

let extended_color_to_int = function
    | `RGBA (r,g,b,a) -> 256 + a + b * 6 + g * 36 + r * 216
    | `Grey x -> 2000 + x
    | (`Basic _ | `RGB _ | `Gray _) as color -> color_to_int color
```

In the preceding code, we did something funny to the definition of
extended_color_to_int that highlights some of the downsides of polymorphic variants. In particular, we added some special-case handling for the color gray, rather than
using color_to_int. Unfortunately, we misspelled Gray as Grey. This is exactly the
kind of error that the compiler would catch with ordinary variants, but with polymorphic variants, this compiles without issue. All that happened was that the compiler
inferred a wider type for extended_color_to_int, which happens to be compatible
with the narrower type that was listed in the mli. As a result, this library builds without
error.

```
$ dune build @all
```

If we add an explicit type annotation to the code itself (rather than just in the mli),
then the compiler has enough information to warn us:

```
let extended_color_to_int : extended_color -> int = function
    | `RGBA (r,g,b,a) -> 256 + a + b * 6 + g * 36 + r * 216
```

```
        | `Grey x -> 2000 + x
        | (`Basic _ | `RGB _ | `Gray _) as color -> color_to_int color
```

In particular, the compiler will complain that the `Grey case is unused:

```
$ dune build @all
File "terminal_color.ml", line 30, characters 4-11:
30 |     | `Grey x -> 2000 + x
         ^^^^^^^
Error: This pattern matches values of type [? `Grey of 'a ]
       but a pattern was expected which matches values of type
     extended_color
       The second variant type does not allow tag(s) `Grey
[1]
```

Once we have type definitions at our disposal, we can revisit the question of how we write the pattern match that narrows the type. In particular, we can explicitly use the type name as part of the pattern match, by prefixing it with a #:

```
let extended_color_to_int : extended_color -> int = function
  | `RGBA (r,g,b,a) -> 256 + a + b * 6 + g * 36 + r * 216
  | #color as color -> color_to_int color
```

This is useful when you want to narrow down to a type whose definition is long, and you don't want the verbosity of writing the tags down explicitly in the match.

7.4.2   When to Use Polymorphic Variants

At first glance, polymorphic variants look like a strict improvement over ordinary variants. You can do everything that ordinary variants can do, plus it's more flexible and more concise. What's not to like?

In reality, regular variants are the more pragmatic choice most of the time. That's because the flexibility of polymorphic variants comes at a price. Here are some of the downsides:

Complexity The typing rules for polymorphic variants are a lot more complicated than they are for regular variants. This means that heavy use of polymorphic variants can leave you scratching your head trying to figure out why a given piece of code did or didn't compile. It can also lead to absurdly long and hard to decode error messages. Indeed, concision at the value level is often balanced out by more verbosity at the type level.

Error-finding Polymorphic variants are type-safe, but the typing discipline that they impose is, by dint of its flexibility, less likely to catch bugs in your program.

Efficiency This isn't a huge effect, but polymorphic variants are somewhat heavier than regular variants, and OCaml can't generate code for matching on polymorphic variants that is quite as efficient as what it generated for regular variants.

All that said, polymorphic variants are still a useful and powerful feature, but it's worth understanding their limitations and how to use them sensibly and modestly.

Probably the safest and most common use case for polymorphic variants is where ordinary variants would be sufficient but are syntactically too heavyweight. For example, you often want to create a variant type for encoding the inputs or outputs to a function, where it's not worth declaring a separate type for it. Polymorphic variants are very useful here, and as long as there are type annotations that constrain these to have explicit, exact types, this tends to work well.

Variants are most problematic exactly where you take full advantage of their power; in particular, when you take advantage of the ability of polymorphic variant types to overlap in the tags they support. This ties into OCaml's support for subtyping. As we'll discuss further when we cover objects in Chapter 13 (Objects), subtyping brings in a lot of complexity, and most of the time, that's complexity you want to avoid.

8   Error Handling

Nobody likes dealing with errors. It's tedious, it's easy to get wrong, and it's usually just not as fun as thinking about how your program is going to succeed. But error handling is important, and however much you don't like thinking about it, having your software fail due to poor error handling is worse.

Thankfully, OCaml has powerful tools for handling errors reliably and with a minimum of pain. In this chapter we'll discuss some of the different approaches in OCaml to handling errors, and give some advice on how to design interfaces that make error handling easier.

We'll start by describing the two basic approaches for reporting errors in OCaml: error-aware return types and exceptions.

8.1   Error-Aware Return Types

The best way in OCaml to signal an error is to include that error in your return value. Consider the type of the find function in the List module:

```
# open Base;;
# List.find;;
- : 'a list -> f:('a -> bool) -> 'a option = <fun>
```

The option in the return type indicates that the function may not succeed in finding a suitable element:

```
# List.find [1;2;3] ~f:(fun x -> x >= 2);;
- : int option = Some 2
# List.find [1;2;3] ~f:(fun x -> x >= 10);;
- : int option = None
```

Including errors in the return values of your functions requires the caller to handle the error explicitly, allowing the caller to make the choice of whether to recover from the error or propagate it onward.

Consider the compute_bounds function below, which takes a list and a comparison function and returns upper and lower bounds for the list by finding the smallest and largest element on the list. List.hd and List.last, which return None when they encounter an empty list, are used to extract the largest and smallest element of the list:

```
# let compute_bounds ~compare list =
    let sorted = List.sort ~compare list in
```

```
match List.hd sorted, List.last sorted with
| None,_ | _, None -> None
| Some x, Some y -> Some (x,y);;
val compute_bounds : compare:('a -> 'a -> int) -> 'a list -> ('a * 'a)
  option =
<fun>
```

The match expression is used to handle the error cases, propagating a None in hd or last into the return value of compute_bounds.

On the other hand, in the find_mismatches that follows, errors encountered during the computation do not propagate to the return value of the function. find_mismatches takes two hash tables as arguments and searches for keys that have different data in one table than in the other. As such, the failure to find a key in one table isn't a failure of any sort:

```
# let find_mismatches table1 table2 =
    Hashtbl.fold table1 ~init:[] ~f:(fun ~key ~data mismatches ->
      match Hashtbl.find table2 key with
      | Some data' when data' <> data -> key :: mismatches
      | _ -> mismatches
    );;
val find_mismatches :
  ('a, int) Hashtbl.Poly.t -> ('a, int) Hashtbl.Poly.t -> 'a list =
  <fun>
```

The use of options to encode errors underlines the fact that it's not clear whether a particular outcome, like not finding something on a list, is an error or is just another valid outcome. This depends on the larger context of your program, and thus is not something that a general-purpose library can know in advance. One of the advantages of error-aware return types is that they work well in both situations.

8.1.1   Encoding Errors with Result

Options aren't always a sufficiently expressive way to report errors. Specifically, when you encode an error as None, there's nowhere to say anything about the nature of the error.

Result.t is meant to address this deficiency. The type is defined as follows:

```
module Result : sig
  type ('a,'b) t = | Ok of 'a
                   | Error of 'b
end
```

A Result.t is essentially an option augmented with the ability to store other information in the error case. Like Some and None for options, the constructors Ok and Error are available at the toplevel. As such, we can write:

```
# [ Ok 3; Error "abject failure"; Ok 4 ];;
- : (int, string) result list = [Ok 3; Error "abject failure"; Ok 4]
```

without first opening the Result module.

8.1.2   Error and Or_error

`Result.t` gives you complete freedom to choose the type of value you use to represent errors, but it's often useful to standardize on an error type. Among other things, this makes it easier to write utility functions to automate common error handling patterns.

But which type to choose? Is it better to represent errors as strings? Some more structured representation like XML? Or something else entirely?

Base's answer to this question is the `Error.t` type. You can, for example, construct one from a string.

```
# Error.of_string "something went wrong";;
- : Error.t = something went wrong
```

An `Or_error.t` is simply a `Result.t` with the error case specialized to the `Error.t` type. Here's an example.

```
# Error (Error.of_string "failed!");;
- : ('a, Error.t) result = Error failed!
```

The `Or_error` module provides a bunch of useful operators for constructing errors. For example, `Or_error.try_with` can be used for catching exceptions from a computation.

```
# let float_of_string s =
    Or_error.try_with (fun () -> Float.of_string s);;
val float_of_string : string -> float Or_error.t = <fun>
# float_of_string "3.34";;
- : float Or_error.t = Base__.Result.Ok 3.34
# float_of_string "a.bc";;
- : float Or_error.t =
Base__.Result.Error (Invalid_argument "Float.of_string a.bc")
```

Perhaps the most common way to create `Error.t`s is using *s-expressions*. An s-expression is a balanced parenthetical expression where the leaves of the expressions are strings. Here's a simple example:

```
(This (is an) (s expression))
```

S-expressions are supported by the Sexplib package that is distributed with Base and is the most common serialization format used in Base. Indeed, most types in Base come with built-in s-expression converters.

```
# Error.create "Unexpected character" 'c' Char.sexp_of_t;;
- : Error.t = ("Unexpected character" c)
```

We're not restricted to doing this kind of error reporting with built-in types. As we'll discuss in more detail in Chapter 21 (Data Serialization with S-Expressions), Sexplib comes with a syntax extension that can autogenerate sexp converters for specific types. We can enable it in the toplevel with a `#require` statement enabling `ppx_jane`, which is a package that pulls in multiple different syntax extensions, including `ppx_sexp_value`, the one we need here. (Because of technical issues with the toplevel, we can't easily enable these syntax extensions individually.)

```
# #require "ppx_jane";;
```

```
# Error.t_of_sexp
    [%sexp ("List is too long",[1;2;3] : string * int list)];;
- : Error.t = ("List is too long" (1 2 3))
```

Error also supports operations for transforming errors. For example, it's often useful to augment an error with information about the context of the error or to combine multiple errors together. `Error.tag` and `Error.of_list` fulfill these roles:

```
# Error.tag
    (Error.of_list [ Error.of_string "Your tires were slashed";
                     Error.of_string "Your windshield was smashed" ])
    ~tag:"over the weekend";;
- : Error.t =
("over the weekend" "Your tires were slashed" "Your windshield was
    smashed")
```

A very common way of generating errors is the `%message` syntax extension, which provides a compact syntax for providing a string describing the error, along with further values represented as s-expressions. Here's an example.

```
# let a = "foo" and b = ("foo",[3;4]);;
val a : string = "foo"
val b : string * int list = ("foo", [3; 4])
# Or_error.error_s
    [%message "Something went wrong" (a:string) (b: string * int
    list)];;
- : 'a Or_error.t =
Base__.Result.Error ("Something went wrong" (a foo) (b (foo (3 4))))
```

This is the most common idiom for generating `Error.t`'s.

8.1.3   bind and Other Error Handling Idioms

As you write more error handling code in OCaml, you'll discover that certain patterns start to emerge. A number of these common patterns have been codified by functions in modules like `Option` and `Result`. One particularly useful pattern is built around the function `bind`, which is both an ordinary function and an infix operator `>>=`. Here's the definition of `bind` for options:

```
# let bind option ~f =
    match option with
    | None -> None
    | Some x -> f x;;
val bind : 'a option -> f:('a -> 'b option) -> 'b option = <fun>
```

As you can see, `bind None f` returns `None` without calling `f`, and `bind (Some x)` `~f` returns `f x`. `bind` can be used as a way of sequencing together error-producing functions so that the first one to produce an error terminates the computation. Here's a rewrite of `compute_bounds` to use a nested series of binds:

```
# let compute_bounds ~compare list =
    let sorted = List.sort ~compare list in
    Option.bind (List.hd sorted) ~f:(fun first ->
      Option.bind (List.last sorted) ~f:(fun last ->
```

```
        Some (first,last)));;
val compute_bounds : compare:('a -> 'a -> int) -> 'a list -> ('a * 'a)
    option =
  <fun>
```

The preceding code is a little bit hard to swallow, however, on a syntactic level. We can make it easier to read and drop some of the parentheses, by using the infix operator form of bind, which we get access to by locally opening Option.Monad_infix. The module is called Monad_infix because the bind operator is part of a subinterface called Monad, which we'll see again in Chapter 17 (Concurrent Programming with Async).

```
# let compute_bounds ~compare list =
    let open Option.Monad_infix in
    let sorted = List.sort ~compare list in
    List.hd sorted    >>= fun first ->
    List.last sorted >>= fun last  ->
    Some (first,last);;
val compute_bounds : compare:('a -> 'a -> int) -> 'a list -> ('a * 'a)
    option =
  <fun>
```

This use of bind isn't really materially better than the one we started with, and indeed, for small examples like this, direct matching of options is generally better than using bind. But for large, complex examples with many stages of error handling, the bind idiom becomes clearer and easier to manage.

Monads and Let_syntax

We can make this look a little bit more ordinary by using a syntax extension that's designed specifically for monadic binds, called Let_syntax. Here's what the above example looks like using this extension.

```
# #require "ppx_let";;
# let compute_bounds ~compare list =
    let open Option.Let_syntax in
    let sorted = List.sort ~compare list in
    let%bind first = List.hd sorted in
    let%bind last  = List.last sorted in
    Some (first,last);;
val compute_bounds : compare:('a -> 'a -> int) -> 'a list -> ('a * 'a)
    option =
  <fun>
```

Note that we needed a #require statement to enable the extension.

To understand what's going on here, you need to know that let%bind x = some_expr in some_other_expr is rewritten into some_expr >>= fun x -> some_other_expr.

The advantage of Let_syntax is that it makes monadic bind look more like a regular let-binding. This works nicely because you can think of the monadic bind in this case as a special form of let binding that has some built-in error handling semantics.

There are other useful idioms encoded in the functions in Option. One example is Option.both, which takes two optional values and produces a new optional pair that is None if either of its arguments are None. Using Option.both, we can make compute_bounds even shorter:

```
# let compute_bounds ~compare list =
    let sorted = List.sort ~compare list in
    Option.both (List.hd sorted) (List.last sorted);;
val compute_bounds : compare:('a -> 'a -> int) -> 'a list -> ('a * 'a)
    option =
  <fun>
```

These error-handling functions are valuable because they let you express your error handling both explicitly and concisely. We've only discussed these functions in the context of the Option module, but more functionality of this kind can be found in the Result and Or_error modules.

8.2   Exceptions

Exceptions in OCaml are not that different from exceptions in many other languages, like Java, C#, and Python. Exceptions are a way to terminate a computation and report an error, while providing a mechanism to catch and handle (and possibly recover from) exceptions that are triggered by subcomputations.

You can trigger an exception by, for example, dividing an integer by zero:

```
# 3 / 0;;
Exception: Division_by_zero.
```

And an exception can terminate a computation even if it happens nested somewhere deep within it:

```
# List.map ~f:(fun x -> 100 / x) [1;3;0;4];;
Exception: Division_by_zero.
```

If we put a printf in the middle of the computation, we can see that List.map is interrupted partway through its execution, never getting to the end of the list:

```
# List.map ~f:(fun x -> Stdio.printf "%d\n%!" x; 100 / x) [1;3;0;4];;
1
3
0
Exception: Division_by_zero.
```

In addition to built-in exceptions like Divide_by_zero, OCaml lets you define your own:

```
# exception Key_not_found of string;;
exception Key_not_found of string
# raise (Key_not_found "a");;
Exception: Key_not_found("a").
```

Exceptions are ordinary values and can be manipulated just like other OCaml values:

```
# let exceptions = [ Division_by_zero; Key_not_found "b" ];;
val exceptions : exn list = [Division_by_zero; Key_not_found("b")]
# List.filter exceptions  ~f:(function
```

```
      | Key_not_found _ -> true
      | _ -> false);;
- : exn list = [Key_not_found("b")]
```

Exceptions are all of the same type, exn, which is itself something of a special case in the OCaml type system. It is similar to the variant types we encountered in Chapter 7 (Variants), except that it is *open*, meaning that it's not fully defined in any one place. In particular, new tags (specifically, new exceptions) can be added to it by different parts of the program. This is in contrast to ordinary variants, which are defined with a closed universe of available tags. One result of this is that you can never have an exhaustive match on an exn, since the full set of possible exceptions is not known.

The following function uses the Key_not_found exception we defined above to signal an error:

```
# let rec find_exn alist key = match alist with
    | [] -> raise (Key_not_found key)
    | (key',data) :: tl -> if String.(=) key key' then data else
    find_exn tl key;;
val find_exn : (string * 'a) list -> string -> 'a = <fun>
# let alist = [("a",1); ("b",2)];;
val alist : (string * int) list = [("a", 1); ("b", 2)]
# find_exn alist "a";;
- : int = 1
# find_exn alist "c";;
Exception: Key_not_found("c").
```

Note that we named the function find_exn to warn the user that the function routinely throws exceptions, a convention that is used heavily in Base.

In the preceding example, raise throws the exception, thus terminating the computation. The type of raise is a bit surprising when you first see it: [raise]{.idx}

```
# raise;;
- : exn -> 'a = <fun>
```

The return type of 'a makes it look like raise manufactures a value to return that is completely unconstrained in its type. That seems impossible, and it is. Really, raise has a return type of 'a because it never returns at all. This behavior isn't restricted to functions like raise that terminate by throwing exceptions. Here's another example of a function that doesn't return a value:

```
# let rec forever () = forever ();;
val forever : unit -> 'a = <fun>
```

forever doesn't return a value for a different reason: it's an infinite loop.

This all matters because it means that the return type of raise can be whatever it needs to be to fit into the context it is called in. Thus, the type system will let us throw an exception anywhere in a program.

Declaring Exceptions Using [@@deriving sexp]

OCaml can't always generate a useful textual representation of an exception. For example:

```
# type 'a bounds = { lower: 'a; upper: 'a };;
```

```
type 'a bounds = { lower : 'a; upper : 'a; }
# exception Crossed_bounds of int bounds;;
exception Crossed_bounds of int bounds
# Crossed_bounds { lower=10; upper=0 };;
- : exn = Crossed_bounds(_)
```

But if we declare the exception (and the types it depends on) using [@@deriving sexp],
we'll get something with more information:

```
# type 'a bounds = { lower: 'a; upper: 'a } [@@deriving sexp];;
type 'a bounds = { lower : 'a; upper : 'a; }
val bounds_of_sexp : (Sexp.t -> 'a) -> Sexp.t -> 'a bounds = <fun>
val sexp_of_bounds : ('a -> Sexp.t) -> 'a bounds -> Sexp.t = <fun>
# exception Crossed_bounds of int bounds [@@deriving sexp];;
exception Crossed_bounds of int bounds
# Crossed_bounds { lower=10; upper=0 };;
- : exn = (//toplevel//.Crossed_bounds ((lower 10) (upper 0)))
```

The period in front of `Crossed_bounds` is there because the representation generated
by [@@deriving sexp] includes the full module path of the module where the exception
in question is defined. In this case, the string `//toplevel//` is used to indicate that this
was declared at the utop prompt, rather than in a module.

This is all part of the support for s-expressions provided by the Sexplib library and
syntax extension, which is described in more detail in Chapter 21 (Data Serialization
with S-Expressions).

8.2.1   Helper Functions for Throwing Exceptions

Base provides a number of helper functions to simplify the task of throwing exceptions.
The simplest one is `failwith`, which could be defined as follows:

```
# let failwith msg = raise (Failure msg);;
val failwith : string -> 'a = <fun>
```

There are several other useful functions for raising exceptions, which can be found
in the API documentation for the Common and Exn modules in Base.

Another important way of throwing an exception is the `assert` directive. `assert`
is used for situations where a violation of the condition in question indicates a bug.
Consider the following piece of code for zipping together two lists:

```
# let merge_lists xs ys ~f =
    if List.length xs <> List.length ys then None
    else
      let rec loop xs ys =
        match xs,ys with
        | [],[] -> []
        | x::xs, y::ys -> f x y :: loop xs ys
        | _ -> assert false
      in
      Some (loop xs ys);;
val merge_lists : 'a list -> 'b list -> f:('a -> 'b -> 'c) -> 'c list
    option =
```

```
    <fun>
# merge_lists [1;2;3] [-1;1;2] ~f:(+);;
- : int list option = Some [0; 3; 5]
# merge_lists [1;2;3] [-1;1] ~f:(+);;
- : int list option = None
```

Here we use `assert false`, which means that the `assert`, once reached, is guaranteed to trigger. In general, one can put an arbitrary condition in the assertion.

In this case, the `assert` can never be triggered because we have a check that makes sure that the lists are of the same length before we call `loop`. If we change the code so that we drop this test, then we can trigger the `assert`:

```
# let merge_lists xs ys ~f =
    let rec loop xs ys =
      match xs,ys with
      | [],[] -> []
      | x::xs, y::ys -> f x y :: loop xs ys
      | _ -> assert false
    in
    loop xs ys;;
val merge_lists : 'a list -> 'b list -> f:('a -> 'b -> 'c) -> 'c list =
    <fun>
# merge_lists [1;2;3] [-1] ~f:(+);;
Exception: "Assert_failure //toplevel//:6:14"
```

This shows what's special about `assert`: it captures the line number and character offset of the source location from which the assertion was made.

8.2.2 Exception Handlers

So far, we've only seen exceptions fully terminate the execution of a computation. But sometimes, we want a program to be able to respond to and recover from an exception. This is achieved through the use of *exception handlers*.

In OCaml, an exception handler is declared using a `try/with` expression. Here's the basic syntax.

```
try <expr> with
| <pat1> -> <expr1>
| <pat2> -> <expr2>
...
```

A `try/with` clause first evaluates its body, *expr*. If no exception is thrown, then the result of evaluating the body is what the entire `try/with` clause evaluates to.

But if the evaluation of the body throws an exception, then the exception will be fed to the pattern-match clauses following the `with`. If the exception matches a pattern, then we consider the exception caught, and the `try/with` clause evaluates to the expression on the right-hand side of the matching pattern.

Otherwise, the original exception continues up the stack of function calls, to be handled by the next outer exception handler. If the exception is never caught, it terminates the program.

8.2.3   Cleaning Up in the Presence of Exceptions

One headache with exceptions is that they can terminate your execution at unexpected places, leaving your program in an awkward state. Consider the following function for loading a file full of numerical data. This code parses data that matches a simple comma-separated file format, where each field is a floating point number. In this example we open Stdio, to get access to routines for reading from files.

```
# open Stdio;;
# let parse_line line =
    String.split_on_chars ~on:[','] line
    |> List.map ~f:Float.of_string;;
val parse_line : string -> float list = <fun>
# let load filename =
    let inc = In_channel.create filename in
    let data =
      In_channel.input_lines inc
      |> List.map ~f:parse_line
    in
    In_channel.close inc;
    data;;
val load : string -> float list list = <fun>
```

One problem with this code is that the parsing function can throw an exception if the file in question is malformed. Unfortunately, that means that the In_channel.t that was opened will never be closed, leading to a file-descriptor leak.

We can fix this using Base's Exn.protect function, which takes two arguments: a thunk f, which is the main body of the computation to be run; and a thunk finally, which is to be called when f exits, whether it exits normally or with an exception. This is similar to the try/finally construct available in many programming languages, but it is implemented in a library, rather than being a built-in primitive. Here's how it could be used to fix our load function:

```
# let load filename =
    let inc = In_channel.create filename in
    Exn.protect
      ~f:(fun () -> In_channel.input_lines inc |> List.map
      ~f:parse_line)
      ~finally:(fun () -> In_channel.close inc);;
val load : string -> float list list = <fun>
```

This is a common enough problem that In_channel has a function called with_file that automates this pattern:

```
# let load filename =
    In_channel.with_file filename ~f:(fun inc ->
      In_channel.input_lines inc |> List.map ~f:parse_line);;
val load : string -> float list list = <fun>
```

In_channel.with_file is built on top of protect so that it can clean up after itself in the presence of exceptions.

8.2.4   Catching Specific Exceptions

OCaml's exception-handling system allows you to tune your error-recovery logic to the particular error that was thrown. For example, `find_exn`, which we defined earlier in the chapter, throws `Key_not_found` when the element in question can't be found. Let's look at an example of how you could take advantage of this. In particular, consider the following function:

```
# let lookup_weight ~compute_weight alist key =
    try
      let data = find_exn alist key in
      compute_weight data
    with
      Key_not_found _ -> 0.;;
val lookup_weight :
  compute_weight:('a -> float) -> (string * 'a) list -> string ->
    float =
  <fun>
```

As you can see from the type, `lookup_weight` takes an association list, a key for looking up a corresponding value in that list, and a function for computing a floating-point weight from the looked-up value. If no value is found, then a weight of `0.` should be returned.

The use of exceptions in this code, however, presents some problems. In particular, what happens if `compute_weight` throws an exception? Ideally, `lookup_weight` should propagate that exception on, but if the exception happens to be `Key_not_found`, then that's not what will happen:

```
# lookup_weight ~compute_weight:(fun _ -> raise (Key_not_found "foo"))
  ["a",3; "b",4] "a";;
- : float = 0.
```

This kind of problem is hard to detect in advance because the type system doesn't tell you what exceptions a given function might throw. For this reason, it's usually best to avoid relying on the identity of the exception to determine the nature of a failure. A better approach is to narrow the scope of the exception handler, so that when it fires it's very clear what part of the code failed:

```
# let lookup_weight ~compute_weight alist key =
    match
      try Some (find_exn alist key)
      with _ -> None
    with
    | None -> 0.
    | Some data -> compute_weight data;;
val lookup_weight :
  compute_weight:('a -> float) -> (string * 'a) list -> string ->
    float =
  <fun>
```

This nesting of a `try` within a `match` expression is both awkward and involves some unnecessary computation (in particular, the allocation of the option). Happily, OCaml allows for exceptions to be caught by match expressions directly, which lets you write this more concisely as follows.

```
# let lookup_weight ~compute_weight alist key =
    match find_exn alist key with
    | exception _ -> 0.
    | data -> compute_weight data;;
val lookup_weight :
  compute_weight:('a -> float) -> (string * 'a) list -> string ->
    float =
  <fun>
```

Note that the exception keyword is used to mark the exception-handling cases.

Best of all is to avoid exceptions entirely, which we could do by using the exception-free function from Base, List.Assoc.find, instead:

```
# let lookup_weight ~compute_weight alist key =
    match List.Assoc.find ~equal:String.equal alist key with
    | None -> 0.
    | Some data -> compute_weight data;;
val lookup_weight :
  compute_weight:('a -> float) ->
  (string, 'a) Base.List.Assoc.t -> string -> float = <fun>
```

8.2.5   Backtraces

A big part of the value of exceptions is that they provide useful debugging information in the form of a stack backtrace. Consider the following simple program:

```
open Base
open Stdio
exception Empty_list

let list_max = function
  | [] -> raise Empty_list
  | hd :: tl -> List.fold tl ~init:hd ~f:(Int.max)

let () =
  printf "%d\n" (list_max [1;2;3]);
  printf "%d\n" (list_max [])
```

If we build and run this program, we'll get a stack backtrace that will provide some information about where the error occurred and the stack of function calls that were in place at the time of the error:

```
$ dune exec -- ./blow_up.exe
3
Fatal error: exception Dune__exe__Blow_up.Empty_list
Raised at Dune__exe__Blow_up.list_max in file "blow_up.ml", line 6,
    characters 10-26
Called from Dune__exe__Blow_up in file "blow_up.ml", line 11,
    characters 16-29
[2]
```

You can also capture a backtrace within your program by calling Backtrace.Exn.most_recent, which returns the backtrace of the most recently thrown exception. This is useful for reporting detailed information on errors that did not cause your program to fail.

This works well if you have backtraces enabled, but that isn't always the case. In fact, by default, OCaml has backtraces turned off, and even if you have them turned on at runtime, you can't get backtraces unless you have compiled with debugging symbols. Base reverses the default, so if you're linking in Base, you will have backtraces enabled by default.

Even using Base and compiling with debugging symbols, you can turn backtraces off via the OCAMLRUNPARAM environment variable, as shown below.

```
$ OCAMLRUNPARAM=b=0 dune exec -- ./blow_up.exe
3
Fatal error: exception Dune__exe__Blow_up.Empty_list
[2]
```

The resulting error message is considerably less informative. You can also turn backtraces off in your code by calling Backtrace.Exn.set_recording false.

There is a legitimate reason to run without backtraces: speed. OCaml's exceptions are fairly fast, but they're faster still if you disable backtraces. Here's a simple benchmark that shows the effect, using the core_bench package:

```
open Core
open Core_bench

exception Exit

let x = 0

type how_to_end = Ordinary | Raise | Raise_no_backtrace

let computation how_to_end =
  let x = 10 in
  let y = 40 in
  let _z = x + (y * y) in
  match how_to_end with
  | Ordinary -> ()
  | Raise -> raise Exit
  | Raise_no_backtrace -> raise_notrace Exit

let computation_with_handler how = try computation how with Exit -> ()

let () =
  [
    Bench.Test.create ~name:"simple computation" (fun () ->
        computation Ordinary);
    Bench.Test.create ~name:"computation w/handler" (fun () ->
        computation_with_handler Ordinary);
    Bench.Test.create ~name:"end with exn" (fun () ->
        computation_with_handler Raise);
    Bench.Test.create ~name:"end with exn notrace" (fun () ->
        computation_with_handler Raise_no_backtrace);
  ]
  |> Bench.make_command |> Command.run
```

We're testing four cases here:

- a simple computation with no exception,

- the same, but with an exception handler but no exception thrown,
- the same, but where an exception is thrown,
- and finally, the same, but where we throw an exception using `raise_notrace`, which is a version of `raise` which locally avoids the costs of keeping track of the backtrace.

Here are the results.

```
$ dune exec -- \
> ./exn_cost.exe -ascii -quota 1 -clear-columns time cycles
Estimated testing time 4s (4 benchmarks x 1s). Change using '-quota'.

  Name                    Time/Run   Cycls/Run
 ----------------------- ---------- -----------
  simple computation        1.84ns       3.66c
  computation w/handler     3.13ns       6.23c
  end with exn             27.96ns      55.69c
  end with exn notrace     11.69ns      23.28c
```

Note that we lose just a small number of cycles to setting up an exception handler, which means that an unused exception handler is quite cheap indeed. We lose a much bigger chunk, around 55 cycles, to actually raising an exception. If we explicitly raise an exception with no backtrace, it costs us about 25 cycles.

We can also disable backtraces, as we discussed, using `OCAMLRUNPARAM`. That changes the results a bit.

```
$ OCAMLRUNPARAM=b=0 dune exec -- \
> ./exn_cost.exe -ascii -quota 1 -clear-columns time cycles
Estimated testing time 4s (4 benchmarks x 1s). Change using '-quota'.

  Name                    Time/Run   Cycls/Run
 ----------------------- ---------- -----------
  simple computation        1.71ns       3.41c
  computation w/handler     3.04ns       6.05c
  end with exn             19.36ns      38.57c
  end with exn notrace     11.48ns      22.86c
```

The only significant change here is that raising an exception in the ordinary way becomes just a bit cheaper: 20 cycles instead of 55 cycles. But it's still not as fast as using `raise_notrace` explicitly.

Differences on this scale should only matter if you're using exceptions routinely as part of your flow control. That's not a common pattern, and when you do need it, it's better from a performance perspective to use `raise_notrace`. All of which is to say, you should almost always leave stack-traces on.

8.2.6   From Exceptions to Error-Aware Types and Back Again

Both exceptions and error-aware types are necessary parts of programming in OCaml. As such, you often need to move between these two worlds. Happily, Base comes with some useful helper functions to help you do just that. For example, given a piece of code that can throw an exception, you can capture that exception into an option as follows:

```
# let find alist key =
    Option.try_with (fun () -> find_exn alist key);;
val find : (string * 'a) list -> string -> 'a option = <fun>
# find ["a",1; "b",2] "c";;
- : int option = Base.Option.None
# find ["a",1; "b",2] "b";;
- : int option = Base.Option.Some 2
```

Result and Or_error have similar try_with functions. So, we could write:

```
# let find alist key =
    Or_error.try_with (fun () -> find_exn alist key);;
val find : (string * 'a) list -> string -> 'a Or_error.t = <fun>
# find ["a",1; "b",2] "c";;
- : int Or_error.t = Base__.Result.Error ("Key_not_found(\"c\")")
```

We can then reraise that exception:

```
# Or_error.ok_exn (find ["a",1; "b",2] "b");;
- : int = 2
# Or_error.ok_exn (find ["a",1; "b",2] "c");;
Exception: Key_not_found("c").
```

8.3   Choosing an Error-Handling Strategy

Given that OCaml supports both exceptions and error-aware return types, how do you choose between them? The key is to think about the trade-off between concision and explicitness.

Exceptions are more concise because they allow you to defer the job of error handling to some larger scope, and because they don't clutter up your types. But this concision comes at a cost: exceptions are all too easy to ignore. Error-aware return types, on the other hand, are fully manifest in your type definitions, making the errors that your code might generate explicit and impossible to ignore.

The right trade-off depends on your application. If you're writing a rough-and-ready program where getting it done quickly is key and failure is not that expensive, then using exceptions extensively may be the way to go. If, on the other hand, you're writing production software whose failure is costly, then you should probably lean in the direction of using error-aware return types.

To be clear, it doesn't make sense to avoid exceptions entirely. The maxim of "use exceptions for exceptional conditions" applies. If an error occurs sufficiently rarely, then throwing an exception is often the right behavior.

Also, for errors that are omnipresent, error-aware return types may be overkill. A good example is out-of-memory errors, which can occur anywhere, and so you'd need to use error-aware return types everywhere to capture those. Having every operation marked as one that might fail is no more explicit than having none of them marked.

In short, for errors that are a foreseeable and ordinary part of the execution of your production code and that are not omnipresent, error-aware return types are typically the right solution.

9   Imperative Programming

This chapter includes contributions from Jason Hickey.

Most of the code shown so far in this book, and indeed, most OCaml code in general, is *pure*. Pure code works without mutating the program's internal state, performing I/O, reading the clock, or in any other way interacting with changeable parts of the world. Thus, a pure function behaves like a mathematical function, always returning the same results when given the same inputs, and never affecting the world except insofar as it returns the value of its computation. *Imperative* code, on the other hand, operates by side effects that modify a program's internal state or interact with the outside world. An imperative function has a new effect, and potentially returns different results, every time it's called.

Pure code is the default in OCaml, and for good reason—it's generally easier to reason about, less error prone and more composable. But imperative code is of fundamental importance to any practical programming language, because real-world tasks require that you interact with the outside world, which is by its nature imperative. Imperative programming can also be important for performance. While pure code is quite efficient in OCaml, there are many algorithms that can only be implemented efficiently using imperative techniques.

OCaml offers a happy compromise here, making it easy and natural to program in a pure style, but also providing great support for imperative programming. This chapter will walk you through OCaml's imperative features, and help you use them to their fullest.

9.1   Example: Imperative Dictionaries

We'll start with the implementation of a simple imperative dictionary, i.e., a mutable mapping from keys to values. This is very much a toy implementation, and it's really not suitable for any real-world use. That's fine, since both Base and the standard library provide effective imperative dictionaries. There's more advice on using Base's implementation in particular in Chapter 15 (Maps and Hash Tables).

The dictionary we'll describe now, like those in Base and the standard library, will be implemented as a hash table. In particular, we'll use an *open hashing* scheme, where the hash table will be an array of buckets, each bucket containing a list of key/value pairs that have been hashed into that bucket.

Here's the signature we'll match, provided as an interface file, `dictionary.mli`. The type `('a, 'b) t` represents a dictionary with keys of type `'a` and data of type `'b`.

```
open Base

type ('a, 'b) t

val create
  :  hash:('a -> int)
  -> equal:('a -> 'a -> bool)
  -> ('a, 'b) t

val length : ('a, 'b) t -> int
val add : ('a, 'b) t -> key:'a -> data:'b -> unit
val find : ('a, 'b) t -> 'a -> 'b option
val iter : ('a, 'b) t -> f:(key:'a -> data:'b -> unit) -> unit
val remove : ('a, 'b) t -> 'a -> unit
```

This `mli` also includes a collection of helper functions whose purpose and behavior should be largely inferable from their names and type signatures. Note that the `create` function takes as its arguments functions for hashing keys and testing them for equality.

You might notice that some of the functions, like `add` and `iter`, return `unit`. This is unusual for functional code, but common for imperative functions whose primary purpose is to mutate some data structure, rather than to compute a value.

We'll now walk through the implementation (contained in the corresponding `ml` file, `dictionary.ml`) piece by piece, explaining different imperative constructs as they come up.

Our first step is to define the type of a dictionary as a record.

```
open Base

type ('a, 'b) t =
  { mutable length : int
  ; buckets : ('a * 'b) list array
  ; hash : 'a -> int
  ; equal : 'a -> 'a -> bool
  }
```

The first field, `length`, is declared as mutable. In OCaml, records are immutable by default, but individual fields are mutable when marked as such. The second field, `buckets`, is immutable but contains an array, which is itself a mutable data structure. The remaining fields contain the functions for hashing and equality checking.

Now we'll start putting together the basic functions for manipulating a dictionary:

```
let num_buckets = 17
let hash_bucket t key = t.hash key % num_buckets

let create ~hash ~equal =
  { length = 0
  ; buckets = Array.create ~len:num_buckets []
  ; hash
```

```
  ; equal
  }

let length t = t.length

let find t key =
  List.find_map
    t.buckets.(hash_bucket t key)
    ~f:(fun (key', data) ->
      if t.equal key' key then Some data else None)
```

Note that num_buckets is a constant, which means our bucket array is of fixed length. A practical implementation would need to be able to grow the array as the number of elements in the dictionary increases, but we'll omit this to simplify the presentation.

The function hash_bucket is used throughout the rest of the module to choose the position in the array that a given key should be stored at.

The other functions defined above are fairly straightforward:

create Creates an empty dictionary.

length Grabs the length from the corresponding record field, thus returning the number of entries stored in the dictionary.

find Looks for a matching key in the table and returns the corresponding value if found as an option.

Another important piece of imperative syntax shows up in find: we write array.(index) to grab a value from an array. find also uses List.find_map, which you can see the type of by typing it into the toplevel:

```
# open Base;;
# List.find_map;;
- : 'a list -> f:('a -> 'b option) -> 'b option = <fun>
```

List.find_map iterates over the elements of the list, calling f on each one until a Some is returned by f, at which point that value is returned. If f returns None on all values, then None is returned.

Now let's look at the implementation of iter:

```
let iter t ~f =
  for i = 0 to Array.length t.buckets - 1 do
    List.iter t.buckets.(i) ~f:(fun (key, data) -> f ~key ~data)
  done
```

iter is designed to walk over all the entries in the dictionary. In particular, iter t ~f will call f for each key/value pair in dictionary t. Note that f must return unit, since it is expected to work by side effect rather than by returning a value, and the overall iter function returns unit as well.

The code for iter uses two forms of iteration: a for loop to walk over the array of buckets; and within that loop a call to List.iter to walk over the values in a given bucket. We could have done the outer loop with a recursive function instead of a for loop, but for loops are syntactically convenient, and are more familiar and idiomatic in imperative contexts.

The following code is for adding and removing mappings from the dictionary:

```
let bucket_has_key t i key =
  List.exists t.buckets.(i) ~f:(fun (key', _) -> t.equal key' key)

let add t ~key ~data =
  let i = hash_bucket t key in
  let replace = bucket_has_key t i key in
  let filtered_bucket =
    if replace
    then
      List.filter t.buckets.(i) ~f:(fun (key', _) ->
          not (t.equal key' key))
    else t.buckets.(i)
  in
  t.buckets.(i) <- (key, data) :: filtered_bucket;
  if not replace then t.length <- t.length + 1

let remove t key =
  let i = hash_bucket t key in
  if bucket_has_key t i key
  then (
    let filtered_bucket =
      List.filter t.buckets.(i) ~f:(fun (key', _) ->
          not (t.equal key' key))
    in
    t.buckets.(i) <- filtered_bucket;
    t.length <- t.length - 1)
```

This preceding code is made more complicated by the fact that we need to detect whether we are overwriting or removing an existing binding, so we can decide whether t.length needs to be changed. The helper function bucket_has_key is used for this purpose.

Another piece of syntax shows up in both add and remove: the use of the <- operator to update elements of an array (array.(i) <- expr) and for updating a record field (record.field <- expression).

We also use ;, the sequencing operator, to express a sequence of imperative actions. We could have done the same using let bindings:

```
let () = t.buckets.(i) <- (key, data) :: filtered_bucket in
if not replace then t.length <- t.length + 1
```

but ; is more concise and idiomatic. More generally,

```
<expr1>;
<expr2>;
...
<exprN>
```

is equivalent to

```
let () = <expr1> in
let () = <expr2> in
...
<exprN>
```

When a sequence expression expr1; expr2 is evaluated, expr1 is evaluated first, and then expr2. The expression expr1 should have type unit (though this is a warning rather than a hard restriction. The `-strict-sequence` compiler flag makes this a hard restriction, which is generally a good idea), and the value of `expr2` is returned as the value of the entire sequence. For example, the sequence `print_string "hello world"; 1 + 2` first prints the string `"hello world"`, then returns the integer 3.

Note also that we do all of the side-effecting operations at the very end of each function. This is good practice because it minimizes the chance that such operations will be interrupted with an exception, leaving the data structure in an inconsistent state.

9.2   Primitive Mutable Data

Now that we've looked at a complete example, let's take a more systematic look at imperative programming in OCaml. We encountered two different forms of mutable data above: records with mutable fields and arrays. We'll now discuss these in more detail, along with the other primitive forms of mutable data that are available in OCaml.

9.2.1   Array-Like Data

OCaml supports a number of array-like data structures; i.e., mutable integer-indexed containers that provide constant-time access to their elements. We'll discuss several of them in this section.

Ordinary arrays

The `array` type is used for general-purpose polymorphic arrays. The `Array` module has a variety of utility functions for interacting with arrays, including a number of mutating operations. These include `Array.set`, for setting an individual element, and `Array.blit`, for efficiently copying values from one range of indices to another.

Arrays also come with special syntax for retrieving an element from an array:

```
<array_expr>.(<index_expr>)
```

and for setting an element in an array:

```
<array_expr>.(<index_expr>) <- <value_expr>
```

Out-of-bounds accesses for arrays (and indeed for all the array-like data structures) will lead to an exception being thrown.

Array literals are written using `[|` and `|]` as delimiters. Thus, `[| 1; 2; 3 |]` is a literal integer array.

`bytes` and `strings`.

The strings we've encountered thus far are essentially byte arrays, and are most often used for textual data. You could imagine using a `char array` (a `char` represents an 8-bit character) for the same purpose, but strings are considerably more space-efficient; an array uses one 8-byte word on a 64-bit machine—to store a single entry, whereas strings use one byte per character.

Unlike arrays, though, strings are immutable, and sometimes, it's convenient to have a space-efficient, mutable array of bytes. Happily, OCaml has that, via the `bytes` type.

You can set individual characters using `Bytes.set`, and a value of type `bytes` can be converted to and from the `string` type.

```
# let b = Bytes.of_string "foobar";;
val b : bytes = "foobar"
# Bytes.set b 0 (Char.uppercase (Bytes.get b 0));;
- : unit = ()
# Bytes.to_string b;;
- : string = "Foobar"
```

Bigarrays

A `Bigarray.t` is a handle to a block of memory stored outside of the OCaml heap. These are mostly useful for interacting with C or Fortran libraries, and are discussed in Chapter 24 (Memory Representation of Values). Bigarrays too have their own getting and setting syntax:

```
<bigarray_expr>.{<index_expr>}
<bigarray_expr>.{<index_expr>} <- <value_expr>
```

9.2.2   Mutable Record and Object Fields and Ref Cells

As we've seen, records are immutable by default, but individual record fields can be declared as mutable. These mutable fields can be set using the `<-` operator, i.e., `record.field <- expr`.

As we'll see in Chapter 13 (Objects), fields of an object can similarly be declared as mutable, and can then be modified in much the same way as record fields.

Ref cells

Variables in OCaml are never mutable—they can refer to mutable data, but what the variable points to can't be changed. Sometimes, though, you want to do exactly what you would do with a mutable variable in another language: define a single, mutable value. In OCaml this is typically achieved using a `ref`, which is essentially a container with a single mutable polymorphic field.

The definition for the `ref` type is as follows:

```
# type 'a ref = { mutable contents : 'a };;
type 'a ref = { mutable contents : 'a; }
```

The standard library defines the following operators for working with `ref`s.

`ref expr` Constructs a reference cell containing the value defined by the expression `expr`.

`!refcell` Returns the contents of the reference cell.

`refcell := expr` Replaces the contents of the reference cell.

You can see these in action:

```
# let x = ref 1;;
val x : int ref = {Base.Ref.contents = 1}
# !x;;
- : int = 1
# x := !x + 1;;
- : unit = ()
# !x;;
- : int = 2
```

The preceding are just ordinary OCaml functions, which could be defined as follows:

```
# let ref x = { contents = x };;
val ref : 'a -> 'a ref = <fun>
# let (!) r = r.contents;;
val ( ! ) : 'a ref -> 'a = <fun>
# let (:=) r x = r.contents <- x;;
val ( := ) : 'a ref -> 'a -> unit = <fun>
```

This reflects the fact that ref cells are really just a special case of mutable record fields.

9.2.3   Foreign Functions

Another source of imperative operations in OCaml is resources that come from interfacing with external libraries through OCaml's foreign function interface (FFI). The FFI opens OCaml up to imperative constructs that are exported by system calls or other external libraries. Many of these come built in, like access to the write system call or to the clock, while others come from user libraries. OCaml's FFI is discussed in more detail in Chapter 23 (Foreign Function Interface).

9.3   For and While Loops

OCaml provides support for traditional imperative looping constructs, in particular, for and while loops. Neither of these constructs is strictly necessary, since they can be simulated with recursive functions. Nonetheless, explicit for and while loops are both more concise and more idiomatic when programming imperatively.

The for loop is the simpler of the two. Indeed, we've already seen the for loop in action—the iter function in Dictionary is built using it. Here's a simple example of for. Note that we open the Stdio library to get access to the printf function.

```
# open Stdio;;
# for i = 0 to 3 do printf "i = %d\n" i done;;
i = 0
i = 1
i = 2
i = 3
- : unit = ()
```

As you can see, the upper and lower bounds are inclusive. We can also use downto to iterate in the other direction:

```
# for i = 3 downto 0 do printf "i = %d\n" i done;;
i = 3
i = 2
i = 1
i = 0
- : unit = ()
```

Note that the loop variable of a for loop, i in this case, is immutable in the scope of the loop and is also local to the loop, i.e., it can't be referenced outside of the loop.

OCaml also supports while loops, which include a condition and a body. The loop first evaluates the condition, and then, if it evaluates to true, evaluates the body and starts the loop again. Here's a simple example of a function for reversing an array in place:

```
# let rev_inplace ar =
    let i = ref 0 in
    let j = ref (Array.length ar - 1) in
    (* terminate when the upper and lower indices meet *)
    while !i < !j do
      (* swap the two elements *)
      let tmp = ar.(!i) in
      ar.(!i) <- ar.(!j);
      ar.(!j) <- tmp;
      (* bump the indices *)
      Int.incr i;
      Int.decr j
    done;;
val rev_inplace : 'a array -> unit = <fun>
# let nums = [|1;2;3;4;5|];;
val nums : int array = [|1; 2; 3; 4; 5|]
# rev_inplace nums;;
- : unit = ()
# nums;;
- : int array = [|5; 4; 3; 2; 1|]
```

In the preceding example, we used Int.incr and Int.decr, which are built-in functions for incrementing and decrementing an int ref by one, respectively.

9.4   Example: Doubly Linked Lists

Another common imperative data structure is the doubly linked list. Doubly linked lists can be traversed in both directions, and elements can be added and removed from the list in constant time. Core defines a doubly linked list (the module is called Doubly_linked), but we'll define our own linked list library as an illustration.

Here's the mli of the module we'll build:

```
open Base

type 'a t
type 'a element

(** Basic list operations *)
```

```
val create : unit -> 'a t
val is_empty : 'a t -> bool

(** Navigation using [element]s *)

val first : 'a t -> 'a element option
val next : 'a element -> 'a element option
val prev : 'a element -> 'a element option
val value : 'a element -> 'a

(** Whole-data-structure iteration *)

val iter : 'a t -> f:('a -> unit) -> unit
val find_el : 'a t -> f:('a -> bool) -> 'a element option

(** Mutation *)

val insert_first : 'a t -> 'a -> 'a element
val insert_after : 'a element -> 'a -> 'a element
val remove : 'a t -> 'a element -> unit
```

Note that there are two types defined here: 'a t, the type of a list; and 'a element, the type of an element. Elements act as pointers to the interior of a list and allow us to navigate the list and give us a point at which to apply mutating operations.

Now let's look at the implementation. We'll start by defining 'a element and 'a t:

```
open Base

type 'a element =
  { value : 'a
  ; mutable next : 'a element option
  ; mutable prev : 'a element option
  }

type 'a t = 'a element option ref
```

An 'a element is a record containing the value to be stored in that node as well as optional (and mutable) fields pointing to the previous and next elements. At the beginning of the list, the prev field is None, and at the end of the list, the next field is None.

The type of the list itself, 'a t, is a mutable reference to an optional element. This reference is None if the list is empty, and Some otherwise.

Now we can define a few basic functions that operate on lists and elements:

```
let create () = ref None
let is_empty t = Option.is_none !t
let value elt = elt.value
let first t = !t
let next elt = elt.next
let prev elt = elt.prev
```

These all follow relatively straightforwardly from our type definitions.

Cyclic Data Structures

Doubly linked lists are a cyclic data structure, meaning that it is possible to follow a nontrivial sequence of pointers that closes in on itself. In general, building cyclic data structures requires the use of side effects. This is done by constructing the data elements first, and then adding cycles using assignment afterward.

There is an exception to this, though: you can construct fixed-size cyclic data structures using `let rec`:

```
# let rec endless_loop = 1 :: 2 :: 3 :: endless_loop;;
val endless_loop : int list = [1; 2; 3; <cycle>]
```

This approach is quite limited, however. General-purpose cyclic data structures require mutation.

9.4.1   Modifying the List

Now, we'll start considering operations that mutate the list, starting with `insert_first`, which inserts an element at the front of the list:

```
let insert_first t value =
  let new_elt = { prev = None; next = !t; value } in
  (match !t with
  | Some old_first -> old_first.prev <- Some new_elt
  | None -> ());
  t := Some new_elt;
  new_elt
```

`insert_first` first defines a new element `new_elt`, and then links it into the list, finally setting the list itself to point to `new_elt`. Note that the precedence of a `match` expression is very low, so to separate it from the following assignment (`t := Some new_elt`), we surround the match with parentheses. We could have used `begin ... end` for the same purpose, but without some kind of bracketing, the final assignment would incorrectly become part of the `None` case.

We can use `insert_after` to insert elements later in the list. `insert_after` takes as arguments both an `element` after which to insert the new node and a value to insert:

```
let insert_after elt value =
  let new_elt = { value; prev = Some elt; next = elt.next } in
  (match elt.next with
  | Some old_next -> old_next.prev <- Some new_elt
  | None -> ());
  elt.next <- Some new_elt;
  new_elt
```

We also need a remove function:

```
let remove t elt =
  let { prev; next; _ } = elt in
  (match prev with
  | Some prev -> prev.next <- next
  | None -> t := next);
  (match next with
```

```
  | Some next -> next.prev <- prev
  | None -> ());
elt.prev <- None;
elt.next <- None
```

Note that the preceding code is careful to change the `prev` pointer of the following element and the `next` pointer of the previous element, if they exist. If there's no previous element, then the list pointer itself is updated. In any case, the next and previous pointers of the element itself are set to `None`.

These functions are more fragile than they may seem. In particular, misuse of the interface may lead to corrupted data. For example, double-removing an element will cause the main list reference to be set to `None`, thus emptying the list. Similar problems arise from removing an element from a list it doesn't belong to.

This shouldn't be a big surprise. Complex imperative data structures can be quite tricky, considerably trickier than their pure equivalents. The issues described previously can be dealt with by more careful error detection, and such error correction is taken care of in modules like Core's `Doubly_linked`. You should use imperative data structures from a well-designed library when you can. And when you can't, you should make sure to put great care into your error handling.

9.4.2   Iteration Functions

When defining containers like lists, dictionaries, and trees, you'll typically want to define a set of iteration functions like `iter`, `map`, and `fold`, which let you concisely express common iteration patterns.

`Dlist` has two such iterators: `iter`, the goal of which is to call a `unit`-producing function on every element of the list, in order; and `find_el`, which runs a provided test function on each value stored in the list, returning the first `element` that passes the test. Both `iter` and `find_el` are implemented using simple recursive loops that use `next` to walk from element to element and `value` to extract the element from a given node:

```
let iter t ~f =
  let rec loop = function
    | None -> ()
    | Some el ->
      f (value el);
      loop (next el)
  in
  loop !t

let find_el t ~f =
  let rec loop = function
    | None -> None
    | Some elt -> if f (value elt) then Some elt else loop (next elt)
  in
  loop !t
```

This completes our implementation, but there's still considerably more work to be done to make a really usable doubly linked list. As mentioned earlier, you're probably better off using something like Core `Doubly_linked` module that has a more complete interface and has more of the tricky corner cases worked out. Nonetheless, this example should serve to demonstrate some of the techniques you can use to build nontrivial imperative data structure in OCaml, as well as some of the pitfalls.

9.5 Laziness and Other Benign Effects

There are many instances where you basically want to program in a pure style, but you want to make limited use of side effects to improve the performance of your code. Such side effects are sometimes called *benign effects*, and they are a useful way of leveraging OCaml's imperative features while still maintaining most of the benefits of pure programming.

One of the simplest benign effects is *laziness*. A lazy value is one that is not computed until it is actually needed. In OCaml, lazy values are created using the `lazy` keyword, which can be used to convert any expression of type s into a lazy value of type s `lazy_t`. The evaluation of that expression is delayed until forced with `Lazy.force`:

```
# let v = lazy (print_endline "performing lazy computation";
    Float.sqrt 16.);;
val v : float lazy_t = <lazy>
# Lazy.force v;;
performing lazy computation
- : float = 4.
# Lazy.force v;;
- : float = 4.
```

You can see from the `print` statement that the actual computation was performed only once, and only after `force` had been called.

To better understand how laziness works, let's walk through the implementation of our own lazy type. We'll start by declaring types to represent a lazy value:

```
# type 'a lazy_state =
    | Delayed of (unit -> 'a)
    | Value of 'a
    | Exn of exn;;
type 'a lazy_state = Delayed of (unit -> 'a) | Value of 'a | Exn of exn
# type 'a our_lazy = { mutable state : 'a lazy_state };;
type 'a our_lazy = { mutable state : 'a lazy_state; }
```

A `lazy_state` represents the possible states of a lazy value. A lazy value is `Delayed` before it has been run, where `Delayed` holds a function for computing the value in question. A lazy value is in the `Value` state when it has been forced and the computation ended normally. The `Exn` case is for when the lazy value has been forced, but the computation ended with an exception. A lazy value is simply a record with a single mutable field containing a `lazy_state`, where the mutability makes it possible to change from being in the `Delayed` state to being in the `Value` or `Exn` states.

We can create a lazy value from a thunk, i.e., a function that takes a unit argument. Wrapping an expression in a thunk is another way to suspend the computation of an expression:

```
# let our_lazy f = { state = Delayed f };;
val our_lazy : (unit -> 'a) -> 'a our_lazy = <fun>
# let v =
    our_lazy (fun () ->
      print_endline "performing lazy computation"; Float.sqrt 16.);;
val v : float our_lazy = {state = Delayed <fun>}
```

Now we just need a way to force a lazy value. The following function does just that.

```
# let our_force l =
    match l.state with
    | Value x -> x
    | Exn e -> raise e
    | Delayed f ->
      try
        let x = f () in
        l.state <- Value x;
        x
      with exn ->
        l.state <- Exn exn;
        raise exn;;
val our_force : 'a our_lazy -> 'a = <fun>
```

Which we can use in the same way we used `Lazy.force`:

```
# our_force v;;
performing lazy computation
- : float = 4.
# our_force v;;
- : float = 4.
```

The main user-visible difference between our implementation of laziness and the built-in version is syntax. Rather than writing `our_lazy (fun () -> sqrt 16.)`, we can (with the built-in `lazy`) just write `lazy (sqrt 16.)`, avoiding the necessity of declaring a function.

9.5.1   Memoization and Dynamic Programming

Another benign effect is *memoization*. A memoized function remembers the result of previous invocations of the function so that they can be returned without further computation when the same arguments are presented again.

Here's a function that takes as an argument an arbitrary single-argument function and returns a memoized version of that function. Here we'll use Base's `Hashtbl` module, rather than our toy `Dictionary`.

This implementation requires an argument of a `Hashtbl.Key.t`, which plays the role of the hash and equal from `Dictionary`. `Hashtbl.Key.t` is an example of what's called a first-class module, which we'll see more of in Chapter 12 (First-Class Modules).

```
# let memoize m f =
    let memo_table = Hashtbl.create m in
    (fun x ->
      Hashtbl.find_or_add memo_table x ~default:(fun () -> f x));;
val memoize : 'a Hashtbl.Key.t -> ('a -> 'b) -> 'a -> 'b = <fun>
```

The preceding code is a bit tricky. memoize takes as its argument a function f and then allocates a polymorphic hash table (called memo_table), and returns a new function which is the memoized version of f. When called, this new function uses Hashtbl.find_or_add to try to find a value in the memo_table, and if it fails, to call f and store the result. Note that memo_table is referred to by the function, and so won't be collected until the function returned by memoize is itself collected.

Memoization can be useful whenever you have a function that is expensive to recompute and you don't mind caching old values indefinitely. One important caution: a memoized function by its nature leaks memory. As long as you hold on to the memoized function, you're holding every result it has returned thus far.

Memoization is also useful for efficiently implementing some recursive algorithms. One good example is the algorithm for computing the *edit distance* (also called the Levenshtein distance) between two strings. The edit distance is the number of single-character changes (including letter switches, insertions, and deletions) required to convert one string to the other. This kind of distance metric can be useful for a variety of approximate string-matching problems, like spellcheckers.

Consider the following code for computing the edit distance. Understanding the algorithm isn't important here, but you should pay attention to the structure of the recursive calls:

```
# let rec edit_distance s t =
    match String.length s, String.length t with
    | (0,x) | (x,0) -> x
    | (len_s,len_t) ->
      let s' = String.drop_suffix s 1 in
      let t' = String.drop_suffix t 1 in
      let cost_to_drop_both =
        if Char.(=) s.[len_s - 1] t.[len_t - 1] then 0 else 1
      in
      List.reduce_exn ~f:Int.min
        [ edit_distance s' t  + 1
        ; edit_distance s  t' + 1
        ; edit_distance s' t' + cost_to_drop_both
        ];;
val edit_distance : string -> string -> int = <fun>
# edit_distance "OCaml" "ocaml";;
- : int = 2
```

The thing to note is that if you call edit_distance "OCaml" "ocaml", then that will in turn dispatch the following calls:

```
edit_distance "OCam" "ocaml"
edit_distance "OCaml" "ocam"
edit_distance "OCam" "ocam"
```

And these calls will in turn dispatch other calls:

```
edit_distance "OCam" "ocaml"
  edit_distance "OCa" "ocaml"
  edit_distance "OCam" "ocam"
  edit_distance "OCa" "ocam"
  edit_distance "OCaml" "ocam"
  edit_distance "OCam" "ocam"
  edit_distance "OCaml" "oca"
  edit_distance "OCam" "oca"
edit_distance "OCam" "ocam"
  edit_distance "OCa" "ocam"
  edit_distance "OCam" "oca"
  edit_distance "OCa" "oca"
```

As you can see, some of these calls are repeats. For example, there are two different calls to `edit_distance` `"OCam"` `"oca"`. The number of redundant calls grows exponentially with the size of the strings, meaning that our implementation of `edit_distance` is brutally slow for large strings. We can see this by writing a small timing function, using Core's `Time` module.

```
# let time f =
    let open Core in
    let start = Time.now () in
    let x = f () in
    let stop = Time.now () in
    printf "Time: %F ms\n" (Time.diff stop start |> Time.Span.to_ms);
    x;;
val time : (unit -> 'a) -> 'a = <fun>
```

And now we can use this to try out some examples:

```
# time (fun () -> edit_distance "OCaml" "ocaml");;
Time: 0.655651092529 ms
- : int = 2
# time (fun () -> edit_distance "OCaml 4.13" "ocaml 4.13");;
Time: 2541.6533947 ms
- : int = 2
```

Just those few extra characters made it thousands of times slower!

Memoization would be a huge help here, but to fix the problem, we need to memoize the calls that `edit_distance` makes to itself. Such recursive memoization is closely related to a common algorithmic technique called *dynamic programming*, except that with dynamic programming, you do the necessary sub-computations bottom-up, in anticipation of needing them. With recursive memoization, you go top-down, only doing a sub-computation when you discover that you need it.

To see how to do this, let's step away from `edit_distance` and instead consider a much simpler example: computing the nth element of the Fibonacci sequence. The Fibonacci sequence by definition starts out with two 1s, with every subsequent element being the sum of the previous two. The classic recursive definition of Fibonacci is as follows:

```
# let rec fib i =
```

```
    if i <= 1 then i else fib (i - 1) + fib (i - 2);;
val fib : int -> int = <fun>
```

This is, however, exponentially slow, for the same reason that edit_distance was slow: we end up making many redundant calls to fib. It shows up quite dramatically in the performance:

```
# time (fun () -> fib 20);;
Time: 1.14369392395 ms
- : int = 6765
# time (fun () -> fib 40);;
Time: 14752.7184486 ms
- : int = 102334155
```

As you can see, fib 40 takes thousands of times longer to compute than fib 20.

So, how can we use memoization to make this faster? The tricky bit is that we need to insert the memoization before the recursive calls within fib. We can't just define fib in the ordinary way and memoize it after the fact and expect the first call to fib to be improved.

```
# let fib = memoize (module Int) fib;;
val fib : int -> int = <fun>
# time (fun () -> fib 40);;
Time: 18174.5970249 ms
- : int = 102334155
# time (fun () -> fib 40);;
Time: 0.00524520874023 ms
- : int = 102334155
```

In order to make fib fast, our first step will be to rewrite fib in a way that unwinds the recursion. The following version expects as its first argument a function (called fib) that will be called in lieu of the usual recursive call.

```
# let fib_norec fib i =
    if i <= 1 then i
    else fib (i - 1) + fib (i - 2);;
val fib_norec : (int -> int) -> int -> int = <fun>
```

We can now turn this back into an ordinary Fibonacci function by tying the recursive knot:

```
# let rec fib i = fib_norec fib i;;
val fib : int -> int = <fun>
# fib 20;;
- : int = 6765
```

We can even write a polymorphic function that we'll call make_rec that can tie the recursive knot for any function of this form:

```
# let make_rec f_norec =
    let rec f x = f_norec f x in
    f;;
val make_rec : (('a -> 'b) -> 'a -> 'b) -> 'a -> 'b = <fun>
# let fib = make_rec fib_norec;;
val fib : int -> int = <fun>
# fib 20;;
- : int = 6765
```

This is a pretty strange piece of code, and it may take a few moments of thought to figure out what's going on. Like `fib_norec`, the function `f_norec` passed in to `make_rec` is a function that isn't recursive but takes as an argument a function that it will call. What `make_rec` does is to essentially feed `f_norec` to itself, thus making it a true recursive function.

This is clever enough, but all we've really done is find a new way to implement the same old slow Fibonacci function. To make it faster, we need a variant of `make_rec` that inserts memoization when it ties the recursive knot. We'll call that function `memo_rec`:

```
# let memo_rec m f_norec x =
    let fref = ref (fun _ -> assert false) in
    let f = memoize m (fun x -> f_norec !fref x) in
    fref := f;
    f x;;
val memo_rec : 'a Hashtbl.Key.t -> (('a -> 'b) -> 'a -> 'b) -> 'a -> 'b =
  <fun>
```

Note that `memo_rec` has almost the same signature as `make_rec`.

We're using the reference here as a way of tying the recursive knot without using a `let rec`, which for reasons we'll describe later wouldn't work here.

Using `memo_rec`, we can now build an efficient version of `fib`:

```
# let fib = memo_rec (module Int) fib_norec;;
val fib : int -> int = <fun>
# time (fun () -> fib 40);;
Time: 0.121355056763 ms
- : int = 102334155
```

As you can see, the exponential time complexity is now gone.

The memory behavior here is important. If you look back at the definition of `memo_rec`, you'll see that the call `memo_rec fib_norec` does not trigger a call to `memoize`. Only when `fib` is called and thereby the final argument to `memo_rec` is presented does `memoize` get called. The result of that call falls out of scope when the `fib` call returns, and so calling `memo_rec` on a function does not create a memory leak—the memoization table is collected after the computation completes.

We can use `memo_rec` as part of a single declaration that makes this look like it's little more than a special form of `let rec`:

```
# let fib = memo_rec (module Int) (fun fib i ->
    if i <= 1 then 1 else fib (i - 1) + fib (i - 2));;
val fib : int -> int = <fun>
```

Memoization is overkill for implementing Fibonacci, and indeed, the `fib` defined above is not especially efficient, allocating space linear in the number passed into `fib`. It's easy enough to write a Fibonacci function that takes a constant amount of space.

But memoization is a good approach for optimizing `edit_distance`, and we can apply the same approach we used on `fib` here. We will need to change `edit_distance` to take a pair of strings as a single argument, since `memo_rec` only works on single-argument functions. (We can always recover the original interface with a wrapper function.) With just that change and the addition of the `memo_rec` call, we can get a memoized version of `edit_distance`. The memoization key is going to be a pair of strings, so we need to get our hands on a module with the necessary functionality for building a hash-table in Base.

Writing hash-functions and equality tests and the like by hand can be tedious and error prone, so instead we'll use a few different syntax extensions for deriving the necessary functionality automatically. By enabling ppx_jane, we pull in a collection of such derivers, three of which we use in defining String_pair below.

```
# #require "ppx_jane";;
# module String_pair = struct
    type t = string * string [@@deriving sexp_of, hash, compare]
  end;;
module String_pair :
  sig
    type t = string * string
    val sexp_of_t : t -> Sexp.t
    val hash_fold_t : Hash.state -> t -> Hash.state
    val hash : t -> int
    val compare : t -> t -> int
  end
```

With that in hand, we can define our optimized form of edit_distance.

```
# let edit_distance = memo_rec (module String_pair)
    (fun edit_distance (s,t) ->
       match String.length s, String.length t with
       | (0,x) | (x,0) -> x
       | (len_s,len_t) ->
         let s' = String.drop_suffix s 1 in
         let t' = String.drop_suffix t 1 in
         let cost_to_drop_both =
           if Char.(=) s.[len_s - 1] t.[len_t - 1] then 0 else 1
         in
         List.reduce_exn ~f:Int.min
           [ edit_distance (s',t ) + 1
           ; edit_distance (s ,t') + 1
           ; edit_distance (s',t') + cost_to_drop_both
    ]);;
val edit_distance : String_pair.t -> int = <fun>
```

This new version of edit_distance is much more efficient than the one we started with; the following call is many thousands of times faster than it was without memoization.

```
# time (fun () -> edit_distance ("OCaml 4.09","ocaml 4.09"));;
Time: 0.964403152466 ms
- : int = 2
```

Limitations of let rec

You might wonder why we didn't tie the recursive knot in memo_rec using let rec, as we did for make_rec earlier. Here's code that tries to do just that:

```
# let memo_rec m f_norec =
    let rec f = memoize m (fun x -> f_norec f x) in
    f;;
Line 2, characters 17-49:
```

```
Error: This kind of expression is not allowed as right-hand side of
    `let rec'
```

OCaml rejects the definition because OCaml, as a strict language, has limits on what it can put on the right-hand side of a `let rec`. In particular, imagine how the following code snippet would be compiled:

```
let rec x = x + 1
```

Note that `x` is an ordinary value, not a function. As such, it's not clear how this definition should be handled by the compiler. You could imagine it compiling down to an infinite loop, but `x` is of type `int`, and there's no `int` that corresponds to an infinite loop. As such, this construct is effectively impossible to compile.

To avoid such impossible cases, the compiler only allows three possible constructs to show up on the right-hand side of a `let rec`: a function definition, a constructor, or the lazy keyword. This excludes some reasonable things, like our definition of `memo_rec`, but it also blocks things that don't make sense, like our definition of `x`.

It's worth noting that these restrictions don't show up in a lazy language like Haskell. Indeed, we can make something like our definition of x work if we use OCaml's laziness:

```
# let rec x = lazy (force x + 1);;
val x : int lazy_t = <lazy>
```

Of course, actually trying to compute this will fail. OCaml's `lazy` throws an exception when a lazy value tries to force itself as part of its own evaluation.

```
# force x;;
Exception: Lazy.Undefined
```

But we can also create useful recursive definitions with `lazy`. In particular, we can use laziness to make our definition of `memo_rec` work without explicit mutation:

```
# let lazy_memo_rec m f_norec x =
    let rec f = lazy (memoize m (fun x -> f_norec (force f) x)) in
    (force f) x;;
val lazy_memo_rec : 'a Hashtbl.Key.t -> (('a -> 'b) -> 'a -> 'b) -> 'a ->
    'b =
  <fun>
# time (fun () -> lazy_memo_rec (module Int) fib_norec 40);;
Time: 0.181913375854 ms
- : int = 102334155
```

Laziness is more constrained than explicit mutation, and so in some cases can lead to code whose behavior is easier to think about.

9.6   Input and Output

Imperative programming is about more than modifying in-memory data structures. Any function that doesn't boil down to a deterministic transformation from its arguments to its return value is imperative in nature. That includes not only things that mutate your program's data, but also operations that interact with the world outside of your program. An important example of this kind of interaction is I/O, i.e., operations for reading or writing data to things like files, terminal input and output, and network sockets.

There are multiple I/O libraries in OCaml. In this section we'll discuss OCaml's buffered I/O library that can be used through the In_channel and Out_channel modules in Stdio. Other I/O primitives are also available through the Unix module in Core as well as Async, the asynchronous I/O library that is covered in Chapter 17 (Concurrent Programming with Async). Most of the functionality in Core's In_channel and Out_channel (and in Core's Unix module) derives from the standard library, but we'll use Core's interfaces here.

9.6.1   Terminal I/O

OCaml's buffered I/O library is organized around two types: in_channel, for channels you read from, and out_channel, for channels you write to. The In_channel and Out_channel modules only have direct support for channels corresponding to files and terminals; other kinds of channels can be created through the Unix module.

We'll start our discussion of I/O by focusing on the terminal. Following the UNIX model, communication with the terminal is organized around three channels, which correspond to the three standard file descriptors in Unix:

In_channel.stdin The "standard input" channel. By default, input comes from the terminal, which handles keyboard input.

Out_channel.stdout The "standard output" channel. By default, output written to stdout appears on the user terminal.

Out_channel.stderr The "standard error" channel. This is similar to stdout but is intended for error messages.

The values stdin, stdout, and stderr are useful enough that they are also available in the top level of Core's namespace directly, without having to go through the In_channel and Out_channel modules.

Let's see this in action in a simple interactive application. The following program, time_converter, prompts the user for a time zone, and then prints out the current time in that time zone. Here, we use Core's Zone module for looking up a time zone, and the Time module for computing the current time and printing it out in the time zone in question:

```
open Core

let () =
  Out_channel.output_string stdout "Pick a timezone: ";
  Out_channel.flush stdout;
  match In_channel.(input_line stdin) with
  | None -> failwith "No timezone provided"
  | Some zone_string ->
    let zone = Time.Zone.find_exn zone_string in
    let time_string = Time.to_string_abs (Time.now ()) ~zone in
    Out_channel.output_string stdout
```

```
        (String.concat
            ["The time in ";Time.Zone.to_string zone;" is
        ";time_string;".\n"]);
        Out_channel.flush stdout
```

We can build this program using dune and run it, though you'll need to add a
dune-project and dune file, as described in Chapter 5 (Files, Modules, and Programs).
You'll see that it prompts you for input, as follows:

```
$ dune exec ./time_converter.exe
Pick a timezone:
```

You can then type in the name of a time zone and hit Return, and it will print out
the current time in the time zone in question:

```
Pick a timezone: Europe/London
The time in Europe/London is 2013-08-15 00:03:10.666220+01:00.
```

We called Out_channel.flush on stdout because out_channels are buffered, which
is to say that OCaml doesn't immediately do a write every time you call output_string.
Instead, writes are buffered until either enough has been written to trigger the flushing
of the buffers, or until a flush is explicitly requested. This greatly increases the efficiency
of the writing process by reducing the number of system calls.

Note that In_channel.input_line returns a string option, with None indicating that the input stream has ended (i.e., an end-of-file condition).
Out_channel.output_string is used to print the final output, and Out_channel.flush
is called to flush that output to the screen. The final flush is not technically required,
since the program ends after that instruction, at which point all remaining output will
be flushed anyway, but the explicit flush is nonetheless good practice.

9.6.2   Formatted Output with printf

Generating output with functions like Out_channel.output_string is simple and easy
to understand, but can be a bit verbose. OCaml also supports formatted output using
the printf function, which is modeled after printf in the C standard library. printf
takes a *format string* that describes what to print and how to format it, as well as
arguments to be printed, as determined by the formatting directives embedded in the
format string. So, for example, we can write:

```
# printf
    "%i is an integer, %F is a float, \"%s\" is a string\n"
    3 4.5 "five";;
3 is an integer, 4.5 is a float, "five" is a string
- : unit = ()
```

Unlike C's printf, the printf in OCaml is type-safe. In particular, if we provide
an argument whose type doesn't match what's presented in the format string, we'll get
a type error:

```
# printf "An integer: %i\n" 4.5;;
Line 1, characters 27-30:
```

```
Error: This expression has type float but an expression was expected
     of type
          int
```

Understanding Format Strings

The format strings used by `printf` turn out to be quite different from ordinary strings. This difference ties to the fact that OCaml's `printf` facility, unlike the equivalent in C, is type-safe. In particular, the compiler checks that the types referred to by the format string match the types of the rest of the arguments passed to `printf`.

To check this, OCaml needs to analyze the contents of the format string at compile time, which means the format string needs to be available as a string literal at compile time. Indeed, if you try to pass an ordinary string to `printf`, the compiler will complain:

```
# let fmt = "%i is an integer\n";;
val fmt : string = "%i is an integer\n"
# printf fmt 3;;
Line 1, characters 8-11:
Error: This expression has type string but an expression was expected
     of type
          ('a -> 'b, Stdio.Out_channel.t, unit) format =
             ('a -> 'b, Stdio.Out_channel.t, unit, unit, unit, unit)
     format6
```

If OCaml infers that a given string literal is a format string, then it parses it at compile time as such, choosing its type in accordance with the formatting directives it finds. Thus, if we add a type annotation indicating that the string we're defining is actually a format string, it will be interpreted as such. (Here, we open the CamlinternalFormatBasics so that the representation of the format string that's printed out won't fill the whole page.)

```
# open CamlinternalFormatBasics;;
# let fmt : ('a, 'b, 'c) format =
    "%i is an integer\n";;
val fmt : (int -> 'c, 'b, 'c) format =
    Format
      (Int (Int_i, No_padding, No_precision,
        String_literal (" is an integer\n", End_of_format)),
      "%i is an integer\n")
```

And accordingly, we can pass it to `printf`:

```
# printf fmt 3;;
3 is an integer
- : unit = ()
```

If this looks different from everything else you've seen so far, that's because it is. This is really a special case in the type system. Most of the time, you don't need to know about this special handling of format strings—you can just use `printf` and not worry about the details. But it's useful to keep the broad outlines of the story in the back of your head.

Now let's see how we can rewrite our time conversion program to be a little more concise using `printf`:

```
open Core

let () =
  printf "Pick a timezone: %!";
  match In_channel.input_line In_channel.stdin with
  | None -> failwith "No timezone provided"
  | Some zone_string ->
    let zone = Time.Zone.find_exn zone_string in
    let time_string = Time.to_string_abs (Time.now ()) ~zone in
    printf "The time in %s is %s.\n%!" (Time.Zone.to_string zone)
    time_string
```

In the preceding example, we've used only two formatting directives: %s, for including a string, and %! which causes `printf` to flush the channel.

`printf`'s formatting directives offer a significant amount of control, allowing you to specify things like:

- Alignment and padding
- Escaping rules for strings
- Whether numbers should be formatted in decimal, hex, or binary
- Precision of float conversions

There are also `printf`-style functions that target outputs other than `stdout`, including:

- `eprintf`, which prints to `stderr`
- `fprintf`, which prints to an arbitrary `out_channel`
- `sprintf`, which returns a formatted string

All of this, and a good deal more, is described in the API documentation for the `Printf` module in the OCaml Manual.

9.6.3   File I/O

Another common use of `in_channels` and `out_channels` is for working with files. Here are a couple of functions—one that creates a file full of numbers, and the other that reads in such a file and returns the sum of those numbers:

```
# let create_number_file filename numbers =
    let outc = Out_channel.create filename in
    List.iter numbers ~f:(fun x -> Out_channel.fprintf outc "%d\n" x);
    Out_channel.close outc;;
val create_number_file : string -> int list -> unit = <fun>
# let sum_file filename =
    let file = In_channel.create filename in
    let numbers = List.map ~f:Int.of_string (In_channel.input_lines
    file) in
    let sum = List.fold ~init:0 ~f:(+) numbers in
    In_channel.close file;
```

```
      sum;;
val sum_file : string -> int = <fun>
# create_number_file "numbers.txt" [1;2;3;4;5];;
- : unit = ()
# sum_file "numbers.txt";;
- : int = 15
```

For both of these functions, we followed the same basic sequence: we first create the channel, then use the channel, and finally close the channel. The closing of the channel is important, since without it, we won't release resources associated with the file back to the operating system.

One problem with the preceding code is that if it throws an exception in the middle of its work, it won't actually close the file. If we try to read a file that doesn't actually contain numbers, we'll see such an error:

```
# sum_file "/etc/hosts";;
Exception:
(Failure
   "Int.of_string: \"127.0.0.1    localhost localhost.localdomain
      localhost4 localhost4.localdomain4\"")
```

And if we do this over and over in a loop, we'll eventually run out of file descriptors:

```
# for i = 1 to 10000 do try ignore (sum_file "/etc/hosts") with _ ->
      () done;;
- : unit = ()
# sum_file "numbers.txt";;
Error: I/O error: ...: Too many open files
```

And now, you'll need to restart your toplevel if you want to open any more files!

To avoid this, we need to make sure that our code cleans up after itself. We can do this using the `protect` function described in Chapter 8 (Error Handling), as follows:

```
# let sum_file filename =
    let file = In_channel.create filename in
    Exn.protect ~f:(fun () ->
      let numbers = List.map ~f:Int.of_string (In_channel.input_lines
      file) in
      List.fold ~init:0 ~f:(+) numbers)
      ~finally:(fun () -> In_channel.close file);;
val sum_file : string -> int = <fun>
```

And now, the file descriptor leak is gone:

```
# for i = 1 to 10000 do try ignore (sum_file "/etc/hosts" : int) with
      _ -> () done;;
- : unit = ()
# sum_file "numbers.txt";;
- : int = 15
```

This is really an example of a more general issue with imperative programming and exceptions. If you're changing the internal state of your program and you're interrupted by an exception, you need to consider quite carefully if it's safe to continue working from your current state.

`In_channel` has functions that automate the handling of some of these details. For example, `In_channel.with_file` takes a filename and a function for processing data from an `in_channel` and takes care of the bookkeeping associated with opening and closing the file. We can rewrite `sum_file` using this function, as shown here:

```
# let sum_file filename =
    In_channel.with_file filename ~f:(fun file ->
      let numbers = List.map ~f:Int.of_string (In_channel.input_lines
      file) in
      List.fold ~init:0 ~f:(+) numbers);;
val sum_file : string -> int = <fun>
```

Another misfeature of our implementation of `sum_file` is that we read the entire file into memory before processing it. For a large file, it's more efficient to process a line at a time. You can use the `In_channel.fold_lines` function to do just that:

```
# let sum_file filename =
    In_channel.with_file filename ~f:(fun file ->
      In_channel.fold_lines file ~init:0 ~f:(fun sum line ->
        sum + Int.of_string line));;
val sum_file : string -> int = <fun>
```

This is just a taste of the functionality of `In_channel` and `Out_channel`. To get a fuller understanding, you should review the API documentation.

9.7   Order of Evaluation

The order in which expressions are evaluated is an important part of the definition of a programming language, and it is particularly important when programming imperatively. Most programming languages you're likely to have encountered are *strict*, and OCaml is too. In a strict language, when you bind an identifier to the result of some expression, the expression is evaluated before the variable is bound. Similarly, if you call a function on a set of arguments, those arguments are evaluated before they are passed to the function.

Consider the following simple example. Here, we have a collection of angles, and we want to determine if any of them have a negative `sin`. The following snippet of code would answer that question:

```
# let x = Float.sin 120. in
  let y = Float.sin 75.  in
  let z = Float.sin 128. in
  List.exists ~f:(fun x -> Float.0.(x < 0.)) [x;y;z];;
- : bool = true
```

In some sense, we don't really need to compute the `sin` 128 because `sin` 75 is negative, so we could know the answer before even computing `sin` 128.

It doesn't have to be this way. Using the `lazy` keyword, we can write the original computation so that `sin` 128 won't ever be computed:

```
# let x = lazy (Float.sin 120.) in
  let y = lazy (Float.sin 75.)  in
  let z = lazy (Float.sin 128.) in
```

```
  List.exists ~f:(fun x -> Float.O.(Lazy.force x < 0.)) [x;y;z];;
- : bool = true
```

We can confirm that fact by a few well-placed `printf`s:

```
# let x = lazy (printf "1\n"; Float.sin 120.) in
  let y = lazy (printf "2\n"; Float.sin 75.)  in
  let z = lazy (printf "3\n"; Float.sin 128.) in
  List.exists ~f:(fun x -> Float.O.(Lazy.force x < 0.)) [x;y;z];;
1
2
- : bool = true
```

OCaml is strict by default for a good reason: lazy evaluation and imperative programming generally don't mix well because laziness makes it harder to reason about
when a given side effect is going to occur. Understanding the order of side effects is
essential to reasoning about the behavior of an imperative program.

Because OCaml is strict, we know that expressions that are bound by a sequence
of `let` bindings will be evaluated in the order that they're defined. But what about the
evaluation order within a single expression? Officially, the answer is that evaluation
order within an expression is undefined. In practice, OCaml has only one compiler,
and that behavior is a kind of *de facto* standard. Unfortunately, the evaluation order in
this case is often the opposite of what one might expect.

Consider the following example:

```
# List.exists ~f:(fun x -> Float.O.(x < 0.))
    [ (printf "1\n"; Float.sin 120.);
      (printf "2\n"; Float.sin 75.);
      (printf "3\n"; Float.sin 128.); ];;
3
2
1
- : bool = true
```

Here, you can see that the subexpression that came last was actually evaluated first!
This is generally the case for many different kinds of expressions. If you want to make
sure of the evaluation order of different subexpressions, you should express them as a
series of `let` bindings.

9.8   Side Effects and Weak Polymorphism

Consider the following simple, imperative function:

```
# let remember =
    let cache = ref None in
    (fun x ->
       match !cache with
       | Some y -> y
       | None -> cache := Some x; x);;
val remember : '_weak1 -> '_weak1 = <fun>
```

`remember` simply caches the first value that's passed to it, returning that value on every call. That's because `cache` is created and initialized once and is shared across invocations of `remember`.

`remember` is not a terribly useful function, but it raises an interesting question: what should its type be?

On its first call, `remember` returns the same value it's passed, which means its input type and return type should match. Accordingly, `remember` should have type `t -> t` for some type `t`. There's nothing about `remember` that ties the choice of `t` to any particular type, so you might expect OCaml to generalize, replacing `t` with a polymorphic type variable. It's this kind of generalization that gives us polymorphic types in the first place. The identity function, as an example, gets a polymorphic type in this way:

```
# let identity x = x;;
val identity : 'a -> 'a = <fun>
# identity 3;;
- : int = 3
# identity "five";;
- : string = "five"
```

As you can see, the polymorphic type of `identity` lets it operate on values with different types.

This is not what happens with `remember`, though. As you can see from the above examples, the type that OCaml infers for `remember` looks almost, but not quite, like the type of the identity function. Here it is again:

```
val remember : '_weak1 -> '_weak1 = <fun>
```

The underscore in the type variable `'_weak1` tells us that the variable is only *weakly polymorphic*, which is to say that it can be used with any *single* type. That makes sense because, unlike `identity`, `remember` always returns the value it was passed on its first invocation, which means its return value must always have the same type.

OCaml will convert a weakly polymorphic variable to a concrete type as soon as it gets a clue as to what concrete type it is to be used as:

```
# let remember_three () = remember 3;;
val remember_three : unit -> int = <fun>
# remember;;
- : int -> int = <fun>
# remember "avocado";;
Line 1, characters 10-19:
Error: This expression has type string but an expression was expected
       of type
           int
```

Note that the type of `remember` was settled by the definition of `remember_three`, even though `remember_three` was never called!

9.8.1   The Value Restriction

So, when does the compiler infer weakly polymorphic types? As we've seen, we need weakly polymorphic types when a value of unknown type is stored in a persistent mutable cell. Because the type system isn't precise enough to determine all cases where this might happen, OCaml uses a rough rule to flag cases that don't introduce any persistent mutable cells, and to only infer polymorphic types in those cases. This rule is called *the value restriction*.

The core of the value restriction is the observation that some kinds of expressions, which we'll refer to as *simple values*, by their nature can't introduce persistent mutable cells, including:

- Constants (i.e., things like integer and floating-point literals)
- Constructors that only contain other simple values
- Function declarations, i.e., expressions that begin with `fun` or `function`, or the equivalent let binding, `let f x = ...`
- `let` bindings of the form `let var = expr1 in expr2`, where both `expr1` and `expr2` are simple values

Thus, the following expression is a simple value, and as a result, the types of values contained within it are allowed to be polymorphic:

```
# (fun x -> [x;x]);;
- : 'a -> 'a list = <fun>
```

But, if we write down an expression that isn't a simple value by the preceding definition, we'll get different results.

```
# identity (fun x -> [x;x]);;
- : '_weak2 -> '_weak2 list = <fun>
```

In principle, it would be safe to infer a fully polymorphic variable here, but because OCaml's type system doesn't distinguish between pure and impure functions, it can't separate those two cases.

The value restriction doesn't require that there is no mutable state, only that there is no *persistent* mutable state that could share values between uses of the same function. Thus, a function that produces a fresh reference every time it's called can have a fully polymorphic type:

```
# let f () = ref None;;
val f : unit -> 'a option ref = <fun>
```

But a function that has a mutable cache that persists across calls, like `memoize`, can only be weakly polymorphic.

9.8.2   Partial Application and the Value Restriction

Most of the time, when the value restriction kicks in, it's for a good reason, i.e., it's because the value in question can actually only safely be used with a single type. But sometimes, the value restriction kicks in when you don't want it. The most common such case is partially applied functions. A partially applied function, like any function application, is not a simple value, and as such, functions created by partial application are sometimes less general than you might expect.

Consider the `List.init` function, which is used for creating lists where each element is created by calling a function on the index of that element:

```
# List.init;;
- : int -> f:(int -> 'a) -> 'a list = <fun>
# List.init 10 ~f:Int.to_string;;
- : string list = ["0"; "1"; "2"; "3"; "4"; "5"; "6"; "7"; "8"; "9"]
```

Imagine we wanted to create a specialized version of `List.init` that always created lists of length 10. We could do that using partial application, as follows:

```
# let list_init_10 = List.init 10;;
val list_init_10 : f:(int -> '_weak3) -> '_weak3 list = <fun>
```

As you can see, we now infer a weakly polymorphic type for the resulting function. That's because there's nothing that guarantees that `List.init` isn't creating a persistent `ref` somewhere inside of it that would be shared across multiple calls to `list_init_10`. We can eliminate this possibility, and at the same time get the compiler to infer a polymorphic type, by avoiding partial application:

```
# let list_init_10 ~f = List.init 10 ~f;;
val list_init_10 : f:(int -> 'a) -> 'a list = <fun>
```

This transformation is referred to as *eta expansion* and is often useful to resolve problems that arise from the value restriction.

9.8.3   Relaxing the Value Restriction

OCaml is actually a little better at inferring polymorphic types than was suggested previously. The value restriction as we described it is basically a syntactic check: you can do a few operations that count as simple values, and anything that's a simple value can be generalized.

But OCaml actually has a relaxed version of the value restriction that can make use of type information to allow polymorphic types for things that are not simple values.

For example, we saw that a function application, even a simple application of the identity function, is not a simple value and thus can turn a polymorphic value into a weakly polymorphic one:

```
# identity (fun x -> [x;x]);;
- : '_weak4 -> '_weak4 list = <fun>
```

But that's not always the case. When the type of the returned value is immutable, then OCaml can typically infer a fully polymorphic type:

```
# identity [];;
- : 'a list = []
```

On the other hand, if the returned type is mutable, then the result will be weakly polymorphic:

```
# [||];;
- : 'a array = [||]
# identity [||];;
- : '_weak5 array = [||]
```

A more important example of this comes up when defining abstract data types. Consider the following simple data structure for an immutable list type that supports constant-time concatenation:

```
# module Concat_list : sig
    type 'a t
    val empty : 'a t
    val singleton : 'a -> 'a t
    val concat  : 'a t -> 'a t -> 'a t   (* constant time *)
    val to_list : 'a t -> 'a list        (* linear time   *)
  end = struct

    type 'a t = Empty | Singleton of 'a | Concat of 'a t * 'a t

    let empty = Empty
    let singleton x = Singleton x
    let concat x y = Concat (x,y)

    let rec to_list_with_tail t tail =
      match t with
      | Empty -> tail
      | Singleton x -> x :: tail
      | Concat (x,y) -> to_list_with_tail x (to_list_with_tail y tail)

    let to_list t =
      to_list_with_tail t []

  end;;
module Concat_list :
  sig
    type 'a t
    val empty : 'a t
    val singleton : 'a -> 'a t
    val concat : 'a t -> 'a t -> 'a t
    val to_list : 'a t -> 'a list
  end
```

The details of the implementation don't matter so much, but it's important to note that a `Concat_list.t` is unquestionably an immutable value. However, when it comes to the value restriction, OCaml treats it as if it were mutable:

```
# Concat_list.empty;;
- : 'a Concat_list.t = <abstr>
# identity Concat_list.empty;;
- : '_weak6 Concat_list.t = <abstr>
```

The issue here is that the signature, by virtue of being abstract, has obscured the fact that `Concat_list.t` is in fact an immutable data type. We can resolve this in one of two ways: either by making the type concrete (i.e., exposing the implementation in the `mli`), which is often not desirable; or by marking the type variable in question as *covariant*. We'll learn more about covariance and contravariance in Chapter 13 (Objects), but for now, you can think of it as an annotation that can be put in the interface of a pure data structure.

In particular, if we replace `type 'a t` in the interface with `type +'a t`, that will make it explicit in the interface that the data structure doesn't contain any persistent references to values of type `'a`, at which point, OCaml can infer polymorphic types for expressions of this type that are not simple values:

```
# module Concat_list : sig
```

```
        type +'a t
        val empty : 'a t
        val singleton : 'a -> 'a t
        val concat  : 'a t -> 'a t -> 'a t   (* constant time *)
        val to_list : 'a t -> 'a list        (* linear time   *)
      end = struct

        type 'a t = Empty | Singleton of 'a | Concat of 'a t * 'a t

        let empty = Empty
        let singleton x = Singleton x
        let concat x y = Concat (x,y)

        let rec to_list_with_tail t tail =
          match t with
          | Empty -> tail
          | Singleton x -> x :: tail
          | Concat (x,y) -> to_list_with_tail x (to_list_with_tail y tail)

        let to_list t =
          to_list_with_tail t []

      end;;
    module Concat_list :
      sig
        type +'a t
        val empty : 'a t
        val singleton : 'a -> 'a t
        val concat : 'a t -> 'a t -> 'a t
        val to_list : 'a t -> 'a list
      end
```

Now, we can apply the identity function to `Concat_list.empty` without losing any polymorphism:

```
# identity Concat_list.empty;;
- : 'a Concat_list.t = <abstr>
```

9.9   Summary

This chapter has covered quite a lot of ground, including:

- Discussing the building blocks of mutable data structures as well as the basic imperative constructs like `for` loops, `while` loops, and the sequencing operator ;
- Walking through the implementation of a couple of classic imperative data structures
- Discussing so-called benign effects like memoization and laziness
- Covering OCaml's API for blocking I/O
- Discussing how language-level issues like order of evaluation and weak polymorphism interact with OCaml's imperative features

The scope and sophistication of the material here is an indication of the importance of OCaml's imperative features. The fact that OCaml defaults to immutability shouldn't obscure the fact that imperative programming is a fundamental part of building any serious application, and that if you want to be an effective OCaml programmer, you need to understand OCaml's approach to imperative programming.

10 GADTs

Generalized Algebraic Data Types, or GADTs for short, are an extension of the variants we saw in Chapter 7 (Variants). GADTs are more expressive than regular variants, which helps you create types that more precisely match the shape of the program you want to write. That can help you write code that's safer, more concise, and more efficient.

At the same time, GADTs are an advanced feature of OCaml, and their power comes at a distinct cost. GADTs are harder to use and less intuitive than ordinary variants, and it can sometimes be a bit of a puzzle to figure out how to use them effectively. All of which is to say that you should only use a GADT when it makes a big qualitative improvement to your design.

That said, for the right use-case, GADTs can be really transformative, and this chapter will walk through several examples that demonstrate the range of use-cases that GADTs support.

At their heart, GADTs provide two extra features above and beyond ordinary variants:

- They let the compiler learn more type information when you descend into a case of a pattern match.
- They make it easy to use *existential types*, which let you work with data of a specific but unknown type.

It's a little hard to understand these features without working through some examples, so we'll do that next.

10.1 A Little Language

One classic use-case for GADTs is for writing typed expression languages, similar to the boolean expression language described in Chapter 7.3 (Variants and Recursive Data Structures). In this section, we'll create a slightly richer language that lets us mix arithmetic and boolean expressions. This means that we have to deal with the possibility of ill-typed expressions, e.g., an expression that adds a bool and an int.

Let's first try to do this with an ordinary variant. We'll declare two types here: value, which represents a primitive value in the language (i.e., an int or a bool), and expr, which represents the full set of possible expressions.

```
open Base

type value =
  | Int of int
  | Bool of bool

type expr =
  | Value of value
  | Eq of expr * expr
  | Plus of expr * expr
  | If of expr * expr * expr
```

We can write a recursive evaluator for this type in a pretty straight-ahead style. First, we'll declare an exception that can be thrown when we hit an ill-typed expression, e.g., when encountering an expression that tries to add a bool and an int.

```
exception Ill_typed
```

With that in hand, we can write the evaluator itself.

```
# let rec eval expr =
    match expr with
    | Value v -> v
    | If (c, t, e) ->
      (match eval c with
        | Bool b -> if b then eval t else eval e
        | Int _ -> raise Ill_typed)
    | Eq (x, y) ->
      (match eval x, eval y with
        | Bool _, _ | _, Bool _ -> raise Ill_typed
        | Int f1, Int f2 -> Bool (f1 = f2))
    | Plus (x, y) ->
      (match eval x, eval y with
        | Bool _, _ | _, Bool _ -> raise Ill_typed
        | Int f1, Int f2 -> Int (f1 + f2));;
val eval : expr -> value = <fun>
```

This implementation is a bit ugly because it has a lot of dynamic checks to detect type errors. Indeed, it's entirely possible to create an ill-typed expression which will trip these checks.

```
# let i x = Value (Int x)
  and b x = Value (Bool x)
  and (+:) x y = Plus (x,y);;
val i : int -> expr = <fun>
val b : bool -> expr = <fun>
val ( +: ) : expr -> expr -> expr = <fun>
# eval (i 3 +: b false);;
Exception: Ill_typed.
```

This possibility of ill-typed expressions doesn't just complicate the implementation: it's also a problem for users, since it's all too easy to create ill-typed expressions by mistake.

10.1.1   Making the Language Type-Safe

Let's consider what a type-safe version of this API might look like in the absence of
GADTs. To even express the type constraints, we'll need expressions to have a type
parameter to distinguish integer expressions from boolean expressions. Given such a
parameter, the signature for such a language might look like this.

```
module type Typesafe_lang_sig = sig
  type 'a t

  (** functions for constructing expressions *)

  val int : int -> int t
  val bool : bool -> bool t
  val if_ : bool t -> 'a t -> 'a t -> 'a t
  val eq : 'a t -> 'a t -> bool t
  val plus : int t -> int t -> int t

  (** Evaluation functions *)

  val int_eval : int t -> int
  val bool_eval : bool t -> bool
end
```

The functions int_eval and bool_eval deserve some explanation. You might expect
there to be a single evaluation function, with this signature.

```
val eval : 'a t -> 'a
```

But as we'll see, we're not going to be able to implement that, at least, not without
using GADTs. So for now, we're stuck with two different evaluators, one for each type
of expression.

Now let's write an implementation that matches this signature.

```
module Typesafe_lang : Typesafe_lang_sig = struct
  type 'a t = expr

  let int x = Value (Int x)
  let bool x = Value (Bool x)
  let if_ c t e = If (c, t, e)
  let eq x y = Eq (x, y)
  let plus x y = Plus (x, y)

  let int_eval expr =
    match eval expr with
    | Int x -> x
    | Bool _ -> raise Ill_typed

  let bool_eval expr =
    match eval expr with
    | Bool x -> x
    | Int _ -> raise Ill_typed
end
```

As you can see, the ill-typed expression we had trouble with before can't be constructed, because it's rejected by OCaml's type-system.

```
# let expr = Typesafe_lang.(plus (int 3) (bool false));;
Line 1, characters 40-52:
Error: This expression has type bool t but an expression was expected
    of type
          int t
        Type bool is not compatible with type int
```

So, what happened here? How did we add the type-safety we wanted? The fundamental trick is to add what's called a *phantom type*. In this definition:

```
type 'a t = expr
```

the type parameter 'a is the phantom type, since it doesn't show up in the body of the
definition of t.

Because the type parameter is unused, it's free to take on any value. That means
we can constrain the use of that type parameter arbitrarily in the signature, which is a
freedom we use to add the type-safety rules that we wanted.

This all amounts to an improvement in terms of the API, but the implementation is
if anything worse. We still have the same evaluator with all of its dynamic checking
for type errors. But we've had to write yet more wrapper code to make this work.

Also, the phantom-type discipline is quite error prone. You might have missed the
fact that the type on the eq function above is wrong!

```
# Typesafe_lang.eq;;
- : 'a Typesafe_lang.t -> 'a Typesafe_lang.t -> bool Typesafe_lang.t =
    <fun>
```

It looks like it's polymorphic over the type of expressions, but the evaluator only
supports checking equality on integers. As a result, we can still construct an ill-typed
expression, phantom-types notwithstanding.

```
# let expr = Typesafe_lang.(eq (bool true) (bool false));;
val expr : bool Typesafe_lang.t = <abstr>
# Typesafe_lang.bool_eval expr;;
Exception: Ill_typed.
```

This highlights why we still need the dynamic checks in the implementation: the
types within the implementation don't necessarily rule out ill-typed expressions. The
same fact explains why we needed two different eval functions: the implementation
of eval doesn't have any type-level guarantee of when it's handling a bool expression
versus an int expression, so it can't safely give results where the type of the result varies
based on the result of the expression.

10.1.2   Trying to Do Better with Ordinary Variants

To see why we need GADTs, let's see how far we can get without them. In particular,
let's see what happens when we try to encode the typing rules we want for our DSL
directly into the definition of the expression type. We'll do that by putting an ordinary
type parameter on our expr and value types, in order to represent the type of an
expression or value.

```
type 'a value =
  | Int of 'a
  | Bool of 'a

type 'a expr =
  | Value of 'a value
  | Eq of 'a expr * 'a expr
  | Plus of 'a expr * 'a expr
  | If of bool expr * 'a expr * 'a expr
```

This looks promising at first, but it doesn't quite do what we want. Let's experiment a little.

```
# let i x = Value (Int x)
  and b x = Value (Bool x)
  and (+:) x y = Plus (x,y);;
val i : 'a -> 'a expr = <fun>
val b : 'a -> 'a expr = <fun>
val ( +: ) : 'a expr -> 'a expr -> 'a expr = <fun>
# i 3;;
- : int expr = Value (Int 3)
# b false;;
- : bool expr = Value (Bool false)
# i 3 +: i 4;;
- : int expr = Plus (Value (Int 3), Value (Int 4))
```

So far so good. But if you think about it for a minute, you'll realize this doesn't actually do what we want. For one thing, the type of the outer expression is always just equal to the type of the inner expression, which means that some things that should type-check don't.

```
# If (Eq (i 3, i 4), i 0, i 1);;
Line 1, characters 9-12:
Error: This expression has type int expr
        but an expression was expected of type bool expr
        Type int is not compatible with type bool
```

Also, some things that shouldn't typecheck do.

```
# b 3;;
- : int expr = Value (Bool 3)
```

The problem here is that the way we want to use the type parameter isn't supported by ordinary variants. In particular, we want the type parameter to be populated in different ways in the different tags, and to depend in non-trivial ways on the types of the data associated with each tag. That's where GADTs can help.

10.1.3   GADTs to the Rescue

Now we're ready to write our first GADT. Here's a new version of our value and expr types that correctly encode our desired typing rules.

```
type _ value =
  | Int : int -> int value
  | Bool : bool -> bool value
```

```
type _ expr =
  | Value : 'a value -> 'a expr
  | Eq : int expr * int expr -> bool expr
  | Plus : int expr * int expr -> int expr
  | If : bool expr * 'a expr * 'a expr -> 'a expr
```

The syntax here requires some decoding. The colon to the right of each tag is what tells you that this is a GADT. To the right of the colon, you'll see what looks like an ordinary, single-argument function type, and you can almost think of it that way; specifically, as the type signature for that particular tag, viewed as a type constructor. The left-hand side of the arrow states the types of the arguments to the constructor, and the right-hand side determines the type of the constructed value.

In the definition of each tag in a GADT, the right-hand side of the arrow is an instance of the type of the overall GADT, with independent choices for the type parameter in each case. Importantly, the type parameter can depend both on the tag and on the type of the arguments. Eq is an example where the type parameter is determined entirely by the tag: it always corresponds to a bool expr. If is an example where the type parameter depends on the arguments to the tag, in particular the type parameter of the If is the type parameter of the then and else clauses.

Let's try some examples.

```
# let i x = Value (Int x)
  and b x = Value (Bool x)
  and (+:) x y = Plus (x,y);;
val i : int -> int expr = <fun>
val b : bool -> bool expr = <fun>
val ( +: ) : int expr -> int expr -> int expr = <fun>
# i 3;;
- : int expr = Value (Int 3)
# b 3;;
Line 1, characters 3-4:
Error: This expression has type int but an expression was expected of
       type
           bool
# i 3 +: i 6;;
- : int expr = Plus (Value (Int 3), Value (Int 6))
# i 3 +: b false;;
Line 1, characters 8-15:
Error: This expression has type bool expr
          but an expression was expected of type int expr
          Type bool is not compatible with type int
```

What we see here is that the type-safety rules we previously enforced with signature-level restrictions on phantom types are now directly encoded in the definition of the expression type.

These type-safety rules apply not just when constructing an expression, but also when deconstructing one, which means we can write a simpler and more concise evaluator that doesn't need any type-safety checks.

```
# let eval_value : type a. a value -> a = function
    | Int x -> x
```

```
    | Bool x -> x;;
val eval_value : 'a value -> 'a = <fun>
# let rec eval : type a. a expr -> a = function
    | Value v -> eval_value v
    | If (c, t, e) -> if eval c then eval t else eval e
    | Eq (x, y) -> eval x = eval y
    | Plus (x, y) -> eval x + eval y;;
val eval : 'a expr -> 'a = <fun>
```

Note that we now have a single polymorphic eval function, as opposed to the two type-specific evaluators we needed when using phantom types.

10.1.4   GADTs, Locally Abstract Types, and Polymorphic Recursion

The above example lets us see one of the downsides of GADTs, which is that code using them needs extra type annotations. Look at what happens if we write the definition of value without the annotation.

```
# let eval_value = function
    | Int x -> x
    | Bool x -> x;;
Line 3, characters 7-13:
Error: This pattern matches values of type bool value
       but a pattern was expected which matches values of type int
       value
         Type bool is not compatible with type int
```

The issue here is that OCaml by default isn't willing to instantiate ordinary type variables in different ways in the body of the same function, which is what is required here. We can fix that by adding a *locally abstract type*, which doesn't have that restriction.

```
# let eval_value (type a) (v : a value) : a =
    match v with
    | Int x -> x
    | Bool x -> x;;
val eval_value : 'a value -> 'a = <fun>
```

This isn't the same annotation we wrote earlier, and indeed, if we try this approach with eval, we'll see that it doesn't work.

```
# let rec eval (type a) (e : a expr) : a =
    match e with
    | Value v -> eval_value v
    | If (c, t, e) -> if eval c then eval t else eval e
    | Eq (x, y) -> eval x = eval y
    | Plus (x, y) -> eval x + eval y;;
Line 4, characters 43-44:
Error: This expression has type a expr but an expression was expected
       of type
         bool expr
         The type constructor a would escape its scope
```

This is a pretty unhelpful error message, but the basic problem is that eval is recursive, and inference of GADTs doesn't play well with recursive calls.

More specifically, the issue is that the type-checker is trying to merge the locally abstract type a into the type of the recursive function eval, and merging it into the outer scope within which eval is defined is the way in which a is escaping its scope.

We can fix this by explicitly marking eval as polymorphic, which OCaml has a handy type annotation for.

```
# let rec eval : 'a. 'a expr -> 'a =
    fun (type a) (x : a expr) ->
      match x with
      | Value v -> eval_value v
      | If (c, t, e) -> if eval c then eval t else eval e
      | Eq (x, y) -> eval x = eval y
      | Plus (x, y) -> eval x + eval y;;
val eval : 'a expr -> 'a = <fun>
```

This works because by marking eval as polymorphic, the type of eval isn't specialized to a, and so a doesn't escape its scope.

It's also helpful here because eval itself is an example of *polymorphic recursion*, which is to say that eval needs to call itself at multiple different types. This comes up, for example, with If, since the If itself must be of type bool, but the type of the then and else clauses could be of type int. This means that when evaluating If, we'll dispatch eval at a different type than it was called on.

As such, eval needs to see itself as polymorphic. This kind of polymorphism is basically impossible to infer automatically, which is a second reason we need to annotate eval's polymorphism explicitly.

The above syntax is a bit verbose, so OCaml has syntactic sugar to combine the polymorphism annotation and the creation of the locally abstract types:

```
# let rec eval : type a. a expr -> a = function
    | Value v -> eval_value v
    | If (c, t, e) -> if eval c then eval t else eval e
    | Eq (x, y) -> eval x = eval y
    | Plus (x, y) -> eval x + eval y;;
val eval : 'a expr -> 'a = <fun>
```

This type of annotation is the right one to pick when you write any recursive function that makes use of GADTs.

10.2   When Are GADTs Useful?

The typed language we showed above is a perfectly reasonable example, but GADTs are useful for a lot more than designing little languages. In this section, we'll try to give you a broader sampling of the kinds of things you can do with GADTs.

10.2.1   Varying Your Return Type

Sometimes, you want to write a single function that can effectively have different types in different circumstances. In some sense, this is totally ordinary. After all, OCaml's polymorphism means that values can take on different types in different contexts. List.find is a fine example. The signature indicates that the type of the result varies with the type of the input list.

```
# List.find;;
- : 'a list -> f:('a -> bool) -> 'a option = <fun>
```

And of course you can use List.find to produce values of different types.

```
# List.find ~f:(fun x -> x > 3) [1;3;5;2];;
- : int option = Some 5
# List.find ~f:(Char.is_uppercase) ['a';'B';'C'];;
- : char option = Some B
```

But this approach is limited to simple dependencies between types that correspond to how data flows through your code. Sometimes you want types to vary in a more flexible way.

To make this concrete, let's say we wanted to create a version of find that is configurable in terms of how it handles the case of not finding an item. There are three different behaviors you might want:

• Throw an exception.
• Return None.
• Return a default value.

Let's try to write a function that exhibits these behaviors without using GADTs. First, we'll create a variant type that represents the three possible behaviors.

```
module If_not_found = struct
  type 'a t =
    | Raise
    | Return_none
    | Default_to of 'a
end
```

Now we can write flexible_find, which takes an If_not_found.t as a parameter and varies its behavior accordingly.

```
# let rec flexible_find list ~f (if_not_found : _ If_not_found.t) =
    match list with
    | hd :: tl ->
      if f hd then Some hd else flexible_find ~f tl if_not_found
    | [] ->
      (match if_not_found with
       | Raise -> failwith "Element not found"
       | Return_none -> None
       | Default_to x -> Some x);;
val flexible_find :
  'a list -> f:('a -> bool) -> 'a If_not_found.t -> 'a option = <fun>
```

Here are some examples of the above function in action:

```
# flexible_find ~f:(fun x -> x > 10) [1;2;5] Return_none;;
- : int option = None
# flexible_find ~f:(fun x -> x > 10) [1;2;5] (Default_to 10);;
- : int option = Some 10
```

```
# flexible_find ~f:(fun x -> x > 10) [1;2;5] Raise;;
Exception: (Failure "Element not found")
# flexible_find ~f:(fun x -> x > 10) [1;2;20] Raise;;
- : int option = Some 20
```

This mostly does what we want, but the problem is that `flexible_find` always returns an option, even when it's passed `Raise` or `Default_to`, which guarantees that the `None` case is never used.

To eliminate the unnecessary option in the `Raise` and `Default_to` cases, we're going to turn `If_not_found.t` into a GADT. In particular, we'll mint it as a GADT with two type parameters: one for the type of the list element, and one for the return type of the function.

```
module If_not_found = struct
  type (_, _) t =
    | Raise : ('a, 'a) t
    | Return_none : ('a, 'a option) t
    | Default_to : 'a -> ('a, 'a) t
end
```

As you can see, `Raise` and `Default_to` both have the same element type and return type, but `Return_none` provides an optional return value.

Here's a definition of `flexible_find` that takes advantage of this GADT.

```
# let rec flexible_find
    : type a b. f:(a -> bool) -> a list -> (a, b) If_not_found.t -> b =
    fun ~f list if_not_found ->
    match list with
    | [] ->
      (match if_not_found with
       | Raise -> failwith "No matching item found"
       | Return_none -> None
       | Default_to x -> x)
    | hd :: tl ->
      if f hd
      then (
        match if_not_found with
        | Raise -> hd
        | Return_none -> Some hd
        | Default_to _ -> hd)
      else flexible_find ~f tl if_not_found;;
val flexible_find :
  f:('a -> bool) -> 'a list -> ('a, 'b) If_not_found.t -> 'b = <fun>
```

As you can see from the signature of `flexible_find`, the return value now depends on the type of `If_not_found.t`, which means it can depend on the particular variant of `If_not_found.t` that's in use. As a result, `flexible_find` only returns an option when it needs to.

```
# flexible_find ~f:(fun x -> x > 10) [1;2;5] Return_none;;
- : int option = Base.Option.None
# flexible_find ~f:(fun x -> x > 10) [1;2;5] (Default_to 10);;
- : int = 10
# flexible_find ~f:(fun x -> x > 10) [1;2;5] Raise;;
Exception: (Failure "No matching item found")
```

```
# flexible_find ~f:(fun x -> x > 10) [1;2;20] Raise;;
- : int = 20
```

10.2.2   Capturing the Unknown

Code that works with unknown types is routine in OCaml, and comes up in the simplest
of examples:

```
# let tuple x y = (x,y);;
val tuple : 'a -> 'b -> 'a * 'b = <fun>
```

The type variables 'a and 'b indicate that there are two unknown types here, and
these type variables are *universally quantified*. Which is to say, the type of tuple is:
for all types a and b, a -> b -> a * b.

And indeed, we can restrict the type of tuple to any 'a and 'b we want.

```
# (tuple : int -> float -> int * float);;
- : int -> float -> int * float = <fun>
# (tuple : string -> string * string -> string * (string * string));;
- : string -> string * string -> string * (string * string) = <fun>
```

Sometimes, however, we want type variables that are *existentially quantified*, meaning that instead of being compatible with all types, the type represents a particular but
unknown type.

GADTs provide one natural way of encoding such type variables. Here's a simple
example.

```
type stringable =
  Stringable : { value: 'a; to_string: 'a -> string } -> stringable
```

This type packs together a value of some arbitrary type, along with a function for
converting values of that type to strings.

We can tell that 'a is existentially quantified because it shows up on the left-hand
side of the arrow but not on the right, so the 'a that shows up internally doesn't appear
in a type parameter for stringable itself. Essentially, the existentially quantified type
is bound within the definition of stringable.

The following function can print an arbitrary stringable:

```
# let print_stringable (Stringable s) =
    Stdio.print_endline (s.to_string s.value);;
val print_stringable : stringable -> unit = <fun>
```

We can use print_stringable on a collection of stringables of different underlying
types.

```
# let stringables =
    (let s value to_string = Stringable { to_string; value } in
     [ s 100 Int.to_string
     ; s 12.3 Float.to_string
     ; s "foo" Fn.id
     ]);;
val stringables : stringable list =
  [Stringable {value = <poly>; to_string = <fun>};
```

```
    Stringable {value = <poly>; to_string = <fun>};
    Stringable {value = <poly>; to_string = <fun>}]
# List.iter ~f:print_stringable stringables;;
100
12.3
foo
- : unit = ()
```

The thing that lets this all work is that the type of the underlying object is existentially bound within the type stringable. As such, the type of the underlying values can't escape the scope of stringable, and any function that tries to return such a value won't type-check.

```
# let get_value (Stringable s) = s.value;;
Line 1, characters 32-39:
Error: This expression has type $Stringable_'a
       but an expression was expected of type 'a
       The type constructor $Stringable_'a would escape its scope
```

It's worth spending a moment to decode this error message, and the meaning of the type variable $Stringable_'a in particular. You can think of this variable as having three parts:

- The $ marks the variable as an existential.
- Stringable is the name of the GADT tag that this variable came from.
- 'a is the name of the type variable from inside that tag.

10.2.3 Abstracting Computational Machines

A common idiom in OCaml is to combine small components into larger computational machines, using a collection of component-combining functions, or *combinators*.

GADTs can be helpful for writing such combinators. To see how, let's consider an example: *pipelines*. Here, a pipeline is a sequence of steps where each step consumes the output of the previous step, potentially does some side effects, and returns a value to be passed to the next step. This is analogous to a shell pipeline, and is useful for all sorts of system automation tasks.

But, can't we write pipelines already? After all, OCaml comes with a perfectly serviceable pipeline operator:

```
# open Core;;
# let sum_file_sizes () =
    Sys.ls_dir "."
    |> List.filter ~f:Sys.is_file_exn
    |> List.map ~f:(fun file_name -> (Unix.lstat file_name).st_size)
    |> List.sum (module Int) ~f:Int64.to_int_exn;;
val sum_file_sizes : unit -> int = <fun>
```

This works well enough, but the advantage of a custom pipeline type is that it lets you build extra services beyond basic execution of the pipeline, e.g.:

- Profiling, so that when you run a pipeline, you get a report of how long each step of the pipeline took.

- Control over execution, like allowing users to pause the pipeline mid-execution, and restart it later.
- Custom error handling, so, for example, you could build a pipeline that kept track of where it failed, and offered the possibility of restarting it.

The type signature of such a pipeline type might look something like this:

```
module type Pipeline = sig
  type ('input,'output) t

  val ( @> ) : ('a -> 'b) -> ('b,'c) t -> ('a,'c) t
  val empty : ('a,'a) t
end
```

Here, the type `('a,'b) t` represents a pipeline that consumes values of type `'a` and emits values of type `'b`. The operator `@>` lets you add a step to a pipeline by providing a function to prepend on to an existing pipeline, and `empty` gives you an empty pipeline, which can be used to seed the pipeline.

The following shows how we could use this API for building a pipeline like our earlier example using `|>`. Here, we're using a *functor*, which we'll see in more detail in Chapter 11 (Functors), as a way to write code using the pipeline API before we've implemented it.

```
# module Example_pipeline (Pipeline : Pipeline) = struct
    open Pipeline
    let sum_file_sizes =
      (fun () -> Sys.ls_dir ".")
      @> List.filter ~f:Sys.is_file_exn
      @> List.map ~f:(fun file_name -> (Unix.lstat file_name).st_size)
      @> List.sum (module Int) ~f:Int64.to_int_exn
      @> empty
  end;;
module Example_pipeline :
  functor (Pipeline : Pipeline) ->
    sig val sum_file_sizes : (unit, int) Pipeline.t end
```

If all we want is a pipeline capable of a no-frills execution, we can define our pipeline itself as a simple function, the `@>` operator as function composition. Then executing the pipeline is just function application.

```
module Basic_pipeline : sig
    include Pipeline
    val exec : ('a,'b) t -> 'a -> 'b
  end= struct
    type ('input, 'output) t = 'input -> 'output

    let empty = Fn.id

    let ( @> ) f t input =
      t (f input)

    let exec t input = t input
end
```

But this way of implementing a pipeline doesn't give us any of the extra services we discussed. All we're really doing is step-by-step building up the same kind of function that we could have gotten using the |> operator.

We could get a more powerful pipeline by simply enhancing the pipeline type, providing it with extra runtime structures to track profiles, or handle exceptions, or provide whatever else is needed for the particular use-case. But this approach is awkward, since it requires us to pre-commit to whatever services we're going to support, and to embed all of them in our pipeline representation.

GADTs provide a simpler approach. Instead of concretely building a machine for executing a pipeline, we can use GADTs to abstractly represent the pipeline we want, and then build the functionality we want on top of that representation.

Here's what such a representation might look like.

```
type (_, _) pipeline =
  | Step : ('a -> 'b) * ('b, 'c) pipeline -> ('a, 'c) pipeline
  | Empty : ('a, 'a) pipeline
```

The tags here represent the two building blocks of a pipeline: Step corresponds to the @> operator, and Empty corresponds to the empty pipeline, as you can see below.

```
# let ( @> ) f pipeline = Step (f,pipeline);;
val ( @> ) : ('a -> 'b) -> ('b, 'c) pipeline -> ('a, 'c) pipeline = <fun>
# let empty = Empty;;
val empty : ('a, 'a) pipeline = Empty
```

With that in hand, we can do a no-frills pipeline execution easily enough.

```
# let rec exec : type a b. (a, b) pipeline -> a -> b =
    fun pipeline input ->
    match pipeline with
    | Empty -> input
    | Step (f, tail) -> exec tail (f input);;
val exec : ('a, 'b) pipeline -> 'a -> 'b = <fun>
```

But we can also do more interesting things. For example, here's a function that executes a pipeline and produces a profile showing how long each step of a pipeline took.

```
# let exec_with_profile pipeline input =
    let rec loop
        : type a b.
          (a, b) pipeline -> a -> Time_ns.Span.t list -> b *
    Time_ns.Span.t list
      =
     fun pipeline input rev_profile ->
      match pipeline with
      | Empty -> input, rev_profile
      | Step (f, tail) ->
        let start = Time_ns.now () in
        let output = f input in
        let elapsed = Time_ns.diff (Time_ns.now ()) start in
        loop tail output (elapsed :: rev_profile)
    in
    let output, rev_profile = loop pipeline input [] in
    output, List.rev rev_profile;;
```

```
val exec_with_profile : ('a, 'b) pipeline -> 'a -> 'b * Time_ns.Span.t
    list =
<fun>
```

The more abstract GADT approach for creating a little combinator library like this has several advantages over having combinators that build a more concrete computational machine:

- The core types are simpler, since they are typically built out of GADT tags that are just reflections of the types of the base combinators.
- The design is more modular, since your core types don't need to contemplate every possible use you want to make of them.
- The code tends to be more efficient, since the more concrete approach typically involves allocating closures to wrap up the necessary functionality, and closures are more heavyweight than GADT tags.

10.2.4   Narrowing the Possibilities

Another use-case for GADTs is to narrow the set of possible states for a given data-type in different circumstances.

One context where this can be useful is when managing complex application state, where the available data changes over time. Let's consider a simple example, where we're writing code to handle a logon request from a user, and we want to check if the user in question is authorized to logon.

We'll assume that the user logging in is authenticated as a particular name, but that in order to authenticate, we need to do two things: to translate that user-name into a numeric user-id, and to fetch permissions for the service in question; once we have both, we can check if the user-id is permitted to log on.

Without GADTs, we might model the state of a single logon request as follows.

```
type logon_request =
  { user_name : User_name.t
  ; user_id : User_id.t option
  ; permissions : Permissions.t option
  }
```

Here, User_name.t represents a textual name, User_id.t represents an integer identifier associated with a user, and a Permissions.t lets you determine which User_id.t's are authorized to log in.

Here's how we might write a function for testing whether a given request is authorized.

```
# let authorized request =
    match request.user_id, request.permissions with
    | None, _ | _, None ->
      Error "Can't check authorization: data incomplete"
    | Some user_id, Some permissions ->
      Ok (Permissions.check permissions user_id);;
val authorized : logon_request -> (bool, string) result = <fun>
```

The intent is to only call this function once the data is complete, i.e., when the `user_id` and `permissions` fields have been filled in, which is why it errors out if the data is incomplete.

The code above works just fine for a simple case like this. But in a real system, your code can get more complicated in multiple ways, e.g.,

- more fields to manage, including more optional fields,
- more operations that depend on these optional fields,
- multiple requests to be handled in parallel, each of which might be in a different state of completion.

As this kind of complexity creeps in, it can be useful to be able to track the state of a given request at the type level, and to use that to narrow the set of states a given request can be in, thereby removing some extra case analysis and error handling, which can reduce the complexity of the code and remove opportunities for mistakes.

One way of doing this is to mint different types to represent different states of the request, e.g., one type for an incomplete request where various fields are optional, and a different type where all of the data is mandatory.

While this works, it can be awkward and verbose. With GADTs, we can track the state of the request in a type parameter, and have that parameter be used to narrow the set of available cases, without duplicating the type.

A Completion-Sensitive Option Type

We'll start by creating an option type that is sensitive to whether our request is in a complete or incomplete state. To do that, we'll mint types to represent the states of being complete and incomplete.

```
type incomplete = Incomplete
type complete = Complete
```

The definition of the types doesn't really matter, since we're never instantiating these types, just using them as markers of different states. All that matters is that the types are distinct.

Now we can mint a completeness-sensitive option type. Note the two type variables: the first indicates the type of the contents of the option, and the second indicates whether this is being used in an incomplete state.

```
type (_, _) coption =
  | Absent : (_, incomplete) coption
  | Present : 'a -> ('a, _) coption
```

We use `Absent` and `Present` rather than `Some` or `None` to make the code less confusing when both `option` and `coption` are used together.

You might notice that we haven't used `complete` here explicitly. Instead, what we've done is to ensure that only an `incomplete` `coption` can be `Absent`. Accordingly, a `coption` that's complete (and therefore not `incomplete`) can only be `Present`.

This is easier to understand with some examples. Consider the following function for getting the value out of a `coption`, returning a default value if `Absent` is found.

```
# let get ~default o =
    match o with
    | Present x -> x
    | Absent -> default;;
val get : default:'a -> ('a, incomplete) coption -> 'a = <fun>
```

Note that the incomplete type was inferred here. If we annotate the coption as complete, the code no longer compiles.

```
# let get ~default (o : (_,complete) coption) =
    match o with
    | Absent -> default
    | Present x -> x;;
Line 3, characters 7-13:
Error: This pattern matches values of type ('a, incomplete) coption
       but a pattern was expected which matches values of type
          ('a, complete) coption
       Type incomplete is not compatible with type complete
```

We can make this compile by deleting the Absent branch (and the now useless default argument).

```
# let get (o : (_,complete) coption) =
    match o with
    | Present x -> x;;
val get : ('a, complete) coption -> 'a = <fun>
```

We could write this more simply as:

```
# let get (Present x : (_,complete) coption) = x;;
val get : ('a, complete) coption -> 'a = <fun>
```

As we can see, when the coption is known to be complete, the pattern matching is narrowed to just the Present case.

A Completion-Sensitive Request Type

We can use coption to define a completion-sensitive version of logon_request.

```
type 'c logon_request =
  { user_name : User_name.t
  ; user_id : (User_id.t, 'c) coption
  ; permissions : (Permissions.t, 'c) coption
  }
```

There's a single type parameter for the logon_request that marks whether it's complete, at which point, both the user_id and permissions fields will be complete as well.

As before, it's easy to fill in the user_id and permissions fields.

```
# let set_user_id request x = { request with user_id = Present x };;
val set_user_id : 'a logon_request -> User_id.t -> 'a logon_request =
    <fun>
# let set_permissions request x = { request with permissions =
    Present x };;
val set_permissions : 'a logon_request -> Permissions.t -> 'a
    logon_request =
    <fun>
```

Note that filling in the fields doesn't automatically mark a request as complete. To do that, we need to explicitly test for completeness, and then construct a version of the record with just the completed fields filled in.

```
# let check_completeness request =
    match request.user_id, request.permissions with
    | Absent, _ | _, Absent -> None
    | (Present _ as user_id), (Present _ as permissions) ->
      Some { request with user_id; permissions };;
val check_completeness : incomplete logon_request -> 'a logon_request
    option =
  <fun>
```

The result is polymorphic, meaning it can return a logon request of any kind, which includes the possibility of returning a complete request. In practice, the function type is easier to understand if we constrain the return value to explicitly return a complete request.

```
# let check_completeness request : complete logon_request option =
    match request.user_id, request.permissions with
    | Absent, _ | _, Absent -> None
    | (Present _ as user_id), (Present _ as permissions) ->
      Some { request with user_id; permissions };;
val check_completeness :
  incomplete logon_request -> complete logon_request option = <fun>
```

Finally, we can write an authorization checker that works unconditionally on a complete login request.

```
# let authorized (request : complete logon_request) =
    let { user_id = Present user_id; permissions = Present
    permissions; _ } = request in
    Permissions.check permissions user_id;;
val authorized : complete logon_request -> bool = <fun>
```

After all that work, the result may seem a bit underwhelming, and indeed, most of the time, this kind of narrowing isn't worth the complexity of setting it up. But for a sufficiently complex state machine, cutting down on the possibilities that your code needs to contemplate can make a big difference to the comprehensibility and correctness of the result.

Type Distinctness and Abstraction

In the example in this section, we used two types, complete and incomplete to mark different states, and we defined those types so as to be in some sense obviously different.

```
type incomplete = Incomplete
type complete = Complete
```

This isn't strictly necessary. Here's another way of defining these types that makes them less obviously distinct.

```
type incomplete = Z
type complete = Z
```

OCaml's variant types are nominal, so `complete` and `incomplete` are distinct types, despite having variants of the same name, as you can see when we try to put instances of each type in the same list.

```
# let i = (Z : incomplete) and c = (Z : complete);;
val i : incomplete = Z
val c : complete = Z
# [i; c];;
Line 1, characters 5-6:
Error: This expression has type complete
       but an expression was expected of type incomplete
```

As a result, we can narrow a pattern match using these types as indices, much as we did earlier. First, we set up the `coption` type:

```
type ('a, _) coption =
  | Absent : (_, incomplete) coption
  | Present : 'a -> ('a, _) coption
```

Then, we write a function that requires the `coption` to be complete, and accordingly, need only contemplate the `Present` case.

```
# let assume_complete (coption : (_,complete) coption) =
    match coption with
    | Present x -> x;;
val assume_complete : ('a, complete) coption -> 'a = <fun>
```

An easy-to-miss issue here is that the way we expose these types through an interface can cause OCaml to lose track of the distinctness of the types in question. Consider this version, where we entirely hide the definition of `complete` and `incomplete`.

```
module M : sig
  type incomplete
  type complete
end = struct
  type incomplete = Z
  type complete = Z
end
include M

type ('a, _) coption =
  | Absent : (_, incomplete) coption
  | Present : 'a -> ('a, _) coption
```

Now, the `assume_complete` function we wrote is no longer found to be exhaustive.

```
# let assume_complete (coption : (_,complete) coption) =
    match coption with
    | Present x -> x;;
Lines 2-3, characters 5-21:
Warning 8 [partial-match]: this pattern-matching is not exhaustive.
Here is an example of a case that is not matched:
Absent
val assume_complete : ('a, complete) coption -> 'a = <fun>
```

That's because by leaving the types abstract, we've entirely hidden the underlying types, leaving the type system with no evidence that the types are distinct.

Let's see what happens if we expose the implementation of these types.

```
module M : sig
  type incomplete = Z
  type complete = Z
end = struct
  type incomplete = Z
  type complete = Z
end
include M

type ('a, _) coption =
  | Absent : (_, incomplete) coption
  | Present : 'a -> ('a, _) coption
```

But the result is still not exhaustive!

```
# let assume_complete (coption : (_,complete) coption) =
    match coption with
    | Present x -> x;;
Lines 2-3, characters 5-21:
Warning 8 [partial-match]: this pattern-matching is not exhaustive.
Here is an example of a case that is not matched:
Absent
val assume_complete : ('a, complete) coption -> 'a = <fun>
```

In order to be exhaustive, we need the types that are exposed to be definitively different, which would be the case if we defined them as variants with differently named tags, as we did originally.

The reason for this is that types that appear to be different in an interface may turn out to be the same in the implementation, as we can see below.

```
module M : sig
  type incomplete = Z
  type complete = Z
end = struct
  type incomplete = Z
  type complete = incomplete = Z
end
```

All of which is to say: when creating types to act as abstract markers for the type parameter of a GADT, you should choose definitions that make the distinctness of those types clear, and you should expose those definitions in your mlis.

Narrowing Without GADTs

Thus far, we've only seen narrowing in the context of GADTs, but OCaml can eliminate impossible cases from ordinary variants too. As with GADTs, to eliminate a case you need to demonstrate that the case in question is impossible at the type level.

One way to do this is via an *uninhabited type*, which is a type that has no associated values. You can declare such a value by creating a variant with no tags.

```
type nothing = |
```

This turns out to be useful enough that Base has a standard uninhabited type, Nothing.t.

So, how does an uninhabited type help? Well, consider the Result.t type, discussed

in as described in Chapter 8.1.1 (Encoding Errors with Result). Normally, to match a
`Result.t`, you need to handle both the `Ok` and `Error` cases.

```
# open Stdio;;
# let print_result (x : (int,string) Result.t) =
    match x with
    | Ok x -> printf "%d\n" x
    | Error x -> printf "ERROR: %s\n" x;;
val print_result : (int, string) result -> unit = <fun>
```

But if the `Error` case contains an uninhabitable type, well, that case can never be
instantiated, and OCaml will tell you as much.

```
# let print_result (x : (int, Nothing.t) Result.t) =
    match x with
    | Ok x -> printf "%d\n" x
    | Error _ -> printf "ERROR\n";;
Line 4, characters 7-14:
Warning 56 [unreachable-case]: this match case is unreachable.
Consider replacing it with a refutation case '<pat> -> .'
val print_result : (int, Nothing.t) result -> unit = <fun>
```

We can follow the advice above, and add a so-called *refutation case*.

```
# let print_result (x : (int, Nothing.t) Result.t) =
    match x with
    | Ok x -> printf "%d\n" x
    | Error _ -> .;;
val print_result : (int, Nothing.t) result -> unit = <fun>
```

The period in the final case tells the compiler that we believe this case can never
be reached, and OCaml will verify that it's true. In some simple cases, however, the
compiler can automatically add the refutation case for you, so you don't need to write
it out explicitly.

```
# let print_result (x : (int, Nothing.t) Result.t) =
    match x with
    | Ok x -> printf "%d\n" x;;
val print_result : (int, Nothing.t) result -> unit = <fun>
```

Narrowing with uninhabitable types can be useful when using a highly configurable
library that supports multiple different modes of use, not all of which are necessarily
needed for a given application. One example of this comes from `Async`'s RPC (remote
procedure-call) library. Async RPCs support a particular flavor of interaction called
a `State_rpc`. Such an RPC is parameterized by four types, for four different kinds of
data:

- query, for the initial client request,
- state, for the initial snapshot returned by the server,
- update, for the sequence of updates to that snapshot, and
- error, for an error to terminate the stream.

Now, imagine you want to use a `State_rpc` in a context where you don't need to
terminate the stream with a custom error. We could just instantiate the `State_rpc` using
the type `unit` for the error type.

```
open Core
open Async
let rpc =
  Rpc.State_rpc.create
    ~name:"int-map"
    ~version:1
    ~bin_query:[%bin_type_class: unit]
    ~bin_state:[%bin_type_class: int Map.M(String).t]
    ~bin_update:[%bin_type_class: int Map.M(String).t]
    ~bin_error:[%bin_type_class: unit]
    ()
```

But with this approach, you still have to handle the error case when writing code to dispatch the RPC.

```
# let dispatch conn =
    match%bind Rpc.State_rpc.dispatch rpc conn () >>| ok_exn with
    | Ok (initial_state, updates, _) -> handle_state_changes
    initial_state updates
    | Error () -> failwith "this is not supposed to happen";;
val dispatch : Rpc.Connection.t -> unit Deferred.t = <fun>
```

An alternative approach is to use an uninhabited type for the error:

```
let rpc =
  Rpc.State_rpc.create
    ~name:"foo"
    ~version:1
    ~bin_query:[%bin_type_class: unit]
    ~bin_state:[%bin_type_class: int Map.M(String).t]
    ~bin_update:[%bin_type_class: int Map.M(String).t]
    ~bin_error:[%bin_type_class: Nothing.t]
    ()
```

Now, we've essentially banned the use of the error type, and as a result, our dispatch function needs only deal with the Ok case.

```
# let dispatch conn =
    match%bind Rpc.State_rpc.dispatch rpc conn () >>| ok_exn with
    | Ok (initial_state, updates, _) -> handle_state_changes
    initial_state updates;;
val dispatch : Rpc.Connection.t -> unit Deferred.t = <fun>
```

What's nice about this example is that it shows that narrowing can be applied to code that isn't designed with narrowing in mind.

10.3   Limitations of GADTs

Hopefully, we've demonstrated the utility of GADTs, while at the same time showing some of the attendant complexities. In this final section, we're going to highlight some remaining difficulties with using GADTs that you may run into, as well as how to work around them.

10.3.1   Or-Patterns

GADTs don't work well with or-patterns. Consider the following type that represents various ways we might use for obtaining some piece of data.

```
open Core
module Source_kind = struct
  type _ t =
    | Filename : string t
    | Host_and_port : Host_and_port.t t
    | Raw_data : string t
end
```

We can write a function that takes a `Source_kind.t` and the corresponding source, and prints it out.

```
# let source_to_sexp (type a) (kind : a Source_kind.t) (source : a) =
    match kind with
    | Filename -> String.sexp_of_t source
    | Host_and_port -> Host_and_port.sexp_of_t source
    | Raw_data -> String.sexp_of_t source;;
val source_to_sexp : 'a Source_kind.t -> 'a -> Sexp.t = <fun>
```

But, observing that the right-hand side of `Raw_data` and `Filename` are the same, you might try to merge those cases together with an or-pattern. Unfortunately, that doesn't work.

```
# let source_to_sexp (type a) (kind : a Source_kind.t) (source : a) =
    match kind with
    | Filename | Raw_data -> String.sexp_of_t source
    | Host_and_port -> Host_and_port.sexp_of_t source;;
Line 3, characters 47-53:
Error: This expression has type a but an expression was expected of
type
        string
```

Or-patterns do sometimes work, but only when you don't make use of the type information that is discovered during the pattern match. Here's an example of a function that uses or-patterns successfully.

```
# let requires_io (type a) (kind : a Source_kind.t) =
    match kind with
    | Filename | Host_and_port -> true
    | Raw_data -> false;;
val requires_io : 'a Source_kind.t -> bool = <fun>
```

In any case, the lack of or-patterns is annoying, but it's not a big deal, since you can reduce the code duplication by pulling out most of the content of the duplicated right-hand sides into functions that can be called in each of the duplicated cases.

10.3.2   Deriving Serializers

As will be discussed in more detail in Chapter 21 (Data Serialization with S-Expressions), s-expressions are a convenient data format for representing structured data. Rather than write the serializers and deserializers by hand, we typically use `ppx_sexp_value`, which is a syntax extension which auto-generates these functions for a given type, based on that type's definition.

Here's an example:

```
# type position = { x: float; y: float } [@@deriving sexp];;
type position = { x : float; y : float; }
val position_of_sexp : Sexp.t -> position = <fun>
val sexp_of_position : position -> Sexp.t = <fun>
# sexp_of_position { x = 3.5; y = -2. };;
- : Sexp.t = ((x 3.5) (y -2))
# position_of_sexp (Sexp.of_string "((x 72) (y 1.2))");;
- : position = {x = 72.; y = 1.2}
```

While `[@@deriving sexp]` works with most types, it doesn't always work with GADTs.

```
# type _ number_kind =
    | Int : int number_kind
    | Float : float number_kind
  [@@deriving sexp];;
Lines 1-4, characters 1-20:
Error: This expression has type int number_kind
       but an expression was expected of type a__001_ number_kind
       Type int is not compatible with type a__001_
```

The error message is pretty awful, but if you stop and think about it, it's not too surprising that we ran into trouble here. What should the type of `number_kind_of_sexp` be anyway? When parsing `"Int"`, the returned type would have to be `int number_kind`, and when parsing `"Float"`, the type would have to be `float number_kind`. That kind of dependency between the value of an argument and the type of the returned value is just not expressible in OCaml's type system.

This argument doesn't stop us from serializing, and indeed, `[@@deriving sexp_of]`, which only creates the serializer, works just fine.

```
# type _ number_kind =
    | Int : int number_kind
    | Float : float number_kind
  [@@deriving sexp_of];;
type _ number_kind = Int : int number_kind | Float : float number_kind
val sexp_of_number_kind :
  ('a__001_ -> Sexp.t) -> 'a__001_ number_kind -> Sexp.t = <fun>
# sexp_of_number_kind Int.sexp_of_t Int;;
- : Sexp.t = Int
```

It is possible to build a deserializer for `number_kind`, but it's tricky. First, we'll need a type that packs up a `number_kind` while hiding its type parameter. This is going to be the value we return from our parser.

```
type packed_number_kind = P : _ number_kind -> packed_number_kind
```

Next, we'll need to create a non-GADT version of our type, for which we'll derive a deserializer.

```
type simple_number_kind = Int | Float [@@deriving of_sexp]
```

Then, we write a function for converting from our non-GADT type to the packed variety.

```
# let simple_number_kind_to_packed_number_kind kind :
    packed_number_kind
  =
  match kind with
  | Int -> P Int
  | Float -> P Float;;
val simple_number_kind_to_packed_number_kind :
  simple_number_kind -> packed_number_kind = <fun>
```

Finally, we combine our generated sexp-converter with our conversion type to produce the full deserialization function.

```
# let number_kind_of_sexp sexp =
    simple_number_kind_of_sexp sexp
    |> simple_number_kind_to_packed_number_kind;;
val number_kind_of_sexp : Sexp.t -> packed_number_kind = <fun>
```

And here's that function in action.

```
# List.map ~f:number_kind_of_sexp
    [ Sexp.of_string "Float"; Sexp.of_string "Int" ];;
- : packed_number_kind list = [P Float; P Int]
```

While all of this is doable, it's definitely awkward, and requires some unpleasant code duplication.

11 Functors

Up until now, we've seen OCaml's modules play an important but limited role. In particular, we've used modules to organize code into units with specified interfaces. But OCaml's module system can do much more than that, serving as a powerful tool for building generic code and structuring large-scale systems. Much of that power comes from functors.

Functors are, roughly speaking, functions from modules to modules, and they can be used to solve a variety of code-structuring problems, including:

Dependency injection Makes the implementations of some components of a system swappable. This is particularly useful when you want to mock up parts of your system for testing and simulation purposes.

Autoextension of modules Functors give you a way of extending existing modules with new functionality in a standardized way. For example, you might want to add a slew of comparison operators derived from a base comparison function. To do this by hand would require a lot of repetitive code for each type, but functors let you write this logic just once and apply it to many different types.

Instantiating modules with state Modules can contain mutable states, and that means that you'll occasionally want to have multiple instantiations of a particular module, each with its own separate and independent mutable state. Functors let you automate the construction of such modules.

These are really just some of the uses that you can put functors to. We'll make no attempt to provide examples of all of the uses of functors here. Instead, this chapter will try to provide examples that illuminate the language features and design patterns that you need to master in order to use functors effectively.

11.1 A Trivial Example

Let's create a functor that takes a module containing a single integer variable x and returns a new module with x incremented by one. This is intended to serve as a way to walk through the basic mechanics of functors, even though it's not something you'd want to do in practice.

First, let's define a signature for a module that contains a single value of type int:

```
# open Base;;
# module type X_int = sig val x : int end;;
module type X_int = sig val x : int end
```

Now we can define our functor. We'll use X_int both to constrain the argument to the functor and to constrain the module returned by the functor:

```
# module Increment (M : X_int) : X_int = struct
    let x = M.x + 1
  end;;
module Increment : functor (M : X_int) -> X_int
```

One thing that immediately jumps out is that functors are more syntactically heavyweight than ordinary functions. For one thing, functors require explicit (module) type annotations, which ordinary functions do not. Technically, only the type on the input is mandatory, although in practice, you should usually constrain the module returned by the functor, just as you should use an mli, even though it's not mandatory.

The following shows what happens when we omit the module type for the output of the functor:

```
# module Increment (M : X_int) = struct
    let x = M.x + 1
  end;;
module Increment : functor (M : X_int) -> sig val x : int end
```

We can see that the inferred module type of the output is now written out explicitly, rather than being a reference to the named signature X_int.

We can use Increment to define new modules:

```
# module Three = struct let x = 3 end;;
module Three : sig val x : int end
# module Four = Increment(Three);;
module Four : sig val x : int end
# Four.x - Three.x;;
- : int = 1
```

In this case, we applied Increment to a module whose signature is exactly equal to X_int. But we can apply Increment to any module that *satisfies* the interface X_int, in the same way that the contents of an ml file must satisfy the mli. That means that the module type can omit some information available in the module, either by dropping fields or by leaving some fields abstract. Here's an example:

```
# module Three_and_more = struct
    let x = 3
    let y = "three"
  end;;
module Three_and_more : sig val x : int val y : string end
# module Four = Increment(Three_and_more);;
module Four : sig val x : int end
```

The rules for determining whether a module matches a given signature are similar in spirit to the rules in an object-oriented language that determine whether an object satisfies a given interface. As in an object-oriented context, the extra information that doesn't match the signature you're looking for (in this case, the variable y) is simply ignored.

11.2   A Bigger Example: Computing with Intervals

Let's consider a more realistic example of how to use functors: a library for computing with intervals. Intervals are a common computational object, and they come up in different contexts and for different types. You might need to work with intervals of floating-point values or strings or times, and in each of these cases, you want similar operations: testing for emptiness, checking for containment, intersecting intervals, and so on.

We can use functors to build a generic interval library that can be used with any type that supports a total ordering on the underlying set.

First we'll define a module type that captures the information we'll need about the endpoints of the intervals. This interface, which we'll call Comparable, contains just two things: a comparison function and the type of the values to be compared:

```
# module type Comparable = sig
    type t
    val compare : t -> t -> int
  end;;
module type Comparable = sig type t val compare : t -> t -> int end
```

The comparison function follows the standard OCaml idiom for such functions, returning 0 if the two elements are equal, a positive number if the first element is larger than the second, and a negative number if the first element is smaller than the second. Thus, we could rewrite the standard comparison functions on top of compare.

```
compare x y < 0      (* x < y *)
compare x y = 0      (* x = y *)
compare x y > 0      (* x > y *)
```

(This idiom is a bit of a historical error. It would be better if compare returned a variant with three cases for less than, greater than, and equal. But it's a well-established idiom at this point, and unlikely to change.)

The functor for creating the interval module follows. We represent an interval with a variant type, which is either Empty or Interval (x,y), where x and y are the bounds of the interval. In addition to the type, the body of the functor contains implementations of a number of useful primitives for interacting with intervals:

```
# module Make_interval(Endpoint : Comparable) = struct

    type t = | Interval of Endpoint.t * Endpoint.t
             | Empty

    (** [create low high] creates a new interval from [low] to
        [high].  If [low > high], then the interval is empty *)
    let create low high =
      if Endpoint.compare low high > 0 then Empty
      else Interval (low,high)

    (** Returns true iff the interval is empty *)
    let is_empty = function
      | Empty -> true
      | Interval _ -> false
```

```
(** [contains t x] returns true iff [x] is contained in the
      interval [t] *)
let contains t x =
  match t with
  | Empty -> false
  | Interval (l,h) ->
      Endpoint.compare x l >= 0 && Endpoint.compare x h <= 0

  (** [intersect t1 t2] returns the intersection of the two input
        intervals *)
  let intersect t1 t2 =
    let min x y = if Endpoint.compare x y <= 0 then x else y in
    let max x y = if Endpoint.compare x y >= 0 then x else y in
    match t1,t2 with
    | Empty, _ | _, Empty -> Empty
    | Interval (l1,h1), Interval (l2,h2) ->
        create (max l1 l2) (min h1 h2)

end;;
module Make_interval :
  functor (Endpoint : Comparable) ->
    sig
      type t = Interval of Endpoint.t * Endpoint.t | Empty
      val create : Endpoint.t -> Endpoint.t -> t
      val is_empty : t -> bool
      val contains : t -> Endpoint.t -> bool
      val intersect : t -> t -> t
    end
```

We can instantiate the functor by applying it to a module with the right signature. In the following code, rather than name the module first and then call the functor, we provide the functor input as an anonymous module:

```
# module Int_interval =
    Make_interval(struct
      type t = int
      let compare = Int.compare
  end);;
module Int_interval :
  sig
    type t = Interval of int * int | Empty
    val create : int -> int -> t
    val is_empty : t -> bool
    val contains : t -> int -> bool
    val intersect : t -> t -> t
  end
```

If the input interface for your functor is aligned with the standards of the libraries you use, then you don't need to construct a custom module to feed to the functor. In this case, we can directly use the Int or String modules provided by Base:

```
# module Int_interval = Make_interval(Int);;
module Int_interval :
  sig
    type t = Make_interval(Base.Int).t = Interval of int * int | Empty
    val create : int -> int -> t
```

```
    val is_empty : t -> bool
    val contains : t -> int -> bool
    val intersect : t -> t -> t
  end
# module String_interval = Make_interval(String);;
module String_interval :
  sig
    type t =
      Make_interval(Base.String).t =
        Interval of string * string
      | Empty
    val create : string -> string -> t
    val is_empty : t -> bool
    val contains : t -> string -> bool
    val intersect : t -> t -> t
  end
```

This works because many modules in Base, including Int and String, satisfy an extended version of the Comparable signature described previously. Such standardized signatures are good practice, both because they make functors easier to use, and because they encourage standardization that makes your codebase easier to navigate.

We can use the newly defined Int_interval module like any ordinary module:

```
# let i1 = Int_interval.create 3 8;;
val i1 : Int_interval.t = Int_interval.Interval (3, 8)
# let i2 = Int_interval.create 4 10;;
val i2 : Int_interval.t = Int_interval.Interval (4, 10)
# Int_interval.intersect i1 i2;;
- : Int_interval.t = Int_interval.Interval (4, 8)
```

This design gives us the freedom to use any comparison function we want for comparing the endpoints. We could, for example, create a type of integer interval with the order of the comparison reversed, as follows:

```
# module Rev_int_interval =
    Make_interval(struct
      type t = int
      let compare x y = Int.compare y x
  end);;
module Rev_int_interval :
  sig
    type t = Interval of int * int | Empty
    val create : int -> int -> t
    val is_empty : t -> bool
    val contains : t -> int -> bool
    val intersect : t -> t -> t
  end
```

The behavior of Rev_int_interval is of course different from Int_interval:

```
# let interval = Int_interval.create 4 3;;
val interval : Int_interval.t = Int_interval.Empty
# let rev_interval = Rev_int_interval.create 4 3;;
val rev_interval : Rev_int_interval.t = Rev_int_interval.Interval (4,
    3)
```

Importantly, Rev_int_interval.t is a different type than Int_interval.t, even though its physical representation is the same. Indeed, the type system will prevent us from confusing them.

```
# Int_interval.contains rev_interval 3;;
Line 1, characters 23-35:
Error: This expression has type Rev_int_interval.t
       but an expression was expected of type Int_interval.t
```

This is important, because confusing the two kinds of intervals would be a semantic error, and it's an easy one to make. The ability of functors to mint new types is a useful trick that comes up a lot.

11.2.1   Making the Functor Abstract

There's a problem with `Make_interval`. The code we wrote depends on the invariant that the upper bound of an interval is greater than its lower bound, but that invariant can be violated. The invariant is enforced by the `create` function, but because `Int_interval.t` is not abstract, we can bypass the `create` function:

```
# Int_interval.is_empty (* going through create *)
  (Int_interval.create 4 3);;
- : bool = true
# Int_interval.is_empty (* bypassing create *)
  (Int_interval.Interval (4,3));;
- : bool = false
```

To make `Int_interval.t` abstract, we need to restrict the output of `Make_interval` with an interface. Here's an explicit interface that we can use for that purpose:

```
# module type Interval_intf = sig
    type t
    type endpoint
    val create : endpoint -> endpoint -> t
    val is_empty : t -> bool
    val contains : t -> endpoint -> bool
    val intersect : t -> t -> t
  end;;
module type Interval_intf =
  sig
    type t
    type endpoint
    val create : endpoint -> endpoint -> t
    val is_empty : t -> bool
    val contains : t -> endpoint -> bool
    val intersect : t -> t -> t
  end
```

This interface includes the type `endpoint` to give us a way of referring to the endpoint type. Given this interface, we can redo our definition of `Make_interval`. Notice that we added the type `endpoint` to the implementation of the module to match `Interval_intf`:

```
# module Make_interval(Endpoint : Comparable) : Interval_intf = struct
    type endpoint = Endpoint.t
    type t = | Interval of Endpoint.t * Endpoint.t
             | Empty
```

```
      (** [create low high] creates a new interval from [low] to
          [high].  If [low > high], then the interval is empty *)
      let create low high =
        if Endpoint.compare low high > 0 then Empty
        else Interval (low,high)

      (** Returns true iff the interval is empty *)
      let is_empty = function
        | Empty -> true
        | Interval _ -> false

      (** [contains t x] returns true iff [x] is contained in the
          interval [t] *)
      let contains t x =
        match t with
        | Empty -> false
        | Interval (l,h) ->
          Endpoint.compare x l >= 0 && Endpoint.compare x h <= 0

      (** [intersect t1 t2] returns the intersection of the two input
          intervals *)
      let intersect t1 t2 =
        let min x y = if Endpoint.compare x y <= 0 then x else y in
        let max x y = if Endpoint.compare x y >= 0 then x else y in
        match t1,t2 with
        | Empty, _ | _, Empty -> Empty
        | Interval (l1,h1), Interval (l2,h2) ->
          create (max l1 l2) (min h1 h2)

  end;;
module Make_interval : functor (Endpoint : Comparable) ->
    Interval_intf
```

11.2.2 Sharing Constraints

The resulting module is abstract, but it's unfortunately too abstract. In particular, we haven't exposed the type endpoint, which means that we can't even construct an interval anymore:

```
# module Int_interval = Make_interval(Int);;
module Int_interval :
  sig
    type t = Make_interval(Base.Int).t
    type endpoint = Make_interval(Base.Int).endpoint
    val create : endpoint -> endpoint -> t
    val is_empty : t -> bool
    val contains : t -> endpoint -> bool
    val intersect : t -> t -> t
  end
# Int_interval.create 3 4;;
Line 1, characters 21-22:
Error: This expression has type int but an expression was expected of
    type
        Int_interval.endpoint
```

To fix this, we need to expose the fact that `endpoint` is equal to `Int.t` (or more generally, `Endpoint.t`, where `Endpoint` is the argument to the functor). One way of doing this is through a *sharing constraint*, which allows you to tell the compiler to expose the fact that a given type is equal to some other type. The syntax for a simple sharing constraint is as follows:

```
<Module_type> with type <type> = <type'>
```

The result of this expression is a new signature that's been modified so that it exposes the fact that *type* defined inside of the module type is equal to *type'* whose definition is outside of it. One can also apply multiple sharing constraints to the same signature:

```
<Module_type> with type <type1> = <type1'> and type <type2> = <type2'>
```

We can use a sharing constraint to create a specialized version of `Interval_intf` for integer intervals:

```
# module type Int_interval_intf =
    Interval_intf with type endpoint = int;;
module type Int_interval_intf =
  sig
    type t
    type endpoint = int
    val create : endpoint -> endpoint -> t
    val is_empty : t -> bool
    val contains : t -> endpoint -> bool
    val intersect : t -> t -> t
  end
```

We can also use sharing constraints in the context of a functor. The most common use case is where you want to expose that some of the types of the module being generated by the functor are related to the types in the module fed to the functor.

In this case, we'd like to expose an equality between the type `endpoint` in the new module and the type `Endpoint.t`, from the module `Endpoint` that is the functor argument. We can do this as follows:

```
# module Make_interval(Endpoint : Comparable)
    : (Interval_intf with type endpoint = Endpoint.t)
  = struct

    type endpoint = Endpoint.t
    type t = | Interval of Endpoint.t * Endpoint.t
             | Empty

    (** [create low high] creates a new interval from [low] to
        [high].  If [low > high], then the interval is empty *)
    let create low high =
      if Endpoint.compare low high > 0 then Empty
      else Interval (low,high)

    (** Returns true iff the interval is empty *)
    let is_empty = function
      | Empty -> true
      | Interval _ -> false
```

```
(** [contains t x] returns true iff [x] is contained in the
    interval [t] *)
let contains t x =
  match t with
  | Empty -> false
  | Interval (l,h) ->
    Endpoint.compare x l >= 0 && Endpoint.compare x h <= 0

(** [intersect t1 t2] returns the intersection of the two input
    intervals *)
let intersect t1 t2 =
  let min x y = if Endpoint.compare x y <= 0 then x else y in
  let max x y = if Endpoint.compare x y >= 0 then x else y in
  match t1,t2 with
  | Empty, _ | _, Empty -> Empty
  | Interval (l1,h1), Interval (l2,h2) ->
    create (max l1 l2) (min h1 h2)

  end;;
module Make_interval :
  functor (Endpoint : Comparable) ->
    sig
      type t
      type endpoint = Endpoint.t
      val create : endpoint -> endpoint -> t
      val is_empty : t -> bool
      val contains : t -> endpoint -> bool
      val intersect : t -> t -> t
    end
```

Now the interface is as it was, except that endpoint is known to be equal to Endpoint.t. As a result of that type equality, we can again do things that require that endpoint be exposed, like constructing intervals:

```
# module Int_interval = Make_interval(Int);;
module Int_interval :
  sig
    type t = Make_interval(Base.Int).t
    type endpoint = int
    val create : endpoint -> endpoint -> t
    val is_empty : t -> bool
    val contains : t -> endpoint -> bool
    val intersect : t -> t -> t
  end
# let i = Int_interval.create 3 4;;
val i : Int_interval.t = <abstr>
# Int_interval.contains i 5;;
- : bool = false
```

11.2.3 Destructive Substitution

Sharing constraints basically do the job, but they have some downsides. In particular, we've now been stuck with the useless type declaration of endpoint that clutters up both the interface and the implementation. A better solution would be to modify the

`Interval_intf` signature by replacing endpoint with `Endpoint.t` everywhere it shows up, and deleting the definition of endpoint from the signature. We can do just this using what's called *destructive substitution*. Here's the basic syntax:

```
<Module_type> with type <type> := <type'>
```

This looks just like a sharing constraint, except that we use `:=` instead of `=`. The following shows how we could use this with `Make_interval`.

```
# module type Int_interval_intf =
    Interval_intf with type endpoint := int;;
module type Int_interval_intf =
  sig
    type t
    val create : int -> int -> t
    val is_empty : t -> bool
    val contains : t -> int -> bool
    val intersect : t -> t -> t
  end
```

There's now no endpoint type: all of its occurrences have been replaced by `int`. As with sharing constraints, we can also use this in the context of a functor:

```
# module Make_interval(Endpoint : Comparable)
    : Interval_intf with type endpoint := Endpoint.t =
  struct

    type t = | Interval of Endpoint.t * Endpoint.t
             | Empty

    (** [create low high] creates a new interval from [low] to
        [high].  If [low > high], then the interval is empty *)
    let create low high =
      if Endpoint.compare low high > 0 then Empty
      else Interval (low,high)

    (** Returns true iff the interval is empty *)
    let is_empty = function
      | Empty -> true
      | Interval _ -> false

    (** [contains t x] returns true iff [x] is contained in the
        interval [t] *)
    let contains t x =
      match t with
      | Empty -> false
      | Interval (l,h) ->
        Endpoint.compare x l >= 0 && Endpoint.compare x h <= 0

    (** [intersect t1 t2] returns the intersection of the two input
        intervals *)
    let intersect t1 t2 =
      let min x y = if Endpoint.compare x y <= 0 then x else y in
      let max x y = if Endpoint.compare x y >= 0 then x else y in
      match t1,t2 with
      | Empty, _ | _, Empty -> Empty
      | Interval (l1,h1), Interval (l2,h2) ->
```

```
              create (max l1 l2) (min h1 h2)

    end;;
module Make_interval :
  functor (Endpoint : Comparable) ->
    sig
      type t
      val create : Endpoint.t -> Endpoint.t -> t
      val is_empty : t -> bool
      val contains : t -> Endpoint.t -> bool
      val intersect : t -> t -> t
    end
```

The interface is precisely what we want: the type t is abstract, and the type of the endpoint is exposed; so we can create values of type Int_interval.t using the creation function, but not directly using the constructors and thereby violating the invariants of the module.

```
# module Int_interval = Make_interval(Int);;
module Int_interval :
  sig
    type t = Make_interval(Base.Int).t
    val create : int -> int -> t
    val is_empty : t -> bool
    val contains : t -> int -> bool
    val intersect : t -> t -> t
  end
# Int_interval.is_empty
    (Int_interval.create 3 4);;
- : bool = false
# Int_interval.is_empty (Int_interval.Interval (4,3));;
Line 1, characters 24-45:
Error: Unbound constructor Int_interval.Interval
```

In addition, the endpoint type is gone from the interface, meaning we no longer need to define the endpoint type alias in the body of the module.

It's worth noting that the name is somewhat misleading, in that there's nothing destructive about destructive substitution; it's really just a way of creating a new signature by transforming an existing one.

11.2.4   Using Multiple Interfaces

Another feature that we might want for our interval module is the ability to *serialize*, i.e., to be able to read and write intervals as a stream of bytes. In this case, we'll do this by converting to and from s-expressions, which were mentioned already in Chapter 8 (Error Handling). To recall, an s-expression is essentially a parenthesized expression whose atoms are strings, and it is a serialization format that is used commonly in Base. Here's an example:

```
# Sexp.List [ Sexp.Atom "This"; Sexp.Atom "is"
    ; Sexp.List [Sexp.Atom "an"; Sexp.Atom "s-expression"]];;
- : Sexp.t = (This is (an s-expression))
```

Base is designed to work well with a syntax extension called `ppx_sexp_conv` which will generate s-expression conversion functions for any type annotated with `[@@deriving sexp]`. We can enable `ppx_sexp_conv` along with a collection of other useful extensions by enabling `ppx_jane`:

```
# #require "ppx_jane";;
```

Now, we can use the deriving annotation to create sexp-converters for a given type.

```
# type some_type = int * string list [@@deriving sexp];;
type some_type = int * string list
val some_type_of_sexp : Sexp.t -> some_type = <fun>
val sexp_of_some_type : some_type -> Sexp.t = <fun>
# sexp_of_some_type (33, ["one"; "two"]);;
- : Sexp.t = (33 (one two))
# Core.Sexp.of_string "(44 (five six))" |> some_type_of_sexp;;
- : some_type = (44, ["five"; "six"])
```

We'll discuss s-expressions and Sexplib in more detail in Chapter 21 (Data Serialization with S-Expressions), but for now, let's see what happens if we attach the `[@@deriving sexp]` declaration to the definition of t within the functor:

```
# module Make_interval(Endpoint : Comparable)
    : (Interval_intf with type endpoint := Endpoint.t) = struct

    type t = | Interval of Endpoint.t * Endpoint.t
             | Empty
    [@@deriving sexp]

    (** [create low high] creates a new interval from [low] to
        [high].  If [low > high], then the interval is empty *)
    let create low high =
      if Endpoint.compare low high > 0 then Empty
      else Interval (low,high)

    (** Returns true iff the interval is empty *)
    let is_empty = function
      | Empty -> true
      | Interval _ -> false

    (** [contains t x] returns true iff [x] is contained in the
        interval [t] *)
    let contains t x =
      match t with
      | Empty -> false
      | Interval (l,h) ->
        Endpoint.compare x l >= 0 && Endpoint.compare x h <= 0

    (** [intersect t1 t2] returns the intersection of the two input
        intervals *)
    let intersect t1 t2 =
      let min x y = if Endpoint.compare x y <= 0 then x else y in
      let max x y = if Endpoint.compare x y >= 0 then x else y in
      match t1,t2 with
      | Empty, _ | _, Empty -> Empty
      | Interval (l1,h1), Interval (l2,h2) ->
        create (max l1 l2) (min h1 h2)
```

```
   end;;
Line 4, characters 28-38:
Error: Unbound value Endpoint.t_of_sexp
```

The problem is that [@@deriving sexp] adds code for defining the s-expression converters, and that code assumes that Endpoint has the appropriate sexp-conversion functions for Endpoint.t. But all we know about Endpoint is that it satisfies the Comparable interface, which doesn't say anything about s-expressions.

Happily, Base comes with a built-in interface for just this purpose called Sexpable.S, which is defined as follows:

```
sig
  type t
  val sexp_of_t : t -> Sexp.t
  val t_of_sexp : Sexp.t -> t
end
```

We can modify Make_interval to use the Sexpable.S interface, for both its input and its output. First, let's create an extended version of the Interval_intf interface that includes the functions from the Sexpable.S interface. We can do this using destructive substitution on the Sexpable.S interface, to avoid having multiple distinct type t's clashing with each other:

```
# module type Interval_intf_with_sexp = sig
    include Interval_intf
    include Sexpable.S with type t := t
  end;;
module type Interval_intf_with_sexp =
  sig
    type t
    type endpoint
    val create : endpoint -> endpoint -> t
    val is_empty : t -> bool
    val contains : t -> endpoint -> bool
    val intersect : t -> t -> t
    val t_of_sexp : Sexp.t -> t
    val sexp_of_t : t -> Sexp.t
  end
```

Equivalently, we can define a type t within our new module, and apply destructive substitutions to all of the included interfaces, Interval_intf included, as shown in the following example. This is somewhat cleaner when combining multiple interfaces, since it correctly reflects that all of the signatures are being handled equivalently:

```
# module type Interval_intf_with_sexp = sig
    type t
    include Interval_intf with type t := t
    include Sexpable.S with type t := t
  end;;
module type Interval_intf_with_sexp =
  sig
    type t
    type endpoint
    val create : endpoint -> endpoint -> t
```

```
    val is_empty : t -> bool
    val contains : t -> endpoint -> bool
    val intersect : t -> t -> t
    val t_of_sexp : Sexp.t -> t
    val sexp_of_t : t -> Sexp.t
  end
```

Now we can write the functor itself. We have been careful to override the sexp converter here to ensure that the data structure's invariants are still maintained when reading in from an s-expression:

```
# module Make_interval(Endpoint : sig
      type t
      include Comparable with type t := t
      include Sexpable.S with type t := t
    end)
    : (Interval_intf_with_sexp with type endpoint := Endpoint.t)
  = struct

    type t = | Interval of Endpoint.t * Endpoint.t
             | Empty
    [@@deriving sexp]

    (** [create low high] creates a new interval from [low] to
        [high].  If [low > high], then the interval is empty *)
    let create low high =
      if Endpoint.compare low high > 0 then Empty
      else Interval (low,high)

    (* put a wrapper around the autogenerated [t_of_sexp] to enforce
       the invariants of the data structure *)
    let t_of_sexp sexp =
      match t_of_sexp sexp with
      | Empty -> Empty
      | Interval (x,y) -> create x y

    (** Returns true iff the interval is empty *)
    let is_empty = function
      | Empty -> true
      | Interval _ -> false

    (** [contains t x] returns true iff [x] is contained in the
        interval [t] *)
    let contains t x =
      match t with
      | Empty -> false
      | Interval (l,h) ->
        Endpoint.compare x l >= 0 && Endpoint.compare x h <= 0

    (** [intersect t1 t2] returns the intersection of the two input
        intervals *)
    let intersect t1 t2 =
      let min x y = if Endpoint.compare x y <= 0 then x else y in
      let max x y = if Endpoint.compare x y >= 0 then x else y in
      match t1,t2 with
      | Empty, _ | _, Empty -> Empty
      | Interval (l1,h1), Interval (l2,h2) ->
```

```
             create (max l1 l2) (min h1 h2)
      end;;
  module Make_interval :
    functor
      (Endpoint : sig
                    type t
                    val compare : t -> t -> int
                    val t_of_sexp : Sexp.t -> t
                    val sexp_of_t : t -> Sexp.t
                  end)
      ->
      sig
        type t
        val create : Endpoint.t -> Endpoint.t -> t
        val is_empty : t -> bool
        val contains : t -> Endpoint.t -> bool
        val intersect : t -> t -> t
        val t_of_sexp : Sexp.t -> t
        val sexp_of_t : t -> Sexp.t
      end
```

Finally, we can use that sexp converter in the ordinary way:

```
# module Int_interval = Make_interval(Int);;
module Int_interval :
  sig
    type t = Make_interval(Base.Int).t
    val create : int -> int -> t
    val is_empty : t -> bool
    val contains : t -> int -> bool
    val intersect : t -> t -> t
    val t_of_sexp : Sexp.t -> t
    val sexp_of_t : t -> Sexp.t
  end
# Int_interval.sexp_of_t (Int_interval.create 3 4);;
- : Sexp.t = (Interval 3 4)
# Int_interval.sexp_of_t (Int_interval.create 4 3);;
- : Sexp.t = Empty
```

11.3 Extending Modules

Another common use of functors is to generate type-specific functionality for a given module in a standardized way. Let's see how this works in the context of a functional queue, which is just a functional version of a FIFO (first-in, first-out) queue. Being functional, operations on the queue return new queues, rather than modifying the queues that were passed in.

Here's a reasonable `mli` for such a module:

```
type 'a t

val empty : 'a t

(** [enqueue q el] adds [el] to the back of [q] *)
```

```
val enqueue : 'a t -> 'a -> 'a t

(** [dequeue q] returns None if the [q] is empty, otherwise returns
    the first element of the queue and the remainder of the queue *)
val dequeue : 'a t -> ('a * 'a t) option

(** Folds over the queue, from front to back *)
val fold : 'a t -> init:'acc -> f:('acc -> 'a -> 'acc) -> 'acc
```

The signature of the fold function requires some explanation. It follows the same pattern as the List.fold function we described in Chapter 4.4 (Using the List Module Effectively). Essentially, Fqueue.fold q ~init ~f walks over the elements of q from front to back, starting with an accumulator of init and using f to update the accumulator value as it walks over the queue, returning the final value of the accumulator at the end of the computation. fold is a quite powerful operation, as we'll see.

We'll implement Fqueue using the well known trick of maintaining an input and an output list so that one can both efficiently enqueue on the input list and dequeue from the output list. If you attempt to dequeue when the output list is empty, the input list is reversed and becomes the new output list. Here's the implementation:

```
open Base

type 'a t = 'a list * 'a list

let empty = ([],[])

let enqueue (in_list, out_list) x =
  (x :: in_list,out_list)

let dequeue (in_list, out_list) =
  match out_list with
  | hd :: tl -> Some (hd, (in_list, tl))
  | [] ->
    match List.rev in_list with
    | [] -> None
    | hd :: tl -> Some (hd, ([], tl))

let fold (in_list, out_list) ~init ~f =
  let after_out = List.fold ~init ~f out_list in
  List.fold_right ~init:after_out ~f:(fun x acc -> f acc x) in_list
```

One problem with Fqueue is that the interface is quite skeletal. There are lots of useful helper functions that one might want that aren't there. The List module, by way of contrast, has functions like List.iter, which runs a function on each element; and List.for_all, which returns true if and only if the given predicate evaluates to true on every element of the list. Such helper functions come up for pretty much every container type, and implementing them over and over is a dull and repetitive affair.

As it happens, many of these helper functions can be derived mechanically from the fold function we already implemented. Rather than write all of these helper functions by hand for every new container type, we can instead use a functor to add this functionality to any container that has a fold function.

We'll create a new module, Foldable, that automates the process of adding helper functions to a fold-supporting container. As you can see, `Foldable` contains a module signature S which defines the signature that is required to support folding; and a functor `Extend` that allows one to extend any module that matches `Foldable.S`:

```
open Base

module type S = sig
  type 'a t
  val fold : 'a t -> init:'acc -> f:('acc -> 'a -> 'acc) -> 'acc
end

module type Extension = sig
  type 'a t
  val iter    : 'a t -> f:('a -> unit) -> unit
  val length  : 'a t -> int
  val count   : 'a t -> f:('a -> bool) -> int
  val for_all : 'a t -> f:('a -> bool) -> bool
  val exists  : 'a t -> f:('a -> bool) -> bool
end

(* For extending a Foldable module *)
module Extend(Arg : S)
  : (Extension with type 'a t := 'a Arg.t) =
struct
  open Arg

  let iter t ~f =
    fold t ~init:() ~f:(fun () a -> f a)

  let length t =
    fold t ~init:0  ~f:(fun acc _ -> acc + 1)

  let count t ~f =
    fold t ~init:0  ~f:(fun count x -> count + if f x then 1 else 0)

  exception Short_circuit

  let for_all c ~f =
    try iter c ~f:(fun x -> if not (f x) then raise Short_circuit);
    true
    with Short_circuit -> false

  let exists c ~f =
    try iter c ~f:(fun x -> if f x then raise Short_circuit); false
    with Short_circuit -> true
end
```

Now we can apply this to `Fqueue`. We can create an interface for an extended version of `Fqueue` as follows:

```
type 'a t
include (module type of Fqueue) with type 'a t := 'a t
include Foldable.Extension with type 'a t := 'a t
```

In order to apply the functor, we'll put the definition of `Fqueue` in a submodule called `T`, and then call `Foldable.Extend` on `T`:

```
include Fqueue
include Foldable.Extend(Fqueue)
```

Base comes with a number of functors for extending modules that follow this same basic pattern, including:

- `Container.Make` : Very similar to `Foldable.Extend`.
- `Comparable.Make` : Adds support for functionality that depends on the presence of a comparison function, including support for containers like maps and sets.
- `Hashable.Make` : Adds support for hashing-based data structures including hash tables, hash sets, and hash heaps.
- `Monad.Make` : For so-called monadic libraries, like those discussed in Chapters Chapter 8 (Error Handling) and Chapter 17 (Concurrent Programming with Async). Here, the functor is used to provide a collection of standard helper functions based on the `bind` and `return` operators.

These functors come in handy when you want to add the same kind of functionality that is commonly available in Base to your own types.

We've really only covered some of the possible uses of functors. Functors are really a quite powerful tool for modularizing your code. The cost is that functors are syntactically heavyweight compared to the rest of the language, and that there are some tricky issues you need to understand to use them effectively, with sharing constraints and destructive substitution being high on that list.

All of this means that for small and simple programs, heavy use of functors is probably a mistake. But as your programs get more complicated and you need more effective modular architectures, functors become a highly valuable tool.

12 First-Class Modules

You can think of OCaml as being broken up into two parts: a core language that is concerned with values and types, and a module language that is concerned with modules and module signatures. These sublanguages are stratified, in that modules can contain types and values, but ordinary values can't contain modules or module types. That means you can't do things like define a variable whose value is a module, or a function that takes a module as an argument.

OCaml provides a way around this stratification in the form of *first-class modules*. First-class modules are ordinary values that can be created from and converted back to regular modules.

First-class modules are a sophisticated technique, and you'll need to get comfortable with some advanced aspects of the language to use them effectively. But it's worth learning, because letting modules into the core language is quite powerful, increasing the range of what you can express and making it easier to build flexible and modular systems.

12.1 Working with First-Class Modules

We'll start out by covering the basic mechanics of first-class modules by working through some toy examples. We'll get to more realistic examples in the next section.

12.1.1 Creating First-Class Modules

In that light, consider the following signature of a module with a single integer variable:

```
# open Base;;
# module type X_int = sig val x : int end;;
module type X_int = sig val x : int end
```

We can also create a module that matches this signature:

```
# module Three : X_int = struct let x = 3 end;;
module Three : X_int
# Three.x;;
- : int = 3
```

A first-class module is created by packaging up a module with a signature that it satisfies. This is done using the `module` keyword.

```
(module <Module> : <Module_type>)
```

We can convert `Three` into a first-class module as follows:

```
# let three = (module Three : X_int);;
val three : (module X_int) = <module>
```

12.1.2   Inference and Anonymous Modules

The module type doesn't need to be part of the construction of a first-class module if it can be inferred. Thus, we can write:

```
# module Four = struct let x = 4 end;;
module Four : sig val x : int end
# let numbers = [ three; (module Four) ];;
val numbers : (module X_int) list = [<module>; <module>]
```

We can also create a first-class module from an anonymous module:

```
# let numbers = [three; (module struct let x = 4 end)];;
val numbers : (module X_int) list = [<module>; <module>]
```

12.1.3   Unpacking First-Class Modules

In order to access the contents of a first-class module, you need to unpack it into an ordinary module. This can be done using the `val` keyword, using this syntax:

```
(val <first_class_module> : <Module_type>)
```

Here's an example:

```
# module New_three = (val three : X_int);;
module New_three : X_int
# New_three.x;;
- : int = 3
```

12.1.4   Functions for Manipulating First-Class Modules

We can also write ordinary functions which consume and create first-class modules. The following shows the definition of two functions: `to_int`, which converts a (module `X_int`) into an int; and plus, which returns the sum of two (module `X_int`):

```
# let to_int m =
    let module M = (val m : X_int) in
    M.x;;
val to_int : (module X_int) -> int = <fun>
# let plus m1 m2 =
    (module struct
       let x = to_int m1 + to_int m2
    end : X_int);;
val plus : (module X_int) -> (module X_int) -> (module X_int) = <fun>
```

You can also unpack a first-class module with a pattern match, which lets us write to_int more concisely:

```
# let to_int (module M : X_int) = M.x;;
val to_int : (module X_int) -> int = <fun>
```

With these functions in hand, we can now work with values of type (module X_int) in a more natural style, taking advantage of the concision and simplicity of the core language:

```
# let six = plus three three;;
val six : (module X_int) = <module>
# to_int (List.fold ~init:six ~f:plus [three;three]);;
- : int = 12
```

12.1.5 Richer First-Class Modules

First-class modules can contain types and functions in addition to simple values like int. Here's an interface that contains a type and a corresponding bump operation that takes a value of the type and produces a new one:

```
# module type Bumpable = sig
    type t
    val bump : t -> t
  end;;
module type Bumpable = sig type t val bump : t -> t end
```

We can create multiple instances of this module with different underlying types:

```
# module Int_bumper = struct
    type t = int
    let bump n = n + 1
  end;;
module Int_bumper : sig type t = int val bump : t -> t end
# module Float_bumper = struct
    type t = float
    let bump n = n +. 1.
  end;;
module Float_bumper : sig type t = float val bump : t -> t end
```

And we can convert these to first-class modules:

```
# let int_bumper = (module Int_bumper : Bumpable);;
val int_bumper : (module Bumpable) = <module>
```

12.1.6 Exposing types

You can't do much with int_bumper because it's fully abstract, so we can't take advantage of the fact that the type in question is int, which makes it impossible to construct or really do anything with values of type Bumper.t.

```
# let (module Bumper) = int_bumper in
  Bumper.bump 3;;
Line 2, characters 15-16:
```

```
Error: This expression has type int but an expression was expected of
    type
        Bumper.t
```

To make `int_bumper` usable, we need to expose that the type `Bumpable.t` is actually equal to `int`. Below we'll do that for `int_bumper`, and also provide the corresponding definition for `float_bumper`.

```
# let int_bumper = (module Int_bumper : Bumpable with type t = int);;
val int_bumper : (module Bumpable with type t = int) = <module>
# let float_bumper = (module Float_bumper : Bumpable with type t =
    float);;
val float_bumper : (module Bumpable with type t = float) = <module>
```

The addition of the sharing constraint has exposed the type `t`, which lets us actually use the values within the module.

```
# let (module Bumper) = int_bumper in
  Bumper.bump 3;;
- : int = 4
# let (module Bumper) = float_bumper in
  Bumper.bump 3.5;;
- : float = 4.5
```

We can also use these first-class modules polymorphically. The following function takes two arguments: a `Bumpable` module and a list of elements of the same type as the type `t` of the module:

```
# let bump_list
        (type a)
        (module Bumper : Bumpable with type t = a)
        (l: a list)
    =
    List.map ~f:Bumper.bump l;;
val bump_list : (module Bumpable with type t = 'a) -> 'a list -> 'a
    list =
  <fun>
```

In this example, a is a *locally abstract type*. For any function, you can declare a pseudoparameter of the form (type a) which introduces a fresh type named a. This type acts like an abstract type within the context of the function. In the example above, the locally abstract type was used as part of a sharing constraint that ties the type B.t with the type of the elements of the list passed in.

The resulting function is polymorphic in both the type of the list element and the type `Bumpable.t`. We can see this function in action:

```
# bump_list int_bumper [1;2;3];;
- : int list = [2; 3; 4]
# bump_list float_bumper [1.5;2.5;3.5];;
- : float list = [2.5; 3.5; 4.5]
```

Polymorphic first-class modules are important because they allow you to connect the types associated with a first-class module to the types of other values you're working with.

More on Locally Abstract Types

One of the key properties of locally abstract types is that they're dealt with as abstract types in the function they're defined within, but are polymorphic from the outside. Consider the following example:

```
# let wrap_in_list (type a) (x:a) = [x];;
val wrap_in_list : 'a -> 'a list = <fun>
```

The type a is used in a way that is compatible with it being abstract, but the type of the function that is inferred is polymorphic.

If, on the other hand, we try to use the type a as if it were equivalent to some concrete type, say, int, then the compiler will complain.

```
# let double_int (type a) (x:a) = x + x;;
Line 1, characters 33-34:
Error: This expression has type a but an expression was expected of
       type int
```

One common use of locally abstract types is to create a new type that can be used in constructing a module. Here's an example of doing this to create a new first-class module:

```
# module type Comparable = sig
    type t
    val compare : t -> t -> int
  end;;
module type Comparable = sig type t val compare : t -> t -> int end
# let create_comparable (type a) compare =
    (module struct
       type t = a
       let compare = compare
     end : Comparable with type t = a);;
val create_comparable :
  ('a -> 'a -> int) -> (module Comparable with type t = 'a) = <fun>
# create_comparable Int.compare;;
- : (module Comparable with type t = int) = <module>
# create_comparable Float.compare;;
- : (module Comparable with type t = float) = <module>
```

This technique is useful beyond first-class modules. For example, we can use the same approach to construct a local module to be fed to a functor.

12.2   Example: A Query-Handling Framework

Now let's look at first-class modules in the context of a more complete and realistic example. In particular, we're going to implement a system for responding to user-generated queries.

This system will use *s-expressions* for formatting queries and responses, as well as the configuration for the query handler. S-expressions are a simple, flexible, and human-readable serialization format commonly used in Base and related libraries. For now, it's enough to think of them as balanced parenthetical expressions whose atomic values are strings, e.g., (this (is an) (s expression)). S-expressions are covered in more detail in Chapter 21 (Data Serialization with S-Expressions).

The following signature for a module that implements a system for responding to user-generated queries. Here, we use Base's Sexp module for handling s-expressions. Note that we could just as easily have used another serialization format, like JSON, as discussed in Chapter 19 (Handling JSON Data).

```
module type Query_handler = sig

  (** Configuration for a query handler *)
  type config

  val sexp_of_config : config -> Sexp.t
  val config_of_sexp : Sexp.t -> config

  (** The name of the query-handling service *)
  val name : string

  (** The state of the query handler *)
  type t

  (** Creates a new query handler from a config *)
  val create : config -> t

  (** Evaluate a given query, where both input and output are
      s-expressions *)
  val eval : t -> Sexp.t -> Sexp.t Or_error.t
end;;
```

Implementing s-expression converters by hand is tedious and error-prone, but happily, we have an alternative. ppx_sexp_conv is a syntax extension which can be used to automatically generate s-expression converters based on their type definition. We'll enable ppx_sexp_conv by enabling ppx_jane, which brings in a larger family of syntax extensions.

```
# #require "ppx_jane";;
```

Here's an example of the extension in action. Note that we need the annotation [@@deriving sexp] to kick off the generation of the converters.

```
# type u = { a: int; b: float } [@@deriving sexp];;
type u = { a : int; b : float; }
val u_of_sexp : Sexp.t -> u = <fun>
val sexp_of_u : u -> Sexp.t = <fun>
# sexp_of_u {a=3;b=7.};;
- : Sexp.t = ((a 3) (b 7))
# u_of_sexp (Core.Sexp.of_string "((a 43) (b 3.4))");;
- : u = {a = 43; b = 3.4}
```

The same annotations can be attached within a signature to add the appropriate type signature.

```
# module type M = sig type t [@@deriving sexp] end;;
module type M =
```

```
sig type t val t_of_sexp : Sexp.t -> t val sexp_of_t : t -> Sexp.t
end
```

12.2.1 Implementing a Query Handler

Now we can construct an example of a query handler that satisfies the `Query_handler` interface. We'll start with a handler that produces unique integer IDs, which works by keeping an internal counter that's bumped every time a new value is requested. The input to the query in this case is just the trivial s-expression (), otherwise known as `Sexp.unit`:

```
module Unique = struct
  type config = int [@@deriving sexp]
  type t = { mutable next_id: int }

  let name = "unique"
  let create start_at = { next_id = start_at }

  let eval t sexp =
    match Or_error.try_with (fun () -> unit_of_sexp sexp) with
    | Error _ as err -> err
    | Ok () ->
      let response = Ok (Int.sexp_of_t t.next_id) in
      t.next_id <- t.next_id + 1;
      response
end;;
```

We can use this module to create an instance of the `Unique` query handler and interact with it directly:

```
# let unique = Unique.create 0;;
val unique : Unique.t = {Unique.next_id = 0}
# Unique.eval unique (Sexp.List []);;
- : (Sexp.t, Error.t) result = Ok 0
# Unique.eval unique (Sexp.List []);;
- : (Sexp.t, Error.t) result = Ok 1
```

Here's another example: a query handler that does directory listings. Here, the config is the default directory that relative paths are interpreted within:

```
module List_dir = struct
  type config = string [@@deriving sexp]
  type t = { cwd: string }

  (** [is_abs p] Returns true if [p] is an absolute path  *)
  let is_abs p =
    String.length p > 0 && Char.(=) p.[0] '/'

  let name = "ls"
  let create cwd = { cwd }

  let eval t sexp =
    match Or_error.try_with (fun () -> string_of_sexp sexp) with
    | Error _ as err -> err
    | Ok dir ->
```

```
        let dir =
          if is_abs dir then dir
          else Core.Filename.concat t.cwd dir
        in
          Ok (Array.sexp_of_t String.sexp_of_t (Core.Sys.readdir dir))
end;;
```

Again, we can create an instance of this query handler and interact with it directly:

```
# let list_dir = List_dir.create "/var";;
val list_dir : List_dir.t = {List_dir.cwd = "/var"}
# List_dir.eval list_dir (sexp_of_string ".");;
- : (Sexp.t, Error.t) result =
Ok
  (yp networkd install empty ma mail spool jabberd vm msgs audit root
     lib db
   at log folders netboot run rpc tmp backups agentx rwho)
# List_dir.eval list_dir (sexp_of_string "yp");;
- : (Sexp.t, Error.t) result = Ok (binding)
```

12.2.2   Dispatching to Multiple Query Handlers

Now, what if we want to dispatch queries to any of an arbitrary collection of handlers? Ideally, we'd just like to pass in the handlers as a simple data structure like a list. This is awkward to do with modules and functors alone, but it's quite natural with first-class modules. The first thing we'll need to do is create a signature that combines a Query_handler module with an instantiated query handler:

```
# module type Query_handler_instance = sig
    module Query_handler : Query_handler
    val this : Query_handler.t
  end;;
module type Query_handler_instance =
  sig module Query_handler : Query_handler val this : Query_handler.t
    end
```

With this signature, we can create a first-class module that encompasses both an instance of the query and the matching operations for working with that query.

We can create an instance as follows:

```
# let unique_instance =
    (module struct
      module Query_handler = Unique
      let this = Unique.create 0
    end : Query_handler_instance);;
val unique_instance : (module Query_handler_instance) = <module>
```

Constructing instances in this way is a little verbose, but we can write a function that eliminates most of this boilerplate. Note that we are again making use of a locally abstract type:

```
# let build_instance
      (type a)
      (module Q : Query_handler with type config = a)
```

```
        config
    =
    (module struct
       module Query_handler = Q
       let this = Q.create config
     end : Query_handler_instance);;
val build_instance :
  (module Query_handler with type config = 'a) ->
  'a -> (module Query_handler_instance) = <fun>
```

Using build_instance, constructing a new instance becomes a one-liner:

```
# let unique_instance = build_instance (module Unique) 0;;
val unique_instance : (module Query_handler_instance) = <module>
# let list_dir_instance = build_instance (module List_dir)  "/var";;
val list_dir_instance : (module Query_handler_instance) = <module>
```

We can now write code that lets you dispatch queries to one of a list of query handler instances. We assume that the shape of the query is as follows:

```
(query-name query)
```

where *query-name* is the name used to determine which query handler to dispatch the query to, and *query* is the body of the query.

The first thing we'll need is a function that takes a list of query handler instances and constructs a dispatch table from it:

```
# let build_dispatch_table handlers =
    let table = Hashtbl.create (module String) in
    List.iter handlers
      ~f:(fun ((module I : Query_handler_instance) as instance) ->
        Hashtbl.set table ~key:I.Query_handler.name ~data:instance);
    table;;
val build_dispatch_table :
  (module Query_handler_instance) list ->
  (string, (module Query_handler_instance)) Hashtbl.Poly.t = <fun>
```

Next, we'll need a function that dispatches to a handler using a dispatch table:

```
# let dispatch dispatch_table name_and_query =
    match name_and_query with
    | Sexp.List [Sexp.Atom name; query] ->
      begin match Hashtbl.find dispatch_table name with
      | None ->
        Or_error.error "Could not find matching handler"
          name String.sexp_of_t
      | Some (module I : Query_handler_instance) ->
        I.Query_handler.eval I.this query
      end
    | _ ->
      Or_error.error_string "malformed query";;
val dispatch :
  (string, (module Query_handler_instance)) Hashtbl.Poly.t ->
  Sexp.t -> Sexp.t Or_error.t = <fun>
```

This function interacts with an instance by unpacking it into a module I and then using the query handler instance (I.this) in concert with the associated module (I.Query_handler).

The bundling together of the module and the value is in many ways reminiscent of object-oriented languages. One key difference is that first-class modules allow you to package up more than just functions or methods. As we've seen, you can also include types and even modules. We've only used it in a small way here, but this extra power allows you to build more sophisticated components that involve multiple interdependent types and values.

We can turn this into a complete, running example by adding a command-line interface:

```
# open Stdio;;
# let rec cli dispatch_table =
    printf ">>> %!";
    let result =
      match In_channel.(input_line stdin) with
      | None -> `Stop
      | Some line ->
        match Or_error.try_with (fun () ->
          Core.Sexp.of_string line)
        with
        | Error e -> `Continue (Error.to_string_hum e)
        | Ok (Sexp.Atom "quit") -> `Stop
        | Ok query ->
          begin match dispatch dispatch_table query with
          | Error e -> `Continue (Error.to_string_hum e)
          | Ok s    -> `Continue (Sexp.to_string_hum s)
          end;
    in
    match result with
    | `Stop -> ()
    | `Continue msg ->
      printf "%s\n%!" msg;
      cli dispatch_table;;
val cli : (string, (module Query_handler_instance)) Hashtbl.Poly.t ->
  unit =
  <fun>
```

We'll run this command-line interface from a standalone program by putting the above code in a file, and adding the following to launch the interface.

```
let () =
  cli (build_dispatch_table [unique_instance; list_dir_instance])
```

Here's an example of a session with this program:

```
$ dune exec -- ./query_handler.exe
>>> (unique ())
0
>>> (unique ())
1
>>> (ls .)
(agentx at audit backups db empty folders jabberd lib log mail msgs
    named
 netboot pgsql_socket_alt root rpc run rwho spool tmp vm yp)
>>> (ls vm)
(sleepimage swapfile0 swapfile1 swapfile2 swapfile3 swapfile4
    swapfile5
```

```
swapfile6)
```

12.2.3   Loading and Unloading Query Handlers

One of the advantages of first-class modules is that they afford a great deal of dynamism and flexibility. For example, it's a fairly simple matter to change our design to allow query handlers to be loaded and unloaded at runtime.

We'll do this by creating a query handler whose job is to control the set of active query handlers. The module in question will be called Loader, and its configuration is a list of known Query_handler modules. Here are the basic types:

```
module Loader = struct
  type config = (module Query_handler) list [@sexp.opaque]
  [@@deriving sexp]

  type t = { known  : (module Query_handler)          String.Table.t
           ; active : (module Query_handler_instance) String.Table.t
           }

  let name = "loader"
```

Note that a Loader.t has two tables: one containing the known query handler modules, and one containing the active query handler instances. The Loader.t will be responsible for creating new instances and adding them to the table, as well as for removing instances, all in response to user queries.

Next, we'll need a function for creating a Loader.t. This function requires the list of known query handler modules. Note that the table of active modules starts out as empty:

```
let create known_list =
  let active = String.Table.create () in
  let known  = String.Table.create () in
  List.iter known_list
    ~f:(fun ((module Q : Query_handler) as q) ->
      Hashtbl.set known ~key:Q.name ~data:q);
  { known; active }
```

Now we can write the functions for manipulating the table of active query handlers. We'll start with the function for loading an instance. Note that it takes as an argument both the name of the query handler and the configuration for instantiating that handler in the form of an s-expression. These are used for creating a first-class module of type (module Query_handler_instance), which is then added to the active table:

```
let load t handler_name config =
  if Hashtbl.mem t.active handler_name then
    Or_error.error "Can't re-register an active handler"
      handler_name String.sexp_of_t
  else
    match Hashtbl.find t.known handler_name with
    | None ->
      Or_error.error "Unknown handler" handler_name String.sexp_of_t
    | Some (module Q : Query_handler) ->
```

```
let instance =
  (module struct
     module Query_handler = Q
     let this = Q.create (Q.config_of_sexp config)
   end : Query_handler_instance)
in
Hashtbl.set t.active ~key:handler_name ~data:instance;
Ok Sexp.unit
```

Since the `load` function will refuse to `load` an already active handler, we also need the ability to unload a handler. Note that the handler explicitly refuses to unload itself:

```
let unload t handler_name =
  if not (Hashtbl.mem t.active handler_name) then
    Or_error.error "Handler not active" handler_name
  String.sexp_of_t
  else if String.(=) handler_name name then
    Or_error.error_string "It's unwise to unload yourself"
  else (
    Hashtbl.remove t.active handler_name;
    Ok Sexp.unit
  )
```

Finally, we need to implement the `eval` function, which will determine the query interface presented to the user. We'll do this by creating a variant type, and using the s-expression converter generated for that type to parse the query from the user:

```
type request =
  | Load of string * Sexp.t
  | Unload of string
  | Known_services
  | Active_services
[@@deriving sexp]
```

The eval function itself is fairly straightforward, dispatching to the appropriate functions to respond to each type of query. Note that we write <:sexp_of<string list>> to autogenerate a function for converting a list of strings to an s-expression, as described in Chapter 21 (Data Serialization with S-Expressions).

This function ends the definition of the `Loader` module:

```
let eval t sexp =
  match Or_error.try_with (fun () -> request_of_sexp sexp) with
  | Error _ as err -> err
  | Ok resp ->
    match resp with
    | Load (name,config) -> load   t name config
    | Unload name         -> unload t name
    | Known_services ->
      Ok ([%sexp_of: string list] (Hashtbl.keys t.known))
    | Active_services ->
      Ok ([%sexp_of: string list] (Hashtbl.keys t.active))
  end
```

Finally, we can put this all together with the command-line interface. We first create an instance of the loader query handler and then add that instance to the loader's active table. We can then launch the command-line interface, passing it the active table.

```
let () =
  let loader = Loader.create [(module Unique); (module List_dir)] in
  let loader_instance =
    (module struct
       module Query_handler = Loader
       let this = loader
     end : Query_handler_instance)
  in
  Hashtbl.set loader.Loader.active
    ~key:Loader.name ~data:loader_instance;
  cli loader.active
```

The resulting command-line interface behaves much as you'd expect, starting out with no query handlers available but giving you the ability to load and unload them. Here's an example of it in action. As you can see, we start out with `loader` itself as the only active handler.

```
$ dune exec -- ./query_handler_loader.exe
>>> (loader known_services)
(ls unique)
>>> (loader active_services)
(loader)
```

Any attempt to use an inactive query handler will fail:

```
>>> (ls .)
Could not find matching handler: ls
```

But, we can load the `ls` handler with a config of our choice, at which point it will be available for use. And once we unload it, it will be unavailable yet again and could be reloaded with a different config.

```
>>> (loader (load ls /var))
()
>>> (ls .)
(agentx at audit backups db empty folders jabberd lib log mail msgs
    named
 netboot pgsql_socket_alt root rpc run rwho spool tmp vm yp)
>>> (loader (unload ls))
()
>>> (ls .)
Could not find matching handler: ls
```

Notably, the loader can't be loaded (since it's not on the list of known handlers) and can't be unloaded either:

```
>>> (loader (unload loader))
It's unwise to unload yourself
```

Although we won't describe the details here, we can push this dynamism yet further using OCaml's dynamic linking facilities, which allow you to compile and link in new code to a running program. This can be automated using libraries like `ocaml_plugin`, which can be installed via OPAM, and which takes care of much of the workflow around setting up dynamic linking.

12.3   Living Without First-Class Modules

It's worth noting that most designs that can be done with first-class modules can be simulated without them, with some level of awkwardness. For example, we could rewrite our query handler example without first-class modules using the following types:

```
# type query_handler_instance =
    { name : string
    ; eval : Sexp.t -> Sexp.t Or_error.t };;
type query_handler_instance = {
  name : string;
  eval : Sexp.t -> Sexp.t Or_error.t;
}
# type query_handler = Sexp.t -> query_handler_instance;;
type query_handler = Sexp.t -> query_handler_instance
```

The idea here is that we hide the true types of the objects in question behind the functions stored in the closure. Thus, we could put the Unique query handler into this framework as follows:

```
# let unique_handler config_sexp =
    let config = Unique.config_of_sexp config_sexp in
    let unique = Unique.create config in
    { name = Unique.name
    ; eval = (fun config -> Unique.eval unique config)
    };;
val unique_handler : Sexp.t -> query_handler_instance = <fun>
```

For an example on this scale, the preceding approach is completely reasonable, and first-class modules are not really necessary. But the more functionality you need to hide away behind a set of closures, and the more complicated the relationships between the different types in question, the more awkward this approach becomes, and the better it is to use first-class modules.

13 Objects

This chapter was written by Leo White and Jason Hickey.

We've already seen several tools that OCaml provides for organizing programs, particularly modules. In addition, OCaml also supports object-oriented programming. There are objects, classes, and their associated types. In this chapter, we'll introduce you to OCaml objects and subtyping. In the next chapter, Chapter 14 (Classes), we'll introduce you to classes and inheritance.

What Is Object-Oriented Programming?

Object-oriented programming (often shortened to OOP) is a programming style that encapsulates computation and data within logical *objects*. Each object contains some data stored in *fields* and has *method* functions that can be invoked against the data within the object (also called "sending a message" to the object). The code definition behind an object is called a *class*, and objects are constructed from a class definition by calling a constructor with the data that the object will use to build itself.

There are five fundamental properties that differentiate OOP from other styles:

Abstraction The details of the implementation are hidden in the object, and the external interface is just the set of publicly accessible methods.

Dynamic lookup When a message is sent to an object, the method to be executed is determined by the implementation of the object, not by some static property of the program. In other words, different objects may react to the same message in different ways.

Subtyping If an object a has all the functionality of an object b, then we may use a in any context where b is expected.

Inheritance The definition of one kind of object can be reused to produce a new kind of object. This new definition can override some behavior, but also share code with its parent.

Open recursion An object's methods can invoke another method in the same object using a special variable (often called self or this). When objects are created from classes, these calls use dynamic lookup, allowing a method defined in one class to invoke methods defined in another class that inherits from the first.

Almost every notable modern programming language has been influenced by OOP, and you'll have run across these terms if you've ever used C++, Java, C#, Ruby, Python, or JavaScript.

13.1   OCaml Objects

If you already know about object-oriented programming in a language like Java or C++, the OCaml object system may come as a surprise. Foremost is the complete separation of objects and their types from the class system. In a language like Java, a class name is also used as the type of objects created by instantiating it, and the relationships between these object types correspond to inheritance. For example, if we implement a class Deque in Java by inheriting from a class Stack, we would be allowed to pass a deque anywhere a stack is expected.

OCaml is entirely different. Classes are used to construct objects and support inheritance, but classes are not types. Instead, objects have *object types*, and if you want to use objects, you aren't required to use classes at all. Here's an example of a simple object:

```
# open Base;;
# let s = object
    val mutable v = [0; 2]

    method pop =
      match v with
      | hd :: tl ->
        v <- tl;
        Some hd
      | [] -> None

    method push hd =
      v <- hd :: v
  end;;
val s : < pop : int option; push : int -> unit > = <obj>
```

The object has an integer list value v, a method pop that returns the head of v, and a method push that adds an integer to the head of v.

The object type is enclosed in angle brackets < ... >, containing just the types of the methods. Fields, like v, are not part of the public interface of an object. All interaction with an object is through its methods. The syntax for a method invocation uses the # character:

```
# s#pop;;
- : int option = Some 0
# s#push 4;;
- : unit = ()
# s#pop;;
- : int option = Some 4
```

Note that unlike functions, methods can have zero parameters, since the method call is routed to a concrete object instance. That's why the pop method doesn't have a unit argument, as the equivalent functional version would.

Objects can also be constructed by functions. If we want to specify the initial value of the object, we can define a function that takes the value and returns an object:

```
# let stack init = object
    val mutable v = init

    method pop =
      match v with
      | hd :: tl ->
        v <- tl;
        Some hd
      | [] -> None

    method push hd =
      v <- hd :: v
  end;;
val stack : 'a list -> < pop : 'a option; push : 'a -> unit > = <fun>
# let s = stack [3; 2; 1];;
val s : < pop : int option; push : int -> unit > = <obj>
# s#pop;;
- : int option = Some 3
```

Note that the types of the function `stack` and the returned object now use the polymorphic type `'a`. When `stack` is invoked on a concrete value `[3; 2; 1]`, we get the same object type as before, with type `int` for the values on the stack.

13.2   Object Polymorphism

Like polymorphic variants, methods can be used without an explicit type declaration:

```
# let area sq = sq#width * sq#width;;
val area : < width : int; .. > -> int = <fun>
# let minimize sq : unit = sq#resize 1;;
val minimize : < resize : int -> unit; .. > -> unit = <fun>
# let limit sq = if (area sq) > 100 then minimize sq;;
val limit : < resize : int -> unit; width : int; .. > -> unit = <fun>
```

As you can see, object types are inferred automatically from the methods that are invoked on them.

The type system will complain if it sees incompatible uses of the same method:

```
# let toggle sq b : unit =
    if b then sq#resize `Fullscreen else minimize sq;;
Line 2, characters 51-53:
Error: This expression has type < resize : [> `Fullscreen ] -> unit;
       .. >
       but an expression was expected of type < resize : int -> unit;
       .. >
       Types for method resize are incompatible
```

The `..` in the inferred object types are ellipses, standing for other unspecified methods that the object may have. The type `< width : float; .. >` specifies an object that must have at least a `width` method, and possibly some others as well. Such object types are said to be *open*.

We can manually *close* an object type using a type annotation:

```
# let area_closed (sq: < width : int >) = sq#width * sq#width;;
val area_closed : < width : int > -> int = <fun>
# let sq = object
    method width = 30
    method name = "sq"
  end;;
val sq : < name : string; width : int > = <obj>
# area_closed sq;;
Line 1, characters 13-15:
Error: This expression has type < name : string; width : int >
       but an expression was expected of type < width : int >
       The second object type has no method name
```

Elisions Are Polymorphic

The `..` in an open object type is an elision, standing for "possibly more methods." It may not be apparent from the syntax, but an elided object type is actually polymorphic. For example, if we try to write a type definition, we get an "unbound type variable" error:

```
# type square = < width : int; ..>;;
Line 1, characters 1-33:
Error: A type variable is unbound in this type declaration.
       In type < width : Base.int; .. > as 'a the variable 'a is
       unbound
```

This is because `..` is really a special kind of type variable called a *row variable*.

This kind of typing scheme using row variables is called *row polymorphism*. Row polymorphism is also used in polymorphic variant types, and there is a close relationship between objects and polymorphic variants: objects are to records what polymorphic variants are to ordinary variants.

An object of type `< pop : int option; .. >` can be any object with a method `pop : int option`; it doesn't matter how it is implemented. When the method `#pop` is invoked, the actual method that is run is determined by the object. Consider the following function.

```
# let print_pop st = Option.iter ~f:(Stdio.printf "Popped: %d\n")
    st#pop;;
val print_pop : < pop : int option; .. > -> unit = <fun>
```

We can run it on the stack type we defined above, which is based on linked lists.

```
# print_pop (stack [5;4;3;2;1]);;
Popped: 5
- : unit = ()
```

But we could also create a totally different implementation of stacks, using Base's array-based `Stack` module.

```
# let array_stack l = object
    val stack = Stack.of_list l
    method pop = Stack.pop stack
```

```
   end;;
val array_stack : 'a list -> < pop : 'a option > = <fun>
```

And `print_pop` will work just as well on this kind of stack object, despite having a completely different implementation.

```
# print_pop (array_stack [5;4;3;2;1]);;
Popped: 5
- : unit = ()
```

13.3   Immutable Objects

Many people consider object-oriented programming to be intrinsically imperative, where an object is like a state machine. Sending a message to an object causes it to change state, possibly sending messages to other objects.

Indeed, in many programs this makes sense, but it is by no means required. Let's define a function that creates immutable stack objects:

```
# let imm_stack init = object
      val v = init

      method pop =
         match v with
         | hd :: tl -> Some (hd, {< v = tl >})
         | [] -> None

      method push hd =
         {< v = hd :: v >}
   end;;
val imm_stack :
   'a list -> (< pop : ('a * 'b) option; push : 'a -> 'b > as 'b) = <fun>
```

The key parts of this implementation are in the pop and push methods. The expression `{< ... >}` produces a copy of the current object, with the same type, and the specified fields updated. In other words, the push hd method produces a copy of the object, with v replaced by hd :: v. The original object is not modified:

```
# let s = imm_stack [3; 2; 1];;
val s : < pop : (int * 'a) option; push : int -> 'a > as 'a = <obj>
# let r = s#push 4;;
val r : < pop : (int * 'a) option; push : int -> 'a > as 'a = <obj>
# s#pop;;
- : (int * (< pop : 'a; push : int -> 'b > as 'b)) option as 'a =
Some (3, <obj>)
# r#pop;;
- : (int * (< pop : 'a; push : int -> 'b > as 'b)) option as 'a =
Some (4, <obj>)
```

There are some restrictions on the use of the expression `{< ... >}`. It can be used only within a method body, and only the values of fields may be updated. Method implementations are fixed at the time the object is created; they cannot be changed dynamically.

13.4   When to Use Objects

You might wonder when to use objects in OCaml, which has a multitude of alternative mechanisms to express similar concepts. First-class modules are more expressive (a module can include types, while classes and objects cannot). Modules, functors, and data types also offer a wide range of ways to express program structure. In fact, many seasoned OCaml programmers rarely use classes and objects, if at all.

Objects have some advantages over records: they don't require type definitions, and their support for row polymorphism makes them more flexible. However, the heavy syntax and additional runtime cost means that objects are rarely used in place of records.

The real benefits of objects come from the class system. Classes support inheritance and open recursion. Open recursion allows interdependent parts of an object to be defined separately. This works because calls between the methods of an object are determined when the object is instantiated, a form of *late* binding. This makes it possible (and necessary) for one method to refer to other methods in the object without knowing statically how they will be implemented.

In contrast, modules use early binding. If you want to parameterize your module code so that some part of it can be implemented later, you would write a function or functor. This is more explicit, but often more verbose than overriding a method in a class.

In general, a rule of thumb is: use classes and objects in situations where open recursion is a big win. Two good examples are Xavier Leroy's Cryptokit[1], which provides a variety of cryptographic primitives that can be combined in building-block style; and the Camlimages[2] library, which manipulates various graphical file formats. Camlimages also provides a module-based version of the same library, letting you choose between functional and object-oriented styles depending on your problem domain.

We'll introduce you to classes, and examples using open recursion, in Chapter 14 (Classes).

13.5   Subtyping

Subtyping is a central concept in object-oriented programming. It governs when an object with one type A can be used in an expression that expects an object of another type B. When this is true, we say that A is a *subtype* of B. More concretely, subtyping restricts when the coercion operator e :> t can be applied. This coercion works only if the type of e is a subtype of t.

---

[1] http://gallium.inria.fr/~xleroy/software.html#cryptokit
[2] http://cristal.inria.fr/camlimages/

13.5.1   Width Subtyping

To explore this, let's define some simple object types for geometric shapes. The generic type shape just has a method to compute the area.

```
# type shape = < area : float >;;
type shape = < area : float >
```

Now let's add a type representing a specific kind of shape, as well as a function for creating objects of that type.

```
# type square = < area : float; width : int >;;
type square = < area : float; width : int >
# let square w = object
     method area = Float.of_int (w * w)
     method width = w
   end;;
val square : int -> < area : float; width : int > = <fun>
```

A square has a method area just like a shape, and an additional method width. Still, we expect a square to be a shape, and it is. Note, however, that the coercion :> must be explicit:

```
# (square 10 : shape);;
Line 1, characters 2-11:
Error: This expression has type < area : float; width : int >
       but an expression was expected of type shape
       The second object type has no method width
# (square 10 :> shape);;
- : shape = <obj>
```

This form of object subtyping is called *width* subtyping. Width subtyping means that an object type *A* is a subtype of *B*, if *A* has all of the methods of *B*, and possibly more. A square is a subtype of shape because it implements all of the methods of shape, which in this case means the area method.

13.5.2   Depth Subtyping

We can also use *depth* subtyping with objects. Depth subtyping allows us to coerce an object if its individual methods could safely be coerced. So an object type < m: t1 > is a subtype of < m: t2 > if t1 is a subtype of t2.

First, let's add a new shape type, circle:

```
# type circle = < area : float; radius : int >;;
type circle = < area : float; radius : int >
# let circle r = object
     method area = 3.14 *. (Float.of_int r) **. 2.0
     method radius = r
   end;;
val circle : int -> < area : float; radius : int > = <fun>
```

Using that, let's create a couple of objects that each have a shape method, one returning a shape of type circle:

```
# let coin = object
    method shape = circle 5
    method color = "silver"
  end;;
val coin : < color : string; shape : < area : float; radius : int > >
    = <obj>
```

And the other returning a shape of type `square`:

```
# let map = object
    method shape = square 10
  end;;
val map : < shape : < area : float; width : int > > = <obj>
```

Both these objects have a shape method whose type is a subtype of the shape type, so they can both be coerced into the object type < shape : shape >:

```
# type item = < shape : shape >;;
type item = < shape : shape >
# let items = [ (coin :> item) ; (map :> item) ];;
val items : item list = [<obj>; <obj>]
```

Polymorphic Variant Subtyping

Subtyping can also be used to coerce a polymorphic variant into a larger polymorphic variant type. A polymorphic variant type *A* is a subtype of *B*, if the tags of *A* are a subset of the tags of *B*:

```
# type num = [ `Int of int | `Float of float ];;
type num = [ `Float of float | `Int of int ]
# type const = [ num | `String of string ];;
type const = [ `Float of float | `Int of int | `String of string ]
# let n : num = `Int 3;;
val n : num = `Int 3
# let c : const = (n :> const);;
val c : const = `Int 3
```

13.5.3   Variance

What about types built from object types? If a `square` is a `shape`, we expect a `square` `list` to be a `shape` `list`. OCaml does indeed allow such coercions:

```
# let squares: square list = [ square 10; square 20 ];;
val squares : square list = [<obj>; <obj>]
# let shapes: shape list = (squares :> shape list);;
val shapes : shape list = [<obj>; <obj>]
```

Note that this relies on lists being immutable. It would not be safe to treat a `square` `array` as a `shape` `array` because it would allow you to store non-square shapes into what should be an array of squares. OCaml recognizes this and does not allow the coercion:

```
# let square_array: square array = [| square 10; square 20 |];;
val square_array : square array = [|<obj>; <obj>|]
```

```
# let shape_array: shape array = (square_array :> shape array);;
Line 1, characters 32-61:
Error: Type square array is not a subtype of shape array
        The second object type has no method width
```

We say that 'a list is *covariant* (in 'a), while 'a array is *invariant*.

Subtyping function types requires a third class of variance. A function with type square -> string cannot be used with type shape -> string because it expects its argument to be a square and would not know what to do with a circle. However, a function with type shape -> string can safely be used with type square -> string:

```
# let shape_to_string: shape -> string =
    fun s -> Printf.sprintf "Shape(%F)" s#area;;
val shape_to_string : shape -> string = <fun>
# let square_to_string: square -> string =
    (shape_to_string :> square -> string);;
val square_to_string : square -> string = <fun>
```

We say that 'a -> string is *contravariant* in 'a. In general, function types are contravariant in their arguments and covariant in their results.

Variance Annotations

OCaml works out the variance of a type using that type's definition. Consider the following simple immutable Either type.

```
# module Either = struct
    type ('a, 'b) t =
      | Left of 'a
      | Right of 'b
    let left x = Left x
    let right x = Right x
  end;;
module Either :
  sig
    type ('a, 'b) t = Left of 'a | Right of 'b
    val left : 'a -> ('a, 'b) t
    val right : 'a -> ('b, 'a) t
  end
```

By looking at what coercions are allowed, we can see that the type parameters of the immutable Either type are covariant.

```
# let left_square = Either.left (square 40);;
val left_square : (< area : float; width : int >, 'a) Either.t =
  Either.Left <obj>
# (left_square :> (shape,_) Either.t);;
- : (shape, 'a) Either.t = Either.Left <obj>
```

The story is different, however, if the definition is hidden by a signature.

```
# module Abs_either : sig
    type ('a, 'b) t
    val left: 'a -> ('a, 'b) t
    val right: 'b -> ('a, 'b) t
  end = Either;;
module Abs_either :
```

```
sig
  type ('a, 'b) t
  val left : 'a -> ('a, 'b) t
  val right : 'b -> ('a, 'b) t
end
```

In this case, OCaml is forced to assume that the type is invariant.

```
# (Abs_either.left (square 40) :> (shape, _) Abs_either.t);;
Line 1, characters 2-29:
Error: This expression cannot be coerced to type (shape, 'b)
    Abs_either.t;
      it has type (< area : float; width : int >, 'a) Abs_either.t
      but is here used with type (shape, 'b) Abs_either.t
      Type < area : float; width : int > is not compatible with type
        shape = < area : float >
      The second object type has no method width
```

We can fix this by adding *variance annotations* to the type's parameters in the signature: + for covariance or - for contravariance:

```
# module Var_either : sig
    type (+'a, +'b) t
    val left: 'a -> ('a, 'b) t
    val right: 'b -> ('a, 'b) t
  end = Either;;
module Var_either :
  sig
    type (+'a, +'b) t
    val left : 'a -> ('a, 'b) t
    val right : 'b -> ('a, 'b) t
  end
```

As you can see, this now allows the coercion once again.

```
# (Var_either.left (square 40) :> (shape, _) Var_either.t);;
- : (shape, 'a) Var_either.t = <abstr>
```

For a more concrete example of variance, let's create some stacks containing shapes by applying our stack function to some squares and some circles:

```
# type 'a stack = < pop: 'a option; push: 'a -> unit >;;
type 'a stack = < pop : 'a option; push : 'a -> unit >
# let square_stack: square stack = stack [square 30; square 10];;
val square_stack : square stack = <obj>
# let circle_stack: circle stack = stack [circle 20; circle 40];;
val circle_stack : circle stack = <obj>
```

If we wanted to write a function that took a list of such stacks and found the total area of their shapes, we might try:

```
# let total_area (shape_stacks: shape stack list) =
    let stack_area acc st =
      let rec loop acc =
        match st#pop with
        | Some s -> loop (acc +. s#area)
        | None -> acc
      in
```

```
        loop acc
     in
  List.fold ~init:0.0 ~f:stack_area shape_stacks;;
val total_area : shape stack list -> float = <fun>
```

However, when we try to apply this function to our objects, we get an error:

```
# total_area [(square_stack :> shape stack); (circle_stack :> shape
    stack)];;
Line 1, characters 13-42:
Error: Type square stack = < pop : square option; push : square ->
    unit >
       is not a subtype of
         shape stack = < pop : shape option; push : shape -> unit >
       Type shape = < area : float > is not a subtype of
         square = < area : float; width : int >
       The first object type has no method width
```

As you can see, square stack and circle stack are not subtypes of shape stack. The problem is with the push method. For shape stack, the push method takes an arbitrary shape. So if we could coerce a square stack to a shape stack, then it would be possible to push an arbitrary shape onto square stack, which would be an error.

Another way of looking at this is that < push: 'a -> unit; .. > is contravariant in 'a, so < push: square -> unit; pop: square option > cannot be a subtype of < push: shape -> unit; pop: shape option >.

Still, the total_area function should be fine, in principle. It doesn't call push, so it isn't making that error. To make it work, we need to use a more precise type that indicates we are not going to be using the push method. We define a type readonly_stack and confirm that we can coerce the list of stacks to it:

```
# type 'a readonly_stack = < pop : 'a option >;;
type 'a readonly_stack = < pop : 'a option >
# let total_area (shape_stacks: shape readonly_stack list) =
    let stack_area acc st =
      let rec loop acc =
        match st#pop with
        | Some s -> loop (acc +. s#area)
        | None -> acc
      in
        loop acc
    in
  List.fold ~init:0.0 ~f:stack_area shape_stacks;;
val total_area : shape readonly_stack list -> float = <fun>
# total_area [(square_stack :> shape readonly_stack); (circle_stack :>
    shape readonly_stack)];;
- : float = 7280.
```

Aspects of this section may seem fairly complicated, but it should be pointed out that this typing *works*, and in the end, the type annotations are fairly minor. In most typed object-oriented languages, these coercions would simply not be possible. For example, in C++, a STL type list<T> is invariant in T, so it is simply not possible to use list<square> where list<shape> is expected (at least safely). The situation is similar in Java, although Java has an escape hatch that allows the program to fall back to dynamic typing. The situation in OCaml is much better: it works, it is statically checked, and the annotations are pretty simple.

13.5.4   Narrowing

Narrowing, also called *down casting*, is the ability to coerce an object to one of its subtypes. For example, if we have a list of shapes shape list, we might know (for some reason) what the actual type of each shape is. Perhaps we know that all objects in the list have type square. In this case, *narrowing* would allow the recasting of the object from type shape to type square. Many languages support narrowing through dynamic type checking. For example, in Java, a coercion (Square) x is allowed if the value x has type Square or one of its subtypes; otherwise the coercion throws an exception.

Narrowing is *not permitted* in OCaml. Period.

Why? There are two reasonable explanations, one based on a design principle, and another technical (the technical reason is simple: it is hard to implement).

The design argument is this: narrowing violates abstraction. In fact, with a structural typing system like in OCaml, narrowing would essentially provide the ability to enumerate the methods in an object. To check whether an object obj has some method foo : int, one would attempt a coercion (obj :> < foo : int >).

More pragmatically, narrowing leads to poor object-oriented style. Consider the following Java code, which returns the name of a shape object:

```
String GetShapeName(Shape s) {
  if (s instanceof Square) {
    return "Square";
  } else if (s instanceof Circle) {
    return "Circle";
  } else {
    return "Other";
  }
}
```

Most programmers would consider this code to be awkward, at the least. Instead of performing a case analysis on the type of object, it would be better to define a method to return the name of the shape. Instead of calling GetShapeName(s), we should call s.Name() instead.

However, the situation is not always so obvious. The following code checks whether an array of shapes looks like a barbell, composed of two Circle objects separated by a Line, where the circles have the same radius:

```
boolean IsBarbell(Shape[] s) {
  return s.length == 3 && (s[0] instanceof Circle) &&
    (s[1] instanceof Line) && (s[2] instanceof Circle) &&
      ((Circle) s[0]).radius() == ((Circle) s[2]).radius();
}
```

In this case, it is much less clear how to augment the Shape class to support this kind of pattern analysis. It is also not obvious that object-oriented programming is well-suited for this situation. Pattern matching seems like a better fit:

```
# type shape = Circle of { radius : int } | Line of { length: int };;
type shape = Circle of { radius : int; } | Line of { length : int; }
# let is_barbell = function
  | [Circle {radius=r1}; Line _; Circle {radius=r2}] when r1 = r2 ->
    true
  | _ -> false;;
val is_barbell : shape list -> bool = <fun>
```

Regardless, there is a solution if you find yourself in this situation, which is to augment the classes with variants. You can define a method `variant` that injects the actual object into a variant type.

```
# type shape = < variant : repr >
  and circle = < variant : repr; radius : int >
  and line = < variant : repr; length : int >
  and repr =
  | Circle of circle
  | Line of line;;
type shape = < variant : repr >
and circle = < radius : int; variant : repr >
and line = < length : int; variant : repr >
and repr = Circle of circle | Line of line
# let is_barbell = function
  | [s1; s2; s3] ->
    (match s1#variant, s2#variant, s3#variant with
      | Circle c1, Line _, Circle c2 when c1#radius = c2#radius ->
      true
      | _ -> false)
  | _ -> false;;
val is_barbell : < variant : repr; .. > list -> bool = <fun>
```

This pattern works, but it has drawbacks. In particular, the recursive type definition should make it clear that this pattern is essentially equivalent to using variants, and that objects do not provide much value here.

13.5.5   Subtyping Versus Row Polymorphism

There is considerable overlap between subtyping and row polymorphism. Both mechanisms allow you to write functions that can be applied to objects of different types. In these cases, row polymorphism is usually preferred over subtyping because it does not require explicit coercions, and it preserves more type information, allowing functions like the following:

```
# let remove_large l =
  List.filter ~f:(fun s -> Float.(s#area <= 100.)) l;;
val remove_large : (< area : float; .. > as 'a) list -> 'a list = <fun>
```

The return type of this function is built from the open object type of its argument, preserving any additional methods that it may have, as we can see below.

```
# let squares : < area : float; width : int > list =
  [square 5; square 15; square 10];;
val squares : < area : float; width : int > list = [<obj>; <obj>;
  <obj>]
```

```
# remove_large squares;;
- : < area : float; width : int > list = [<obj>; <obj>]
```

Writing a similar function with a closed type and applying it using subtyping does not preserve the methods of the argument: the returned object is only known to have an area method:

```
# let remove_large (l: < area : float > list) =
    List.filter ~f:(fun s -> Float.(s#area <= 100.)) l;;
val remove_large : < area : float > list -> < area : float > list =
    <fun>
# remove_large (squares :> < area : float > list );;
- : < area : float > list = [<obj>; <obj>]
```

There are some situations where we cannot use row polymorphism. In particular, row polymorphism cannot be used to place different types of objects in the same container. For example, lists of heterogeneous elements cannot be created using row polymorphism:

```
# let hlist: < area: float; ..> list = [square 10; circle 30];;
Line 1, characters 50-59:
Error: This expression has type < area : float; radius : int >
       but an expression was expected of type < area : float; width :
    int >
       The second object type has no method radius
```

Similarly, we cannot use row polymorphism to store different types of object in the same reference:

```
# let shape_ref: < area: float; ..> ref = ref (square 40);;
val shape_ref : < area : float; width : int > ref =
    {Base.Ref.contents = <obj>}
# shape_ref := circle 20;;
Line 1, characters 14-23:
Error: This expression has type < area : float; radius : int >
       but an expression was expected of type < area : float; width :
    int >
       The second object type has no method radius
```

In both these cases we must use subtyping:

```
# let hlist: shape list = [(square 10 :> shape); (circle 30 :>
    shape)];;
val hlist : shape list = [<obj>; <obj>]
# let shape_ref: shape ref = ref (square 40 :> shape);;
val shape_ref : shape ref = {Base.Ref.contents = <obj>}
# shape_ref := (circle 20 :> shape);;
- : unit = ()
```

14 Classes

This chapter was written by Leo White and Jason Hickey.

Programming with objects directly is great for encapsulation, but one of the main goals of object-oriented programming is code reuse through inheritance. For inheritance, we need to introduce *classes*. In object-oriented programming, a class is essentially a recipe for creating objects. The recipe can be changed by adding new methods and fields, or it can be changed by modifying existing methods.

14.1   OCaml Classes

In OCaml, class definitions must be defined as toplevel statements in a module. The syntax for a class definition uses the keyword `class`:

```
# open Base;;
# class istack = object
    val mutable v = [0; 2]

    method pop =
      match v with
      | hd :: tl ->
        v <- tl;
        Some hd
      | [] -> None

    method push hd =
      v <- hd :: v
  end;;
class istack :
  object
    val mutable v : int list
    method pop : int option
    method push : int -> unit
  end
```

The `class istack : object ... end` result shows that we have created a class `istack` with *class type* `object ... end`. Like module types, class types are completely separate from regular OCaml types (e.g., `int`, `string`, and `list`) and, in particular, should not be confused with object types (e.g., `< get : int; .. >`). The class type describes the class itself rather than the objects that the class creates. This particular

class type specifies that the istack class defines a mutable field v, a method pop that
returns an int option, and a method push with type int -> unit.

To produce an object, classes are instantiated with the keyword new:

```
# let s = new istack;;
val s : istack = <obj>
# s#pop;;
- : int option = Some 0
# s#push 5;;
- : unit = ()
# s#pop;;
- : int option = Some 5
```

You may have noticed that the object s has been given the type istack. But wait,
we've stressed *classes are not types*, so what's up with that? In fact, what we've said
is entirely true: classes and class names *are not* types. However, for convenience, the
definition of the class istack also defines an object type istack with the same methods
as the class. This type definition is equivalent to:

```
# type istack = < pop: int option; push: int -> unit >;;
type istack = < pop : int option; push : int -> unit >
```

Note that this type represents any object with these methods: objects created using
the istack class will have this type, but objects with this type may not have been
created by the istack class.

14.2   Class Parameters and Polymorphism

A class definition serves as the *constructor* for the class. In general, a class definition
may have parameters that must be provided as arguments when the object is created
with new.

Let's implement a variant of the istack class that can hold any values, not just
integers. When defining the class, the type parameters are placed in square brackets
before the class name in the class definition. We also add a parameter init for the
initial contents of the stack:

```
# class ['a] stack init = object
    val mutable v : 'a list = init

    method pop =
      match v with
      | hd :: tl ->
        v <- tl;
        Some hd
      | [] -> None

    method push hd =
      v <- hd :: v
  end;;
class ['a] stack :
  'a list ->
```

```
object
  val mutable v : 'a list
  method pop : 'a option
  method push : 'a -> unit
end
```

Note that the type parameter `['a]` in the definition uses square brackets, but for other uses of the type they are omitted (or replaced with parentheses if there is more than one type parameter).

The type annotation on the declaration of `v` is used to constrain type inference. If we omit this annotation, the type inferred for the class will be "too polymorphic": `init` could have some type `'b list`:

```
# class ['a] stack init = object
    val mutable v = init

    method pop =
      match v with
      | hd :: tl ->
        v <- tl;
        Some hd
      | [] -> None

    method push hd =
      v <- hd :: v
  end;;
Lines 1-13, characters 1-6:
Error: Some type variables are unbound in this type:
       class ['a] stack :
         'b list ->
         object
           val mutable v : 'b list
           method pop : 'b option
           method push : 'b -> unit
         end
       The method pop has type 'b option where 'b is unbound
```

In general, we need to provide enough constraints so that the compiler will infer the correct type. We can add type constraints to the parameters, to the fields, and to the methods. It is a matter of preference how many constraints to add. You can add type constraints in all three places, but the extra text may not help clarity. A convenient middle ground is to annotate the fields and/or class parameters, and add constraints to methods only if necessary.

14.3   Object Types as Interfaces

We may wish to traverse the elements on our stack. One common style for doing this in object-oriented languages is to define a class for an `iterator` object. An iterator provides a generic mechanism to inspect and traverse the elements of a collection.

There are two common styles for defining abstract interfaces like this. In Java, an iterator would normally be specified with an interface, which specifies a set of method types:

```
// Java-style iterator, specified as an interface.
interface <T> iterator {
  T Get();
  boolean HasValue();
  void Next();
};
```

In languages without interfaces, like C++, the specification would normally use *abstract* classes to specify the methods without implementing them (C++ uses the "= 0" definition to mean "not implemented"):

```
// Abstract class definition in C++.
template<typename T>
class Iterator {
 public:
  virtual ~Iterator() {}
  virtual T get() const = 0;
  virtual bool has_value() const = 0;
  virtual void next() = 0;
};
```

OCaml supports both styles. In fact, OCaml is more flexible than these approaches because an object type can be implemented by any object with the appropriate methods; it does not have to be specified by the object's class *a priori*. We'll leave abstract classes for later. Let's demonstrate the technique using object types.

First, we'll define an object type iterator that specifies the methods in an iterator:

```
# type 'a iterator = < get : 'a; has_value : bool; next : unit >;;
type 'a iterator = < get : 'a; has_value : bool; next : unit >
```

Next, we'll define an actual iterator for lists. We can use this to iterate over the contents of our stack:

```
# class ['a] list_iterator init = object
    val mutable current : 'a list = init

    method has_value = not (List.is_empty current)

    method get =
      match current with
      | hd :: tl -> hd
      | [] -> raise (Invalid_argument "no value")

    method next =
      match current with
      | hd :: tl -> current <- tl
      | [] -> raise (Invalid_argument "no value")
  end;;
class ['a] list_iterator :
  'a list ->
  object
    val mutable current : 'a list
    method get : 'a
```

```
    method has_value : bool
    method next : unit
  end
```

Finally, we add a method `iterator` to the `stack` class to produce an iterator. To do so, we construct a `list_iterator` that refers to the current contents of the stack:

```
# class ['a] stack init = object
    val mutable v : 'a list = init

    method pop =
      match v with
      | hd :: tl ->
        v <- tl;
        Some hd
      | [] -> None

    method push hd =
      v <- hd :: v

    method iterator : 'a iterator =
      new list_iterator v
  end;;
class ['a] stack :
  'a list ->
  object
    val mutable v : 'a list
    method iterator : 'a iterator
    method pop : 'a option
    method push : 'a -> unit
  end
```

Now we can build a new stack, push some values to it, and iterate over them:

```
# let s = new stack [];;
val s : '_weak1 stack = <obj>
# s#push 5;;
- : unit = ()
# s#push 4;;
- : unit = ()
# let it = s#iterator;;
val it : int iterator = <obj>
# it#get;;
- : int = 4
# it#next;;
- : unit = ()
# it#get;;
- : int = 5
# it#next;;
- : unit = ()
# it#has_value;;
- : bool = false
```

14.3.1   Functional Iterators

In practice, most OCaml programmers avoid iterator objects in favor of functional-style techniques. For example, the alternative `stack` class that follows takes a function `f` and applies it to each of the elements on the stack:

```
# class ['a] stack init = object
    val mutable v : 'a list = init

    method pop =
      match v with
      | hd :: tl ->
        v <- tl;
        Some hd
      | [] -> None

    method push hd =
      v <- hd :: v

    method iter f =
      List.iter ~f v
  end;;
class ['a] stack :
  'a list ->
  object
    val mutable v : 'a list
    method iter : ('a -> unit) -> unit
    method pop : 'a option
    method push : 'a -> unit
  end
```

What about functional operations like `map` and `fold`? In general, these methods take a function that produces a value of some other type than the elements of the set.

For example, a fold method for our `['a] stack` class should have type `('b -> 'a -> 'b) -> 'b -> 'b`, where the `'b` is polymorphic. To express a polymorphic method type like this, we must use a type quantifier, as shown in the following example:

```
# class ['a] stack init = object
    val mutable v : 'a list = init

    method pop =
      match v with
      | hd :: tl ->
        v <- tl;
        Some hd
      | [] -> None

    method push hd =
      v <- hd :: v

    method fold : 'b. ('b -> 'a -> 'b) -> 'b -> 'b =
      (fun f init -> List.fold ~f ~init v)
  end;;
class ['a] stack :
  'a list ->
  object
```

```
      val mutable v : 'a list
      method fold : ('b -> 'a -> 'b) -> 'b -> 'b
      method pop : 'a option
      method push : 'a -> unit
    end
```

The type quantifier `'b.` can be read as "for all `'b`." Type quantifiers can only be used *directly after* the method name, which means that method parameters must be expressed using a fun or function expression.

14.4   Inheritance

Inheritance uses an existing class to define a new one. For example, the following class definition inherits from our `stack` class for strings and adds a new method `print` that prints all the strings on the stack:

```
# class sstack init = object
    inherit [string] stack init

    method print =
        List.iter ~f:Stdio.print_endline v
  end;;
class sstack :
  string list ->
  object
    val mutable v : string list
    method pop : string option
    method print : unit
    method push : string -> unit
  end
```

A class can override methods from classes it inherits. For example, this class creates stacks of integers that double the integers before they are pushed onto the stack:

```
# class double_stack init = object
    inherit [int] stack init as super

    method push hd =
        super#push (hd * 2)
  end;;
class double_stack :
  int list ->
  object
    val mutable v : int list
    method pop : int option
    method push : int -> unit
  end
```

The preceding as super statement creates a special object called super which can be used to call superclass methods. Note that super is not a real object and can only be used to call methods.

14.5   Class Types

To allow code in a different file or module to inherit from a class, we must expose it and give it a class type. What is the class type?

As an example, let's wrap up our `stack` class in an explicit module (we'll use explicit modules for illustration, but the process is similar when we want to define a `.mli` file). In keeping with the usual style for modules, we define a type `'a t` to represent the type of our stacks:

```
module Stack = struct
  class ['a] stack init = object
    ...
  end

  type 'a t = 'a stack

  let make init = new stack init
end
```

We have multiple choices in defining the module type, depending on how much of the implementation we want to expose. At one extreme, a maximally abstract signature would completely hide the class definitions:

```
module AbstractStack : sig
  type 'a t = < pop: 'a option; push: 'a -> unit >

  val make : 'a list -> 'a t
end = Stack
```

The abstract signature is simple because we ignore the classes. But what if we want to include them in the signature so that other modules can inherit from the class definitions? For this, we need to specify types for the classes, called *class types*.

Class types do not appear in mainstream object-oriented programming languages, so you may not be familiar with them, but the concept is pretty simple. A class type specifies the type of each of the visible parts of the class, including both fields and methods. Just as with module types, you don't have to give a type for everything; anything you omit will be hidden:

```
module VisibleStack : sig

  type 'a t = < pop: 'a option; push: 'a -> unit >

  class ['a] stack : object
    val mutable v : 'a list
    method pop : 'a option
    method push : 'a -> unit
  end

  val make : 'a list -> 'a t
end = Stack
```

In this signature, we've chosen to make everything visible. The class type for `stack` specifies the types of the field `v`, as well as the types of each of the methods.

14.6   Open Recursion

Open recursion allows an object's methods to invoke other methods on the same object. These calls are looked up dynamically, allowing a method in one class to call a method from another class, if both classes are inherited by the same object. This allows mutually recursive parts of an object to be defined separately.

This ability to define mutually recursive methods from separate components is a key feature of classes: achieving similar functionality with data types or modules is much more cumbersome and verbose.

For example, consider writing recursive functions over a simple document format. This format is represented as a tree with three different types of node:

```
type doc =
  | Heading of string
  | Paragraph of text_item list
  | Definition of string list_item list

and text_item =
  | Raw of string
  | Bold of text_item list
  | Enumerate of int list_item list
  | Quote of doc

and 'a list_item =
  { tag: 'a;
    text: text_item list }
```

It is quite easy to write a function that operates by recursively traversing this data. However, what if you need to write many similar recursive functions? How can you factor out the common parts of these functions to avoid repetitive boilerplate?

The simplest way is to use classes and open recursion. For example, the following class defines objects that fold over the document data:

```
class ['a] folder = object(self)
  method doc acc = function
  | Heading _ -> acc
  | Paragraph text -> List.fold ~f:self#text_item ~init:acc text
  | Definition list -> List.fold ~f:self#list_item ~init:acc list

  method list_item: 'b. 'a -> 'b list_item -> 'a =
    fun acc {tag; text} ->
      List.fold ~f:self#text_item ~init:acc text

  method text_item acc = function
  | Raw _ -> acc
  | Bold text -> List.fold ~f:self#text_item ~init:acc text
  | Enumerate list -> List.fold ~f:self#list_item ~init:acc list
  | Quote doc -> self#doc acc doc
end
```

The `object (self)` syntax binds `self` to the current object, allowing the `doc`, `list_item`, and `text_item` methods to call each other.

By inheriting from this class, we can create functions that fold over the document data. For example, the `count_doc` function counts the number of bold tags in the document that are not within a list:

```
class counter = object
  inherit [int] folder as super

  method list_item acc li = acc

  method text_item acc ti =
    let acc = super#text_item acc ti in
    match ti with
    | Bold _ -> acc + 1
    | _ -> acc
end

let count_doc = (new counter)#doc
```

Note how the super special object is used in `text_item` to call the `[int]` folder class's `text_item` method to fold over the children of the `text_item` node.

14.7   Private Methods

Methods can be declared *private*, which means that they may be called by subclasses, but they are not visible otherwise (similar to a *protected* method in C++).

For example, we may want to include methods in our `folder` class for handling each of the different cases in doc and `text_item`. However, we may not want to force subclasses of `folder` to expose these methods, as they probably shouldn't be called directly:

```
class ['a] folder2 = object(self)
  method doc acc = function
  | Heading str -> self#heading acc str
  | Paragraph text -> self#paragraph acc text
  | Definition list -> self#definition acc list

  method list_item: 'b. 'a -> 'b list_item -> 'a =
    fun acc {tag; text} ->
      List.fold ~f:self#text_item ~init:acc text

  method text_item acc = function
  | Raw str -> self#raw acc str
  | Bold text -> self#bold acc text
  | Enumerate list -> self#enumerate acc list
  | Quote doc -> self#quote acc doc

  method private heading acc str = acc
  method private paragraph acc text =
    List.fold ~f:self#text_item ~init:acc text
  method private definition acc list =
    List.fold ~f:self#list_item ~init:acc list

  method private raw acc str = acc
  method private bold acc text =
```

```
      List.fold ~f:self#text_item ~init:acc text
   method private enumerate acc list =
      List.fold ~f:self#list_item ~init:acc list
   method private quote acc doc = self#doc acc doc
end

let f :
   < doc : int -> doc -> int;
     list_item : 'a . int -> 'a list_item -> int;
     text_item : int -> text_item -> int >  = new folder2
```

The final statement that builds the value f shows how the instantiation of a folder2 object has a type that hides the private methods.

To be precise, the private methods are part of the class type, but not part of the object type. This means, for example, that the object f has no method bold. However, the private methods are available to subclasses: we can use them to simplify our counter class:

```
class counter_with_private_method = object
   inherit [int] folder2 as super

   method list_item acc li = acc

   method private bold acc txt =
      let acc = super#bold acc txt in
      acc + 1
end
```

The key property of private methods is that they are visible to subclasses, but not anywhere else. If you want the stronger guarantee that a method is *really* private, not even accessible in subclasses, you can use an explicit class type that omits the method. In the following code, the private methods are explicitly omitted from the class type of counter_with_sig and can't be invoked in subclasses of counter_with_sig:

```
class counter_with_sig : object
   method doc : int -> doc -> int
   method list_item : int -> 'b list_item -> int
   method text_item : int -> text_item -> int
end = object
   inherit [int] folder2 as super

   method list_item acc li = acc

   method private bold acc txt =
      let acc = super#bold acc txt in
      acc + 1
end
```

14.8   Binary Methods

A *binary method* is a method that takes an object of self type. One common example is defining a method for equality:

```
# class square w = object(self : 'self)
    method width = w
    method area = Float.of_int (self#width * self#width)
    method equals (other : 'self) = other#width = self#width
  end;;
class square :
  int ->
  object ('a)
    method area : float
    method equals : 'a -> bool
    method width : int
  end
# class circle r = object(self : 'self)
    method radius = r
    method area = 3.14 *. (Float.of_int self#radius) **. 2.0
    method equals (other : 'self) = other#radius = self#radius
  end;;
class circle :
  int ->
  object ('a)
    method area : float
    method equals : 'a -> bool
    method radius : int
  end
```

Note how we can use the type annotation (self: 'self) to obtain the type of the current object.

We can now test different object instances for equality by using the equals binary method:

```
# (new square 5)#equals (new square 5);;
- : bool = true
# (new circle 10)#equals (new circle 7);;
- : bool = false
```

This works, but there is a problem lurking here. The method equals takes an object of the exact type square or circle. Because of this, we can't define a common base class shape that also includes an equality method:

```
# type shape = < equals : shape -> bool; area : float >;;
type shape = < area : float; equals : shape -> bool >
# (new square 5 :> shape);;
Line 1, characters 1-24:
Error: Type square = < area : float; equals : square -> bool; width :
       int >
         is not a subtype of shape = < area : float; equals : shape ->
       bool >
       Type shape = < area : float; equals : shape -> bool >
       is not a subtype of
         square = < area : float; equals : square -> bool; width :
       int >
         The first object type has no method width
```

The problem is that a square expects to be compared with a square, not an arbitrary shape; likewise for circle. This problem is fundamental. Many languages solve it either with narrowing (with dynamic type checking), or by method overloading. Since OCaml has neither of these, what can we do?

Since the problematic method is equality, one proposal we could consider is to just drop it from the base type shape and use polymorphic equality instead. However, the built-in polymorphic equality has very poor behavior when applied to objects:

```
# Poly.(=)
    (object method area = 5 end)
    (object method area = 5 end);;
- : bool = false
```

The problem here is that two objects are considered equal by the built-in polymorphic equality if and only if they are physically equal. There are other reasons not to use the built-in polymorphic equality, but these false negatives are a showstopper.

If we want to define equality for shapes in general, the remaining solution is to use the same approach as we described for narrowing. That is, introduce a *representation* type implemented using variants, and implement the comparison based on the representation type:

```
# type shape_repr =
    | Square of int
    | Circle of int;;
type shape_repr = Square of int | Circle of int
# type shape =
  < repr : shape_repr; equals : shape -> bool; area : float >;;
type shape = < area : float; equals : shape -> bool; repr :
    shape_repr >
# class square w = object(self)
      method width = w
      method area = Float.of_int (self#width * self#width)
      method repr = Square self#width
      method equals (other : shape) =
        match (self#repr, other#repr) with
        | Square x, Square x' -> Int.(=) x x'
        | _ -> false
  end;;
class square :
  int ->
  object
    method area : float
    method equals : shape -> bool
    method repr : shape_repr
    method width : int
  end
```

The binary method equals is now implemented in terms of the concrete type shape_repr. When using this pattern, you will not be able to hide the repr method, but you can hide the type definition using the module system:

```
module Shapes : sig
  type shape_repr
  type shape =
    < repr : shape_repr; equals : shape -> bool; area: float >

  class square : int ->
```

```
      object
        method width : int
        method area : float
        method repr : shape_repr
        method equals : shape -> bool
      end
  end = struct
    type shape_repr =
    | Square of int
    | Circle of int
    ...
  end
```

Note that this solution prevents us from adding new kinds of shapes without adding new constructors to the shape_repr type, which is quite restrictive. We can fix this, however, by using OCaml's rarely-used but still useful *extensible variants*.

Extensible variants let you separate the definition of a variant type from the definition of its constructors. The resulting type is by definition open, in the sense that new variants can always be added. As a result, the compiler can't check whether pattern matching on such a variant is exhaustive. Happily, exhaustivity is not what we need here.

Here's how we'd rewrite the above example with extensible variants.

```
# type shape_repr = ..;;
type shape_repr = ..
# type shape =
    < repr : shape_repr; equals : shape -> bool; area : float >;;
type shape = < area : float; equals : shape -> bool; repr :
      shape_repr >
# type shape_repr += Square of int;;
type shape_repr += Square of int
# class square w = object(self)
      method width = w
      method area = Float.of_int (self#width * self#width)
      method repr = Square self#width
      method equals (other : shape) =
          match (self#repr, other#repr) with
          | Square x, Square x' -> Int.(=) x x'
          | _ -> false
    end;;
class square :
  int ->
  object
    method area : float
    method equals : shape -> bool
    method repr : shape_repr
    method width : int
  end
```

One oddity of the representation type approach is that the objects created by these classes are in one-to-one correspondence with members of the representation type, making the objects seem somewhat redundant.

But equality is an extreme instance of a binary method: it needs access to all the information of the other object. Many other binary methods need only partial information about the object. For instance, consider a method that compares shapes by their sizes:

```
# class square w = object(self)
    method width = w
    method area = Float.of_int (self#width * self#width)
    method larger (other : shape) = Float.(self#area > other#area)
  end;;
class square :
  int ->
  object
    method area : float
    method larger : shape -> bool
    method width : int
  end
```

The `larger` method can be used on a `square`, but it can also be applied to any object of type `shape`.

14.9   Virtual Classes and Methods

A *virtual* class is a class where some methods or fields are declared but not implemented. This should not be confused with the word `virtual` as it is used in C++. A virtual method in C++ uses dynamic dispatch, while regular, nonvirtual methods are statically dispatched. In OCaml, *all* methods use dynamic dispatch, but the keyword `virtual` means that the method or field is not implemented. A class containing virtual methods must also be flagged `virtual` and cannot be directly instantiated (i.e., no object of this class can be created).

To explore this, let's extend our shapes examples to simple, interactive graphics. We will use the Async concurrency library and the Async_graphics [1] library, which provides an asynchronous interface to OCaml's built-in Graphics library. Concurrent programming with Async will be explored later in Chapter 17 (Concurrent Programming with Async); for now you can safely ignore the details. You just need to run `opam install async_graphics` to get the library installed on your system.

We will give each shape a `draw` method that describes how to draw the shape on the `Async_graphics` display:

```
open Core
open Async
open Async_graphics

type drawable = < draw: unit >
```

14.9.1   Create Some Simple Shapes

Now let's add classes for making squares and circles. We include an `on_click` method for adding event handlers to the shapes:

[1] http://github.com/lpw25/async_graphics/

```
class square w x y = object(self)
  val mutable x: int = x
  method x = x

  val mutable y: int = y
  method y = y

  val mutable width = w
  method width = width

  method draw = fill_rect x y width width

  method private contains x' y' =
    x <= x' && x' <= x + width &&
      y <= y' && y' <= y + width

  method on_click ?start ?stop f =
    on_click ?start ?stop
      (fun ev ->
          if self#contains ev.mouse_x ev.mouse_y then
            f ev.mouse_x ev.mouse_y)
end
```

The square class is pretty straightforward, and the circle class below also looks very similar:

```
class circle r x y = object(self)
  val mutable x: int = x
  method x = x

  val mutable y: int = y
  method y = y

  val mutable radius = r
  method radius = radius

  method draw = fill_circle x y radius

  method private contains x' y' =
    let dx = x' - x in
    let dy = y' - y in
      dx * dx + dy * dy <= radius * radius

  method on_click ?start ?stop f =
    on_click ?start ?stop
      (fun ev ->
          if self#contains ev.mouse_x ev.mouse_y then
            f ev.mouse_x ev.mouse_y)
end
```

These classes have a lot in common, and it would be useful to factor out this common functionality into a superclass. We can easily move the definitions of x and y into a superclass, but what about on_click? Its definition depends on contains, which has a different definition in each class. The solution is to create a *virtual* class. This class will declare a contains method but leave its definition to the subclasses.

Here is the more succinct definition, starting with a virtual shape class that implements on_click and on_mousedown:

```
class virtual shape x y = object(self)
  method virtual private contains: int -> int -> bool

  val mutable x: int = x
  method x = x

  val mutable y: int = y
  method y = y

  method on_click ?start ?stop f =
    on_click ?start ?stop
      (fun ev ->
         if self#contains ev.mouse_x ev.mouse_y then
           f ev.mouse_x ev.mouse_y)

  method on_mousedown ?start ?stop f =
    on_mousedown ?start ?stop
      (fun ev ->
         if self#contains ev.mouse_x ev.mouse_y then
           f ev.mouse_x ev.mouse_y)
end
```

Now we can define square and circle by inheriting from shape:

```
class square w x y = object
  inherit shape x y

  val mutable width = w
  method width = width

  method draw = fill_rect x y width width

  method private contains x' y' =
    x <= x' && x' <= x + width &&
    y <= y' && y' <= y + width
end

class circle r x y = object
  inherit shape x y

  val mutable radius = r
  method radius = radius

  method draw = fill_circle x y radius

  method private contains x' y' =
    let dx = x' - x in
    let dy = y' - y in
      dx * dx + dy * dy <= radius * radius
end
```

One way to view a virtual class is that it is like a functor, where the "inputs" are the declared—but not defined—virtual methods and fields. The functor application is implemented through inheritance, when virtual methods are given concrete implementations.

14.10   Initializers

You can execute expressions during the instantiation of a class by placing them before the object expression or in the initial value of a field:

```
# class obj x =
    let () = Stdio.printf "Creating obj %d\n" x in
    object
      val field = Stdio.printf "Initializing field\n"; x
  end;;
class obj : int -> object val field : int end
# let o = new obj 3;;
Creating obj 3
Initializing field
val o : obj = <obj>
```

However, these expressions are executed before the object has been created and cannot refer to the methods of the object. If you need to use an object's methods during instantiation, you can use an initializer. An initializer is an expression that will be executed during instantiation but after the object has been created.

For example, suppose we wanted to extend our previous shapes module with a growing_circle class for circles that expand when clicked. We could inherit from circle and use the inherited on_click to add a handler for click events:

```
class growing_circle r x y = object(self)
  inherit circle r x y

  initializer
    self#on_click (fun _x _y -> radius <- radius * 2)
end
```

14.11   Multiple Inheritance

When a class inherits from more than one superclass, it is using *multiple inheritance*. Multiple inheritance extends the variety of ways that classes can be combined, and it can be quite useful, particularly with virtual classes. However, it can be tricky to use, particularly when the inheritance hierarchy is a graph rather than a tree, so it should be used with care.

14.11.1   How Names Are Resolved

The main trickiness of multiple inheritance is due to naming—what happens when a method or field with some name is defined in more than one class?

If there is one thing to remember about inheritance in OCaml, it is this: inheritance is like textual inclusion. If there is more than one definition for a name, the last definition wins.

For example, consider this class, which inherits from square and defines a new draw method that uses draw_rect instead of fill_rect to draw the square:

```
class square_outline w x y = object
  inherit square w x y
  method draw = draw_rect x y width width
end
```

Since the inherit declaration comes before the method definition, the new draw method overrides the old one, and the square is drawn using draw_rect. But, what if we had defined square_outline as follows?

```
class square_outline w x y = object
  method draw = draw_rect x y w w
  inherit square w x y
end
```

Here the inherit declaration comes after the method definition, so the draw method from square will override the other definition, and the square will be drawn using fill_rect.

To reiterate, to understand what inheritance means, replace each inherit directive with its definition, and take the last definition of each method or field. Note that the methods and fields added by an inheritance are those listed in its class type, so private methods that are hidden by the type will not be included.

14.11.2   Mixins

When should you use multiple inheritance? If you ask multiple people, you're likely to get multiple (perhaps heated) answers. Some will argue that multiple inheritance is overly complicated; others will argue that inheritance is problematic in general, and one should use object composition instead. But regardless of who you talk to, you will rarely hear that multiple inheritance is great and that you should use it widely.

In any case, if you're programming with objects, there's one general pattern for multiple inheritance that is both useful and reasonably simple: the *mixin* pattern. Generically, a *mixin* is just a virtual class that implements a feature based on another one. If you have a class that implements methods *A*, and you have a mixin *M* that provides methods *B* from *A*, then you can inherit from *M*—"mixing" it in—to get features *B*.

That's too abstract, so let's give some examples based on our interactive shapes. We may wish to allow a shape to be dragged by the mouse. We can define this functionality for any object that has mutable x and y fields and an on_mousedown method for adding event handlers:

```
class virtual draggable = object(self)
  method virtual on_mousedown:
    ?start:unit Deferred.t ->
    ?stop:unit Deferred.t ->
```

```
      (int -> int -> unit) -> unit
  val virtual mutable x: int
  val virtual mutable y: int

  val mutable dragging = false
  method dragging = dragging

  initializer
    self#on_mousedown
      (fun mouse_x mouse_y ->
          let offset_x = x - mouse_x in
          let offset_y = y - mouse_y in
          let mouse_up = Ivar.create () in
          let stop = Ivar.read mouse_up in
          dragging <- true;
          on_mouseup ~stop
            (fun _ ->
                Ivar.fill mouse_up ();
                dragging <- false);
          on_mousemove ~stop
            (fun ev ->
                x <- ev.mouse_x + offset_x;
                y <- ev.mouse_y + offset_y))
end
```

This allows us to create draggable shapes using multiple inheritance:

```
class small_square = object
  inherit square 20 40 40
  inherit draggable
end
```

We can also use mixins to create animated shapes. Each animated shape has a list of update functions to be called during animation. We create an `animated` mixin to provide this update list and ensure that the functions in it are called at regular intervals when the shape is animated:

```
class virtual animated span = object(self)
  method virtual on_click:
    ?start:unit Deferred.t ->
    ?stop:unit Deferred.t ->
    (int -> int -> unit) -> unit
  val mutable updates: (int -> unit) list = []
  val mutable step = 0
  val mutable running = false

  method running = running

  method animate =
    step <- 0;
    running <- true;
    let stop =
      Clock.after span
      >>| fun () -> running <- false
    in
    Clock.every ~stop (Time.Span.of_sec (1.0 /. 24.0))
      (fun () ->
```

```
             step <- step + 1;
             List.iter ~f:(fun f -> f step) updates
        )

   initializer
      self#on_click (fun _x _y -> if not self#running then self#animate)
   end
```

We use initializers to add functions to this update list. For example, this class will produce circles that move to the right for a second when clicked:

```
class my_circle = object
   inherit circle 20 50 50
   inherit animated Time.Span.second
   initializer updates <- [fun _ -> x <- x + 5]
end
```

These initializers can also be added using mixins:

```
class virtual linear x' y' = object
   val virtual mutable updates: (int -> unit) list
   val virtual mutable x: int
   val virtual mutable y: int

   initializer
     let update _ =
       x <- x + x';
       y <- y + y'
     in
     updates <- update :: updates
end

let pi = (Float.atan 1.0) *. 4.0

class virtual harmonic offset x' y' = object
   val virtual mutable updates: (int -> unit) list
   val virtual mutable x: int
   val virtual mutable y: int

   initializer
     let update step =
       let m = Float.sin (offset +. ((Float.of_int step) *. (pi /.
       64.))) in
         let x' = Float.to_int (m *. Float.of_int x') in
         let y' = Float.to_int (m *. Float.of_int y') in
         x <- x + x';
         y <- y + y'
     in
     updates <- update :: updates
end
```

Since the linear and harmonic mixins are only used for their side effects, they can be inherited multiple times within the same object to produce a variety of different animations:

```
class my_square x y = object
   inherit square 40 x y
```

```
    inherit draggable
    inherit animated (Time.Span.of_int_sec 5)
    inherit linear 5 0
    inherit harmonic 0.0 7 ~-10
end

let my_circle = object
    inherit circle 30 250 250
    inherit animated (Time.Span.minute)
    inherit harmonic 0.0 10 0
    inherit harmonic (pi /. 2.0) 0 10
end
```

14.11.3   Displaying the Animated Shapes

We finish our shapes module by creating a main function to draw some shapes on the graphical display and running that function using the Async scheduler:

```
let main () =
  let shapes = [
      (my_circle :> drawable);
      (new my_square 50 350 :> drawable);
      (new my_square 50 200 :> drawable);
      (new growing_circle 20 70 70 :> drawable);
  ] in
  let repaint () =
    clear_graph ();
    List.iter ~f:(fun s -> s#draw) shapes;
    synchronize ()
  in
    open_graph "";
    auto_synchronize false;
    Clock.every (Time.Span.of_sec (1.0 /. 24.0)) repaint

let () = never_returns (Scheduler.go_main ~main ())
```

Our main function creates a list of shapes to be displayed and defines a repaint function that actually draws them on the display. We then open a graphical display and ask Async to run repaint at regular intervals.

Finally, build the binary by linking against the async_graphics package, which will pull in all the other dependencies:

```
(executable
  (name      shapes)
  (modules   shapes)
  (libraries async_graphics))
```

```
$ dune build shapes.exe
```

When you run the binary, a new graphical window should appear (on macOS, you will need to install the X11 package first, which you will be prompted for). Try clicking on the various widgets, and gasp in awe at the sophisticated animations that unfold as a result.

The graphics library described here is the one built into OCaml and is more useful as a learning tool than anything else. There are several third-party libraries that provide more sophisticated bindings to various graphics subsystems:

Lablgtk[2] A strongly typed interface to the GTK widget library.

LablGL[3] An interface between OCaml and OpenGL, a widely supported standard for 3D rendering.

js_of_ocaml[4] Compiles OCaml code to JavaScript and has bindings to WebGL. This is the emerging standard for 3D rendering in web browsers.

Part II

Tools and Techniques

Part II builds on the basics by working through useful tools and techniques for addressing common practical applications, from command-line parsing to asynchronous network programming. Along the way, you'll see how some of the concepts from Part I are glued together into real libraries and tools that combine different features of the language to good effect.

15 Maps and Hash Tables

Lots of programming problems require dealing with data organized as key/value pairs. Maybe the simplest way of representing such data in OCaml is an *association list*, which is simply a list of pairs of keys and values. For example, you could represent a mapping between the 10 digits and their English names as follows:

```
# open Base;;
# let digit_alist =
    [ 0, "zero"; 1, "one"; 2, "two"  ; 3, "three"; 4, "four"
    ; 5, "five"; 6, "six"; 7, "seven"; 8, "eight"; 9, "nine" ];;
val digit_alist : (int * string) list =
    [(0, "zero"); (1, "one"); (2, "two"); (3, "three"); (4, "four");
     (5, "five"); (6, "six"); (7, "seven"); (8, "eight"); (9, "nine")]
```

We can use functions from the List.Assoc module to manipulate this data:

```
# List.Assoc.find ~equal:Int.equal digit_alist 6;;
- : string option = Some "six"
# List.Assoc.find ~equal:Int.equal digit_alist 22;;
- : string option = None
# List.Assoc.add ~equal:Int.equal digit_alist 0 "zilch";;
- : (int, string) Base.List.Assoc.t =
[(0, "zilch"); (1, "one"); (2, "two"); (3, "three"); (4, "four");
 (5, "five"); (6, "six"); (7, "seven"); (8, "eight"); (9, "nine")]
```

Association lists are simple and easy to use, but their performance is not ideal, since almost every nontrivial operation on an association list requires a linear-time scan of the list.

In this chapter, we'll talk about two more efficient alternatives to association lists: *maps* and *hash tables*. A map is an immutable tree-based data structure where most operations take time logarithmic in the size of the map, whereas a hash table is a mutable data structure where most operations have constant time complexity. We'll describe both of these data structures in detail and provide some advice as to how to choose between them.

15.1   Maps

Let's consider an example of how one might use a map in practice. In Chapter 5 (Files, Modules, and Programs), we showed a module Counter for keeping frequency counts on a set of strings. Here's the interface:

```
open Base

(** A collection of string frequency counts *)
type t

(** The empty set of frequency counts *)
val empty : t

(** Bump the frequency count for the given string. *)
val touch : t -> string -> t

(** Converts the set of frequency counts to an association list. Every
      string in the list will show up at most once, and the integers
      will be at least 1. *)
val to_list : t -> (string * int) list
```

The intended behavior here is straightforward. Counter.empty represents an empty collection of frequency counts; touch increments the frequency count of the specified string by 1; and to_list returns the list of nonzero frequencies.

Here's the implementation.

```
open Base

type t = (string, int, String.comparator_witness) Map.t

let empty = Map.empty (module String)
let to_list t = Map.to_alist t

let touch t s =
  let count =
    match Map.find t s with
    | None -> 0
    | Some x -> x
  in
  Map.set t ~key:s ~data:(count + 1)
```

Take a look at the definition of the type t above. You'll see that the Map.t has three type parameters. The first two are what you might expect; one for the type of the key, and one for the type of the data. The third type parameter, the *comparator witness*, requires some explaining.

The comparator witness is used to indicate which comparison function was used to construct the map, rather than saying something about the type of data stored in the map. The type String.comparator_witness in particular indicates that this map was built with the default comparison function from the String module. We'll talk about why the comparator witness is important later in the chapter.

The call to Map.empty is also worth explaining, in that, unusually, it takes a first-class module as an argument. The point of the first class module is to provide the comparison function that is required for building the map, along with an s-expression converter for generating useful error messages (we'll talk more about s-expressions in Chapter 21 (Data Serialization with S-Expressions)). We don't need to provide the module again for functions like Map.find or Map.add, because the map itself contains a reference to the comparison function it uses.

Not every module can be used for creating maps, but the standard ones in Base can. Later in the chapter, we'll show how you can set up a module of your own so it can be used in this way.

15.1.1 Sets

In addition to maps, Base also provides a set data type that's designed along similar lines. In some sense, sets are little more than maps where you ignore the data. But while you could encode sets in terms of maps, it's more natural, and more efficient, to use Base's specialized set type. Here's a simple example.

```
# Set.of_list (module Int) [1;2;3] |> Set.to_list;;
- : int list = [1; 2; 3]
# Set.union
    (Set.of_list (module Int) [1;2;3;2])
    (Set.of_list (module Int) [3;5;1])
  |> Set.to_list;;
- : int list = [1; 2; 3; 5]
```

In addition to the operators you would expect to have for maps, sets support the traditional set operations, including union, intersection, and set difference.

15.1.2 Modules and Comparators

It's easy enough to create a map or set based on a type represented by a module in Base. Here, we'll create a map from digits to their English names, based on digit_alist, which was defined earlier in the chapter.

```
# let digit_map = Map.of_alist_exn (module Int) digit_alist;;
val digit_map : (int, string, Int.comparator_witness) Map.t = <abstr>
# Map.find digit_map 3;;
- : string option = Some "three"
```

The function Map.of_alist_exn constructs a map from a provided association list, throwing an exception if a key is used more than once. Let's take a look at the type signature of Map.of_alist_exn.

```
# #show Map.of_alist_exn;;
val of_alist_exn :
  ('a, 'cmp) Map.comparator -> ('a * 'b) list -> ('a, 'b, 'cmp) Map.t
```

The type Map.comparator is actually an alias for a first-class module type, representing any module that matches the signature Comparator.S, shown below.

```
# #show Base.Comparator.S;;
module type S =
  sig
    type t
    type comparator_witness
    val comparator : (t, comparator_witness) Comparator.t
  end
```

Such a module must contain the type of the key itself, as well as the `comparator_witness` type, which serves as a type-level identifier of the comparison function in question, and finally, the concrete comparator itself, a value that contains the necessary comparison function.

Modules from `Base` like `Int` and `String` already satisfy this interface. But what if you want to satisfy this interface with a new module? Consider, for example, the following type representing a book, for which we've written a comparison function and an s-expression serializer.

```
# module Book = struct

    type t = { title: string; isbn: string }

    let compare t1 t2 =
      let cmp_title = String.compare t1.title t2.title in
      if cmp_title <> 0 then cmp_title
      else String.compare t1.isbn t2.isbn

    let sexp_of_t t : Sexp.t =
      List [ Atom t.title; Atom t.isbn ]
  end;;
module Book :
  sig
    type t = { title : string; isbn : string; }
    val compare : t -> t -> int
    val sexp_of_t : t -> Sexp.t
  end
```

This module has the basic functionality we need, but doesn't satisfy the `Comparator.S` interface, so we can't use it for creating a map, as you can see.

```
# Map.empty (module Book);;
Line 1, characters 19-23:
Error: Signature mismatch:
       ...
       The type `comparator_witness' is required but not provided
       File "duniverse/base/src/comparator.mli", line 19, characters
  2-25:
         Expected declaration
       The value `comparator' is required but not provided
       File "duniverse/base/src/comparator.mli", line 21, characters
  2-53:
         Expected declaration
```

In order to satisfy the interface, we need to use the `Comparator.Make` functor to extend the module. Here, we use a common idiom where we create a submodule, called `T` containing the basic functionality for the type in question, and then include both that module and the result of applying a functor to that module.

```
module Book = struct
  module T = struct

    type t = { title: string; isbn: string }

    let compare t1 t2 =
```

```
      let cmp_title = String.compare t1.title t2.title in
      if cmp_title <> 0 then cmp_title
      else String.compare t1.isbn t2.isbn

    let sexp_of_t t : Sexp.t =
      List [ Atom t.title; Atom t.isbn ]

  end
  include T
  include Comparator.Make(T)
end;;
```

With this module in hand, we can now build a set of Book.t's.

```
# let some_programming_books =
    Set.of_list (module Book)
      [ { title = "Real World OCaml"
        ; isbn = "978-1449323912" }
      ; { title = "Structure and Interpretation of Computer Programs"
        ; isbn = "978-0262510875" }
      ; { title = "The C Programming Language"
        ; isbn = "978-0131101630" } ];;
val some_programming_books : (Book.t, Book.comparator_witness) Set.t =
  <abstr>
```

While we used Comparator.Make in the above, it's often preferable to use Comparable.Make instead, since it provides extra helper functions, like infix comparison operators and min and max functions, in addition to the comparator itself.

15.1.3 Why Do We Need Comparator Witnesses?

The comparator witness is quite different from other types that we've seen. Instead of tracking the kind of data being used, it's used to single out a particular value, a comparison function. Why do we even need such a thing?

The comparator witness matters because some of the operations on maps and sets, in particular those that combine multiple maps or sets together, depend for their correctness on the fact that both objects being combined are ordered according to the same total order, which in turn is determined by the comparison function.

Consider, for example, Map.symmetric_diff, which computes the difference between two maps.

```
# let left = Map.of_alist_exn (module String) ["foo",1; "bar",3;
    "snoo",0];;
val left : (string, int, String.comparator_witness) Map.t = <abstr>
# let right = Map.of_alist_exn (module String) ["foo",0; "snoo",0];;
val right : (string, int, String.comparator_witness) Map.t = <abstr>
# Map.symmetric_diff ~data_equal:Int.equal left right |>
    Sequence.to_list;;
- : (string, int) Map.Symmetric_diff_element.t list =
[("bar", `Left 3); ("foo", `Unequal (1, 0))]
```

As you can see below, the type of Map.symmetric_diff requires that the two maps it compares have the same comparator witness, in addition to the same key and value type.

```
# #show Map.symmetric_diff;;
val symmetric_diff :
  ('k, 'v, 'cmp) Map.t ->
  ('k, 'v, 'cmp) Map.t ->
  data_equal:('v -> 'v -> bool) ->
  ('k, 'v) Map.Symmetric_diff_element.t Sequence.t
```

Without this constraint, we could run `Map.symmetric_diff` on maps that are sorted in different orders, which could lead to garbled results.

To see this constraint in action, we'll need to create two maps with the same key and data types, but different comparison functions. In the following, we do this by minting a new module `Reverse`, which represents strings sorted in the reverse of the usual lexicographic order.

```
module Reverse = struct
  module T = struct
    type t = string
    let sexp_of_t = String.sexp_of_t
    let t_of_sexp = String.t_of_sexp
    let compare x y = String.compare y x
  end
  include T
  include Comparator.Make(T)
end;;
```

As you can see in the following, both `Reverse` and `String` can be used to create maps with a key type of `string`:

```
# let alist = ["foo", 0; "snoo", 3];;
val alist : (string * int) list = [("foo", 0); ("snoo", 3)]
# let ord_map = Map.of_alist_exn (module String) alist;;
val ord_map : (string, int, String.comparator_witness) Map.t = <abstr>
# let rev_map = Map.of_alist_exn (module Reverse) alist;;
val rev_map : (string, int, Reverse.comparator_witness) Map.t =
    <abstr>
```

`Map.min_elt` returns the key and value for the smallest key in the map, which confirms that these two maps do indeed use different comparison functions.

```
# Map.min_elt ord_map;;
- : (string * int) option = Some ("foo", 0)
# Map.min_elt rev_map;;
- : (string * int) option = Some ("snoo", 3)
```

As a result, the algorithm in `Map.symmetric_diff` just wouldn't work correctly when applied to these values. Happily, the type system will give us a compile-time error if we try, instead of throwing an error at run time, or worse, silently returning the wrong result.

```
# Map.symmetric_diff ord_map rev_map;;
Line 1, characters 28-35:
Error: This expression has type
       (string, int, Reverse.comparator_witness) Map.t
```

```
    but an expression was expected of type
      (string, int, String.comparator_witness) Map.t
    Type Reverse.comparator_witness is not compatible with type
      String.comparator_witness
```

15.1.4   The Polymorphic Comparator

We don't need to generate specialized comparators for every type we want to build a map on. We can instead build a map based on OCaml's built-in polymorphic comparison function, which was discussed in Chapter 4 (Lists and Patterns).

```
# Map.Poly.of_alist_exn digit_alist;;
- : (int, string) Map.Poly.t = <abstr>
```

Note that maps based on the polymorphic comparator have different comparator witnesses than those based on the type-specific comparison function. Thus, the compiler rejects the following:

```
# Map.symmetric_diff
    (Map.Poly.singleton 3 "three")
    (Map.singleton (module Int) 3 "four" );;
Line 3, characters 5-43:
Error: This expression has type (int, string, Int.comparator_witness)
    Map.t
      but an expression was expected of type
        (int, string, Comparator.Poly.comparator_witness) Map.t
      Type Int.comparator_witness is not compatible with type
        Comparator.Poly.comparator_witness
```

This is rejected for good reason: there's no guarantee that the comparator associated with a given type will order things in the same way that polymorphic compare does.

The Perils of Polymorphic Compare

Polymorphic compare is awfully convenient, but it has serious downsides and should mostly be avoided in production code. To understand why, it helps to understand how polymorphic compare works.

Polymorphic compare operates directly on the runtime representation of OCaml values, walking the structure of those values without regard for their type.

And despite ignoring types, it mostly behaves as you would hope. Comparisons on ints and floats respect the ordinary ordering of numeric values, and containers like strings, lists, and arrays are compared lexicographically. And it works on almost every OCaml type, with some important exceptions like functions.

But the type-oblivious nature of polymorphic compare means that it peeks under ordinary abstraction boundaries, and that can lead to some deeply confusing results. Maps themselves provide a great example of this. Consider the following two maps.

```
# let m1 = Map.of_alist_exn (module Int) [1, "one";2, "two"];;
val m1 : (int, string, Int.comparator_witness) Map.t = <abstr>
# let m2 = Map.of_alist_exn (module Int) [2, "two";1, "one"];;
val m2 : (int, string, Int.comparator_witness) Map.t = <abstr>
```

Logically, these two maps should be equal, and that's the result that you get if you call `Map.equal` on them:

```
# Map.equal String.equal m1 m2;;
- : bool = true
```

But because the elements were added in different orders, the layout of the trees underlying the maps will be different. As such, polymorphic compare will conclude that they're different.

We can see this below. Note that `Base` hides polymorphic comparison by default, but it is available within the `Poly` module.

```
# Poly.(m1 = m2);;
Exception: (Invalid_argument "compare: functional value")
```

This comparison failed because polymorphic compare doesn't work on functions, and maps store the comparison function they were created with. Happily, there's a function, `Map.Using_comparator.to_tree` which exposes the underlying binary tree without the attached comparison function. We can use that to compare the underlying trees:

```
# Poly.((Map.Using_comparator.to_tree m1) =
    (Map.Using_comparator.to_tree m2));;
- : bool = false
```

As you can see, polymorphic compare now produces a result, but it's not the result we want.

The abstraction-breaking nature of polymorphic compare can cause real and quite subtle bugs. If, for example, you build a map whose keys are sets (which have the same issues with polymorphic compare that maps do), then the map built with the polymorphic comparator will behave incorrectly, separating out keys that should be aggregated together. Even worse, it will behave inconsistently, since the behavior of polymorphic compare will depend on the order in which the sets were built.

15.1.5   Satisfying `Comparator.S` with `[@@deriving]`

Using maps and sets on a new type requires satisfying the `Comparator.S` interface, which in turn requires s-expression converters and comparison functions for the type in question. Writing such functions by hand is annoying and error prone, but there's a better way. `Base` comes along with a set of syntax extensions that automate these tasks away.

Let's return to an example from earlier in the chapter, where we created a type `Book.t` and set it up for use in creating maps and sets.

```
module Book = struct
  module T = struct

    type t = { title: string; isbn: string }

    let compare t1 t2 =
```

```
        let cmp_title = String.compare t1.title t2.title in
        if cmp_title <> 0 then cmp_title
        else String.compare t1.isbn t2.isbn

      let sexp_of_t t : Sexp.t =
        List [ Atom t.title; Atom t.isbn ]

    end
    include T
    include Comparator.Make(T)
  end
```

Much of the code here is devoted to creating a comparison function and s-expression converter for the type `Book.t`. But if we have the `ppx_sexp_conv` and `ppx_compare` syntax extensions enabled, then we can request that default implementations of these functions be created for us. We can enable both of these extensions via the omnibus `ppx_jane` package.

```
# #require "ppx_jane";;
```

And we can use the extensions in our definition of `Book` as follows:

```
module Book = struct
  module T = struct
    type t = { title: string; isbn: string }
    [@@deriving compare, sexp_of]
  end
  include T
  include Comparator.Make(T)
end;;
```

If you want a comparison function that orders things in a particular way, you can always write your own by hand; but if all you need is a total order suitable for creating maps and sets with, then `[@@deriving compare]` is a good choice.

=, ==, and phys_equal

OCaml has multiple notions of equality, and picking the right one can be tricky. If you don't open `Base`, you'll find that the `==` operator tests for *physical* equality, while the `=` operator is the polymorphic equality function.

Two values are considered physically equal if they are the same pointer in memory. Two data structures that have identical contents but are constructed separately will not be considered equal by `==`. Polymorphic equality, on the other hand, is *structural*, which effectively means that it considers values to be equal if they have the same contents.

Most of the time you don't want either of these forms of equality! Polymorphic equality is problematic for reasons we explained earlier in the chapter, and physical equality, while useful, is something that's needed in particular cases, most often when you're dealing with mutable objects, where the physical identity of the object matters.

Base hides polymorphic equality, instead reserving `=` for equality functions associated with particular types. At the top-level `=` is specialized to integers.

```
# 1 = 2;;
- : bool = false
```

```
# "one" = "two";;
Line 1, characters 1-6:
Error: This expression has type string but an expression was expected
       of type
              int
```

Other type-specific equality functions are found in their associated modules

```
# String.("one" = "two");;
- : bool = false
```

It's quite easy to mix up = and ==, and so Base deprecates == and provides phys_equal instead, a function with a clear and descriptive name.

```
# ref 1 == ref 1;;
Line 1, characters 7-9:
Alert deprecated: Base.==
[2016-09] this element comes from the stdlib distributed with OCaml.
Use [phys_equal] instead.
- : bool = false
# phys_equal (ref 1) (ref 1);;
- : bool = false
```

This is just a small way in which Base tries to avoid error-prone APIs.

15.1.6   Applying [@@deriving] to Maps and Sets

In the previous section, we showed how to use [@@deriving] annotations to set up a type so it could be used to create a map or set type. But what if we want to put a [@@deriving] annotation on a map or set type itself?

```
# type string_int_map =
    (string,int,String.comparator_witness) Map.t [@@deriving sexp];;
Line 2, characters 44-49:
Error: Unbound value Map.t_of_sexp
Hint: Did you mean m__t_of_sexp?
```

This fails because there is no existing Map.t_of_sexp. This isn't a simple omission; there's no reasonable way to define a useful Map.t_of_sexp, because a comparator witness isn't something that can be parsed out of the s-expression.

Happily, there's another way of writing the type of a map that does work with the various [@@deriving] extensions, which you can see below.

```
# type string_int_map = int Map.M(String).t [@@deriving sexp];;
type string_int_map = int Base.Map.M(Base.String).t
val string_int_map_of_sexp : Sexp.t -> string_int_map = <fun>
val sexp_of_string_int_map : string_int_map -> Sexp.t = <fun>
```

Here, we use a functor, Map.M, to define the type we need. While this looks different than the ordinary type signature, the meaning of the type is the same, as we can see below.

```
# let m = Map.singleton (module String) "one" 1;;
val m : (string, int, String.comparator_witness) Map.t = <abstr>
```

```
# (m : int Map.M(String).t);;
- : int Base.Map.M(Base.String).t = <abstr>
```

This same type works with other derivers as well, like those for comparison and hash functions. Since this way of writing the type is also shorter, it's what you should use most of the time.

15.1.7 Trees

As we've discussed, maps carry within them the comparator that they were created with. Sometimes, for space efficiency reasons, you want a version of the map data structure that doesn't include the comparator. You can get such a representation with `Map.Using_comparator.to_tree`, which returns just the tree underlying the map, without the comparator.

```
# let ord_tree = Map.Using_comparator.to_tree ord_map;;
val ord_tree :
  (string, int, String.comparator_witness)
    Map.Using_comparator.Tree.t =
  <abstr>
```

Even though the tree doesn't physically include a comparator, it does include the comparator in its type. This is what is known as a *phantom type*, because it reflects something about the logic of the value in question, even though it doesn't correspond to any values directly represented in the underlying physical structure of the value.

Since the comparator isn't included in the tree, we need to provide the comparator explicitly when we, say, search for a key, as shown below:

```
# Map.Using_comparator.Tree.find ~comparator:String.comparator
    ord_tree "snoo";;
- : int option = Some 3
```

The algorithm of `Map.Tree.find` depends on the fact that it's using the same comparator when looking up a value as you were when you stored it. That's the invariant that the phantom type is there to enforce. As you can see in the following example, using the wrong comparator will lead to a type error:

```
# Map.Using_comparator.Tree.find ~comparator:Reverse.comparator
    ord_tree "snoo";;
Line 1, characters 63-71:
Error: This expression has type
         (string, int, String.comparator_witness)
       Map.Using_comparator.Tree.t
         but an expression was expected of type
         (string, int, Reverse.comparator_witness)
         Map.Using_comparator.Tree.t
       Type String.comparator_witness is not compatible with type
         Reverse.comparator_witness
```

15.2   Hash Tables

Hash tables are the imperative cousin of maps. We walked through a basic hash table implementation in Chapter 9 (Imperative Programming), so in this section we'll mostly discuss the pragmatics of Core's `Hashtbl` module. We'll cover this material more briefly than we did with maps because many of the concepts are shared.

Hash tables differ from maps in a few key ways. First, hash tables are mutable, meaning that adding a key/value pair to a hash table modifies the table, rather than creating a new table with the binding added. Second, hash tables generally have better time-complexity than maps, providing constant-time lookup and modifications, as opposed to logarithmic for maps. And finally, just as maps depend on having a comparison function for creating the ordered binary tree that underlies a map, hash tables depend on having a *hash function*, i.e., a function for converting a key to an integer.

15.2.1   Time Complexity of Hash Tables

The statement that hash tables provide constant-time access hides some complexities. First of all, most hash table implementations, OCaml's included, need to resize the table when it gets too full. A resize requires allocating a new backing array for the hash table and copying over all entries, and so it is quite an expensive operation. That means adding a new element to the table is only *amortized* constant, which is to say, it's constant on average over a long sequence of operations, but some of the individual operations can cost more.

Another hidden cost of hash tables has to do with the hash function you use. If you end up with a pathologically bad hash function that hashes all of your data to the same number, then all of your insertions will hash to the same underlying bucket, meaning you no longer get constant-time access at all. Base's hash table implementation uses binary trees for the hash-buckets, so this case only leads to logarithmic time, rather than linear for a traditional implementation.

The logarithmic behavior of Base's hash tables in the presence of hash collisions also helps protect against some denial-of-service attacks. One well-known type of attack is to send queries to a service with carefully chosen keys to cause many collisions. This, in combination with the linear behavior of most hashtables, can cause the service to become unresponsive due to high CPU load. Base's hash tables would be much less susceptible to such an attack because the amount of degradation would be far less.

We create a hashtable in a way that's similar to how we create maps, by providing a first-class module from which the required operations for building a hashtable can be obtained.

```
# let table = Hashtbl.create (module String);;
val table : (string, '_weak1) Base.Hashtbl.t = <abstr>
# Hashtbl.set table ~key:"three" ~data:3;;
- : unit = ()
# Hashtbl.find table "three";;
```

```
- : int option = Some 3
```

As with maps, most modules in Base are ready to be used for this purpose, but if you want to create a hash table from one of your own types, you need to do some work to prepare it. In order for a module to be suitable for passing to Hashtbl.create, it has to match the following interface.

```
# #show Base.Hashtbl.Key.S;;
module type S =
  sig
    type t
    val compare : t -> t -> int
    val sexp_of_t : t -> Sexp.t
    val hash : t -> int
  end
```

Note that there's no equivalent to the comparator witness that came up for maps and sets. That's because the requirement for multiple objects to share a comparison function or a hash function mostly just doesn't come up for hash tables. That makes building a module suitable for use with a hash table simpler.

```
# module Book = struct
    type t = { title: string; isbn: string }
    [@@deriving compare, sexp_of, hash]
  end;;
module Book :
  sig
    type t = { title : string; isbn : string; }
    val compare : t -> t -> int
    val sexp_of_t : t -> Sexp.t
    val hash_fold_t :
      Base_internalhash_types.state -> t ->
      Base_internalhash_types.state
    val hash : t -> int
  end
# let table = Hashtbl.create (module Book);;
val table : (Book.t, '_weak2) Base.Hashtbl.t = <abstr>
```

You can also create a hashtable based on OCaml's polymorphic hash and comparison functions.

```
# let table = Hashtbl.Poly.create ();;
val table : ('_weak3, '_weak4) Base.Hashtbl.t = <abstr>
# Hashtbl.set table ~key:("foo",3,[1;2;3]) ~data:"random data!";;
- : unit = ()
# Hashtbl.find table ("foo",3,[1;2;3]);;
- : string option = Some "random data!"
```

This is highly convenient, but polymorphic comparison can behave in surprising ways, so it's generally best to avoid this for code where correctness matters.

15.2.2 Collisions with the Polymorphic Hash Function

The polymorphic hash function, like polymorphic compare, has problems that derive from the fact that it doesn't pay any attention to the type, just blindly walking down the structure of a data type and computing a hash from what it sees. That means that for data structures like maps and sets where equivalent instances can have different structures, it will do the wrong thing.

But there's another problem with polymorphic hash, which is that it is prone to creating hash collisions. OCaml's polymorphic hash function works by walking over the data structure it's given using a breadth-first traversal that is bounded in the number of nodes it's willing to traverse. By default, that bound is set at 10 "meaningful" nodes.

The bound on the traversal means that the hash function may ignore part of the data structure, and this can lead to pathological cases where every value you store has the same hash value. We'll demonstrate this below, using the function `List.range` to allocate lists of integers of different length:

```
# Hashtbl.Poly.hashable.hash (List.range 0 9);;
- : int = 209331808
# Hashtbl.Poly.hashable.hash (List.range 0 10);;
- : int = 182325193
# Hashtbl.Poly.hashable.hash (List.range 0 11);;
- : int = 182325193
# Hashtbl.Poly.hashable.hash (List.range 0 100);;
- : int = 182325193
```

As you can see, the hash function stops after the first 10 elements. The same can happen with any large data structure, including records and arrays. When building hash functions over large custom data structures, it is generally a good idea to write one's own hash function, or to use the ones provided by [@@deriving], which don't have this problem, as you can see below.

```
# [%hash: int list] (List.range 0 9);;
- : int = 999007935
# [%hash: int list] (List.range 0 10);;
- : int = 195154657
# [%hash: int list] (List.range 0 11);;
- : int = 527899773
# [%hash: int list] (List.range 0 100);;
- : int = 594983280
```

Note that rather than declaring a type and using [@@deriving hash] to invoke ppx_hash, we use [%hash], a shorthand for creating a hash function inline in an expression.

15.3   Choosing Between Maps and Hash Tables

Maps and hash tables overlap enough in functionality that it's not always clear when to choose one or the other. Maps, by virtue of being immutable, are generally the default choice in OCaml. OCaml also has good support for imperative programming, though, and when programming in an imperative idiom, hash tables are often the more natural choice.

Programming idioms aside, there are significant performance differences between maps and hash tables. For code that is dominated by updates and lookups, hash tables are a clear performance win, and the win is clearer the larger the amount of data.

The best way of answering a performance question is by running a benchmark, so let's do just that. The following benchmark uses the core_bench library, and it compares maps and hash tables under a very simple workload. Here, we're keeping track of a set of 1,000 different integer keys and cycling over the keys and updating the values they contain. Note that we use the Map.change and Hashtbl.change functions to update the respective data structures:

```
open Base
open Core_bench

let map_iter ~num_keys ~iterations =
  let rec loop i map =
    if i <= 0
    then ()
    else
      loop
        (i - 1)
        (Map.change map (i % num_keys) ~f:(fun current ->
             Some (1 + Option.value ~default:0 current)))
  in
  loop iterations (Map.empty (module Int))

let table_iter ~num_keys ~iterations =
  let table = Hashtbl.create (module Int) ~size:num_keys in
  let rec loop i =
    if i <= 0
    then ()
    else (
      Hashtbl.change table (i % num_keys) ~f:(fun current ->
          Some (1 + Option.value ~default:0 current));
      loop (i - 1))
  in
  loop iterations

let tests ~num_keys ~iterations =
  let t name f = Bench.Test.create f ~name in
  [ t "table" (fun () -> table_iter ~num_keys ~iterations)
  ; t "map" (fun () -> map_iter ~num_keys ~iterations)
  ]

let () =
  tests ~num_keys:1000 ~iterations:100_000
  |> Bench.make_command
  |> Core.Command.run
```

The results show the hash table version to be around four times faster than the map version:

```
(executable
  (name       map_vs_hash)
  (libraries base core_bench))
```

```
$ dune build map_vs_hash.exe
$ ./_build/default/map_vs_hash.exe -ascii -quota 1 -clear-columns
    time speedup
Estimated testing time 2s (2 benchmarks x 1s). Change using -quota
    SECS.

  Name     Time/Run    Speedup
  -------  ----------  ---------
  table    13.34ms       1.00
  map      44.54ms       3.34
```

We can make the speedup smaller or larger depending on the details of the test; for example, it will vary with the number of distinct keys. But overall, for code that is heavy on sequences of querying and updating a set of key/value pairs, hash tables will significantly outperform maps.

Hash tables are not always the faster choice, though. In particular, maps excel in situations where you need to keep multiple related versions of the data structure in memory at once. That's because maps are immutable, and so operations like `Map.add` that modify a map do so by creating a new map, leaving the original undisturbed. Moreover, the new and old maps share most of their physical structure, so keeping multiple versions around can be space-efficient.

Here's a benchmark that demonstrates this. In it, we create a list of maps (or hash tables) that are built up by iteratively applying small updates, keeping these copies around. In the map case, this is done by using `Map.change` to update the map. In the hash table implementation, the updates are done using `Hashtbl.change`, but we also need to call `Hashtbl.copy` to take snapshots of the table:

```
open Base
open Core_bench

let create_maps ~num_keys ~iterations =
  let rec loop i map =
    if i <= 0
    then []
    else (
      let new_map =
        Map.change map (i % num_keys) ~f:(fun current ->
            Some (1 + Option.value ~default:0 current))
      in
      new_map :: loop (i - 1) new_map)
  in
  loop iterations (Map.empty (module Int))

let create_tables ~num_keys ~iterations =
  let table = Hashtbl.create (module Int) ~size:num_keys in
  let rec loop i =
    if i <= 0
    then []
    else (
      Hashtbl.change table (i % num_keys) ~f:(fun current ->
          Some (1 + Option.value ~default:0 current));
      let new_table = Hashtbl.copy table in
      new_table :: loop (i - 1))
```

```
   in
   loop iterations

let tests ~num_keys ~iterations =
  let t name f = Bench.Test.create f ~name in
  [ t "table" (fun () -> ignore (create_tables ~num_keys ~iterations))
  ; t "map" (fun () -> ignore (create_maps ~num_keys ~iterations))
  ]

let () =
  tests ~num_keys:50 ~iterations:1000
  |> Bench.make_command
  |> Core.Command.run
```

Unsurprisingly, maps perform far better than hash tables on this benchmark, in this case by more than a factor of 10:

```
(executable
  (name        map_vs_hash2)
  (libraries core_bench))
```

```
$ dune build map_vs_hash2.exe
$ ./_build/default/map_vs_hash2.exe -ascii -clear-columns time speedup
Estimated testing time 20s (2 benchmarks x 10s). Change using -quota
     SECS.

   Name       Time/Run    Speedup
  -------  ------------  ---------
   table   4_453.95us      25.80
   map       172.61us       1.00
```

These numbers can be made more extreme by increasing the size of the tables or the length of the list.

As you can see, the relative performance of trees and maps depends a great deal on the details of how they're used, and so whether to choose one data structure or the other will depend on the details of the application.

16   Command-Line Parsing

Many of the OCaml programs that you'll write will end up as binaries that need to be run from a command prompt. Any nontrivial command line should support a collection of basic features:

- Parsing of command-line arguments
- Generation of error messages in response to incorrect inputs
- Help for all the available options
- Interactive autocompletion

It's tedious and error-prone to code all of this manually for every program you write. Core provides the Command library, which simplifies all of this by letting you declare your command-line options in one place and by deriving all of the above functionality from these declarations.

Command is simple to use for simple applications but also scales well as your needs grow more complex. In particular, Command provides a sophisticated subcommand mode that groups related commands together as the complexity of your user interface grows. You may already be familiar with this command-line style from the Git or Mercurial version control systems.

In this chapter, we'll:

- Learn how to use Command to construct basic and grouped command-line interfaces
- Build simple equivalents to the cryptographic md5 and shasum utilities
- Demonstrate how to declare complex command-line interfaces in a type-safe and elegant way

16.1   Basic Command-Line Parsing

Let's start by working through a clone of the md5sum command that is present on most Linux installations (the equivalent command on macOS is simply md5). The following function defined below reads in the contents of a file, applies the MD5 one-way cryptographic hash function to the data, and outputs an ASCII hex representation of the result:

```
open Core
```

```
let do_hash file =
  Md5.digest_file_blocking file |> Md5.to_hex |> print_endline
```

The do_hash function accepts a `filename` parameter and prints the human-readable MD5 string to the console standard output. The first step toward turning this function into a command-line program is to create a parser for the command line arguments. The module `Command.Param` provides a set of combinators that can be combined together to define a parameter parser for optional flags and positional arguments, including documentation, the types they should map to, and whether to take special actions such as pausing for interactive input if certain inputs are encountered.

16.1.1   Defining an Anonymous Argument

Let's build a parser for a command line UI with a single *anonymous* argument, i.e., an argument that is passed in without a flag.

```
let filename_param =
  let open Command.Param in
  anon ("filename" %: string)
```

Here, anon is used to signal the parsing of an anonymous argument, and the expression `("filename" %: string)` indicates the textual name of the argument and specification that describes the kind of value that is expected. The textual name is used for generating help text, and the specification, which has type `Command.Arg_type.t`, is used both to nail down the OCaml type of the returned value (`string`, in this case) and to guide features like input validation. The values anon, string and %: all come from the `Command.Param` module.

16.1.2   Defining Basic Commands

Once we've defined a specification, we need to put it to work on real input. The simplest way is to directly create a command-line interface with `Command.basic`.

```
let command =
  Command.basic
    ~summary:"Generate an MD5 hash of the input data"
    ~readme:(fun () -> "More detailed information")
    (Command.Param.map filename_param ~f:(fun filename () ->
       do_hash filename))
```

The summary argument is a one-line description which goes at the top of the help screen, while the (optional) readme argument is for providing a more detailed description that will be provided on demand.

The final argument is the most interesting one, which is the parameter parser. This will be easier to understand if we first learn a bit more about the type signatures of the various components we've been using. Let's do that by recreating some of this code in the toplevel.

```
# let filename_param = Command.Param.(anon ("filename" %: string));;
val filename_param : string Command.Spec.param = <abstr>
```

The type parameter of `filename_param` is there to indicate the type of the value returned by the parser; in this case, `string`.

But `Command.basic` requires a parameter parser that returns a value of type `unit -> unit`. We can see that by using `#show` to explore the types.

```
# #show Command.basic;;
val basic : unit Command.basic_command
# #show Command.basic_command;;
type nonrec 'result basic_command =
    summary:string ->
    ?readme:(unit -> string) ->
    (unit -> 'result) Command.Spec.param -> Command.t
```

Note that the `'result` parameter of the type alias `basic_command` is instantiated as `unit` for the type of `Command.basic`.

It makes sense that `Command.basic` wants a parser that returns a function; after all, in the end, it needs a function it can run that constitutes the execution of the program. But how do we get such a parser, given the parser we have returns just a filename?

The answer is to use a `map` function to change the value returned by the parser. As you can see below, the type of `Command.Param.map` is very similar to the type of `List.map`.

```
# #show Command.Param.map;;
val map : 'a Command.Spec.param -> f:('a -> 'b) -> 'b Command.Spec.param
```

In our program, we used `map` to convert the `filename_param` parser, which returns a string representing the file name, into a parser that returns a function of type `unit -> unit` containing the body of the command. It might not be obvious that the function passed to map returns a function, but remember that, due to currying, the invocation of map above could be written equivalently as follows.

```
Command.Param.map filename_param ~f:(fun filename ->
    fun () -> do_hash filename)
```

16.1.3   Running Commands

Once we've defined the basic command, running it is just one function call away.

```
let () = Command.run ~version:"1.0" ~build_info:"RWO" command
```

`Command.run` takes a couple of optional arguments that are useful to identify which version of the binary you are running in production. You'll need the following dune file:

```
(executable
    (name       md5)
    (libraries  core)
    (preprocess (pps ppx_jane)))
```

At which point we can build and execute the program using dune exec. Let's use this to query version information from the binary.

```
$ dune exec -- ./md5.exe -version
1.0
$ dune exec -- ./md5.exe -build-info
RWO
```

The versions that you see in the output were defined via the optional arguments to Command.run. You can leave these blank in your own programs or get your build system to generate them directly from your version control system. Dune provides a dune-build-info library[1] that automates this process for most common workflows.

We can invoke our binary with -help to see the auto-generated help.

```
$ dune exec -- ./md5.exe -help
Generate an MD5 hash of the input data

  md5.exe FILENAME

More detailed information

=== flags ===

  [-build-info]  print info about this build and exit
  [-version]     print the version of this build and exit
  [-help]        print this help text and exit
                 (alias: -?)
```

If you supply the filename argument, then do_hash is called with the argument and the MD5 output is displayed to the standard output.

```
$ dune exec -- ./md5.exe md5.ml
2ae55d17ff11d337492a1ca5510ee01b
```

And that's all it takes to build our little MD5 utility! Here's a complete version of the example we just walked through, made slightly more succinct by removing intermediate variables.

```
open Core

let do_hash file =
  Md5.digest_file_blocking file |> Md5.to_hex |> print_endline

let command =
  Command.basic
    ~summary:"Generate an MD5 hash of the input data"
    ~readme:(fun () -> "More detailed information")
    Command.Param.(
      map
        (anon ("filename" %: string))
        ~f:(fun filename () -> do_hash filename))

let () = Command.run ~version:"1.0" ~build_info:"RWO" command
```

---

[1] https://dune.readthedocs.io/en/stable/executables.html#
embedding-build-information-into-executables

16.1.4   Multi-Argument Commands

All the examples thus far have involved a single argument, but we can of course create multi-argument commands as well. We can make a parser for multiple arguments by binding together simpler parsers, using the function `Command.Param.both`. Here is its type.

```
# #show Command.Param.both;;
val both :
  'a Command.Spec.param ->
  'b Command.Spec.param -> ('a * 'b) Command.Spec.param
```

both allows us to take two parameter parsers and combine them into a single parser that returns the two arguments as a pair. In the following, we rewrite our md5 program so it takes two anonymous arguments: the first is an integer saying how many characters of the hash to print out, and the second is the filename.

```
open Core

let do_hash hash_length filename =
  Md5.digest_file_blocking filename
  |> Md5.to_hex
  |> (fun s -> String.prefix s hash_length)
  |> print_endline

let command =
  Command.basic
    ~summary:"Generate an MD5 hash of the input data"
    ~readme:(fun () -> "More detailed information")
    Command.Param.(
      map
        (both
          (anon ("hash_length" %: int))
          (anon ("filename" %: string)))
      ~f:(fun (hash_length, filename) () ->
        do_hash hash_length filename))

let () = Command.run ~version:"1.0" ~build_info:"RWO" command
```

Building and running this command, we can see that it now indeed expects two arguments.

```
$ dune exec -- ./md5.exe 5 md5.ml
f8824
```

This works well enough for two parameters, but if you want longer parameter lists, this approach gets old fast. A better way is to use let-syntax, which was discussed in Chapter 8.1.3 (bind and Other Error Handling Idioms).

```
let command =
  Command.basic
    ~summary:"Generate an MD5 hash of the input data"
    ~readme:(fun () -> "More detailed information")
    (let open Command.Let_syntax in
    let open Command.Param in
    let%map hash_length = anon ("hash_length" %: int)
```

```
      and filename = anon ("filename" %: string) in
      fun () -> do_hash hash_length filename)
```

Here, we take advantage of let-syntax's support for parallel let bindings, using and to join the definitions together. This syntax translates down to the same pattern based on both that we showed above, but it's easier to read and use, and scales better to more arguments.

The need to open both modules is a little awkward, and the Param module in particular you really only need on the right-hand-side of the equals-sign. This is achieved automatically by using the let%map_open syntax, demonstrated below. We'll also drop the open of Command.Let_syntax in favor of explicitly using let%map_open.Command to mark the let-syntax as coming from the Command module

```
let command =
  Command.basic
    ~summary:"Generate an MD5 hash of the input data"
    ~readme:(fun () -> "More detailed information")
    (let%map_open.Command hash_length = anon ("hash_length" %: int)
    and filename = anon ("filename" %: string) in
    fun () -> do_hash hash_length filename)
```

Let-syntax is the most common way of writing parsers for Command, and we'll use that idiom from here on.

Now that we have the basics in place, the rest of the chapter will examine some of the more advanced features of Command.

16.2 Argument Types

You aren't just limited to parsing command lines of strings and ints. There are some other argument types defined in Command.Param, like date and percent. But most of the time, argument types for specific types in Core and other associated libraries are defined in the module that defines the type in question.

As an example, we can tighten up the specification of the command to Filename.arg_type to reflect that the argument must be a valid filename, and not just any string.

```
let command =
  Command.basic
    ~summary:"Generate an MD5 hash of the input data"
    ~readme:(fun () -> "More detailed information")
    (let%map_open.Command file =
      anon ("filename" %: Filename.arg_type)
    in
    fun () -> do_hash file)
```

This doesn't change the validation of the provided value, but it does enable interactive command-line completion. We'll explain how to enable that later in the chapter.

16.2.1   Defining Custom Argument Types

We can also define our own argument types if the predefined ones aren't sufficient. For instance, let's make a `regular_file` argument type that ensures that the input file isn't a character device or some other odd UNIX file type that can't be fully read.

```
open Core

let do_hash file =
  Md5.digest_file_blocking file |> Md5.to_hex |> print_endline

let regular_file =
  Command.Arg_type.create (fun filename ->
      match Sys.is_file filename with
      | `Yes -> filename
      | `No -> failwith "Not a regular file"
      | `Unknown ->
          failwith "Could not determine if this was a regular file")

let command =
  Command.basic
    ~summary:"Generate an MD5 hash of the input data"
    ~readme:(fun () -> "More detailed information")
    (let%map_open.Command filename =
        anon ("filename" %: regular_file)
     in
     fun () -> do_hash filename)

let () = Command.run ~version:"1.0" ~build_info:"RWO" command
```

The `regular_file` function transforms a `filename` string parameter into the same string but first checks that the file exists and is a regular file type. When you build and run this code, you will see the new error messages if you try to open a special device such as `/dev/null`:

```
$ dune exec -- ./md5.exe md5.ml
5df5ec6301ea37bebc22912ceaa6b2e2
$ dune exec -- ./md5.exe /dev/null
Error parsing command line:

  failed to parse FILENAME value "/dev/null"
  (Failure "Not a regular file")

For usage information, run

  md5.exe -help

[1]
```

16.2.2   Optional and Default Arguments

A more realistic `md5` binary could also read from the standard input if a `filename` isn't specified. To do this, we need to declare the filename argument as optional, which we can do with the maybe operator.

```
let command =
  Command.basic
    ~summary:"Generate an MD5 hash of the input data"
    ~readme:(fun () -> "More detailed information")
    (let%map_open.Command filename =
       anon (maybe ("filename" %: string))
     in
     fun () -> do_hash filename)
```

But building this results in a compile-time error.

```
$ dune build md5.exe
File "md5.ml", line 15, characters 23-31:
15 |      fun () -> do_hash filename)
                            ^^^^^^^^
Error: This expression has type string option
       but an expression was expected of type string
[1]
```

This is because changing the argument type has also changed the type of the value that is returned by the parser. It now produces a string option instead of a string, reflecting the optionality of the argument. We can adapt our example to use the new information and read from standard input if no file is specified.

```
open Core

let get_contents = function
  | None | Some "-" -> In_channel.input_all In_channel.stdin
  | Some filename -> In_channel.read_all filename

let do_hash filename =
  get_contents filename
  |> Md5.digest_string
  |> Md5.to_hex
  |> print_endline

let command =
  Command.basic
    ~summary:"Generate an MD5 hash of the input data"
    ~readme:(fun () -> "More detailed information")
    (let%map_open.Command filename =
       anon (maybe ("filename" %: Filename.arg_type))
     in
     fun () -> do_hash filename)

let () = Command.run ~version:"1.0" ~build_info:"RWO" command
```

The filename parameter to do_hash is now a string option type. This is resolved into a string via get_contents to determine whether to read the standard input or a file, and then the rest of the command is similar to our previous examples.

```
$ cat md5.ml | dune exec -- ./md5.exe
54fd98cd30f8faa76be46be0005f00bf
```

Another possible way to handle this would be to supply a dash as the default filename if one isn't specified. The maybe_with_default function can do just this, with the benefit of not having to change the callback parameter type.

The following example behaves exactly the same as the previous example, but
replaces maybe with maybe_with_default:

```
open Core

let get_contents = function
  | "-" -> In_channel.input_all In_channel.stdin
  | filename -> In_channel.read_all filename

let do_hash filename =
  get_contents filename
  |> Md5.digest_string
  |> Md5.to_hex
  |> print_endline

let command =
  Command.basic
    ~summary:"Generate an MD5 hash of the input data"
    ~readme:(fun () -> "More detailed information")
    (let%map_open.Command filename =
       anon (maybe_with_default "-" ("filename" %: Filename.arg_type))
     in
     fun () -> do_hash filename)

let () = Command.run ~version:"1.0" ~build_info:"RWO" command
```

Building and running this confirms that it has the same behavior as before.

```
$ cat md5.ml | dune exec -- ./md5.exe
f0ea4085ca226eef2c0d70026619a244
```

16.2.3   Sequences of Arguments

Another common way of parsing anonymous arguments is as a variable length list. As
an example, let's modify our MD5 code to take a collection of files to process on the
command line.

```
open Core

let get_contents = function
  | "-" -> In_channel.input_all In_channel.stdin
  | filename -> In_channel.read_all filename

let do_hash filename =
  get_contents filename
  |> Md5.digest_string
  |> Md5.to_hex
  |> fun md5 -> printf "MD5 (%s) = %s\n" filename md5

let command =
  Command.basic
    ~summary:"Generate an MD5 hash of the input data"
    ~readme:(fun () -> "More detailed information")
    (let%map_open.Command files =
       anon (sequence ("filename" %: Filename.arg_type))
```

```
    in
    fun () ->
      match files with
      | [] -> do_hash "-"
      | _ -> List.iter files ~f:do_hash)

let () = Command.run ~version:"1.0" ~build_info:"RWO" command
```

The callback function is a little more complex now, to handle the extra options. The `files` are now a `string list`, and an empty list reverts to using standard input, just as our previous `maybe` and `maybe_with_default` examples did. If the list of files isn't empty, then it opens up each file and runs them through `do_hash` sequentially.

```
$ dune exec -- ./md5.exe /etc/services ./_build/default/md5.exe
MD5 (/etc/services) = 6501e9c7bf20b1dc56f015e341f79833
MD5 (./_build/default/md5.exe) = 6602408aa98478ba5617494f7460d3d9
```

16.3   Adding Labeled Flags

You aren't limited to anonymous arguments on the command line. A *flag* is a named field that can be followed by an optional argument. These flags can appear in any order on the command line, or multiple times, depending on how they're declared in the specification.

Let's add two arguments to our `md5` command that mimics the macOS version. A `-s` flag specifies the string to be hashed directly on the command line and `-t` runs a self-test. The complete example follows.

```
open Core

let checksum_from_string buf =
  Md5.digest_string buf |> Md5.to_hex |> print_endline

let checksum_from_file filename =
  let contents =
    match filename with
    | "-" -> In_channel.input_all In_channel.stdin
    | filename -> In_channel.read_all filename
  in
  Md5.digest_string contents |> Md5.to_hex |> print_endline

let command =
  Command.basic
    ~summary:"Generate an MD5 hash of the input data"
    (let%map_open.Command use_string =
       flag
         "-s"
         (optional string)
         ~doc:"string Checksum the given string"
     and trial = flag "-t" no_arg ~doc:" run a built-in time trial"
     and filename =
       anon (maybe_with_default "-" ("filename" %: Filename.arg_type))
     in
```

```
    fun () ->
      if trial
      then printf "Running time trial\n"
      else (
        match use_string with
        | Some buf -> checksum_from_string buf
        | None -> checksum_from_file filename))

let () = Command.run command
```

The specification now uses the `flag` function to define the two new labeled, command-line arguments. The doc string is formatted so that the first word is the short name that appears in the usage text, with the remainder being the full help text. Notice that the -t flag has no argument, and so we prepend its doc text with a blank space. The help text for the preceding code looks like this:

```
$ dune exec -- ./md5.exe -help
Generate an MD5 hash of the input data

  md5.exe [FILENAME]

=== flags ===

  [-s string]    Checksum the given string
  [-t]           run a built-in time trial
  [-build-info]  print info about this build and exit
  [-version]     print the version of this build and exit
  [-help]        print this help text and exit
                 (alias: -?)

$ dune exec -- ./md5.exe -s "ocaml rocks"
5a118fe92ac3b6c7854c595ecf6419cb
```

The -s flag in our specification requires a `string` argument and isn't optional. The Command parser outputs an error message if the flag isn't supplied, as with the anonymous arguments in earlier examples. There are a number of other functions that you can wrap flags in to control how they are parsed:

- `required <arg>` will return `<arg>` and error if not present
- `optional <arg>` with return `<arg>` option
- `optional_with_default <val> <arg>` will return `<arg>` with default `<val>` if not present
- `listed <arg>` will return `<arg>` `list` (this flag may appear multiple times)
- `no_arg` will return a `bool` that is true if the flag is present

The flags affect the type of the callback function in exactly the same way as anonymous arguments do. This lets you change the specification and ensure that all the callback functions are updated appropriately, without runtime errors.

16.4   Grouping Subcommands Together

You can get pretty far by using flags and anonymous arguments to assemble complex, command-line interfaces. After a while, though, too many options can make the program very confusing for newcomers to your application. One way to solve this is by grouping common operations together and adding some hierarchy to the command-line interface.

You'll have run across this style already when using the opam package manager (or, in the non-OCaml world, the Git or Mercurial commands). opam exposes commands in this form:

```
$ opam env
$ opam remote list -k git
$ opam install --help
$ opam install core --verbose
```

The config, remote, and install keywords form a logical grouping of commands that factor out a set of flags and arguments. This lets you prevent flags that are specific to a particular subcommand from leaking into the general configuration space.

This usually only becomes a concern when your application organically grows features. Luckily, it's simple to extend your application to do this in Command: just use Command.group, which lets you merge a collection of Command.t's into one.

```
# Command.group;;
- : summary:string ->
    ?readme:(unit -> string) ->
    ?preserve_subcommand_order:unit ->
    ?body:(path:string list -> unit) ->
    (string * Command.t) list -> Command.t
= <fun>
```

The group signature accepts a list of basic Command.t values and their corresponding names. When executed, it looks for the appropriate subcommand from the name list, and dispatches it to the right command handler.

Let's build the outline of a calendar tool that does a few operations over dates from the command line. We first need to define a command that adds days to an input date and prints the resulting date:

```
open Core

let add =
  Command.basic
    ~summary:"Add [days] to the [base] date and print day"
    (let%map_open.Command base = anon ("base" %: date)
     and days = anon ("days" %: int) in
     fun () ->
       Date.add_days base days |> Date.to_string |> print_endline)

let () = Command.run add
```

Everything in this command should be familiar to you by now, and it works as you might expect.

```
$ dune exec -- ./cal.exe -help
Add [days] to the [base] date and print day

  cal.exe BASE DAYS

=== flags ===

  [-build-info]  print info about this build and exit
  [-version]     print the version of this build and exit
  [-help]        print this help text and exit
                 (alias: -?)

$ dune exec -- ./cal.exe 2012-12-25 40
2013-02-03
```

Now, let's also add the ability to take the difference between two dates, but, instead of creating a new binary, we'll group both operations as subcommands using `Command.group`.

```
open Core

let add =
  Command.basic
    ~summary:"Add [days] to the [base] date"
    Command.Let_syntax.(
      let%map_open base = anon ("base" %: date)
      and days = anon ("days" %: int) in
      fun () ->
        Date.add_days base days |> Date.to_string |> print_endline)

let diff =
  Command.basic
    ~summary:"Show days between [date1] and [date2]"
    (let%map_open.Command date1 = anon ("date1" %: date)
     and date2 = anon ("date2" %: date) in
     fun () -> Date.diff date1 date2 |> printf "%d days\n")

let command =
  Command.group
    ~summary:"Manipulate dates"
    [ "add", add; "diff", diff ]

let () = Command.run command
```

And that's all you really need to add subcommand support! Let's build the example first in the usual way and inspect the help output, which now reflects the subcommands we just added.

```
(executable
  (name         cal)
  (libraries    core)
  (preprocess (pps ppx_jane)))

$ dune exec -- ./cal.exe -help
Manipulate dates
```

```
  cal.exe SUBCOMMAND

=== subcommands ===

  add      Add [days] to the [base] date
  diff     Show days between [date1] and [date2]
  version  print version information
  help     explain a given subcommand (perhaps recursively)
```

We can invoke the two commands we just defined to verify that they work and see the date parsing in action:

```
$ dune exec -- ./cal.exe add 2012-12-25 40
2013-02-03
$ dune exec -- ./cal.exe diff 2012-12-25 2012-11-01
54 days
```

16.5   Prompting for Interactive Input

Sometimes, if a value isn't provided on the command line, you want to prompt for it instead. Let's return to the calendar tool we built before.

```
open Core

let add =
  Command.basic
    ~summary:"Add [days] to the [base] date and print day"
    (let%map_open.Command base = anon ("base" %: date)
     and days = anon ("days" %: int) in
     fun () ->
       Date.add_days base days |> Date.to_string |> print_endline)

let () = Command.run add
```

This program requires you to specify both the base date and the number of days to add onto it. If days isn't supplied on the command line, an error is output. Now let's modify it to interactively prompt for a number of days if only the base date is supplied.

```
open Core

let add_days base days =
  Date.add_days base days |> Date.to_string |> print_endline

let prompt_for_string name of_string =
  printf "enter %s: %!" name;
  match In_channel.input_line In_channel.stdin with
  | None -> failwith "no value entered. aborting."
  | Some line -> of_string line

let add =
  Command.basic
    ~summary:"Add [days] to the [base] date and print day"
    (let%map_open.Command base = anon ("base" %: date)
     and days = anon (maybe ("days" %: int)) in
```

```
      let days =
        match days with
        | Some x -> x
        | None -> prompt_for_string "days" Int.of_string
      in
      fun () -> add_days base days)

let () = Command.run add
```

The days anonymous argument is now an optional integer in the spec, and when it isn't there, we simply prompt for the value as part of the ordinary execution of our program.

Sometimes, it's convenient to pack the prompting behavior into the parser itself. For one thing, this would allow you to easily share the prompting behavior among multiple commands. This is easy enough to do by adding a new function, anon_prompt, which creates a parser that automatically prompts if the value isn't provided.

```
let anon_prompt name of_string =
  let arg = Command.Arg_type.create of_string in
  let%map_open.Command value = anon (maybe (name %: arg)) in
  match value with
  | Some v -> v
  | None -> prompt_for_string name of_string

let add =
  Command.basic
    ~summary:"Add [days] to the [base] date and print day"
    (let%map_open.Command base = anon ("base" %: date)
     and days = anon_prompt "days" Int.of_string in
     fun () -> add_days base days)
```

We can see the prompting behavior if we run the program without providing the second argument.

```
$ echo 35 | dune exec -- ./cal.exe 2013-12-01
enter days: 2014-01-05
```

16.6   Command-Line Autocompletion with bash

Modern UNIX shells usually have a tab-completion feature to interactively help you figure out how to build a command line. These work by pressing the Tab key in the middle of typing a command, and seeing the options that pop up. You've probably used this most often to find the files in the current directory, but it can actually be extended for other parts of the command, too.

The precise mechanism for autocompletion varies depending on what shell you are using, but we'll assume you are using the most common one: bash. This is the default interactive shell on most Linux distributions and macOS, but you may need to switch to it on *BSD or Windows (when using Cygwin). The rest of this section assumes that you're using bash.

Bash autocompletion isn't always installed by default, so check your OS package manager to see if you have it available.

- On Debian Linux, do apt install bash-completion
- On macOS Homebrew, do brew install bash-completion
- On FreeBSD, do pkg install bash-completion.

Once *bash* completion is installed and configured, check that it works by typing the ssh command and pressing the Tab key. This should show you the list of known hosts from your *~/.ssh/known_hosts* file. If it lists some hosts that you've recently connected to, you can continue on. If it lists the files in your current directory instead, then check your OS documentation to configure completion correctly.

One last bit of information you'll need to find is the location of the bash_completion.d directory. This is where all the shell fragments that contain the completion logic are held. On Linux, this is often in /etc/bash_completion.d, and in Homebrew on macOS, it would be /usr/local/etc/bash_completion.d by default.

16.6.1 Generating Completion Fragments from Command

The Command library has a declarative description of all the possible valid options, and it can use this information to generate a shell script that provides completion support for that command. To generate the fragment, just run the command with the COMMAND_OUTPUT_INSTALLATION_BASH environment variable set to any value.

For example, let's try it on our MD5 example from earlier, assuming that the binary is called md5 in the current directory:

```
$ env COMMAND_OUTPUT_INSTALLATION_BASH=1 dune exec -- ./md5.exe
function _jsautocom_32087 {
  export COMP_CWORD
  COMP_WORDS[0]=./md5.exe
  if type readarray > /dev/null
  then readarray -t COMPREPLY < <("${COMP_WORDS[@]}")
  else IFS="
" read -d "" -A COMPREPLY < <("${COMP_WORDS[@]}")
  fi
}
complete -F _jsautocom_32087 ./md5.exe
```

Recall that we used the Arg_type.file to specify the argument type. This also supplies the completion logic so that you can just press Tab to complete files in your current directory.

16.6.2 Installing the Completion Fragment

You don't need to worry about what the preceding output script actually does (unless you have an unhealthy fascination with shell scripting internals, that is). Instead, redirect the output to a file in your current directory and source it into your current shell:

```
$ env COMMAND_OUTPUT_INSTALLATION_BASH=1 ./cal_add_sub_days.native >
    cal.cmd
$ . cal.cmd
$ ./cal_add_sub_days.native <tab>
add     diff    help    version
```

Command completion support works for flags and grouped commands and is very useful when building larger command-line interfaces. Don't forget to install the shell fragment into your global bash_completion.d directory if you want it to be loaded in all of your login shells.

Installing a Generic Completion Handler

Sadly, bash doesn't support installing a generic handler for all Command-based applications. This means you have to install the completion script for every application, but you should be able to automate this in the build and packaging system for your application.

It will help to check out how other applications install tab-completion scripts and follow their lead, as the details are very OS-specific.

16.7   Alternative Command-Line Parsers

This rounds up our tour of the Command library. This isn't the only way to parse command-line arguments of course; there are several alternatives available on opam. Three of the most prominent ones follow:

The Arg module The Arg module is from the OCaml standard library, which is used by the compiler itself to handle its command-line interface. Command is built on top of Arg, but you can also use Arg directly. You can use the Command.Spec.flags_of_args_exn function to convert Arg specifications into ones compatible with Command, which is a simple way of porting an Arg-based command line interface to Command.

ocaml-getopt[2] ocaml-getopt provides the general command-line syntax of GNU getopt and getopt_long. The GNU conventions are widely used in the open source world, and this library lets your OCaml programs obey the same rules.

Cmdliner[3] Cmdliner is a mix between the Command and Getopt libraries. It allows for the declarative definition of command-line interfaces but exposes a more getopt-like interface. It also automates the generation of UNIX man pages as part of the specification. Cmdliner is the parser used by opam to manage its command line.

17 Concurrent Programming with Async

The logic of building programs that interact with the outside world is often dominated by waiting; waiting for the click of a mouse, or for data to be fetched from disk, or for space to be available on an outgoing network buffer. Even mildly sophisticated interactive applications are typically *concurrent*, needing to wait for multiple different events at the same time, responding immediately to whatever happens first.

One approach to concurrency is to use preemptive system threads, which is the dominant approach in languages like Java or C#. In this model, each task that may require simultaneous waiting is given an operating system thread of its own so it can block without stopping the entire program.

Another approach is to have a single-threaded program, where that single thread runs an *event loop* whose job is to react to external events like timeouts or mouse clicks by invoking a callback function that has been registered for that purpose. This approach shows up in languages like JavaScript that have single-threaded runtimes, as well as in many GUI toolkits.

Each of these mechanisms has its own trade-offs. System threads require significant memory and other resources per thread. Also, the operating system can arbitrarily interleave the execution of system threads, requiring the programmer to carefully protect shared resources with locks and condition variables, which is exceedingly error-prone.

Single-threaded event-driven systems, on the other hand, execute a single task at a time and do not require the same kind of complex synchronization that preemptive threads do. However, the inverted control structure of an event-driven program often means that your own control flow has to be threaded awkwardly through the system's event loop, leading to a maze of event callbacks.

This chapter covers the Async library, which offers a hybrid model that aims to provide the best of both worlds, avoiding the performance compromises and synchronization woes of preemptive threads without the confusing inversion of control that usually comes with event-driven systems.

17.1   Async Basics

Recall how I/O is typically done in Core. Here's a simple example.

```
# open Core;;
```

```
# #show In_channel.read_all;;
val read_all : string -> string
# Out_channel.write_all "test.txt" ~data:"This is only a test.";;
- : unit = ()
# In_channel.read_all "test.txt";;
- : string = "This is only a test."
```

From the type of In_channel.read_all, you can see that it must be a blocking operation. In particular, the fact that it returns a concrete string means it can't return until the read has completed. The blocking nature of the call means that no progress can be made on anything else until the call is complete.

In Async, well-behaved functions never block. Instead, they return a value of type Deferred.t that acts as a placeholder that will eventually be filled in with the result. As an example, consider the signature of the Async equivalent of In_channel.read_all.

```
# #require "async";;
# open Async;;
# #show Reader.file_contents;;
val file_contents : string -> string Deferred.t
```

We first load the Async package in the toplevel using #require, and then open the module. Async, like Core, is designed to be an extension to your basic programming environment, and is intended to be opened.

A deferred is essentially a handle to a value that may be computed in the future. As such, if we call Reader.file_contents, the resulting deferred will initially be empty, as you can see by calling Deferred.peek.

```
# let contents = Reader.file_contents "test.txt";;
val contents : string Deferred.t = <abstr>
# Deferred.peek contents;;
- : string option = None
```

The value in contents isn't yet determined partly because nothing running could do the necessary I/O. When using Async, processing of I/O and other events is handled by the Async scheduler. When writing a standalone program, you need to start the scheduler explicitly, but utop knows about Async and can start the scheduler automatically. More than that, utop knows about deferred values, and when you type in an expression of type Deferred.t, it will make sure the scheduler is running and block until the deferred is determined. Thus, we can write:

```
# contents;;
- : string = "This is only a test."
```

Slightly confusingly, the type shown here is not the type of contents, which is string Deferred.t, but rather string, the type of the value contained within that deferred.

If we peek again, we'll see that the value of contents has been filled in.

```
# Deferred.peek contents;;
- : string option = Some "This is only a test."
```

In order to do real work with deferreds, we need a way of waiting for a deferred computation to finish, which we do using Deferred.bind. Here's the type-signature of bind.

```
# #show Deferred.bind;;
val bind : 'a Deferred.t -> f:('a -> 'b Deferred.t) -> 'b Deferred.t
```

bind is effectively a way of sequencing concurrent computations. In particular, Deferred.bind d ~f causes f to be called after the value of d has been determined.

Here's a simple use of bind for a function that replaces a file with an uppercase version of its contents.

```
# let uppercase_file filename =
    Deferred.bind (Reader.file_contents filename)
      ~f:(fun text ->
        Writer.save filename ~contents:(String.uppercase text));;
val uppercase_file : string -> unit Deferred.t = <fun>
# uppercase_file "test.txt";;
- : unit = ()
# Reader.file_contents "test.txt";;
- : string = "THIS IS ONLY A TEST."
```

Again, bind is acting as a sequencing operator, causing the file to be saved via the call to Writer.save only after the contents of the file were first read via Reader.file_contents.

Writing out Deferred.bind explicitly can be rather verbose, and so Async includes an infix operator for it: >>=. Using this operator, we can rewrite uppercase_file as follows:

```
# let uppercase_file filename =
    Reader.file_contents filename
    >>= fun text ->
    Writer.save filename ~contents:(String.uppercase text);;
val uppercase_file : string -> unit Deferred.t = <fun>
```

Here, we've dropped the parentheses around the function on the right-hand side of the bind, and we didn't add a level of indentation for the contents of that function. This is standard practice for using the infix bind operator.

Now let's look at another potential use of bind. In this case, we'll write a function that counts the number of lines in a file:

```
# let count_lines filename =
    Reader.file_contents filename
    >>= fun text ->
    List.length (String.split text ~on:'\n');;
Line 4, characters 5-45:
Error: This expression has type int but an expression was expected of
    type
        'a Deferred.t
```

This looks reasonable enough, but as you can see, the compiler is unhappy. The issue here is that bind expects a function that returns a Deferred.t, but we've provided it with a function that returns the result directly. What we need is return, a function provided by Async that takes an ordinary value and wraps it up in a deferred.

```
# #show_val return;;
val return : 'a -> 'a Deferred.t
# let three = return 3;;
```

```
val three : int Deferred.t = <abstr>
# three;;
- : int = 3
```

Using return, we can make `count_lines` compile:

```
# let count_lines filename =
    Reader.file_contents filename
    >>= fun text ->
    return (List.length (String.split text ~on:'\n'));;
val count_lines : string -> int Deferred.t = <fun>
```

Together, bind and return form a design pattern in functional programming known as a *monad*. You'll run across this signature in many applications beyond just threads. Indeed, we already ran across monads in Chapter 8.1.3 (bind and Other Error Handling Idioms).

Calling bind and return together is a fairly common pattern, and as such there is a standard shortcut for it called `Deferred.map`, which has the following signature:

```
# #show Deferred.map;;
val map : 'a Deferred.t -> f:('a -> 'b) -> 'b Deferred.t
```

and comes with its own infix equivalent, `>>|`. Using it, we can rewrite `count_lines` again a bit more succinctly:

```
# let count_lines filename =
    Reader.file_contents filename
    >>| fun text ->
    List.length (String.split text ~on:'\n');;
val count_lines : string -> int Deferred.t = <fun>
# count_lines "/etc/hosts";;
- : int = 10
```

Note that `count_lines` returns a deferred, but utop waits for that deferred to become determined, and shows us the contents of the deferred instead.

17.1.1   Using Let Syntax

As was discussed in Chapter 8.1.3 (bind and Other Error Handling Idioms), there is a special syntax, which we call *let syntax*, designed for working with monads, which we can enable by enabling ppx_let.

```
# #require "ppx_let";;
```

Here's what the bind-using version of `count_lines` looks like using that syntax.

```
# let count_lines filename =
    let%bind text = Reader.file_contents filename in
    return (List.length (String.split text ~on:'\n'));;
val count_lines : string -> int Deferred.t = <fun>
```

And here's the map-based version of `count_lines`.

```
# let count_lines filename =
    let%map text = Reader.file_contents filename in
    List.length (String.split text ~on:'\n');;
val count_lines : string -> int Deferred.t = <fun>
```

The difference here is just syntactic, with these examples compiling down to the same thing as the corresponding examples written using infix operators. What's nice about let syntax is that it highlights the analogy between monadic bind and OCaml's built-in let-binding, thereby making your code more uniform and more readable.

Let syntax works for any monad, and you decide which monad is in use by opening the appropriate `Let_syntax` module. Opening `Async` also implicitly opens `Deferred.Let_syntax`, but in some contexts you may want to do that explicitly.

For the most part, let syntax is easier to read and work with, and you should default to it when using Async, which is what we'll do for the remainder of the chapter.

17.1.2   Ivars and Upon

Deferreds are usually built using combinations of `bind`, `map` and `return`, but sometimes you want to construct a deferred where you can programmatically decide when it gets filled in. This can be done using an *ivar*. (The term ivar dates back to a language called Concurrent ML that was developed by John Reppy in the early '90s. The "i" in ivar stands for incremental.)

There are three fundamental operations for working with an ivar: you can create one, using `Ivar.create`; you can read off the deferred that corresponds to the ivar in question, using `Ivar.read`; and you can fill an ivar, thus causing the corresponding deferred to become determined, using `Ivar.fill`. These operations are illustrated below:

```
# let ivar = Ivar.create ();;
val ivar : '_weak1 Ivar.t =
  {Async_kernel__.Types.Ivar.cell = Async_kernel__Types.Cell.Empty}
# let def = Ivar.read ivar;;
val def : '_weak2 Deferred.t = <abstr>
# Deferred.peek def;;
- : '_weak3 option = None
# Ivar.fill ivar "Hello";;
- : unit = ()
# Deferred.peek def;;
- : string option = Some "Hello"
```

Ivars are something of a low-level feature; operators like `map`, `bind` and `return` are typically easier to use and think about. But ivars can be useful when you want to build a synchronization pattern that isn't already well supported.

As an example, imagine we wanted a way of scheduling a sequence of actions that would run after a fixed delay. In addition, we'd like to guarantee that these delayed actions are executed in the same order they were scheduled in. Here's a signature that captures this idea:

```
# module type Delayer_intf = sig
    type t
    val create : Time.Span.t -> t
    val schedule : t -> (unit -> 'a Deferred.t) -> 'a Deferred.t
  end;;
module type Delayer_intf =
```

```
sig
  type t
  val create : Time.Span.t -> t
  val schedule : t -> (unit -> 'a Deferred.t) -> 'a Deferred.t
end
```

An action is handed to `schedule` in the form of a deferred-returning thunk (a thunk is a function whose argument is of type `unit`). A deferred is handed back to the caller of `schedule` that will eventually be filled with the contents of the deferred value returned by the thunk. To implement this, we'll use an operator called upon, which has the following signature:

```
# #show upon;;
val upon : 'a Deferred.t -> ('a -> unit) -> unit
```

Like `bind` and `return`, upon schedules a callback to be executed when the deferred it is passed is determined; but unlike those calls, it doesn't create a new deferred for this callback to fill.

Our delayer implementation is organized around a queue of thunks, where every call to `schedule` adds a thunk to the queue and also schedules a job in the future to grab a thunk off the queue and run it. The waiting will be done using the function `after`, which takes a time span and returns a deferred which becomes determined after that time span elapses:

```
# module Delayer : Delayer_intf = struct
    type t = { delay: Time.Span.t;
               jobs: (unit -> unit) Queue.t;
             }

    let create delay =
      { delay; jobs = Queue.create () }

    let schedule t thunk =
      let ivar = Ivar.create () in
      Queue.enqueue t.jobs (fun () ->
        upon (thunk ()) (fun x -> Ivar.fill ivar x));
      upon (after t.delay) (fun () ->
        let job = Queue.dequeue_exn t.jobs in
        job ());
      Ivar.read ivar
  end;;
module Delayer : Delayer_intf
```

This code isn't particularly long, but it is subtle. In particular, note how the queue of thunks is used to ensure that the enqueued actions are run in the order they were scheduled, even if the thunks scheduled by upon are run out of order. This kind of subtlety is typical of code that involves ivars and upon, and because of this, you should stick to the simpler map/bind/return style of working with deferreds when you can.

Understanding bind in Terms of Ivars and upon

Here's roughly what happens when you write `let d' = Deferred.bind d ~f`.

- A new ivar i is created to hold the final result of the computation. The corresponding deferred is returned
- A function is registered to be called when the deferred d becomes determined.
- That function, once run, calls f with the value that was determined for d.
- Another function is registered to be called when the deferred returned by f becomes determined.
- When that function is called, it uses it to fill i, causing the corresponding deferred it to become determined.

That sounds like a lot, but we can implement this relatively concisely.

```
# let my_bind d ~f =
    let i = Ivar.create () in
    upon d (fun x -> upon (f x) (fun y -> Ivar.fill i y));
    Ivar.read i;;
val my_bind : 'a Deferred.t -> f:('a -> 'b Deferred.t) -> 'b Deferred.t
  =
  <fun>
```

Async's real implementation has more optimizations and is therefore more complicated. But the above implementation is still a useful first-order mental model for how bind works under the covers. And it's another good example of how upon and ivars can be useful for building concurrency primitives.

17.2   Example: An Echo Server

Now that we have the basics of Async under our belt, let's look at a small standalone Async program. In particular, we'll write an echo server, *i.e.*, a program that accepts connections from clients and spits back whatever is sent to it.

The first step is to create a function that can copy data from an input to an output. Here, we'll use Async's Reader and Writer modules, which provide a convenient abstraction for working with input and output channels:

```
open Core
open Async

(* Copy data from the reader to the writer, using the provided buffer
   as scratch space *)
let rec copy_blocks buffer r w =
  match%bind Reader.read r buffer with
  | `Eof -> return ()
  | `Ok bytes_read ->
    Writer.write w (Bytes.to_string buffer) ~len:bytes_read;
    let%bind () = Writer.flushed w in
    copy_blocks buffer r w
```

Bind is used in the code to sequence the operations, with a bind marking each place we wait.

- First, we call Reader.read to get a block of input.

- When that's complete and if a new block was returned, we write that block to the writer.
- Finally, we wait until the writer's buffers are flushed, at which point we recurse.

If we hit an end-of-file condition, the loop is ended. The deferred returned by a call to `copy_blocks` becomes determined only once the end-of-file condition is hit.

One important aspect of how `copy_blocks` is written is that it provides *pushback*, which is to say that if the process can't make progress writing, it will stop reading. If you don't implement pushback in your servers, then anything that prevents you from writing (e.g., a client that is unable to keep up) will cause your program to allocate unbounded amounts of memory, as it keeps track of all the data it intends to write but hasn't been able to yet.

Tail-Calls and Chains of Deferreds

There's another memory problem you might be concerned about, which is the allocation of deferreds. If you think about the execution of `copy_blocks`, you'll see it's creating a chain of deferreds, two per time through the loop. The length of this chain is unbounded, and so, naively, you'd think this would take up an unbounded amount of memory as the echo process continues.

Happily, this is a case that Async knows how to optimize. In particular, the whole chain of deferreds should become determined precisely when the final deferred in the chain is determined, in this case, when the `Eof` condition is hit. Because of this, we could safely replace all of these deferreds with a single deferred. Async does just this, and so there's no memory leak after all.

This is essentially a form of tail-call optimization, lifted to the Deferred monad. Indeed, you can tell that the bind in question doesn't lead to a memory leak in more or less the same way you can tell that the tail recursion optimization should apply, which is that the bind that creates the deferred is in tail-position. In other words, nothing is done to that deferred once it's created; it's simply returned as is.

`copy_blocks` provides the logic for handling a client connection, but we still need to set up a server to receive such connections and dispatch to `copy_blocks`. For this, we'll use Async's `Tcp` module, which has a collection of utilities for creating TCP clients and servers:

```
(** Starts a TCP server, which listens on the specified port, invoking
    copy_blocks every time a client connects. *)
let run () =
  let host_and_port =
    Tcp.Server.create
      ~on_handler_error:`Raise
      (Tcp.Where_to_listen.of_port 8765)
      (fun _addr r w ->
        let buffer = Bytes.create (16 * 1024) in
        copy_blocks buffer r w)
  in
  ignore
    (host_and_port
```

```
: (Socket.Address.Inet.t, int) Tcp.Server.t Deferred.t)
```

The result of calling `Tcp.Server.create` is a `Tcp.Server.t`, which is a handle to the server that lets you shut the server down. We don't use that functionality here, so we explicitly ignore `server` to suppress the unused-variables error. We put in a type annotation around the ignored value to make the nature of the value we're ignoring explicit.

The most important argument to `Tcp.Server.create` is the final one, which is the client connection handler. Notably, the preceding code does nothing explicit to close down the client connections when the communication is done. That's because the server will automatically shut down the connection once the deferred returned by the handler becomes determined.

Finally, we need to initiate the server and start the Async scheduler:

```
(* Call [run], and then start the scheduler *)
let () =
  run ();
  never_returns (Scheduler.go ())
```

One of the most common newbie errors with Async is to forget to run the scheduler. It can be a bewildering mistake, because without the scheduler, your program won't do anything at all; even calls to `printf` won't reach the terminal.

It's worth noting that even though we didn't spend much explicit effort on thinking about multiple clients, this server is able to handle many clients concurrently connecting and reading and writing data.

Now that we have the echo server, we can connect to the echo server using the netcat tool, which is invoked as nc. Note that we use dune exec to both build and run the executable. We use the double-dashes so that Dune's parsing of arguments doesn't interfere with argument parsing for the executed program.

```
$ dune exec -- ./echo.exe &
$ echo "This is an echo server" | nc 127.0.0.1 8765
This is an echo server
$ echo "It repeats whatever I write" | nc 127.0.0.1 8765
It repeats whatever I write
$ killall echo.exe
```

Functions that Never Return

The call to `never_returns` around the call to `Scheduler.go` is a little bit surprising, but it has a purpose: to make it clear to whoever invokes `Scheduler.go` that the function never returns.

By default, a function that doesn't return will have an inferred return type of `'a`:

```
# let rec loop_forever () = loop_forever ();;
val loop_forever : unit -> 'a = <fun>
# let always_fail () = assert false;;
val always_fail : unit -> 'a = <fun>
```

This is a little odd, but it does make sense. After all, if a function never returns, we're free to impute any type at all to its non-existent return value. As a result, from a typing perspective, a function that never returns can fit into any context within your program.

But that itself can be problematic, especially with a function like `Scheduler.go`, where the fact that it never returns is perhaps not entirely obvious. The point of `never_returns` is to create an explicit marker so the user knows that the function in question doesn't return.

To do this, `Scheduler.go` is defined to have a return value of `Nothing.t`.

```
# #show Scheduler.go;;
val go : ?raise_unhandled_exn:bool -> unit -> never_returns
```

`never_returns` is just an alias of `Nothing.t`.

`Nothing.t` is *uninhabited*, which means there are no values of that type. As such, a function can't actually return a value of type `Nothing.t`, so only a function that never returns can have `Nothing.t` as its return type! And we can cause a function that never returns to have a return value of `Nothing.t` by just adding a type annotation.

```
# let rec loop_forever () : Nothing.t = loop_forever ();;
val loop_forever : unit -> never_returns = <fun>
```

The function `never_returns` consumes a value of type `Nothing.t` and returns an unconstrained type `'a`.

```
# #show_val never_returns;;
val never_returns : never_returns -> 'a
```

If you try to write a function that uses `Scheduler.go`, and just assumes that it returns `unit`, you'll get a helpful type error.

```
# let do_stuff n =
    let x = 3 in
    if n > 0 then Scheduler.go ();
    x + n;;
Line 3, characters 19-34:
Error: This expression has type never_returns
       but an expression was expected of type unit
       because it is in the result of a conditional with no else
    branch
```

We can fix this by inserting a call to `never_returns`, thus making the fact that `Scheduler.go` doesn't return apparent to the reader.

```
# let do_stuff n =
    let x = 3 in
    if n > 0 then never_returns (Scheduler.go ());
    x + n;;
val do_stuff : int -> int = <fun>
```

17.2.1   Improving the Echo Server

Let's try to go a little bit farther with our echo server by walking through a few improvements. In particular, we will:

- Add a proper command-line interface with `Command`
- Add a flag to specify the port to listen on and a flag to make the server echo back the capitalized version of whatever was sent to it
- Simplify the code using Async's `Pipe` interface

The following code does all of this:

```
open Core
open Async

let run ~uppercase ~port =
  let host_and_port =
    Tcp.Server.create
      ~on_handler_error:`Raise
      (Tcp.Where_to_listen.of_port port)
      (fun _addr r w ->
        Pipe.transfer
          (Reader.pipe r)
          (Writer.pipe w)
          ~f:(if uppercase then String.uppercase else Fn.id))
  in
  ignore
    (host_and_port
      : (Socket.Address.Inet.t, int) Tcp.Server.t Deferred.t);
  Deferred.never ()

let () =
  Command.async
    ~summary:"Start an echo server"
    (let%map_open.Command uppercase =
      flag
        "-uppercase"
        no_arg
        ~doc:" Convert to uppercase before echoing back"
    and port =
      flag
        "-port"
        (optional_with_default 8765 int)
        ~doc:" Port to listen on (default 8765)"
    in
    fun () -> run ~uppercase ~port)
  |> Command.run
```

Note the use of `Deferred.never` in the run function. As you might guess from the name, `Deferred.never` returns a deferred that is never determined. In this case, that indicates that the echo server doesn't ever shut down.

The biggest change in the preceding code is the use of Async's `Pipe`. A `Pipe` is an asynchronous communication channel that's used for connecting different parts of your program. You can think of it as a consumer/producer queue that uses deferreds for communicating when the pipe is ready to be read from or written to. Our use of pipes is fairly minimal here, but they are an important part of Async, so it's worth discussing them in some detail.

Pipes are created in connected read/write pairs:

```
# let (r,w) = Pipe.create ();;
val r : '_weak4 Pipe.Reader.t = <abstr>
val w : '_weak4 Pipe.Writer.t = <abstr>
```

r and w are really just read and write handles to the same underlying object. Note that r and w have weakly polymorphic types, as discussed in Chapter 9 (Imperative Programming), and so can only contain values of a single, yet-to-be-determined type.

If we just try and write to the writer, we'll see that we block indefinitely in utop. You can break out of the wait by hitting **Control-C**:

```
# Pipe.write w "Hello World!";;
Interrupted.
```

That's because a pipe has a certain amount of internal slack, a number of slots in the pipe to which something can be written before the write will block. By default, a pipe has zero slack, which means that the deferred returned by a write is determined only when the value is read out of the pipe.

```
# let (r,w) = Pipe.create ();;
val r : '_weak5 Pipe.Reader.t = <abstr>
val w : '_weak5 Pipe.Writer.t = <abstr>
# let write_complete = Pipe.write w "Hello World!";;
val write_complete : unit Deferred.t = <abstr>
# Pipe.read r;;
- : [ `Eof | `Ok of string ] = `Ok "Hello World!"
# write_complete;;
- : unit = ()
```

In the function run, we're taking advantage of one of the many utility functions provided for pipes in the Pipe module. In particular, we're using Pipe.transfer to set up a process that takes data from a reader-pipe and moves it to a writer-pipe. Here's the type of Pipe.transfer:

```
# Pipe.transfer;;
- : 'a Pipe.Reader.t -> 'b Pipe.Writer.t -> f:('a -> 'b) -> unit
    Deferred.t =
<fun>
```

The two pipes being connected are generated by the Reader.pipe and Writer.pipe call respectively. Note that pushback is preserved throughout the process, so that if the writer gets blocked, the writer's pipe will stop pulling data from the reader's pipe, which will prevent the reader from reading in more data.

Importantly, the deferred returned by Pipe.transfer becomes determined once the reader has been closed and the last element is transferred from the reader to the writer. Once that deferred becomes determined, the server will shut down that client connection. So, when a client disconnects, the rest of the shutdown happens transparently.

The command-line parsing for this program is based on the Command library that we introduced in Chapter 16 (Command-Line Parsing). Opening Async, shadows the Command module with an extended version that contains the async call:

```
# #show Command.async_spec;;
val async_spec :
```

```
('a, unit Deferred.t) Async.Command.basic_spec_command
  Command.with_options
```

This differs from the ordinary `Command.basic` call in that the main function must return a `Deferred.t`, and that the running of the command (using `Command.run`) automatically starts the Async scheduler, without requiring an explicit call to `Scheduler.go`.

17.3   Example: Searching Definitions with DuckDuckGo

DuckDuckGo is a search engine with a freely available search interface. In this section, we'll use Async to write a small command-line utility for querying DuckDuckGo to extract definitions for a collection of terms.

Our code is going to rely on a number of other libraries, all of which can be installed using opam. Refer to the installation instructions [1] if you need help on the installation. Here's the list of libraries we'll need:

textwrap A library for wrapping long lines. We'll use this for printing out our results.
uri A library for handling URIs, or "Uniform Resource Identifiers," of which HTTP URLs are an example.
yojson A JSON parsing library that was described in Handling Json Data [2].
cohttp A library for creating HTTP clients and servers. We need Async support, which comes with the `cohttp-async` package.

Now let's dive into the implementation.

17.3.1   URI Handling

HTTP URLs, which identify endpoints across the Web, are actually part of a more general family known as Uniform Resource Identifiers (URIs). The full URI specification is defined in RFC3986 [3] and is rather complicated. Luckily, the uri library provides a strongly typed interface that takes care of much of the hassle.

We'll need a function for generating the URIs that we're going to use to query the DuckDuckGo servers:

```
open Core
open Async

(* Generate a DuckDuckGo search URI from a query string *)
let query_uri query =
  let base_uri =
    Uri.of_string "http://api.duckduckgo.com/?format=json"
  in
  Uri.add_query_param base_uri ("q", [ query ])
```

---

[1] http://dev.realworldocaml.org/install.html
[2] json.html#handling-json-data
[3] http://tools.ietf.org/html/rfc3986

A `Uri.t` is constructed from the `Uri.of_string` function, and a query parameter q is added with the desired search query. The library takes care of encoding the URI correctly when outputting it in the network protocol.

17.3.2   Parsing JSON Strings

The HTTP response from DuckDuckGo is in JSON, a common (and thankfully simple) format that is specified in RFC4627[4]. We'll parse the JSON data using the Yojson library, which was introduced in Chapter 19 (Handling JSON Data).

We expect the response from DuckDuckGo to come across as a JSON record, which is represented by the `Assoc` tag in Yojson's JSON variant. We expect the definition itself to come across under either the key "Abstract" or "Definition," and so the following code looks under both keys, returning the first one for which a nonempty value is defined:

```
(* Extract the "Definition" or "Abstract" field from the DuckDuckGo
   results *)
let get_definition_from_json json =
  match Yojson.Safe.from_string json with
  | `Assoc kv_list ->
    let find key =
      match List.Assoc.find ~equal:String.equal kv_list key with
      | None | Some (`String "") -> None
      | Some s -> Some (Yojson.Safe.to_string s)
    in
    (match find "Abstract" with
    | Some _ as x -> x
    | None -> find "Definition")
  | _ -> None
```

17.3.3   Executing an HTTP Client Query

Now let's look at the code for dispatching the search queries over HTTP, using the Cohttp library:

```
(* Execute the DuckDuckGo search *)
let get_definition word =
  let%bind _, body = Cohttp_async.Client.get (query_uri word) in
  let%map string = Cohttp_async.Body.to_string body in
  word, get_definition_from_json string
```

To better understand what's going on, it's useful to look at the type for `Cohttp_async.Client.get`, which we can do in utop:

```
# #require "cohttp-async";;
# #show Cohttp_async.Client.get;;
val get :
  ?interrupt:unit Deferred.t ->
  ?ssl_config:Conduit_async.V2.Ssl.Config.t ->
  ?headers:Cohttp.Header.t ->
  Uri.t -> (Cohttp.Response.t * Cohttp_async.Body.t) Deferred.t
```

---

[4] http://www.ietf.org/rfc/rfc4627.txt

The `get` call takes as a required argument a URI and returns a deferred value containing a `Cohttp.Response.t` (which we ignore) and a pipe reader to which the body of the request will be streamed.

In this case, the HTTP body probably isn't very large, so we call `Cohttp_async.Body.to_string` to collect the data from the connection as a single deferred string, rather than consuming the data incrementally.

Running a single search isn't that interesting from a concurrency perspective, so let's write code for dispatching multiple searches in parallel. First, we need code for formatting and printing out the search result:

```
(* Print out a word/definition pair *)
let print_result (word, definition) =
  printf
    "%s\n%s\n\n%s\n\n"
    word
    (String.init (String.length word) ~f:(fun _ -> '-'))
    (match definition with
    | None -> "No definition found"
    | Some def ->
      String.concat ~sep:"\n" (Wrapper.wrap (Wrapper.make 70) def))
```

We use the `Wrapper` module from the `textwrap` package to do the line wrapping. It may not be obvious that this routine is using Async, but it does: the version of `printf` that's called here is actually Async's specialized `printf` that goes through the Async scheduler rather than printing directly. The original definition of `printf` is shadowed by this new one when you open `Async`. An important side effect of this is that if you write an Async program and forget to start the scheduler, calls like `printf` won't actually generate any output!

The next function dispatches the searches in parallel, waits for the results, and then prints:

```
(* Run many searches in parallel, printing out the results after
   they're all done. *)
let search_and_print words =
  let%map results = Deferred.all (List.map words ~f:get_definition) in
  List.iter results ~f:print_result
```

We used `List.map` to call `get_definition` on each word, and `Deferred.all` to wait for all the results. Here's the type of `Deferred.all`:

```
# Deferred.all;;
- : 'a Deferred.t list -> 'a list Deferred.t = <fun>
```

The list returned by `Deferred.all` reflects the order of the deferreds passed to it. As such, the definitions will be printed out in the same order that the search words are passed in, no matter what order the queries return in. It also means that no printing occurs until all results arrive.

We could rewrite this code to print out the results as they're received (and thus potentially out of order) as follows:

```
(* Run many searches in parallel, printing out the results as you
   go *)
```

```
let search_and_print words =
  Deferred.all_unit
    (List.map words ~f:(fun word ->
         get_definition word >>| print_result))
```

The difference is that we both dispatch the query and print out the result in the closure passed to map, rather than wait for all of the results to get back and then print them out together. We use Deferred.all_unit, which takes a list of unit deferreds and returns a single unit deferred that becomes determined when every deferred on the input list is determined. We can see the type of this function in utop:

```
# Deferred.all_unit;;
- : unit Deferred.t list -> unit Deferred.t = <fun>
```

Finally, we create a command-line interface using Command.async:

```
let () =
  Command.async
    ~summary:"Retrieve definitions from duckduckgo search engine"
    (let%map_open.Command words =
       anon (sequence ("word" %: string))
     in
     fun () -> search_and_print words)
  |> Command.run
```

And that's all we need for a simple but usable definition searcher:

```
$ dune exec -- ./search.exe "Concurrent Programming" "OCaml"
Concurrent Programming
----------------------

"Concurrent computing is a form of computing in which several
computations are executed during overlapping time
periodsconcurrentlyinstead of sequentially. This is a property
of a systemthis may be an individual program, a computer, or a
networkand there is a separate execution point or \"thread of
control\" for each computation. A concurrent system is one where a
computation can advance without waiting for all other computations to
complete."

OCaml
-----

"OCaml, originally named Objective Caml, is the main implementation of
the programming language Caml, created by Xavier Leroy, Jérôme
Vouillon, Damien Doligez, Didier Rémy, Ascánder Suárez and others
in 1996. A member of the ML language family, OCaml extends the core
Caml language with object-oriented programming constructs."
```

17.4   Exception Handling

When programming with external resources, errors are everywhere. Everything from a flaky server to a network outage to exhausting of local resources can lead to a runtime error. When programming in OCaml, some of these errors will show up explicitly in a function's return type, and some of them will show up as exceptions. We covered exception handling in OCaml in Chapter 8.2 (Exceptions), but as we'll see, exception handling in a concurrent program presents some new challenges.

Let's get a better sense of how exceptions work in Async by creating an asynchronous computation that (sometimes) fails with an exception. The function maybe_raise blocks for half a second, and then either throws an exception or returns unit, alternating between the two behaviors on subsequent calls:

```
# let maybe_raise =
    let should_fail = ref false in
    fun () ->
      let will_fail = !should_fail in
      should_fail := not will_fail;
      let%map () = after (Time.Span.of_sec 0.5) in
      if will_fail then raise Exit else ();;
val maybe_raise : unit -> unit Deferred.t = <fun>
# maybe_raise ();;
- : unit = ()
# maybe_raise ();;
Exception: (monitor.ml.Error Exit ("Caught by monitor
    block_on_async"))
```

In utop, the exception thrown by maybe_raise () terminates the evaluation of just that expression, but in a standalone program, an uncaught exception would bring down the entire process.

So, how could we capture and handle such an exception? You might try to do this using OCaml's built-in try/with expression, but as you can see that doesn't quite do the trick:

```
# let handle_error () =
    try
      let%map () = maybe_raise () in
      "success"
    with _ -> return "failure";;
val handle_error : unit -> string Deferred.t = <fun>
# handle_error ();;
- : string = "success"
# handle_error ();;
Exception: (monitor.ml.Error Exit ("Caught by monitor
    block_on_async"))
```

This didn't work because try/with only captures exceptions that are thrown by the code executed synchronously within it, while maybe_raise schedules an Async job that will throw an exception in the future, after the try/with expression has exited.

We can capture this kind of asynchronous error using the try_with function provided by Async. try_with f takes as its argument a deferred-returning thunk f and returns a deferred that becomes determined either as Ok of whatever f returned, or Error exn if f threw an exception before its return value became determined.

Here's a trivial example of try_with in action.

```
# let handle_error () =
    match%map try_with (fun () -> maybe_raise ()) with
    | Ok ()    -> "success"
```

```
      | Error _ -> "failure";;
val handle_error : unit -> string Deferred.t = <fun>
# handle_error ();;
- : string = "success"
# handle_error ();;
- : string = "failure"
```

17.4.1   Monitors

try_with is a useful tool for handling exceptions in Async, but it's not the whole story. All of Async's exception-handling mechanisms, try_with included, are built on top of Async's system of *monitors*, which are inspired by the error-handling mechanism in Erlang of the same name. Monitors are fairly low-level and are only occasionally used directly, but it's nonetheless worth understanding how they work.

In Async, a monitor is a context that determines what to do when there is an unhandled exception. Every Async job runs within the context of some monitor, which, when the job is running, is referred to as the current monitor. When a new Async job is scheduled, say, using bind or map, it inherits the current monitor of the job that spawned it.

Monitors are arranged in a tree—when a new monitor is created (say, using Monitor.create), it is a child of the current monitor. You can explicitly run jobs within a monitor using within, which takes a thunk that returns a nondeferred value, or within', which takes a thunk that returns a deferred. Here's an example:

```
# let blow_up () =
    let monitor = Monitor.create ~name:"blow up monitor" () in
    within' ~monitor maybe_raise;;
val blow_up : unit -> unit Deferred.t = <fun>
# blow_up ();;
- : unit = ()
# blow_up ();;
Exception: (monitor.ml.Error Exit ("Caught by monitor blow up
    monitor"))
```

In addition to the ordinary stack-trace, the exception displays the trace of monitors through which the exception traveled, starting at the one we created, called "blow up monitor." The other monitors you see come from utop's special handling of deferreds.

Monitors can do more than just augment the error-trace of an exception. You can also use a monitor to explicitly handle errors delivered to that monitor. The Monitor.detach_and_get_error_stream call is a particularly important one. It detaches the monitor from its parent, handing back the stream of errors that would otherwise have been delivered to the parent monitor. This allows one to do custom handling of errors, which may include reraising errors to the parent. Here is a very simple example of a function that captures and ignores errors in the processes it spawns.

```
# let swallow_error () =
    let monitor = Monitor.create () in
    Stream.iter (Monitor.detach_and_get_error_stream monitor)
      ~f:(fun _exn -> printf "an error happened\n");
```

```
    within' ~monitor (fun () ->
      let%bind () = after (Time.Span.of_sec 0.25) in
      failwith "Kaboom!");;
val swallow_error : unit -> 'a Deferred.t = <fun>
```

The deferred returned by this function is never determined, since the computation ends with an exception rather than a return value. That means that if we run this function in utop, we'll never get our prompt back.

We can fix this by using Deferred.any along with a timeout to get a deferred we know will become determined eventually. Deferred.any takes a list of deferreds, and returns a deferred which will become determined assuming any of its arguments becomes determined.

```
# Deferred.any [ after (Time.Span.of_sec 0.5)
              ; swallow_error () ];;
an error happened
- : unit = ()
```

As you can see, the message "an error happened" is printed out before the timeout expires.

Here's an example of a monitor that passes some exceptions through to the parent and handles others. Exceptions are sent to the parent using Monitor.send_exn, with Monitor.current being called to find the current monitor, which is the parent of the newly created monitor.

```
# exception Ignore_me;;
exception Ignore_me
# let swallow_some_errors exn_to_raise =
    let child_monitor  = Monitor.create  () in
    let parent_monitor = Monitor.current () in
    Stream.iter
      (Monitor.detach_and_get_error_stream child_monitor)
      ~f:(fun error ->
        match Monitor.extract_exn error with
        | Ignore_me -> printf "ignoring exn\n"
        | _ -> Monitor.send_exn parent_monitor error);
    within' ~monitor:child_monitor (fun () ->
      let%bind () = after (Time.Span.of_sec 0.25) in
      raise exn_to_raise);;
val swallow_some_errors : exn -> 'a Deferred.t = <fun>
```

Note that we use Monitor.extract_exn to grab the underlying exception that was thrown. Async wraps exceptions it catches with extra information, including the monitor trace, so you need to grab the underlying exception if you want to depend on the details of the original exception thrown.

If we pass in an exception other than Ignore_me, like, say, the built-in exception Not_found, then the exception will be passed to the parent monitor and delivered as usual:

```
# exception Another_exception;;
exception Another_exception
# Deferred.any [ after (Time.Span.of_sec 0.5)
              ; swallow_some_errors Another_exception ];;
```

```
Exception:
(monitor.ml.Error (Another_exception) ("Caught by monitor (id 69)")).
```

If instead we use `Ignore_me`, the exception will be ignored, and the computation will finish when the timeout expires.

```
# Deferred.any [ after (Time.Span.of_sec 0.5)
                ; swallow_some_errors Ignore_me ];;
ignoring exn
- : unit = ()
```

In practice, you should rarely use monitors directly, and instead use functions like `try_with` and `Monitor.protect` that are built on top of monitors. One example of a library that uses monitors directly is `Tcp.Server.create`, which tracks both exceptions thrown by the logic that handles the network connection and by the callback for responding to an individual request, in either case responding to an exception by closing the connection. It is for building this kind of custom error handling that monitors can be helpful.

17.4.2   Example: Handling Exceptions with DuckDuckGo

Let's now go back and improve the exception handling of our DuckDuckGo client. In particular, we'll change it so that any query that fails is reported without preventing other queries from completing.

The search code as it is fails rarely, so let's make a change that allows us to trigger failures more predictably. We'll do this by making it possible to distribute the requests over multiple servers. Then, we'll handle the errors that occur when one of those servers is misspecified.

First we'll need to change `query_uri` to take an argument specifying the server to connect to:

```
(* Generate a DuckDuckGo search URI from a query string *)
let query_uri ~server query =
  let base_uri =
    Uri.of_string
      (String.concat [ "http://"; server; "/?format=json" ])
  in
  Uri.add_query_param base_uri ("q", [ query ])
```

In addition, we'll make the necessary changes to get the list of servers on the command-line, and to distribute the search queries round-robin across the list of servers.

Now, let's see what happens when we rebuild the application and run it on two servers, one of which won't respond to the query.

```
$ dune exec -- ./search.exe -servers localhost,api.duckduckgo.com
    "Concurrent Programming" "OCaml"
(monitor.ml.Error (Unix.Unix_error "Connection refused" connect
    127.0.0.1:80)
  ("Raised by primitive operation at file
    \"duniverse/async_unix/src/unix_syscalls.ml\", line 1046,
    characters 17-74"
```

```
"Called from file \"duniverse/async_kernel/src/deferred1.ml\"", line
    17, characters 40-45"
"Called from file \"duniverse/async_kernel/src/job_queue.ml\"", line
    170, characters 6-47"
"Caught by monitor Tcp.close_sock_on_error"))
[1]
```

As you can see, we got a "Connection refused" failure, which ends the entire program, even though one of the two queries would have gone through successfully on its own. We can handle the failures of individual connections separately by using the `try_with` function within each call to `get_definition`, as follows:

```
(* Execute the DuckDuckGo search *)
let get_definition ~server word =
  match%map
    try_with (fun () ->
      let%bind _, body =
        Cohttp_async.Client.get (query_uri ~server word)
      in
      let%map string = Cohttp_async.Body.to_string body in
      word, get_definition_from_json string)
  with
  | Ok (word, result) -> word, Ok result
  | Error _ -> word, Error "Unexpected failure"
```

Here, we first use `try_with` to capture the exception, and then use `match%map` (another syntax provided by `ppx_let`) to convert the error into the form we want: a pair whose first element is the word being searched for, and the second element is the (possibly erroneous) result.

Now we just need to change the code for `print_result` so that it can handle the new type:

```
(* Print out a word/definition pair *)
let print_result (word, definition) =
  printf
    "%s\n%s\n\n%s\n\n"
    word
    (String.init (String.length word) ~f:(fun _ -> '-'))
    (match definition with
     | Error s -> "DuckDuckGo query failed: " ^ s
     | Ok None -> "No definition found"
     | Ok (Some def) ->
       String.concat ~sep:"\n" (Wrapper.wrap (Wrapper.make 70) def))
```

Now, if we run that same query, we'll get individualized handling of the connection failures:

```
$ dune exec -- ./search.exe -servers localhost,api.duckduckgo.com
    "Concurrent Programming" OCaml
Concurrent Programming
----------------------

DuckDuckGo query failed: Unexpected failure

OCaml
-----
```

"OCaml, originally named Objective Caml, is the main implementation of the programming language Caml, created by Xavier Leroy, Jérôme Vouillon, Damien Doligez, Didier Rémy, Ascánder Suárez and others in 1996. A member of the ML language family, OCaml extends the core Caml language with object-oriented programming constructs."

Now, only the query that went to localhost failed.

Note that in this code, we're relying on the fact that Cohttp_async.Client.get will clean up after itself after an exception, in particular by closing its file descriptors. If you need to implement such functionality directly, you may want to use the Monitor.protect call, which is analogous to the protect call described in Chapter 8.2.3 (Cleaning Up in the Presence of Exceptions).

17.5   Timeouts, Cancellation, and Choices

In a concurrent program, one often needs to combine results from multiple, distinct concurrent subcomputations going on in the same program. We already saw this in our DuckDuckGo example, where we used Deferred.all and Deferred.all_unit to wait for a list of deferreds to become determined. Another useful primitive is Deferred.both, which lets you wait until two deferreds of different types have returned, returning both values as a tuple. Here, we use the function sec, which is shorthand for creating a time-span equal to a given number of seconds:

```
# let string_and_float =
    Deferred.both
      (let%map () = after (sec 0.5) in "A")
      (let%map () = after (sec 0.25) in 32.33);;
val string_and_float : (string * float) Deferred.t = <abstr>
# string_and_float;;
- : string * float = ("A", 32.33)
```

Sometimes, however, we want to wait only for the first of multiple events to occur. This happens particularly when dealing with timeouts. In that case, we can use the call Deferred.any, which, given a list of deferreds, returns a single deferred that will become determined once any of the values on the list is determined.

```
# Deferred.any
    [ (let%map () = after (sec 0.5) in "half a second")
    ; (let%map () = after (sec 1.0) in "one second")
    ; (let%map () = after (sec 4.0) in "four seconds")
    ];;
- : string = "half a second"
```

Let's use this to add timeouts to our DuckDuckGo searches. The following code is a wrapper for get_definition that takes a timeout (in the form of a Time.Span.t) and returns either the definition, or, if that takes too long, an error:

```
let get_definition_with_timeout ~server ~timeout word =
  Deferred.any
    [ (let%map () = after timeout in
```

```
        word, Error "Timed out")
    ; (match%map get_definition ~server word with
      | word, Error _ -> word, Error "Unexpected failure"
      | word, (Ok _ as x) -> word, x)
    ]
```

We use `let%map` above to transform the deferred values we're waiting for so that `Deferred.any` can choose between values of the same type.

A problem with this code is that the HTTP query kicked off by `get_definition` is not actually shut down when the timeout fires. As such, `get_definition_with_timeout` can leak an open connection. Happily, Cohttp does provide a way of shutting down a client. You can pass a deferred under the label `interrupt` to `Cohttp_async.Client.get`. Once `interrupt` is determined, the client connection will be shut down.

The following code shows how you can change `get_definition` and `get_definition_with_timeout` to cancel the get call if the timeout expires:

```
(* Execute the DuckDuckGo search *)
let get_definition ~server ~interrupt word =
  match%map
    try_with (fun () ->
        let%bind _, body =
          Cohttp_async.Client.get ~interrupt (query_uri ~server word)
        in
        let%map string = Cohttp_async.Body.to_string body in
        word, get_definition_from_json string)
  with
  | Ok (word, result) -> word, Ok result
  | Error _ -> word, Error "Unexpected failure"
```

Next, we'll modify `get_definition_with_timeout` to create a deferred to pass in to `get_definition`, which will become determined when our timeout expires:

```
let get_definition_with_timeout ~server ~timeout word =
  match%map
    get_definition ~server ~interrupt:(after timeout) word
  with
  | word, (Ok _ as x) -> word, x
  | word, Error _ -> word, Error "Unexpected failure"
```

This will cause the connection to shutdown cleanly when we time out; but our code no longer explicitly knows whether or not the timeout has kicked in. In particular, the error message on a timeout will now be "Unexpected failure" rather than "Timed out", which it was in our previous implementation.

We can get more precise handling of timeouts using Async's `choose` function. `choose` lets you pick among a collection of different deferreds, reacting to exactly one of them. Each deferred is paired, using the function `choice`, with a function that is called if and only if that deferred is chosen. Here's the type signature of `choice` and `choose`:

```
# choice;;
- : 'a Deferred.t -> ('a -> 'b) -> 'b Deferred.choice = <fun>
# choose;;
- : 'a Deferred.choice list -> 'a Deferred.t = <fun>
```

Note that there's no guarantee that the winning deferred will be the one that becomes determined first. But choose does guarantee that only one choice will be chosen, and only the chosen choice will execute the attached function.

In the following example, we use choose to ensure that the interrupt deferred becomes determined if and only if the timeout deferred is chosen. Here's the code:

```
let get_definition_with_timeout ~server ~timeout word =
  let interrupt = Ivar.create () in
  choose
    [ choice (after timeout) (fun () ->
          Ivar.fill interrupt ();
          word, Error "Timed out")
    ; choice
        (get_definition ~server ~interrupt:(Ivar.read interrupt) word)
        (fun (word, result) ->
          let result' =
            match result with
            | Ok _ as x -> x
            | Error _ -> Error "Unexpected failure"
          in
          word, result')
    ]
```

Now, if we run this with a suitably small timeout, we'll see that one query succeeds and the other fails reporting a timeout:

```
$ dune exec -- ./search.exe "concurrent programming" ocaml -timeout
    0.1s
concurrent programming
---------------------

"Concurrent computing is a form of computing in which several
computations are executed during overlapping time
periodsconcurrentlyinstead of sequentially. This is a property
of a systemthis may be an individual program, a computer, or a
networkand there is a separate execution point or \"thread of
control\" for each computation. A concurrent system is one where a
computation can advance without waiting for all other computations to
complete."

ocaml
-----

DuckDuckGo query failed: Timed out
```

17.6   Working with System Threads

Although we haven't worked with them yet, OCaml does have built-in support for true system threads, i.e., kernel-level threads whose interleaving is controlled by the operating system. We discussed in the beginning of the chapter the advantages of Async's cooperative threading model over system threads, but even if you mostly use

Async, OCaml's system threads are sometimes necessary, and it's worth understanding them.

The most surprising aspect of OCaml's system threads is that they don't afford you any access to physical parallelism. That's because OCaml's runtime has a single runtime lock that at most one thread can be holding at a time.

Given that threads don't provide physical parallelism, why are they useful at all?

The most common reason for using system threads is that there are some operating system calls that have no nonblocking alternative, which means that you can't run them directly in a system like Async without blocking your entire program. For this reason, Async maintains a thread pool for running such calls. Most of the time, as a user of Async you don't need to think about this, but it is happening under the covers.

Another reason to have multiple threads is to deal with non-OCaml libraries that have their own event loop or for another reason need their own threads. In that case, it's sometimes useful to run some OCaml code on the foreign thread as part of the communication to your main program. OCaml's foreign function interface is discussed in more detail in Chapter 23 (Foreign Function Interface).

Multicore OCaml

OCaml doesn't support truly parallel threads today, but it will soon. The current development branch of OCaml, which is expected to be released in 2022 as OCaml 5.0, has a long awaited multicore-capable garbage collector, which is the result of years of research and hard implementation work.

We won't discuss the multicore gc here in part because it's not yet released, and in part because there's a lot of open questions about how OCaml programs should take advantage of multicore in a way that's safe, convenient, and performant. Given all that, we just don't know enough to write a chapter about multicore today.

In any case, while multicore OCaml isn't here yet, it's an exciting part of OCaml's near-term future.

Another occasional use for system threads is to better interoperate with compute-intensive OCaml code. In Async, if you have a long-running computation that never calls bind or map, then that computation will block out the Async runtime until it completes.

One way of dealing with this is to explicitly break up the calculation into smaller pieces that are separated by binds. But sometimes this explicit yielding is impractical, since it may involve intrusive changes to an existing codebase. Another solution is to run the code in question in a separate thread. Async's In_thread module provides multiple facilities for doing just this, In_thread.run being the simplest. We can simply write:

```
# let def = In_thread.run (fun () -> List.range 1 10);;
val def : int list Deferred.t = <abstr>
# def;;
- : int list = [1; 2; 3; 4; 5; 6; 7; 8; 9]
```

to cause List.range 1 10 to be run on one of Async's worker threads. When the computation is complete, the result is placed in the deferred, where it can be used in the ordinary way from Async.

Interoperability between Async and system threads can be quite tricky. Consider the following function for testing how responsive Async is. The function takes a deferred-returning thunk, and it first runs that thunk, and then uses `Clock.every` to wake up every 100 milliseconds and print out a timestamp, until the returned deferred becomes determined, at which point it prints out one last timestamp:

```
# let log_delays thunk =
    let start = Time.now () in
    let print_time () =
      let diff = Time.diff (Time.now ()) start in
      printf "%s, " (Time.Span.to_string diff)
    in
    let d = thunk () in
    Clock.every (sec 0.1) ~stop:d print_time;
    let%bind () = d in
    printf "\nFinished at: ";
    print_time ();
    printf "\n";
    Writer.flushed (force Writer.stdout);;
val log_delays : (unit -> unit Deferred.t) -> unit Deferred.t = <fun>
```

If we feed this function a simple timeout deferred, it works as you might expect, waking up roughly every 100 milliseconds:

```
# log_delays (fun () -> after (sec 0.5));;
37.670135498046875us, 100.65722465515137ms, 201.19547843933105ms,
    301.85389518737793ms, 402.58693695068359ms,
Finished at: 500.67615509033203ms,
- : unit = ()
```

Now see what happens if, instead of waiting on a clock event, we wait for a busy loop to finish running:

```
# let busy_loop () =
    let x = ref None in
    for i = 1 to 100_000_000 do x := Some i done;;
val busy_loop : unit -> unit = <fun>
# log_delays (fun () -> return (busy_loop ()));;
Finished at: 874.99594688415527ms,
- : unit = ()
```

As you can see, instead of waking up 10 times a second, `log_delays` is blocked out entirely while `busy_loop` churns away.

If, on the other hand, we use `In_thread.run` to offload this to a different system thread, the behavior will be different:

```
# log_delays (fun () -> In_thread.run busy_loop);;
31.709671020507812us, 107.50102996826172ms, 207.65542984008789ms,
    307.95812606811523ms, 458.15873146057129ms,
      608.44659805297852ms, 708.55593681335449ms, 808.81166458129883ms,
Finished at: 840.72136878967285ms,
- : unit = ()
```

Now `log_delays` does get a chance to run, but it's no longer at clean 100 millisecond intervals. The reason is that now that we're using system threads, we are at the mercy of the operating system to decide when each thread gets scheduled. The behavior of threads is very much dependent on the operating system and how it is configured.

Another tricky aspect of dealing with OCaml threads has to do with allocation. When compiling to native code, OCaml's threads only get a chance to give up the runtime lock when they interact with the allocator, so if there's a piece of code that doesn't allocate at all, then it will never allow another OCaml thread to run. Bytecode doesn't have this behavior, so if we run a nonallocating loop in bytecode, our timer process will get to run:

```
# let noalloc_busy_loop () =
    for i = 0 to 100_000_000 do () done;;
val noalloc_busy_loop : unit -> unit = <fun>
# log_delays (fun () -> In_thread.run noalloc_busy_loop);;
32.186508178710938us, 116.56808853149414ms, 216.65477752685547ms,
    316.83063507080078ms, 417.13213920593262ms,
Finished at: 418.69187355041504ms,
- : unit = ()
```

But if we compile this to a native-code executable, then the nonallocating busy loop will block anything else from running:

```
$ dune exec -- native_code_log_delays.exe
197.41058349609375us,
Finished at: 1.2127914428710938s,
```

The takeaway from these examples is that predicting thread interleavings is a subtle business. Staying within the bounds of Async has its limitations, but it leads to more predictable behavior.

17.6.1 Thread-Safety and Locking

Once you start working with system threads, you'll need to be careful about mutable data structures. Most mutable OCaml data structures will behave non-deterministically when accessed concurrently by multiple threads. The issues you can run into range from runtime exceptions to corrupted data structures. That means you should almost always use mutexes when sharing mutable data between different systems threads. Even data structures that seem like they should be safe but are mutable under the covers, like lazy values, can behave in surprising ways when accessed from multiple threads.

There are two commonly available mutex packages for OCaml: the `Mutex` module that's part of the standard library, which is just a wrapper over OS-level mutexes and `Nano_mutex`, a more efficient alternative that takes advantage of some of the locking done by the OCaml runtime to avoid needing to create an OS-level mutex much of the time. As a result, creating a `Nano_mutex.t` is 20 times faster than creating a `Mutex.t`, and acquiring the mutex is about 40 percent faster.

Overall, combining Async and threads is quite tricky, but it's pretty simple if the following two conditions hold:

- There is no shared mutable state between the various threads involved.

- The computations executed by `In_thread.run` do not make any calls to the Async library.

That said, you can safely use threads in ways that violate these constraints. In particular, foreign threads can acquire the Async lock using calls from the `Thread_safe` module in Async, and thereby run Async computations safely. This is a very flexible way of connecting threads to the Async world, but it's a complex use case that is beyond the scope of this chapter.

18 Testing

The goal of this chapter is to teach you how to write effective tests in OCaml, and to show off some tools that can help. Tooling is especially important in the context of testing because one of the things that prevents people from doing as much testing as they should is the tedium of it. But with the right tools in hand, writing tests can be lightweight and fun.

And that's important, because when testing is fun, you'll do more of it, and thorough testing is an essential element of building reliable and evolvable software. People sometimes imagine that tests are less important in a language like OCaml with a rich and expressive type-system, but in some sense the opposite is true. Really, types help you get more value out of your testing effort, both because they prevent you from needing to test all sorts of trivial properties that are automatically enforced by the type system, and because the rigidity of types mean that your code often has a kind of snap-together quality, where a relatively small number of tests can do an outsize amount to ensure that your code is behaving as expected.

Before we start introducing testing tools, it's worth pausing to consider what we want out of our tests in the first place.

Ideally, tests should be:

- **Easy to write and run**. Tests should require a minimum of boilerplate to create and to hook into your development process. Ideally, you should set things up so that tests are run automatically on every proposed change, preventing people from accidentally breaking the build.
- **Easy to update**. Tests that are hard to adjust in the face of code changes can become their own form of technical debt.
- **Fast**, so they don't slow down your development process.
- **Deterministic**. It's hard to take test failures seriously if there's a decent chance that the failure is a random glitch. You want your test failures to be believable indications of a problem, which requires determinism.
- **Understandable**. Good tests should be easy to read, and their failures should be localized and specific, so it's easy to find and fix the problem flagged by a failing test.

No testing framework can ensure that your tests satisfy these properties. But the tools you choose can help or hinder on all these fronts.

As we go through the rest of this chapter and introduce you to some of the available tooling, you should be able to see how each tool helps advance these goals.

18.1   Inline Tests

The first step towards a good testing environment is making it easy to set up and run a test. To that end, we'll show you how to write tests with `ppx_inline_test`, which lets you add tests to any module in a library with a specially annotated `let` binding.

To use inline tests in a library, we need to do two things:

- Tell Dune to expect inline tests to show up in the library, and
- enable `ppx_inline_test` as a preprocessor.

The first of these is achieved by adding an `(inline_tests)` declaration, and the second is achieved by adding `ppx_inline_test` to the set of preprocessors. Here's the resulting dune file.

```
(library
 (name foo)
 (libraries base stdio)
 (inline_tests)
 (preprocess (pps ppx_inline_test)))
```

With this done, any module in this library can host a test. We'll demonstrate this by creating a file called `test.ml`, containing one test.

```
open Base

let%test "rev" =
  List.equal Int.equal (List.rev [ 3; 2; 1 ]) [ 1; 2; 3 ]
```

The test passes if the expression on the right-hand side of the equals-sign evaluates to true. Inline tests are not automatically run with the instantiation of the module, but are instead registered for running via the test runner.

```
$ dune runtest
```

No output is generated because the test passed successfully. But if we break the test,

```
open Base

let%test "rev" =
  List.equal Int.equal (List.rev [ 3; 2; 1 ]) [ 3; 2; 1 ]
```

we'll see an error when we run it.

```
$ dune runtest
File "test.ml", line 3, characters 0-74: rev is false.

FAILED 1 / 1 tests
[1]
```

18.1.1   More Readable Errors with `test_eq`

One problem with the test output we just saw is that it doesn't show the data associated with the failed test, thus making it harder to diagnose and fix the problem when it occurs. We can fix this if we signal a test failure by throwing an exception, rather than by returning false. That exception can then be used to report the details of what went wrong.

To do this, we'll change our test declaration to use `let%test_unit` instead of `let%test`, so that the test no longer expects a body that returns a bool. We're also going to use the `[%test_eq]` syntax, which, given a type, generates code to test for equality and throw a meaningful exception if the arguments are unequal.

To use `[%test_eq]`, we're going to need to add the `ppx_assert` syntax extension, so we'll need to adjust our dune file appropriately.

```
(library
 (name foo)
 (libraries base stdio)
 (preprocess
  (pps ppx_inline_test ppx_assert))
 (inline_tests))
```

Here's what our new test looks like.

```
open Base

let%test_unit "rev" =
  [%test_eq: int list] (List.rev [ 3; 2; 1 ]) [ 3; 2; 1 ]
```

Now we can run the test to see what the output looks like.

```
$ dune runtest
File "test.ml", line 3, characters 0-79: rev threw
(duniverse/ppx_assert/runtime-lib/runtime.ml.E "comparison failed"
  ((1 2 3) vs (3 2 1) (Loc test.ml:4:13))).
  Raised at Base__Exn.protectx in file "duniverse/base/src/exn.ml",
    line 71, characters 4-114
  Called from
    Ppx_inline_test_lib__Runtime.time_and_reset_random_seeds in file
    "duniverse/ppx_inline_test/runtime-lib/runtime.ml", line 356,
    characters 15-52
  Called from Ppx_inline_test_lib__Runtime.test in file
    "duniverse/ppx_inline_test/runtime-lib/runtime.ml", line 444,
    characters 52-83

FAILED 1 / 1 tests
[1]
```

As you can see, the data that caused the comparison to fail is printed out, along with the stack backtrace. Sadly, the backtrace is in this case mostly a distraction. That's a downside of using exceptions to report test failures.

18.1.2   Where Should Tests Go?

The inline test framework lets you put tests into any .ml file that's part of a library. But just because you can do something doesn't mean you should.

Putting tests directly in the library you're building certainly has some benefits. For one thing, it lets you put a test for a given function directly after the definition of that function, which in some cases can be good for readability. This approach also lets you test aspects of your code that aren't exposed by its external interface.

While this sounds appealing at first glance, putting tests in libraries has several downsides.

- **Readability**. Including all of your tests directly in your application code can make that code itself harder to read. This can lead to people writing too few tests in an effort to keep their application code uncluttered.
- **Bloat**. When your tests are written as a part of your library, it means that every user of your library has to link in that testing code in their production application. Even though that code won't be run, it still adds to the size of the executable. It can also require dependencies on libraries that you don't need in production, which can reduce the portability of your code.
- **Testing mindset**. Writing tests on the inside of your libraries lets you write tests against any part of your implementation, rather than just the exposed API. This freedom is useful, but can also put you in the wrong testing mindset. Testing that's phrased in terms of the public API often does a better job of testing what's fundamental about your code, and will better survive refactoring of the implementation. Also, the discipline of keeping tests outside of requires you to write code that can be tested that way, which pushes towards better designs.

For all of these reasons, our recommendation is to put the bulk of your tests in test-only libraries created for that purpose. There are some legitimate reasons to want to put some test directly in your production library, e.g., when you need access to some functionality to do the test that's important but is really awkward to expose. But such cases are very much the exception.

Why Can't Inline Tests Go in Executables?

We've only talked about putting tests into libraries. What about executables? It turns out you can't do this directly, because Dune doesn't support the inline_tests declaration in source files that are directly part of an executable.

There's a good reason for this: the ppx_inline_test test runner needs to instantiate the modules that contain the tests. If those modules have toplevel side-effects, that's a recipe for disaster, since you don't want those top-level effects to be triggered by the test framework.

So, how do we test code that's part of an executable? The solution is to break up your program into two pieces: a directory containing a library that contains the logic of your program, but no top-level effects; and a directory for the executable that links in the library, and is responsible for launching the code.

18.2   Expect Tests

The tests we've shown so far have been mostly about checking some specific properties in a given scenario. Sometimes, though, what you want is not to test this or that property, but to capture and make visible your code's behavior. *Expect tests* let you do just that.

18.2.1   Basic Mechanics

With expect tests, your source file specifies both the code to be executed and the expected output. Upon running an expect test, any discrepancy between the expected output and what was actually generated is reported as a test failure.

Here's a simple example of a test written in this style. While the test generates output (though a call to `print_endline`), that output isn't captured in the source, at least, not yet.

```
open! Base
open Stdio

let%expect_test "trivial" = print_endline "Hello World!"
```

open and open!

In this example, we use open! instead of open because we happen not to be using any values from Base, and so the compiler will warn us about an unused open.

But because Base is effectively our standard library, we want to keep it open anyway, since we want any new code we write to find Base's modules rather than those from the ordinary standard library. The exclamation point at the end of open suppresses that warning.

A sensible idiom is to always use open! when opening a library like Base, so that you don't have to choose when to use the !, and when not to.

If we run the test, we'll be presented with a diff between what we wrote, and a *corrected* version of the source file that now has an `[%expect]` clause containing the output. Note that Dune will use the `patdiff` tool if it's available, which generates easier-to-read diffs. You can install `patdiff` with opam.

```
$ dune runtest
      patdiff (internal) (exit 1)
(cd _build/default && rwo/_build/install/default/bin/patdiff
    -keep-whitespace -location-style omake -ascii test.ml
    test.ml.corrected)
------ test.ml
++++++ test.ml.corrected
File "test.ml", line 5, characters 0-1:
 |open! Base
 |open Stdio
 |
 |let%expect_test "trivial" =
-|  print_endline "Hello World!"
+|  print_endline "Hello World!";
```

```
+|  [%expect {| Hello World! |}]
 [1]
```

The expect test runner also creates a version of the file with the captured output, with
.corrected appended to the end of the filename. If this new output looks correct, we
can *promote* it by copying the corrected file over the original source. The dune promote
command does just this, leaving our source as follows.

```
open Base
open Stdio

let%expect_test "trivial" =
  print_endline "Hello World!";
  [%expect {| Hello World! |}]
```

Now, if we run the test again, we'll see that it passes.

```
$ dune runtest
```

We only have one expect block in this example, but the system supports having
multiple expect blocks:

```
open Base
open Stdio

let%expect_test "multi-block" =
  print_endline "Hello";
  [%expect {| Hello |}];
  print_endline "World!";
  [%expect {| World! |}]
```

18.2.2   What Are Expect Tests Good For?

It's not obvious why one would want to use expect tests in the first place. Why should
this:

```
open Base
open Stdio

let%expect_test _ =
  print_s [%sexp (List.rev [ 3; 2; 1 ] : int list)];
  [%expect {| (1 2 3) |}]
```

be preferable to this:

```
open Base

let%test "rev" =
  List.equal Int.equal (List.rev [ 3; 2; 1 ]) [ 1; 2; 3 ]
```

Indeed, for examples like this, expect tests aren't better: simple example-based
tests like the one above work fine when it's easy and convenient to write out specific
examples in full. And, as we'll discuss later in the chapter, *property tests* are your best
bet when you have a clear set of predicates that you want to test, and examples can be
naturally generated at random.

Where expect tests shine is where you want to make visible some aspect of the behavior of your system that's hard to capture in a predicate. This is more useful than it might seem at first. Let's consider a few different example use-cases to see why.

18.2.3   Exploratory Programming

Expect tests can be especially helpful when you're in exploration mode, where you're trying to solve a problem by playing around with the data, and have no clear specification in advance.

A common programming task of this type is web-scraping, where the goal is generally to extract some useful information from a web page. Figuring out the right way to do so often involves trial and error.

Here's some code that does this kind of data extraction, using the `lambdasoup` package to traverse a chunk of HTML and spit out some data embedded within it. In particular, the function aims to produce the set of hosts that show up in links within a document.

```
open Base
open Stdio

let get_href_hosts soup =
  Soup.select "a[href]" soup
  |> Soup.to_list
  |> List.map ~f:(Soup.R.attribute "href")
  |> Set.of_list (module String)
```

We can use an expect test to demonstrate what this function does on an example page.

```
let%expect_test _ =
  let example_html =
    {|
    <html>
      Some random <b>text</b> with a
      <a href="http://ocaml.org/base">link</a>.
      And here's another
      <a href="http://github.com/ocaml/dune">link</a>.
      And here is <a>link</a> with no href.
    </html>|}
  in
  let soup = Soup.parse example_html in
  let hrefs = get_href_hosts soup in
  print_s [%sexp (hrefs : Set.M(String).t)]
```

Quoted Strings

The example above used a new syntax for string literals, called *quoted strings*. Here's an example.

```
# {|This is a quoted string|};;
- : string = "This is a quoted string"
```

The advantage of this syntax is that it allows the content to be written without the usual escaping required for ordinary string literals. Consider the following examples.

```
# {|This is a literal quote: "|};;
((:- : string = "This is a literal quote: \""::)
```

As you can see, we didn't need to escape the included quote, though the version of the string echoed back by the toplevel uses ordinary string literal syntax, and so the quote there comes out escaped.

Quoted strings are especially useful when writing strings containing text from another language, like HTML. With quoted strings, you can just paste in a snippet of some other source language, and it should work unmodified.

The one tricky corner is if you need to include a literal |} inside your quoted string. The trick is that you can change the delimiter for the quoted string by adding an arbitrary identifier, thereby ensuring that the delimiter won't show up in the body of the string.

```
# {xxx|This is how you quote a {|quoted string|}|xxx};;
- : string = "This is how you quote a {|quoted string|}"
```

If we run the test, we'll see that the output isn't exactly what was intended.

```
$ dune runtest
      patdiff (internal) (exit 1)
...
------ test.ml
++++++ test.ml.corrected
File "test.ml", line 24, characters 0-1:
|   |> List.map ~f:(Soup.R.attribute "href")
|   |> Set.of_list (module String)
|
|[@@@part "1"] ;;
|let%expect_test _ =
|  let example_html = {|
|    <html>
|      Some random <b>text</b> with a
|      <a href="http://ocaml.org/base">link</a>.
|      And here's another
|      <a href="http://github.com/ocaml/dune">link</a>.
|      And here is <a>link</a> with no href.
|    </html>|}
|  in
|  let soup = Soup.parse example_html in
|  let hrefs = get_href_hosts soup in
-|  print_s [%sexp (hrefs : Set.M(String).t)]
+|  print_s [%sexp (hrefs : Set.M(String).t)];
+|  [%expect {| (http://github.com/ocaml/dune http://ocaml.org/base)
    |}]
[1]
```

The problem here is that we failed to extract the host from the URI string. I.e., we ended up with http://github.com/ocaml/dune instead of github.com. We can fix that by using the uri library to parse the string and extract the host. Here's the modified code.

```
let get_href_hosts soup =
  Soup.select "a[href]" soup
  |> Soup.to_list
  |> List.map ~f:(Soup.R.attribute "href")
  |> List.filter_map ~f:(fun uri -> Uri.host (Uri.of_string uri))
  |> Set.of_list (module String)
```

And if we run the test again, we'll see that the output is now as it should be.

```
$ dune runtest
      patdiff (internal) (exit 1)
...
------ test.ml
++++++ test.ml.corrected
File "test.ml", line 26, characters 0-1:
 |  |> Set.of_list (module String)
 |
 |[@@@part "1"] ;;
 |let%expect_test _ =
 |  let example_html = {|
 |    <html>
 |      Some random <b>text</b> with a
 |      <a href="http://ocaml.org/base">link</a>.
 |      And here's another
 |      <a href="http://github.com/ocaml/dune">link</a>.
 |      And here is <a>link</a> with no href.
 |    </html>|}
 |  in
 |  let soup = Soup.parse example_html in
 |  let hrefs = get_href_hosts soup in
 |  print_s [%sexp (hrefs : Set.M(String).t)];
-|  [%expect {| (http://github.com/ocaml/dune http://ocaml.org/base)
 |  |}]
+|  [%expect {| (github.com ocaml.org) |}]
 |[1]
```

One nice aspect of this exploratory workflow is that once you've gotten things working, you can leave the examples you used to develop the code as permanent tests.

18.2.4   Visualizing Complex Behavior

Expect tests can be used to examine the dynamic behavior of a system. Let's walk through a simple example: a rate limiter. The job of a rate limiter is to bound the rate at which a system consumes a particular resource. The following is the `mli` for a library that specifies the logic of a simple rolling-window-style rate limiter, where the intent is to make sure that there's no window of time of the specified period during which more than a specified number of events occurs.

```
open Core

type t

val create : now:Time_ns.t -> period:Time_ns.Span.t -> rate:int -> t
val maybe_consume : t -> now:Time_ns.t -> [ `Consumed | `No_capacity ]
```

We can demonstrate the behavior of the system by running through some examples. First, we'll write some helper functions to make the examples shorter and easier to read.

```
open Core

let start_time = Time_ns.of_string "2021-06-01 7:00:00"

let limiter () =
  Rate_limiter.create
    ~now:start_time
    ~period:(Time_ns.Span.of_sec 1.)
    ~rate:2

let consume lim offset =
  let result =
    Rate_limiter.maybe_consume
      lim
      ~now:(Time_ns.add start_time (Time_ns.Span.of_sec offset))
  in
  printf
    "%4.2f: %s\n"
    offset
    (match result with
    | `Consumed -> "C"
    | `No_capacity -> "N")
```

Here, we define three values: `start_time`, which is just a point in time at which to begin our examples; `limiter`, which is a function for constructing a fresh `Limiter.t` object, with some reasonable defaults; and `consume`, which attempts to consume a resource.

Notably, `consume` doesn't just update the limiter, it also prints out a marker of the result, i.e., whether the consumption succeeded or failed.

Now we can use these helpers to see how the rate limiter would behave in a simple scenario. First, we're going to try to consume three times at time zero; then we're going to wait a half-second and consume again, and then we'll wait one more half-second, and try again.

```
let%expect_test _ =
  let lim = limiter () in
  let consume offset = consume lim offset in
  (* Exhaust the rate limit, without advancing the clock. *)
  for _ = 1 to 3 do
    consume 0.
  done;
  [%expect {| |}];
  (* Wait until a half-second has elapsed, try again *)
  consume 0.5;
  [%expect {| |}];
  (* Wait until a full second has elapsed, try again *)
  consume 1.;
  [%expect {| |}]
```

Running the tests and accepting the promotions will include the execution trace.

```
let%expect_test _ =
  let lim = limiter () in
  let consume offset = consume lim offset in
  (* Exhaust the rate limit, without advancing the clock. *)
  for _ = 1 to 3 do
    consume 0.
  done;
  [%expect {|
    0.00: C
    0.00: C
    0.00: C |}];
  (* Wait until a half-second has elapsed, try again *)
  consume 0.5;
  [%expect {| 0.50: C |}];
  (* Wait until a full second has elapsed, try again *)
  consume 1.;
  [%expect {| 1.00: C |}]
```

The above, however, is not the expected outcome! In particular, all of our calls to consume succeeded, despite us violating the 2-per-second rate limit. That's because there was a bug in our implementation. The implementation has a queue of times where consume events occurred, and we use this function to drain the queue.

```
let rec drain_old_events t =
  match Queue.peek t.events with
  | None -> ()
  | Some time ->
    if Time_ns.Span.( < ) (Time_ns.diff t.now time) t.period
    then (
      ignore (Queue.dequeue_exn t.events : Time_ns.t);
      drain_old_events t)
```

But the comparison goes the wrong way: we should discard events that are older than the limit-period, not younger. If we fix that, we'll see that the trace behaves as we'd expect.

```
let%expect_test _ =
  let lim = limiter () in
  let consume offset = consume lim offset in
  (* Exhaust the rate limit, without advancing the clock. *)
  for _ = 1 to 3 do
    consume 0.
  done;
  [%expect {|
    0.00: C
    0.00: C
    0.00: N |}];
  (* Wait until a half-second has elapsed, try again *)
  consume 0.5;
  [%expect {| 0.50: N |}];
  (* Wait until a full second has elapsed, try again *)
  consume 1.;
  [%expect {| 1.00: C |}]
```

One of the things that makes this test readable is that we went to some trouble to keep the code short and easy to read. Some of this was about creating useful helper functions, and some of it was about having a concise and noise-free format for the data captured by the expect blocks.

18.2.5   End-to-End Tests

The expect tests we've seen so far have been self-contained, not doing any IO or interacting with system resources. As a result, these tests are fast to run and entirely deterministic.

That's a great ideal, but it's not always achievable, especially when you want to run more end-to-end tests of your program. But even if you need to run tests that involve multiple processes interacting with each other and using real IO, expect tests are still a useful tool.

To see how such tests can be built, we'll write some tests for the echo server we developed in Chapter 17.2 (Example: An Echo Server).

We'll start by creating a new test directory with a dune file next to our echo-server implementation.

```
(library
 (name echo_test)
 (libraries core async)
 (preprocess (pps ppx_jane))
 (inline_tests (deps ../bin/echo.exe)))
```

The important line is the last one, where in the `inline_tests` declaration, we declare a dependency on the echo-server binary. Also, note that rather than select useful preprocessors one by one, we used the omnibus `ppx_jane` package, which bundles together a collection of useful extensions.

That done, our next step is to write some helper functions. We won't show the implementation, but here's the signature for our `Helpers` module. Note that there's an argument in the `launch` function that lets you enable the feature in the echo server that causes it to uppercase the text it receives.

```
open! Core
open Async

(** Launches the echo server *)
val launch : port:int -> uppercase:bool -> Process.t Deferred.t

(** Connects to the echo server, returning a reader and writer for
    communicating with the server. *)
val connect : port:int -> (Reader.t * Writer.t) Deferred.t

(** Sends data to the server, printing out the result  *)
val send_data : Reader.t -> Writer.t -> string -> unit Deferred.t

(** Kills the echo server, and waits until it exits  *)
val cleanup : Process.t -> unit Deferred.t
```

With the above, we can now write a test that launches the server, connects to it over TCP, and then sends some data and displays the results.

```
open! Core
open Async
open Helpers

let%expect_test "test uppercase echo" =
  let port = 8081 in
  let%bind process = launch ~port ~uppercase:true in
  Monitor.protect
    (fun () ->
      let%bind r, w = connect ~port in
      let%bind () = send_data r w "one two three\n" in
      let%bind () = [%expect] in
      let%bind () = send_data r w "one 2 three\n" in
      let%bind () = [%expect] in
      return ())
    ~finally:(fun () -> cleanup process)
```

Note that we put in some expect annotations where we want to see data, but we haven't filled them in. We can now run the test to see what happens. The results, however, are not what you might hope for.

```
$ dune runtest
Entering directory
    'rwo/_build/default/book/testing/examples/erroneous/echo_test_original'
    patdiff (internal) (exit 1)
(cd _build/default && rwo/_build/install/default/bin/patdiff
    -keep-whitespace -location-style omake -ascii test/test.ml
    test/test.ml.corrected)
------ test/test.ml
++++++ test/test.ml.corrected
File "test/test.ml", line 11, characters 0-1:
 |open! Core
 |open Async
 |open Helpers
 |
 |let%expect_test "test uppercase echo" =
 |  let port = 8081 in
 |  let%bind process  = launch ~port ~uppercase:true in
 |  Monitor.protect (fun () ->
 |      let%bind (r,w) = connect ~port in
 |      let%bind () = send_data r w "one two three\n" in
-|      let%bind () = [%expect] in
+|      let%bind () = [%expect.unreachable] in
 |      let%bind () = send_data r w "one 2 three\n" in
-|      let%bind () = [%expect] in
+|      let%bind () = [%expect.unreachable] in
 |      return ())
 |    ~finally:(fun () -> cleanup process)
+|[@@expect.uncaught_exn {|
+|  (* CR expect_test_collector: This test expectation appears to
    contain a backtrace.
+|     This is strongly discouraged as backtraces are fragile.
+|     Please change this test to not include a backtrace. *)
+|
+|  (monitor.ml.Error
+|    (Unix.Unix_error "Connection refused" connect 127.0.0.1:8081)
```

```
+|    ("<backtrace elided in test>" "Caught by monitor
      Tcp.close_sock_on_error"))
+|   Raised at Base__Result.ok_exn in file
      "duniverse/base/src/result.ml", line 201, characters 17-26
+|   Called from Expect_test_collector.Make.Instance.exec in file
      "duniverse/ppx_expect/collector/expect_test_collector.ml", line
      244, characters 12-19 |}]
[1]
```

What went wrong here? The issue is that the connect fails, because at the time of the connection, the echo server hasn't finished setting up the server. We can fix this by adding a one second delay before connecting, using Async's Clock.after. With this change, the test now passes, with the expected results.

```
open! Core
open Async
open Helpers

let%expect_test "test uppercase echo" =
  let port = 8081 in
  let%bind process  = launch ~port ~uppercase:true in
  Monitor.protect (fun () ->
      let%bind () = Clock.after (Time.Span.of_sec 1.) in
      let%bind (r,w) = connect ~port in
      let%bind () = send_data r w "one two three\n" in
      let%bind () = [%expect{| ONE TWO THREE |}] in
      let%bind () = send_data r w "one 2 three\n" in
      let%bind () = [%expect{| ONE 2 THREE |}] in
      return ())
    ~finally:(fun () -> cleanup process)
```

We fixed the problem, but the solution should make you uncomfortable. For one thing, why is one second the right timeout, rather than a half a second, or ten? The time we wait is some balance between reducing the likelihood of a non-deterministic failure versus preserving performance of the test, which is a bit of an awkward trade-off to have to make.

We can improve on this by removing the Clock.after call, and instead adding a retry loop to the connect test helper

```
let rec connect ~port =
  match%bind
    Monitor.try_with (fun () ->
        Tcp.connect
          (Tcp.Where_to_connect.of_host_and_port
             { host = "localhost"; port }))
  with
  | Ok (_, r, w) -> return (r, w)
  | Error _ ->
    let%bind () = Clock.after (Time.Span.of_sec 0.01) in
    connect ~port
```

There's still a timeout in this code, in that we wait a bit before retrying. But that timeout is quite aggressive, so you never waste more than 10 milliseconds waiting unnecessarily. That means tests will typically run fast, but if they do run slowly (maybe because your machine is heavily loaded during a big build), the test will still pass.

The lesson here is that keeping tests deterministic in the context of running programs doing real I/O gets messy fast. When possible, you should write your code in a way that allows most of it to be tested without having to connect to real running servers. But when you do need to do it, you can still use expect tests for this purpose.

18.2.6   How to Make a Good Expect Test

Taken together, these examples suggest some guidelines for building good expect tests:

- **Write helper functions** to help you set up your test scenarios more concisely.
- **Write custom pretty-printers** that surface just the information that you need to see in the test. This makes your tests easier to read, and also minimizes unnecessary churn when details that are irrelevant to your test change.
- **Aim for determinism**, ideally by organizing your code so you can put it through its paces without directly interacting with the outside world, which is generally the source of non-determinism. But if you must, be careful to avoid timeouts and other stopgaps that will fall apart under performance pressure.

18.3   Property Testing with Quickcheck

Many tests amount to little more than individual examples decorated with simple assertions to check this or that property. *Property testing* is a useful extension of this approach, which lets you explore a much larger portion of your code's behavior with only a small amount of programmer effort.

The basic idea is simple enough. A property test requires two things: a function that takes an example input and checks that a given property holds on that example; and a way of generating random examples. The test then checks whether the predicate holds over many randomly generated examples.

We can write a property test using only the tools we've learned so far. In this example, we'll check an obvious-seeming invariant connecting three operations:

- `Int.sign`, which computes a `Sign.t` representing the sign of an integer, either `Positive`, `Negative`, or `Zero`
- `Int.neg`, which negates a number
- `Sign.flip`, which flips a `Sign.t`, i.e., mapping `Positive` to `Negative` and vice versa.

The invariant we want to check is that the sign of the negation of any integer x is the flip of the sign of x.

Here's a simple implementation of this test.

```
open Base

let%test_unit "negation flips the sign" =
  for _ = 0 to 100_000 do
    let x = Random.int_incl Int.min_value Int.max_value in
    [%test_eq: Sign.t]
```

```
      (Int.sign (Int.neg x))
      (Sign.flip (Int.sign x))
  done
```

As you might expect, the test passes.

```
$ dune runtest
```

One choice we had to make in our implementation is which probability distribution to use for selecting examples. This may not seem like an important question, but it is. When it comes to testing, not all probability distributions are created equal.

Indeed, the choice we made, which was to pick integers uniformly and at random from the full set of integers, is problematic, since it picks interesting special cases, like zero and one, with the same probability as everything else. Given the number of integers, the chance of testing any of those special cases is rather low, which seems like a problem.

This is a place where Quickcheck can help. Quickcheck is a library to help automate the construction of testing distributions. Let's try rewriting the above example using it. Note that we open Core here because Core has nicely integrated support for Quickcheck, with helper functions already integrated into most common modules. There's also a standalone Base_quickcheck library that can be used without Core.

```
open Core

let%test_unit "negation flips the sign" =
  Quickcheck.test
    ~sexp_of:[%sexp_of: int]
    (Int.gen_incl Int.min_value Int.max_value)
    ~f:(fun x ->
      [%test_eq: Sign.t]
        (Int.sign (Int.neg x))
        (Sign.flip (Int.sign x)))
```

Note that we didn't explicitly state how many examples should be tested. Quickcheck has a built-in default which can be overridden by way of an optional argument.

Running the test uncovers the fact that the property we've been testing doesn't actually hold on all outputs, as you can see below.

```
$ dune runtest
File "test.ml", line 3, characters 0-244: negation flips the sign
    threw
("Base_quickcheck.Test.run: test failed" (input -4611686018427387904)
  (error
    ((duniverse/ppx_assert/runtime-lib/runtime.ml.E "comparison
    failed"
      (Neg vs Pos (Loc test.ml:7:19)))
      "Raised at Ppx_assert_lib__Runtime.failwith in file
    \"duniverse/ppx_assert/runtime-lib/runtime.ml\", line 28,
    characters 28-53\
      \nCalled from Base__Or_error.try_with in file
    \"duniverse/base/src/or_error.ml\", line 76, characters 9-15\
      \n"))).
  Raised at Base__Exn.protectx in file "duniverse/base/src/exn.ml",
    line 71, characters 4-114
```

```
    Called from
      Ppx_inline_test_lib__Runtime.time_and_reset_random_seeds in file
      "duniverse/ppx_inline_test/runtime-lib/runtime.ml", line 356,
      characters 15-52
    Called from Ppx_inline_test_lib__Runtime.test in file
      "duniverse/ppx_inline_test/runtime-lib/runtime.ml", line 444,
      characters 52-83

FAILED 1 / 1 tests
[1]
```

The example that triggers the exception is -4611686018427387904, also known as `Int.min_value`, which is the smallest value of type `Int.t`. This uncovers something about integers which may not have been obvious, which is that the largest int, `Int.max_value`, is smaller in absolute value than `Int.max_value`.

```
# Int.min_value;;
- : int = -4611686018427387904
# Int.max_value;;
- : int = 4611686018427387903
```

That means there's no natural choice for the negation of `min_value`. It turns out that the standard behavior here (not just for OCaml) is for the negation of `min_value` to be equal to itself.

```
# Int.neg Int.min_value;;
- : int = -4611686018427387904
```

Quickcheck's decision to put much larger weight on special cases is what allowed us to discover this unexpected behavior. Note that in this case, it's not really a bug that we've uncovered, it's just that the property that we thought would hold can't in practice. But either way, Quickcheck helped us understand the behavior of our code better.

18.3.1   Handling Complex Types

Tests can't subsist on simple atomic types alone, which is why you'll often want to build probability distributions over more complex types. Here's a simple example, where we want to test the behavior of `List.rev_append`. For this test, we're going to use a probability distribution for generating pairs of lists of integers. The following example shows how that can be done using Quickcheck's combinators.

```
open Core

let gen_int_list_pair =
  let int_list_gen =
    List.gen_non_empty (Int.gen_incl Int.min_value Int.max_value)
  in
  Quickcheck.Generator.both int_list_gen int_list_gen

let%test_unit "List.rev_append is List.append of List.rev" =
  Quickcheck.test
    ~sexp_of:[%sexp_of: int list * int list]
    gen_int_list_pair
```

```
~f:(fun (l1, l2) ->
  [%test_eq: int list]
    (List.rev_append l1 l2)
    (List.append (List.rev l1) l2))
```

Here, we made use of `Quickcheck.Generator.both`, which is useful for creating a generator for pairs from two generators for the constituent types.

```
# open Core;;
# #show Quickcheck.Generator.both;;
val both :
  'a Base_quickcheck.Generator.t ->
  'b Base_quickcheck.Generator.t -> ('a * 'b)
    Base_quickcheck.Generator.t
```

The declaration of the generator is pretty simple, but it's also tedious. Happily, Quickcheck ships with a PPX that can automate creation of the generator given just the type declaration. We can use that to simplify our code, as shown below.

```
open Core

let%test_unit "List.rev_append is List.append of List.rev" =
  Quickcheck.test
    ~sexp_of:[%sexp_of: int list * int list]
    [%quickcheck.generator: int list * int list]
    ~f:(fun (l1, l2) ->
      [%test_eq: int list]
        (List.rev_append l1 l2)
        (List.append (List.rev l1) l2))
```

This also works with other, more complex data-types, like variants. Here's a simple example.

```
type shape =
  | Circle of { radius: float }
  | Rect of { height: float; width: float }
  | Poly of (float * float) list
[@@deriving quickcheck];;
```

This will make a bunch of reasonable default decisions, like picking `Circle`, `Rect`, and `Poly` with equal probability. We can use annotations to adjust this, for example, by specifying the weight on a particular variant.

```
type shape =
  | Circle of { radius: float } [@quickcheck.weight 0.5]
  | Rect of { height: float; width: float }
  | Poly of (float * float) list
[@@deriving quickcheck];;
```

Note that the default weight on each case is 1, so now `Circle` will be generated with probability `0.5 / 2.5` or `0.2`, instead of the 1/3rd probability that it would have natively.

18.3.2   More Control with Let-Syntax

If the annotations associated with `ppx_quickcheck` don't let you do precisely what you want, you can get more control by taking advantage of the fact that Quickcheck's generators form a monad. That means it supports operators like bind and map, which we first presented in an error handling context in Chapter 8.1.3 (bind and Other Error Handling Idioms).

In combination with let syntax, the generator monad gives us a convenient way to specify generators for custom types. Here's an example generator for the shape type above.

```
# let gen_shape =
    let open Quickcheck.Generator.Let_syntax in
    let module G = Base_quickcheck.Generator in
    let circle =
      let%map radius = G.float_positive_or_zero in
      Circle { radius }
    in
    let rect =
      let%bind height = G.float_positive_or_zero in
      let%map width = G.float_inclusive height Float.infinity in
      Rect { height; width }
    in
    let poly =
      let%map points =
        List.gen_non_empty
          (G.both G.float_positive_or_zero G.float_positive_or_zero)
      in
      Poly points
    in
    G.union [ circle; rect; poly ];;
val gen_shape : shape Base_quickcheck.Generator.t = <abstr>
```

Throughout this function we're making choices about the probability distribution. For example, the use of the union operator means that circles, rectangles and polygons will be equally likely. We could have used weighted_union to pick a different distribution. Also, we've ensured that all float values are non-negative, and that the width of the rectangle is no smaller than its height.

The full API for building generators is beyond the scope of this chapter, but it's worth digging into the API docs if you want more control over the distribution of your test examples.

18.4   Other Testing Tools

The testing tools we've described in this chapter cover a lot of ground, but there are other tools worth knowing about.

18.4.1   Other Tools to Do (Mostly) the Same Things

Here are some notable tools that do more or less the same things as the testing tools we've featured in this chapter.

- Alcotest[1], which is another system for registering and running tests.
- qcheck[2], an alternative implementation of quickcheck.
- Dune's cram tests[3], which are expect-like tests that are written in a shell-like syntax. These are great for testing command-line utilities, and are inspired by Mercurial's testing framework.

Which of these you might end up preferring is to some degree a matter of taste.

18.4.2   Fuzzing

There's one other kind of testing tool that we haven't covered in this chapter, but is worth knowing about: *instrumentation-guided fuzzing*. You can think of this as another take on property testing, with a very different approach to generating random examples.

Traditional fuzzing just throws randomly mutated data at a program, and looks for some indication of failure, often simply the program crashing with a segfault. This kind of fuzzing has been surprisingly effective at finding bugs, especially security bugs, in production software. But blind randomization is still quite limited in terms of how much program behavior it can effectively explore.

Instrumentation-guided fuzzing improves on this by instrumenting the program, and then using that instrumentation to guide the randomization in the direction of more code coverage. By far the most successful tool in this space is American Fuzzy Lop[4], or AFL, and OCaml has support for the necessary instrumentation.

AFL can have eerily good results, and can with no guidance do things like constructing nearly-parseable text when fuzzing a parser, just by iteratively randomizing inputs in the direction of more coverage of the program being exercised.

If you're interested in AFL, there are some related tools worth knowing about.

- Crowbar[5] is a quickcheck-style library for writing down properties to be tested by AFL.
- Bun[6] is a library for integrating AFL into your continuous-integration pipeline.

---

[1] https://github.com/mirage/alcotest
[2] https://github.com/c-cube/qcheck
[3] https://dune.readthedocs.io/en/stable/tests.html#cram-tests
[4] https://github.com/google/AFL
[5] https://github.com/stedolan/crowbar
[6] https://github.com/ocurrent/bun

19   Handling JSON Data

Data serialization, i.e., converting data to and from a sequence of bytes that's suitable for writing to disk or sending across the network, is an important and common programming task. You often have to match someone else's data format (such as XML), sometimes you need a highly efficient format, and other times you want something that is easy for humans to edit. To this end, OCaml libraries provide several techniques for data serialization depending on what your problem is.

We'll start by using the popular and simple JSON data format and then look at other serialization formats later in the book. This chapter introduces you to a couple of new techniques that glue together the basic ideas from Part I of the book by using:

- *Polymorphic variants* to write more extensible libraries and protocols (but still retain the ability to extend them if needed)
- *Functional combinators* to compose common operations over data structures in a type-safe way
- External tools to generate boilerplate OCaml modules and signatures from external specification files

19.1   JSON Basics

JSON is a lightweight data-interchange format often used in web services and browsers. It's described in RFC4627 [1] and is easier to parse and generate than alternatives such as XML. You'll run into JSON very often when working with modern web APIs, so we'll cover several different ways to manipulate it in this chapter.

JSON consists of two basic structures: an unordered collection of key/value pairs, and an ordered list of values. Values can be strings, Booleans, floats, integers, or null. Let's see what a JSON record for an example book description looks like:

```
{
  "title": "Real World OCaml",
  "tags" : [ "functional programming", "ocaml", "algorithms" ],
  "pages": 450,
  "authors": [
    { "name": "Jason Hickey", "affiliation": "Google" },
    { "name": "Anil Madhavapeddy", "affiliation": "Cambridge"},
```

---
[1] http://www.ietf.org/rfc/rfc4627.txt

```
      { "name": "Yaron Minsky", "affiliation": "Jane Street"}
    ],
    "is_online": true
  }
```

The outermost JSON value is usually a record (delimited by the curly braces) and contains an unordered set of key/value pairs. The keys must be strings, but values can be any JSON type. In the preceding example, `tags` is a string list, while the `authors` field contains a list of records. Unlike OCaml lists, JSON lists can contain multiple different JSON types within a single list.

This free-form nature of JSON types is both a blessing and a curse. It's very easy to generate JSON values, but code that parses them also has to handle subtle variations in how the values are represented. For example, what if the preceding `pages` value is actually represented as a string value of "450" instead of an integer?

Our first task is to parse the JSON into a more structured OCaml type so that we can use static typing more effectively. When manipulating JSON in Python or Ruby, you might write unit tests to check that you have handled unusual inputs. The OCaml model prefers compile-time static checking as well as unit tests. For example, using pattern matching can warn you if you've not checked that a value can be `Null` as well as contain an actual value.

Installing the Yojson Library

There are several JSON libraries available for OCaml. For this chapter, we've picked the popular Yojson library, which you can install by running `opam install yojson`. Once installed, you can open it in `utop` as follows:

```
# open Core;;
# #require "yojson";;
# open Yojson;;
```

19.2   Parsing JSON with Yojson

The JSON specification has very few data types, and the `Yojson.Basic.t` type that follows is sufficient to express any valid JSON structure:

```
type json = [
  | `Assoc of (string * json) list
  | `Bool of bool
  | `Float of float
  | `Int of int
  | `List of json list
  | `Null
  | `String of string
]
```

Some interesting properties should leap out at you after reading this definition:

- The `json` type is *recursive*, which is to say that some of the tags refer back to the

overall json type. In particular, Assoc and List types can contain references to
further JSON values of different types. This is unlike the OCaml lists, whose
contents must be of a uniform type.

- The definition specifically includes a Null variant for empty fields. OCaml doesn't
  allow null values by default, so this must be encoded explicitly.
- The type definition uses polymorphic variants and not normal variants. This will
  become significant later, when we extend it with custom extensions to the JSON
  format.

Let's parse the earlier JSON example into this type now. The first stop is the
Yojson.Basic documentation, where we find these helpful functions:

```
val from_string : ?buf:Bi_outbuf.t -> ?fname:string -> ?lnum:int ->
  string -> json
(* Read a JSON value from a string.
   [buf]   : use this buffer at will during parsing instead of
             creating a new one.
   [fname] : data file name to be used in error messages. It does not
             have to be a real file.
   [lnum]  : number of the first line of input. Default is 1. *)

val from_file : ?buf:Bi_outbuf.t -> ?fname:string -> ?lnum:int ->
  string -> json
(* Read a JSON value from a file. See [from_string] for the meaning
     of the optional
   arguments. *)

val from_channel : ?buf:Bi_outbuf.t -> ?fname:string -> ?lnum:int ->
  in_channel -> json
  (** Read a JSON value from a channel.
      See [from_string] for the meaning of the optional arguments. *)
```

When first reading these interfaces, you can generally ignore the optional arguments
(which have the question marks in the type signature), since they should have sensible
defaults. In the preceding signature, the optional arguments offer finer control over the
memory buffer allocation and error messages from parsing incorrect JSON.

The type signature for these functions with the optional elements removed makes
their purpose much clearer. The three ways of parsing JSON are either directly from a
string, from a file on a filesystem, or via a buffered input channel:

```
val from_string  : string     -> json
val from_file    : string     -> json
val from_channel : in_channel -> json
```

The next example shows both the string and file functions in action, assuming
the JSON record is stored in a file called *book.json*:

```
open Core

let () =
  (* Read JSON file into an OCaml string *)
  let buf = In_channel.read_all "book.json" in
  (* Use the string JSON constructor *)
  let json1 = Yojson.Basic.from_string buf in
```

```
(* Use the file JSON constructor *)
let json2 = Yojson.Basic.from_file "book.json" in
(* Test that the two values are the same *)
print_endline (if Yojson.Basic.equal json1 json2 then "OK" else
   "FAIL")
```

You can build this by running dune:

```
$ dune exec -- ./read_json.exe
OK
```

The from_file function accepts an input filename and takes care of opening and closing it for you. It's far more common to use from_string to construct JSON values though, since these strings come in via a network connection (we'll see more of this in Chapter 17 (Concurrent Programming with Async)) or a database. Finally, the example checks that the two input mechanisms actually resulted in the same OCaml data structure.

19.3   Selecting Values from JSON Structures

Now that we've figured out how to parse the example JSON into an OCaml value, let's manipulate it from OCaml code and extract specific fields:

```
open Core

let () =
  (* Read the JSON file *)
  let json = Yojson.Basic.from_file "book.json" in

  (* Locally open the JSON manipulation functions *)
  let open Yojson.Basic.Util in
  let title = json |> member "title" |> to_string in
  let tags = json |> member "tags" |> to_list |> filter_string in
  let pages = json |> member "pages" |> to_int in
  let is_online = json |> member "is_online" |> to_bool_option in
  let is_translated = json |> member "is_translated" |>
     to_bool_option in
  let authors = json |> member "authors" |> to_list in
  let names = List.map authors ~f:(fun json -> member "name" json |>
     to_string) in

  (* Print the results of the parsing *)
  printf "Title: %s (%d)\n" title pages;
  printf "Authors: %s\n" (String.concat ~sep:", " names);
  printf "Tags: %s\n" (String.concat ~sep:", " tags);
  let string_of_bool_option =
    function
    | None -> "<unknown>"
    | Some true -> "yes"
    | Some false -> "no" in
  printf "Online: %s\n" (string_of_bool_option is_online);
  printf "Translated: %s\n" (string_of_bool_option is_translated)
```

Now build and run this in the same way as the previous example:

```
(executable
  (name       parse_book)
  (libraries core yojson))
```

```
$ dune build parse_book.exe
$ ./_build/default/parse_book.exe
Title: Real World OCaml (450)
Authors: Jason Hickey, Anil Madhavapeddy, Yaron Minsky
Tags: functional programming, ocaml, algorithms
Online: yes
Translated: <unknown>
```

This code introduces the `Yojson.Basic.Util` module, which contains *combinator* functions that let you easily map a JSON object into a more strongly typed OCaml value.

Functional Combinators

Combinators are a design pattern that crops up quite often in functional programming. John Hughes defines them as "a function which builds program fragments from program fragments." In a functional language, this generally means higher-order functions that combine other functions to apply useful transformations over values.

You've already run across several of these in the `List` module:

```
val map  : 'a list -> f:('a -> 'b)   -> 'b list
val fold : 'a list -> init:'accum -> f:('accum -> 'a -> 'accum) ->
    'accum
```

`map` and `fold` are extremely common combinators that transform an input list by applying a function to each value of the list. The `map` combinator is simplest, with the resulting list being output directly. `fold` applies each value in the input list to a function that accumulates a single result, and returns that instead:

```
val iter : 'a list -> f:('a -> unit) -> unit
```

`iter` is a more specialized combinator that is only useful when writing imperative code. The input function is applied to every value, but no result is supplied. The function must instead apply some side effect such as changing a mutable record field or printing to the standard output.

`Yojson` provides several combinators in the `Yojson.Basic.Util` module to manipulate values:

- `val member : string -> json -> json` selects a named field from a JSON record.
- `val to_string : json -> string` converts a JSON value into an OCaml `string`. It raises an exception if this is impossible.
- `val to_int : json -> int` converts a JSON value into an int. It raises an exception if this is impossible.
- `val filter_string : json list -> string list` filters valid strings from a list of JSON fields, and return them as an OCaml `string list`.

We'll go through each of these uses one by one now. The following examples also use the |> pipe-forward operator that we explained in Chapter 3 (Variables and Functions). This lets us chain together multiple JSON selection functions and feed the output from one into the next one, without having to create separate let bindings for each one.

Let's start with selecting a single title field from the record:

```
# open Yojson.Basic.Util;;
# let title = json |> member "title" |> to_string;;
val title : string = "Real World OCaml"
```

The member function accepts a JSON object and named key and returns the JSON field associated with that key, or Null. Since we know that the title value is always a string in our example schema, we want to convert it to an OCaml string. The to_string function performs this conversion and raises an exception if there is an unexpected JSON type. The |> operator provides a convenient way to chain these operations together:

```
# let tags = json |> member "tags" |> to_list |> filter_string;;
val tags : string list = ["functional programming"; "ocaml";
    "algorithms"]
# let pages = json |> member "pages" |> to_int;;
val pages : int = 450
```

The tags field is similar to title, but the field is a list of strings instead of a single one. Converting this to an OCaml string list is a two-stage process. First, we convert the JSON List to an OCaml list of JSON values and then filter out the String values as an OCaml string list. Remember that OCaml lists must contain values of the same type, so any JSON values that cannot be converted to a string will be skipped from the output of filter_string:

```
# let is_online = json |> member "is_online" |> to_bool_option;;
val is_online : bool option = Some true
# let is_translated = json |> member "is_translated" |>
    to_bool_option;;
val is_translated : bool option = None
```

The is_online and is_translated fields are optional in our JSON schema, so no error should be raised if they are not present. The OCaml type is a bool option to reflect this and can be extracted via to_bool_option. In our example JSON, only is_online is present and is_translated will be None:

```
# let authors = json |> member "authors" |> to_list;;
val authors : Yojson.Basic.t list =
  [`Assoc
    [("name", `String "Jason Hickey"); ("affiliation", `String
    "Google")];
   `Assoc
    [("name", `String "Anil Madhavapeddy");
     ("affiliation", `String "Cambridge")];
   `Assoc
    [("name", `String "Yaron Minsky");
     ("affiliation", `String "Jane Street")]]
```

The final use of JSON combinators is to extract all the name fields from the list of authors. We first construct the author list, and then map it into a string list. Notice that the example explicitly binds authors to a variable name. It can also be written more succinctly using the pipe-forward operator:

```
# let names =
    json |> member "authors" |> to_list
    |> List.map ~f:(fun json -> member "name" json |> to_string);;
val names : string list =
  ["Jason Hickey"; "Anil Madhavapeddy"; "Yaron Minsky"]
```

This style of programming, which omits variable names and chains functions together, is known as *point-free programming*. It's a succinct style but shouldn't be overused due to the increased difficulty of debugging intermediate values. If an explicit name is assigned to each stage of the transformations, debuggers in particular have an easier time making the program flow simpler to represent to the programmer.

This technique of using statically typed parsing functions is very powerful in combination with the OCaml type system. Many errors that don't make sense at runtime (for example, mixing up lists and objects) will be caught statically via a type error.

19.4   Constructing JSON Values

Building and printing JSON values is pretty straightforward given the Yojson.Basic.t type. You can just construct values of type t and call the to_string function on them. Let's remind ourselves of the Yojson.Basic.t type again:

```
type json = [
    | `Assoc of (string * json) list
    | `Bool of bool
    | `Float of float
    | `Int of int
    | `List of json list
    | `Null
    | `String of string
]
```

We can directly build a JSON value against this type and use the pretty-printing functions in the Yojson.Basic module to display JSON output:

```
# let person = `Assoc [ ("name", `String "Anil") ];;
val person : [> `Assoc of (string * [> `String of string ]) list ] =
  `Assoc [("name", `String "Anil")]
```

In the preceding example, we've constructed a simple JSON object that represents a single person. We haven't actually defined the type of person explicitly, as we're relying on the magic of polymorphic variants to make this all work.

The OCaml type system infers a type for person based on how you construct its value. In this case, only the Assoc and String variants are used to define the record, and so the inferred type only contains these fields without knowledge of the other possible allowed variants in JSON records that you haven't used yet (e.g. Int or Null):

```
# Yojson.Basic.pretty_to_string;;
- : ?std:bool -> Yojson.Basic.t -> string = <fun>
```

The `pretty_to_string` function has a more explicit signature that requires an argument of type `Yojson.Basic.t`. When person is applied to `pretty_to_string`, the inferred type of person is statically checked against the structure of the `json` type to ensure that they're compatible:

```
# Yojson.Basic.pretty_to_string person;;
- : string = "{ \"name\": \"Anil\" }"
# Yojson.Basic.pretty_to_channel stdout person;;
{ "name": "Anil" }
- : unit = ()
```

In this case, there are no problems. Our person value has an inferred type that is a valid subtype of `json`, and so the conversion to a string just works without us ever having to explicitly specify a type for person. Type inference lets you write more succinct code without sacrificing runtime reliability, as all the uses of polymorphic variants are still checked at compile time.

Polymorphic Variants and Easier Type Checking

One difficulty you will encounter is that type errors involving polymorphic variants can be quite verbose. For example, suppose you build an `Assoc` and mistakenly include a single value instead of a list of keys:

```
# let person = `Assoc ("name", `String "Anil");;
val person : [> `Assoc of string * [> `String of string ] ] =
  `Assoc ("name", `String "Anil")
# Yojson.Basic.pretty_to_string person;;
Line 1, characters 31-37:
Error: This expression has type
         [> `Assoc of string * [> `String of string ] ]
       but an expression was expected of type Yojson.Basic.t
       Types for tag `Assoc are incompatible
```

The type error is more verbose than it needs to be, which can be inconvenient to wade through for larger values. You can help the compiler to narrow down this error to a shorter form by adding explicit type annotations as a hint about your intentions:

```
# let (person : Yojson.Basic.t) =
    `Assoc ("name", `String "Anil");;
Line 2, characters 10-34:
Error: This expression has type 'a * 'b
         but an expression was expected of type (string *
       Yojson.Basic.t) list
```

We've annotated person as being of type `Yojson.Basic.t`, and as a result, the compiler spots that the argument to the `Assoc` variant has the incorrect type. This illustrates the strengths and weaknesses of polymorphic variants: they're lightweight and flexible, but the error messages can be quite confusing. However, a bit of careful manual type annotation makes tracking down such issues much easier.

We'll discuss more techniques like this that help you interpret type errors more easily in Chapter 26 (The Compiler Frontend: Parsing and Type Checking).

19.5   Using Nonstandard JSON Extensions

The standard JSON types are *really* basic, and OCaml types are far more expressive. Yojson supports an extended JSON format for those times when you're not interoperating with external systems and just want a convenient human-readable, local format. The `Yojson.Safe.json` type is a superset of the `Basic` polymorphic variant and looks like this:

```
type json = [
  | `Assoc of (string * json) list
  | `Bool of bool
  | `Float of float
  | `Floatlit of string
  | `Int of int
  | `Intlit of string
  | `List of json list
  | `Null
  | `String of string
  | `Stringlit of string
  | `Tuple of json list
  | `Variant of string * json option
]
```

The `Safe.json` type includes all of the variants from `Basic.json` and extends it with a few more useful ones. A standard JSON type such as a `String` will type-check against both the `Basic` module and also the nonstandard `Safe` module. If you use the extended values with the `Basic` module, however, the compiler will reject your code until you make it compliant with the portable subset of JSON.

Yojson supports the following JSON extensions:

The lit suffix Denotes that the value is stored as a JSON string. For example, a `Floatlit` will be stored as `"1.234"` instead of `1.234`.

The Tuple type Stored as `("abc", 123)` instead of a list.

The Variant type Encodes OCaml variants more explicitly, as `<"Foo">` or `<"Bar":123>` for a variant with parameters.

The only purpose of these extensions is to have greater control over how OCaml values are represented in JSON (for instance, storing a floating-point number as a JSON string). The output still obeys the same standard format that can be easily exchanged with other languages.

You can convert a `Safe.json` to a `Basic.json` type by using the `to_basic` function as follows:

```
val to_basic : json -> Yojson.Basic.t
(** Tuples are converted to JSON arrays, Variants are converted to
    JSON strings or arrays of a string (constructor) and a json value
    (argument). Long integers are converted to JSON strings.
    Examples:

    `Tuple [ `Int 1; `Float 2.3 ]   ->   `List [ `Int 1; `Float 2.3 ]
    `Variant ("A", None)            ->   `String "A"
    `Variant ("B", Some x)          ->   `List [ `String "B", x ]
```

```
       `Intlit "12345678901234567890"  ->    `String
       "12345678901234567890"
   *)
```

19.6   Automatically Mapping JSON to OCaml Types

The combinators described previously make it easy to write functions that extract fields from JSON records, but the process is still pretty manual. When you implement larger specifications, it's much easier to generate the mappings from JSON schemas to OCaml values more mechanically than writing conversion functions individually.

We'll cover an alternative JSON processing method that is better for larger-scale JSON handling now, using ATD[2], which provides a *domain specific language*, or DSL, that compiles JSON specifications into OCaml modules, which are then used throughout your application.

You can install the atdgen executable by calling opam install atdgen.

```
$ opam install atdgen
$ atdgen -version
2.2.1
```

You may need to run eval $(opam env) in your shell if you don't find atdgen in your path.

19.6.1   ATD Basics

The idea behind ATD is to specify the format of the JSON in a separate file and then run a compiler (atdgen) that outputs OCaml code to construct and parse JSON values. This means that you don't need to write any OCaml parsing code at all, as it will all be autogenerated for you.

Let's go straight into looking at an example of how this works, by using a small portion of the GitHub API. GitHub is a popular code hosting and sharing website that provides a JSON-based web API[3]. The following ATD code fragment describes the GitHub authorization API (which is based on a pseudostandard web protocol known as OAuth):

```
type scope = [
    User <json name="user">
  | Public_repo <json name="public_repo">
  | Repo <json name="repo">
  | Repo_status <json name="repo_status">
  | Delete_repo <json name="delete_repo">
  | Gist <json name="gist">
]

type app = {
```

[2] https://github.com/ahrefs/atd
[3] http://developer.github.com

```
    name: string;
    url: string;
} <ocaml field_prefix="app_">

type authorization_request = {
  scopes: scope list;
  note: string;
} <ocaml field_prefix="auth_req_">

type authorization_response = {
  scopes: scope list;
  token: string;
  app: app;
  url: string;
  id: int;
  ?note: string option;
  ?note_url: string option;
}
```

The ATD specification syntax is deliberately quite similar to OCaml type definitions. Every JSON record is assigned a type name (e.g., app in the preceding example). You can also define variants that are similar to OCaml's variant types (e.g., scope in the example).

19.6.2   ATD Annotations

ATD does deviate from OCaml syntax due to its support for annotations within the specification. The annotations can customize the code that is generated for a particular target (of which the OCaml backend is of most interest to us).

For example, the preceding GitHub scope field is defined as a variant type, with each option starting with an uppercase letter as is conventional for OCaml variants. However, the JSON values that come back from GitHub are actually lowercase and so aren't exactly the same as the option name.

The annotation <json name="user"> signals that the JSON value of the field is user, but that the variable name of the parsed variant in OCaml should be User. These annotations are often useful to map JSON values to reserved keywords in OCaml (e.g., type).

19.6.3   Compiling ATD Specifications to OCaml

The ATD specification we defined can be compiled to OCaml code using the atdgen command-line tool. Let's run the compiler twice to generate some OCaml type definitions and a JSON serializing module that converts between input data and those type definitions.

The atdgen command will generate some new files in your current directory. github_t.ml and github_t.mli will contain an OCaml module with types defined that correspond to the ATD file:

```
$ atdgen -t github.atd
```

```
$ atdgen -j github.atd
$ ocamlfind ocamlc -package atd -i github_t.mli
type scope =
    [ `Delete_repo | `Gist | `Public_repo | `Repo | `Repo_status |
    `User ]
type app = { app_name : string; app_url : string; }
type authorization_response = {
  scopes : scope list;
  token : string;
  app : app;
  url : string;
  id : int;
  note : string option;
  note_url : string option;
}
type authorization_request = {
  auth_req_scopes : scope list;
  auth_req_note : string;
}
```

There is an obvious correspondence to the ATD definition. Note that field names in OCaml records in the same module cannot shadow one another, and so we instruct ATDgen to prefix every field with a name that distinguishes it from other records in the same module. For example, <ocaml field_prefix="auth_req_"> in the ATD spec prefixes every field name in the generated authorization_request record with auth_req.

The Github_t module only contains the type definitions, while Github_j provides serialization functions to and from JSON. You can read the github_j.mli to see the full interface, but the important functions for most uses are the conversion functions to and from a string. For our preceding example, this looks like:

```
val string_of_authorization_request :
  ?len:int -> authorization_request -> string
  (** Serialize a value of type {!authorization_request}
      into a JSON string.
      @param len specifies the initial length
              of the buffer used internally.
              Default: 1024. *)

val string_of_authorization_response :
  ?len:int -> authorization_response -> string
  (** Serialize a value of type {!authorization_response}
      into a JSON string.
      @param len specifies the initial length
              of the buffer used internally.
              Default: 1024. *)
```

This is pretty convenient! We've now written a single ATD file, and all the OCaml boilerplate to convert between JSON and a strongly typed record has been generated for us. You can control various aspects of the serializer by passing flags to atdgen. The important ones for JSON are:

-j-std Converts tuples and variants into standard JSON and refuses to print NaN and infinities. You should specify this if you intend to interoperate with services that aren't using ATD.

-j-custom-fields FUNCTION Calls a custom function for every unknown field encountered, instead of raising a parsing exception.

-j-defaults Always explicitly outputs a JSON value if possible. This requires the default value for that field to be defined in the ATD specification.

The full ATD specification[4] is quite sophisticated and documented online. The ATD compiler can also target formats other than JSON and outputs code for other languages (such as Java) if you need more interoperability.

There are also several similar projects that automate the code generation process. Piqi[5] supports conversions between XML, JSON, and the Google protobuf format; and Thrift[6] supports many other programming languages and includes OCaml bindings.

19.6.4 Example: Querying GitHub Organization Information

Let's finish up with an example of some live JSON parsing from GitHub and build a tool to query organization information via their API. Start by looking at the online API documentation[7] for GitHub to see what the JSON schema for retrieving the organization information looks like.

Now create an ATD file that covers the fields we need. Any extra fields present in the response will be ignored by the ATD parser, so we don't need a completely exhaustive specification of every field that GitHub might send back:

```
type org = {
  login: string;
  id: int;
  url: string;
  ?name: string option;
  ?blog: string option;
  ?email: string option;
  public_repos: int
}
```

Let's build the OCaml type declaration first by calling `atdgen -t` on the specification file:

```
$ dune build github_org_t.mli
$ cat _build/default/github_org_t.mli
(* Auto-generated from "github_org.atd" *)
              [@@@ocaml.warning "-27-32-35-39"]

type org = {
  login: string;
  id: int;
  url: string;
```

[4] https://atd.readthedocs.io/en/latest/
[5] http://piqi.org
[6] http://thrift.apache.org
[7] http://developer.github.com/v3/orgs/

```
  name: string option;
  blog: string option;
  email: string option;
  public_repos: int
}
```

The OCaml type has an obvious mapping to the ATD spec, but we still need the logic to convert JSON buffers to and from this type. Calling atdgen -j will generate this serialization code for us in a new file called github_org_j.ml:

```
$ dune build github_org_j.mli
$ cat _build/default/github_org_j.mli
(* Auto-generated from "github_org.atd" *)
[@@@ocaml.warning "-27-32-35-39"]

type org = Github_org_t.org = {
  login: string;
  id: int;
  url: string;
  name: string option;
  blog: string option;
  email: string option;
  public_repos: int
}

val write_org :
  Bi_outbuf.t -> org -> unit
  (** Output a JSON value of type {!org}. *)

val string_of_org :
  ?len:int -> org -> string
  (** Serialize a value of type {!org}
      into a JSON string.
      @param len specifies the initial length
                 of the buffer used internally.
                 Default: 1024. *)

val read_org :
  Yojson.Safe.lexer_state -> Lexing.lexbuf -> org
  (** Input JSON data of type {!org}. *)

val org_of_string :
  string -> org
  (** Deserialize JSON data of type {!org}. *)
```

The Github_org_j serializer interface contains everything we need to map to and from the OCaml types and JSON. The easiest way to use this interface is by using the string_of_org and org_of_string functions, but there are also more advanced low-level buffer functions available if you need higher performance (but we won't go into that in this tutorial).

All we need to complete our example is an OCaml program that fetches the JSON and uses these modules to output a one-line summary. Our following example does just that.

The following code calls the cURL command-line utility by using the Shell interface to run an external command and capture its output. You'll need to ensure that you have cURL installed on your system before running the example. You might also need to opam install shell if you haven't installed it previously:

```
open Core

let print_org file () =
  let url = sprintf "https://api.github.com/orgs/%s" file in
  Shell.run_full "curl" [url]
  |> Github_org_j.org_of_string
  |> fun org ->
  let open Github_org_t in
  let name = Option.value ~default:"???" org.name in
  printf "%s (%d) with %d public repos\n"
    name org.id org.public_repos

let () =
  Command.basic_spec ~summary:"Print Github organization information"
    Command.Spec.(empty +> anon ("organization" %: string))
    print_org
  |> Command.run
```

The following is a short shell script that generates all of the OCaml code and also builds the final executable:

```
(rule
  (targets github_org_j.ml github_org_j.mli)
  (deps    github_org.atd)
  (mode    fallback)
  (action  (run atdgen -j %{deps})))

(rule
  (targets github_org_t.ml github_org_t.mli)
  (deps    github_org.atd)
  (mode    fallback)
  (action  (run atdgen -t %{deps})))

(executable
  (name      github_org_info)
  (libraries core yojson atdgen shell)
  (flags     :standard -w -32)
  (modules   github_org_info github_org_t github_org_j))
```

```
$ dune build github_org_info.exe
```

You can now run the command-line tool with a single argument to specify the name of the organization, and it will dynamically fetch the JSON from the web, parse it, and render the summary to your console:

```
$ dune exec -- ./github_org_info.exe mirage
MirageOS (131943) with 125 public repos
$ dune exec -- ./github_org_info.exe janestreet
??? (3384712) with 145 public repos
```

The JSON returned from the janestreet query is missing an organization name, but this is explicitly reflected in the OCaml type, since the ATD spec marked name as an optional field. Our OCaml code explicitly handles this case and doesn't have to worry about null-pointer exceptions. Similarly, the JSON integer for the id is mapped into a native OCaml integer via the ATD conversion.

While this tool is obviously quite simple, the ability to specify optional and default fields is very powerful. Take a look at the full ATD specification for the GitHub API in the ocaml-github[8] repository online, which has lots of quirks typical in real-world web APIs.

Our example shells out to curl on the command line to obtain the JSON, which is rather inefficient. You could integrate an Async-based HTTP fetch directly into your OCaml application, as described in Chapter 17 (Concurrent Programming with Async).

[8] http://github.com/avsm/ocaml-github

20 Parsing with OCamllex and Menhir

This chapter includes contributions from Jason Hickey.

Many programming tasks start with the interpretation of some form of structured textual data. *Parsing* is the process of converting such data into data structures that are easy to program against. For simple formats, it's often enough to parse the data in an ad hoc way, say, by breaking up the data into lines, and then using regular expressions for breaking those lines down into their component pieces.

But this simplistic approach tends to fall down when parsing more complicated data, particularly data with the kind of recursive structure you find in full-blown programming languages or flexible data formats like JSON and XML. Parsing such formats accurately and efficiently while providing useful error messages is a complex task.

Often, you can find an existing parsing library that handles these issues for you. But there are tools to simplify the task when you do need to write a parser, in the form of *parser generators*. A parser generator creates a parser from a specification of the data format that you want to parse, and uses that to generate a parser.

Parser generators have a long history, including tools like `lex` and `yacc` that date back to the early 1970s. OCaml has its own alternatives, including `ocamllex`, which replaces `lex`, and `ocamlyacc` and `menhir`, which replace `yacc`. We'll explore these tools in the course of walking through the implementation of a parser for the JSON serialization format that we discussed in Chapter 19 (Handling JSON Data).

Parsing is a broad and often intricate topic, and our purpose here is not to teach all of the theoretical issues, but to provide a pragmatic introduction of how to build a parser in OCaml.

Menhir Versus ocamlyacc

Menhir is an alternative parser generator that is generally superior to the venerable `ocamlyacc`, which dates back quite a few years. Menhir is mostly compatible with `ocamlyacc` grammars, and so you can usually just switch to Menhir and expect older code to work (with some minor differences described in the Menhir manual).

The biggest advantage of Menhir is that its error messages are generally more human-comprehensible, and the parsers that it generates are fully reentrant and can be parameterized in OCaml modules more easily. We recommend that any new code you develop should use Menhir instead of `ocamlyacc`.

Menhir isn't distributed directly with OCaml but is available through OPAM by running `opam install menhir`.

20.1   Lexing and Parsing

Parsing is traditionally broken down into two parts: *lexical analysis*, which is a kind of simplified parsing phase that converts a stream of characters into a stream of logical tokens; and full-on parsing, which involves converting a stream of tokens into the final representation, which is often in the form of a tree-like data structure called an *abstract syntax tree*, or AST.

It's confusing that the term parsing is applied to both the overall process of converting textual data to structured data, and also more specifically to the second phase of converting a stream of tokens to an AST; so from here on out, we'll use the term parsing to refer only to this second phase.

Let's consider lexing and parsing in the context of the JSON format. Here's a snippet of text that represents a JSON object containing a string labeled `title` and an array containing two objects, each with a name and array of zip codes:

```
{
  "title": "Cities",
  "cities": [
    { "name": "Chicago",  "zips": [60601] },
    { "name": "New York", "zips": [10004] }
  ]
}
```

At a syntactic level, we can think of a JSON file as a series of simple logical units, like curly braces, square brackets, commas, colons, identifiers, numbers, and quoted strings. Thus, we could represent our JSON text as a sequence of tokens of the following type:

```
type token =
  | NULL
  | TRUE
  | FALSE
  | STRING of string
  | INT of int
  | FLOAT of float
  | LEFT_BRACK
  | RIGHT_BRACK
  | LEFT_BRACE
  | RIGHT_BRACE
  | COMMA
  | COLON
  | EOF
```

Note that this representation loses some information about the original text. For example, whitespace is not represented. It's common, and indeed useful, for the token stream to forget some details of the original text that are not required for understanding its meaning.

If we converted the preceding example into a list of these tokens, it would look something like this:

```
[ LEFT_BRACE; STRING("title"); COLON; STRING("Cities");
  COMMA; STRING("cities"); ... ]
```

This kind of representation is easier to work with than the original text, since it gets rid of some unimportant syntactic details and adds useful structure. But it's still a good deal more low-level than the simple AST we used for representing JSON data in Chapter 19 (Handling JSON Data):

```
type value =
  [ `Assoc of (string * value) list
  | `Bool of bool
  | `Float of float
  | `Int of int
  | `List of value list
  | `Null
  | `String of string ]
```

This representation is much richer than our token stream, capturing the fact that JSON values can be nested inside each other and that JSON has a variety of value types, including numbers, strings, arrays, and objects. The parser we'll write will convert a token stream into a value of this AST type, as shown below for our earlier JSON example:

```
`Assoc
  ["title", `String "Cities";
   "cities", `List
      [`Assoc ["name", `String "Chicago"; "zips", `List [`Int 60601]];
       `Assoc ["name", `String "New York"; "zips", `List [`Int
      10004]]]]
```

20.2   Defining a Parser

A parser-specification file has suffix .mly and contains two sections that are broken up by separator lines consisting of the characters %% on a line by themselves. The first section of the file is for declarations, including token and type specifications, precedence directives, and other output directives; and the second section is for specifying the grammar of the language to be parsed.

We'll start by declaring the list of tokens. A token is declared using the syntax %token <*type*>*uid*, where the <*type*> is optional and *uid* is a capitalized identifier. For JSON, we need tokens for numbers, strings, identifiers, and punctuation:

```
%token <int> INT
%token <float> FLOAT
%token <string> ID
%token <string> STRING
%token TRUE
%token FALSE
%token NULL
```

```
%token LEFT_BRACE
%token RIGHT_BRACE
%token LEFT_BRACK
%token RIGHT_BRACK
%token COLON
%token COMMA
%token EOF
```

The `<type>` specifications mean that a token carries a value. The `INT` token carries an integer value with it, `FLOAT` has a `float` value, and `STRING` carries a `string` value. The remaining tokens, such as `TRUE`, `FALSE`, or the punctuation, aren't associated with any value, and so we can omit the `<type>` specification.

20.2.1   Describing the Grammar

The next thing we need to do is to specify the grammar of a JSON expression. `menhir`, like many parser generators, expresses grammars as *context-free grammars*. (More precisely, `menhir` supports LR(1) grammars, but we will ignore that technical distinction here.) You can think of a context-free grammar as a set of abstract names, called *non-terminal symbols*, along with a collection of rules for transforming a nonterminal symbol into a sequence of tokens and nonterminal symbols. A sequence of tokens is parsable by a grammar if you can apply the grammar's rules to produce a series of transformations, starting at a distinguished *start symbol* that produces the token sequence in question.

We'll start describing the JSON grammar by declaring the start symbol to be the non-terminal symbol `prog`, and by declaring that when parsed, a `prog` value should be converted into an OCaml value of type `Json.value option`. We then end the declaration section of the parser with a `%%`:

```
%start <Json.value option> prog
%%
```

Once that's in place, we can start specifying the productions. In `menhir`, productions are organized into *rules*, where each rule lists all the possible productions for a given nonterminal symbol. Here, for example, is the rule for `prog`:

```
prog:
  | EOF          { None }
  | v = value { Some v }
  ;
```

The syntax for this is reminiscent of an OCaml `match` expression. The pipes separate the individual productions, and the curly braces contain a *semantic action*: OCaml code that generates the OCaml value corresponding to the production in question. Semantic actions are arbitrary OCaml expressions that are evaluated during parsing to produce values that are attached to the non-terminal in the rule.

We have two cases for `prog`: either there's an `EOF`, which means the text is empty, and so there's no JSON value to read, we return the OCaml value `None`; or we have an instance of the `value` nonterminal, which corresponds to a well-formed JSON value, and we wrap the corresponding Json.value in a Some tag. Note that in the value case, we wrote v = value to bind the OCaml value that corresponds to the variable v, which we can then use within the curly braces for that production.

Now let's consider a more complex example, the rule for the value symbol:

```
value:
    | LEFT_BRACE; obj = object_fields; RIGHT_BRACE
      { `Assoc obj }
    | LEFT_BRACK; vl = array_values; RIGHT_BRACK
      { `List vl }
    | s = STRING
      { `String s }
    | i = INT
      { `Int i }
    | x = FLOAT
      { `Float x }
    | TRUE
      { `Bool true }
    | FALSE
      { `Bool false }
    | NULL
      { `Null }
    ;
```

According to these rules, a JSON value is either:

• An object bracketed by curly braces
• An array bracketed by square braces
• A string, integer, float, bool, or null value

In each of the productions, the OCaml code in curly braces shows what to transform the object in question to. Note that we still have two nonterminals whose definitions we depend on here but have not yet defined: object_fields and array_values. We'll look at how these are parsed next.

20.2.2   Parsing Sequences

The rule for object_fields follows, and is really just a thin wrapper that reverses the list returned by the following rule for rev_object_fields. Note that the first production in rev_object_fields has an empty left-hand side, because what we're matching on in this case is an empty sequence of tokens. The comment (* empty *) is used to make this clear:

```
object_fields: obj = rev_object_fields { List.rev obj };

rev_object_fields:
    | (* empty *) { [] }
    | obj = rev_object_fields; COMMA; k = ID; COLON; v = value
      { (k, v) :: obj }
    ;
```

The rules are structured as they are because menhir generates left-recursive parsers, which means that the constructed pushdown automaton uses less stack space with left-recursive definitions. The following right-recursive rule accepts the same input, but during parsing, it requires linear stack space to read object field definitions:

```
(* Inefficient right-recursive rule *)
object_fields:
  | (* empty *) { [] }
  | k = STRING; COLON; v = value; COMMA; obj = object_fields
    { (k, v) :: obj }
```

Alternatively, we could keep the left-recursive definition and simply construct the returned value in left-to-right order. This is even less efficient, since the complexity of building the list incrementally in this way is quadratic in the length of the list:

```
(* Quadratic left-recursive rule *)
object_fields:
  | (* empty *) { [] }
  | obj = object_fields; COMMA; k = STRING; COLON; v = value
    { obj @ [k, v] }
  ;
```

Assembling lists like this is a pretty common requirement in most realistic grammars, and the preceding rules (while useful for illustrating how parsing works) are rather verbose. Menhir features an extended standard library of built-in rules to simplify this handling. These rules are detailed in the Menhir manual and include optional values, pairs of values with optional separators, and lists of elements (also with optional separators).

A version of the JSON grammar using these more succinct Menhir rules follows. Notice the use of `separated_list` to parse both JSON objects and lists with one rule:

```
%token <int> INT
%token <float> FLOAT
%token <string> STRING
%token TRUE
%token FALSE
%token NULL
%token LEFT_BRACE
%token RIGHT_BRACE
%token LEFT_BRACK
%token RIGHT_BRACK
%token COLON
%token COMMA
%token EOF
%start <Json.value option> prog
%%

prog:
  | v = value { Some v }
  | EOF       { None   } ;

value:
  | LEFT_BRACE; obj = obj_fields; RIGHT_BRACE { `Assoc obj }
  | LEFT_BRACK; vl = list_fields; RIGHT_BRACK { `List vl   }
  | s = STRING                                { `String s  }
  | i = INT                                   { `Int i     }
  | x = FLOAT                                 { `Float x   }
```

```
   | TRUE                                   { `Bool true  }
   | FALSE                                  { `Bool false }
   | NULL                                   { `Null       } ;

obj_fields:
    obj = separated_list(COMMA, obj_field)   { obj } ;

obj_field:
    k = STRING; COLON; v = value             { (k, v) } ;

list_fields:
    vl = separated_list(COMMA, value)        { vl } ;
```

We can hook in `menhir` by adding a `(menhir)` stanza to our dune file, which tells the build system to switch to using `menhir` instead of `ocamlyacc` to handle files with the `.mly` suffix:

```
(menhir
 (modules parser))

(ocamllex lexer)

(library
 (name json_parser)
 (modules parser lexer json)
 (libraries core))
```

20.3 Defining a Lexer

Now we can define a lexer, using `ocamllex`, to convert our input text into a stream of tokens. The specification of the lexer is placed in a file with an `.mll` suffix.

20.3.1 OCaml Prelude

Let's walk through the definition of a lexer section by section. The first section is an optional chunk of OCaml code that is bounded by a pair of curly braces:

```
{
open Lexing
open Parser

exception SyntaxError of string
}
```

This code is there to define utility functions used by later snippets of OCaml code and to set up the environment by opening useful modules and define an exception, `SyntaxError`. Any OCaml functions you define here will be subsequently available in the remainder of the lexer definition.

20.3.2   Regular Expressions

The next section of the lexing file is a collection of named regular expressions. These look syntactically like ordinary OCaml let bindings, but really this is a specialized syntax for declaring regular expressions. Here's an example:

```
let int = '-'? ['0'-'9'] ['0'-'9']*
```

The syntax here is something of a hybrid between OCaml syntax and traditional regular expression syntax. The int regular expression specifies an optional leading -, followed by a digit from 0 to 9, followed by some number of digits from 0 to 9. The question mark is used to indicate an optional component of a regular expression; the square brackets are used to specify ranges; and the * operator is used to indicate a (possibly empty) repetition.

Floating-point numbers are specified similarly, but we deal with decimal points and exponents. We make the expression easier to read by building up a sequence of named regular expressions, rather than creating one big and impenetrable expression:

```
let digit = ['0'-'9']
let frac = '.' digit*
let exp = ['e' 'E'] ['-' '+']? digit+
let float = digit* frac? exp?
```

Finally, we define whitespace, newlines, and identifiers:

```
let white = [' ' '\t']+
let newline = '\r' | '\n' | "\r\n"
let id = ['a'-'z' 'A'-'Z' '_'] ['a'-'z' 'A'-'Z' '0'-'9' '_']*
```

The newline introduces the | operator, which lets one of several alternative regular expressions match (in this case, the various carriage-return combinations of CR, LF, or CRLF).

20.3.3   Lexing Rules

The lexing rules are essentially functions that consume the data, producing OCaml expressions that evaluate to tokens. These OCaml expressions can be quite complicated, using side effects and invoking other rules as part of the body of the rule. Let's look at the read rule for parsing a JSON expression:

```
rule read =
  parse
  | white     { read lexbuf }
  | newline   { next_line lexbuf; read lexbuf }
  | int       { INT (int_of_string (Lexing.lexeme lexbuf)) }
  | float     { FLOAT (float_of_string (Lexing.lexeme lexbuf)) }
  | "true"    { TRUE }
  | "false"   { FALSE }
  | "null"    { NULL }
  | '"'       { read_string (Buffer.create 17) lexbuf }
  | '{'       { LEFT_BRACE }
  | '}'       { RIGHT_BRACE }
  | '['       { LEFT_BRACK }
```

```
| ']'      { RIGHT_BRACK }
| ':'      { COLON }
| ','      { COMMA }
| _ { raise (SyntaxError ("Unexpected char: " ^ Lexing.lexeme
  lexbuf)) }
| eof      { EOF }
```

The rules are structured very similarly to pattern matches, except that the variants are replaced by regular expressions on the left-hand side. The right-hand side clause is the parsed OCaml return value of that rule. The OCaml code for the rules has a parameter called lexbuf that defines the input, including the position in the input file, as well as the text that was matched by the regular expression.

The first white { read lexbuf } calls the lexer recursively. That is, it skips the input whitespace and returns the following token. The action newline { next_line lexbuf; read lexbuf } is similar, but we use it to advance the line number for the lexer using the utility function that we defined at the top of the file. Let's skip to the third action:

```
| int { INT (int_of_string (Lexing.lexeme lexbuf)) }
```

This action specifies that when the input matches the int regular expression, then the lexer should return the expression INT (int_of_string (Lexing.lexeme lexbuf)). The expression Lexing.lexeme lexbuf returns the complete string matched by the regular expression. In this case, the string represents a number, so we use the int_of_string function to convert it to a number.

There are actions for each different kind of token. The string expressions like "true" { TRUE } are used for keywords, and the special characters have actions, too, like '{' { LEFT_BRACE }.

Some of these patterns overlap. For example, the regular expression "true" is also matched by the id pattern. ocamllex used the following disambiguation when a prefix of the input is matched by more than one pattern:

- The longest match always wins. For example, the first input trueX: 167 matches the regular expression "true" for four characters, and it matches id for five characters. The longer match wins, and the return value is ID "trueX".
- If all matches have the same length, then the first action wins. If the input were true: 167, then both "true" and id match the first four characters; "true" is first, so the return value is TRUE.

Unused Lexing Values

In our parser, we have not used all the token regexps that we defined in the lexer. For instance, id is unused since we do not parse unquoted strings for object identifiers (something that is allowed by JavaScript, but not the subset of it that is JSON). If we included a token pattern match for this in the lexer, then we would have to adjust the parser accordingly to add a %token <string> ID. This would in turn trigger an "unused" warning since the parser never constructs a value with type ID:

```
File "parser.mly", line 4, characters 16-18:
```

> Warning: the token ID is unused.

It's completely fine to define unused regexps as we've done, and to hook them into parsers as required. For example, we might use ID if we add an extension to our parser for supporting unquoted string identifiers as a non-standard JSON extension.

20.3.4   Recursive Rules

Unlike many other lexer generators, ocamllex allows the definition of multiple lexers in the same file, and the definitions can be recursive. In this case, we use recursion to match string literals using the following rule definition:

```
and read_string buf =
  parse
  | '"'        { STRING (Buffer.contents buf) }
  | '\\' '/'   { Buffer.add_char buf '/'; read_string buf lexbuf }
  | '\\' '\\'  { Buffer.add_char buf '\\'; read_string buf lexbuf }
  | '\\' 'b'   { Buffer.add_char buf '\b'; read_string buf lexbuf }
  | '\\' 'f'   { Buffer.add_char buf '\012'; read_string buf lexbuf }
  | '\\' 'n'   { Buffer.add_char buf '\n'; read_string buf lexbuf }
  | '\\' 'r'   { Buffer.add_char buf '\r'; read_string buf lexbuf }
  | '\\' 't'   { Buffer.add_char buf '\t'; read_string buf lexbuf }
  | [^ '"' '\\']+
    { Buffer.add_string buf (Lexing.lexeme lexbuf);
      read_string buf lexbuf
    }
  | _ { raise (SyntaxError ("Illegal string character: " ^
    Lexing.lexeme lexbuf)) }
  | eof { raise (SyntaxError ("String is not terminated")) }
```

This rule takes a buf : Buffer.t as an argument. If we reach the terminating double quote ", then we return the contents of the buffer as a STRING.

The other cases are for handling the string contents. The action [^ '"' '\\']+ { ... } matches normal input that does not contain a double quote or backslash. The actions beginning with a backslash \ define what to do for escape sequences. In each of these cases, the final step includes a recursive call to the lexer.

That covers the lexer. Next, we need to combine the lexer with the parser to bring it all together.

Handling Unicode

We've glossed over an important detail here: parsing Unicode characters to handle the full spectrum of the world's writing systems. OCaml has several third-party solutions to handling Unicode, with varying degrees of flexibility and complexity:

- Uutfa is a nonblocking streaming Unicode codec for OCaml, available as a standalone library. It is accompanied by the Uunfb text normalization and Uucdc Unicode character database libraries. There is also a robust parser for JSONd available that illustrates the use of Uutf in your own libraries.

- Camomilee supports the full spectrum of Unicode character types, conversion from around 200 encodings, and collation and locale-sensitive case mappings.
- sedlexf is a lexer generator for Unicode that can serve as a Unicode-aware replacement for `ocamllex`.

All of these libraries are available via opam under their respective names.

a `http://erratique.ch/software/uutf`
b `http://erratique.ch/software/uunf`
c `http://erratique.ch/software/uucd`
d `http://erratique.ch/software/jsonm`
e `https://github.com/yoriyuki/Camomile`
f `https://github.com/ocaml-community/sedlex`

20.4   Bringing It All Together

For the final part, we need to compose the lexer and parser. As we saw in the type definition in `parser.mli`, the parsing function expects a lexer of type `Lexing.lexbuf -> token`, and a lexbuf:

```
val prog : (Lexing.lexbuf -> token) -> Lexing.lexbuf -> Json.value
    option
```

Before we start with the lexing, let's first define some functions to handle parsing errors. There are currently two errors: `Parser.Error` and `Lexer.SyntaxError`. A simple solution when encountering an error is to print the error and give up:

```
open Core
open Lexer
open Lexing

let print_position outx lexbuf =
  let pos = lexbuf.lex_curr_p in
  fprintf outx "%s:%d:%d" pos.pos_fname
    pos.pos_lnum (pos.pos_cnum - pos.pos_bol + 1)

let parse_with_error lexbuf =
  try Parser.prog Lexer.read lexbuf with
  | SyntaxError msg ->
    fprintf stderr "%a: %s\n" print_position lexbuf msg;
    None
  | Parser.Error ->
    fprintf stderr "%a: syntax error\n" print_position lexbuf;
    exit (-1)
```

The "give up on the first error" approach is easy to implement but isn't very friendly. In general, error handling can be pretty intricate, and we won't discuss it here. However, the Menhir parser defines additional mechanisms you can use to try and recover from errors. These are described in detail in its reference manual[1].

The standard lexing library `Lexing` provides a function `from_channel` to read

[1] `http://gallium.inria.fr/~fpottier/menhir/`

the input from a channel. The following function describes the structure, where the
`Lexing.from_channel` function is used to construct a `lexbuf`, which is passed with the
lexing function `Lexer.read` to the `Parser.prog` function. `Parsing.prog` returns `None`
when it reaches end of file. We define a function `Json.output_value`, not shown here,
to print a `Json.value`:

```
let rec parse_and_print lexbuf =
  match parse_with_error lexbuf with
  | Some value ->
    printf "%a\n" Json.output_value value;
    parse_and_print lexbuf
  | None -> ()

let loop filename () =
  let inx = In_channel.create filename in
  let lexbuf = Lexing.from_channel inx in
  lexbuf.lex_curr_p <- { lexbuf.lex_curr_p with pos_fname = filename
    };
  parse_and_print lexbuf;
  In_channel.close inx

let () =
  Command.basic_spec ~summary:"Parse and display JSON"
    Command.Spec.(empty +> anon ("filename" %: string))
    loop
  |> Command.run
```

Here's a test input file we can use to test the code we just wrote:

```
true
false
null
[1, 2, 3., 4.0, .5, 5.5e5, 6.3]
"Hello World"
{ "field1": "Hello",
  "field2": 17e13,
  "field3": [1, 2, 3],
  "field4": { "fieldA": 1, "fieldB": "Hello" }
}
```

Now build and run the example using this file, and you can see the full parser in
action:

```
$ dune exec ./test.exe test1.json
true
false
null
[1, 2, 3.000000, 4.000000, 0.500000, 550000.000000, 6.300000]
"Hello World"
{ "field1": "Hello",
  "field2": 170000000000000.000000,
  "field3": [1, 2, 3],
  "field4": { "fieldA": 1,
  "fieldB": "Hello" } }
```

With our simple error handling scheme, errors are fatal and cause the program to
terminate with a nonzero exit code:

```
$ cat test2.json
{ "name": "Chicago",
  "zips": [12345,
}
{ "name": "New York",
  "zips": [10004]
}
$ dune exec ./test.exe test2.json
test2.json:3:2: syntax error
[255]
```

That wraps up our parsing tutorial. As an aside, notice that the JSON polymorphic variant type that we defined in this chapter is actually structurally compatible with the Yojson representation explained in Chapter 19 (Handling JSON Data). That means that you can take this parser and use it with the helper functions in Yojson to build more sophisticated applications.

21 Data Serialization with S-Expressions

S-expressions are nested parenthetical expressions whose atomic values are strings. They were first popularized by the Lisp programming language in the 1960s, and have remained one of the simplest and most effective ways to encode structured data in a human-readable and editable form.

An example s-expression might look like this.

```
(this (is an) (s expression))
```

S-expressions play a major role in Base and Core, effectively acting as the default serialization format. Indeed, we've encountered s-expressions multiple times already, including in Chapter 8 (Error Handling), Chapter 11 (Functors), and Chapter 12 (First-Class Modules).

This chapter will go into s-expressions in more depth. In particular, we'll discuss:

- The details of the s-expression format, including how to parse it while generating good error messages for debugging malformed inputs
- How to generate converters between s-expressions and arbitrary OCaml types
- How to use annotations to control the behavior of these generated converters
- How to integrate s-expressions into your interfaces, in particular how to add s-expression converters to a module without breaking abstraction boundaries

We'll tie this together at the end of the chapter with a simple s-expression formatted configuration file for a web server

21.1 Basic Usage

The type used to represent an s-expression is quite simple:

```
module Sexp : sig
  type t =
  | Atom of string
  | List of t list
end
```

An s-expression can be thought of as a tree where each node contains a list of its children, and where the leaves of the tree are strings. Core provides good support for s-expressions in its `Sexp` module, including functions for converting s-expressions to and from strings. Let's rewrite our example s-expression in terms of this type:

```
# open Core;;
# Sexp.List [
    Sexp.Atom "this";
    Sexp.List [ Sexp.Atom "is"; Sexp.Atom "an"];
    Sexp.List [ Sexp.Atom "s"; Sexp.Atom "expression" ];
  ];;
- : Sexp.t = (this (is an) (s expression))
```

This prints out nicely because Core registers a pretty printer with the toplevel. This pretty printer is based on the functions in `Sexp` for converting s-expressions to and from strings:

```
# Sexp.to_string (Sexp.List [Sexp.Atom "1"; Sexp.Atom "2"]);;
- : string = "(1 2)"
# Sexp.of_string ("(1 2 (3 4))");;
- : Sexp.t = (1 2 (3 4))
```

Base, Core, and Parsexp

In these examples, we're using Core rather than Base because Core has integrated support for parsing s-expressions, courtesy of the `Parsexp` library. If you just use Base, you'll find that you don't have `Sexp.of_string` at your disposal.

```
# open Base;;
# Sexp.of_string "(1 2 3)";;
Line 1, characters 1-15:
Alert deprecated: Base.Sexp.of_string
[since 2018-02] Use [Parsexp.Single.parse_string_exn]
Line 1, characters 1-15:
Error: This expression has type unit
        This is not a function; it cannot be applied.
```

That's because, in an attempt to keep `Base` light, the s-expression parsing functions aren't included. That said, you can always use them by calling out to the corresponding functions from the `Parsexp` library:

```
# Parsexp.Single.parse_string_exn "(1 2 3)";;
- : Sexp.t = (1 2 3)
```

In addition to providing the `Sexp` module, most of the base types in Base and Core support conversion to and from s-expressions. For example, we can use the conversion functions defined in the respective modules for integers, strings, and exceptions:

```
# Int.sexp_of_t 3;;
- : Sexp.t = 3
# String.sexp_of_t "hello";;
- : Sexp.t = hello
# Exn.sexp_of_t (Invalid_argument "foo");;
- : Sexp.t = (Invalid_argument foo)
```

It's also possible to convert container types such as lists or arrays that are polymorphic over the type of data they contain.

```
# #show List.sexp_of_t;;
val sexp_of_t : ('a -> Sexp.t) -> 'a list -> Sexp.t
```

Notice that `List.sexp_of_t` is polymorphic and takes as its first argument another conversion function to handle the elements of the list to be converted. Base and Core use this scheme more generally for defining sexp converters for polymorphic types. Here's an example of it in action.

```
# List.sexp_of_t Int.sexp_of_t [1; 2; 3];;
- : Sexp.t = (1 2 3)
```

The functions that go in the other direction, *i.e.*, reconstruct an OCaml value from an s-expression, use essentially the same trick for handling polymorphic types, as shown below.

```
# List.t_of_sexp Int.t_of_sexp (Sexp.of_string "(1 2 3)");;
- : int list = [1; 2; 3]
```

Such a function will fail with an exception when presented with an s-expression that doesn't match the structure of the OCaml type in question.

```
# List.t_of_sexp Int.t_of_sexp (Sexp.of_string "(1 2 three)");;
Exception:
(Of_sexp_error "int_of_sexp: (Failure int_of_string)" (invalid_sexp
    three))
```

More on Top-Level Printing

The values of the s-expressions that we created were printed properly as s-expressions in the toplevel, instead of as the tree of `Atom` and `List` variants that they're actually made of.

This is due to OCaml's facility for installing custom *top-level printers* that can rewrite some values into more top-level-friendly equivalents. They are generally installed as `ocamlfind` packages ending in `top`:

```
$ ocamlfind list | grep top
astring.top            (version: 0.8.3)
cohttp.top             (version: n/a)
compiler-libs.toplevel (version: [distributed with Ocaml])
core.top               (version: v0.10.0)
...
uri.top                (version: 1.9.6)
utop                   (version: 2.1.0)
```

The `core.top` package (which you should have loaded by default in your `.ocamlinit` file) loads in printers for the Core extensions already, so you don't need to do anything special to use the s-expression printer.

21.1.1   S-Expression Converters for New Types

But what if you want a function to convert a brand new type to an s-expression? You can of course write it yourself manually. Here's an example.

```
# type t = { foo: int; bar: float };;
type t = { foo : int; bar : float; }
# let sexp_of_t t =
```

```
      let a x = Sexp.Atom x and l x = Sexp.List x in
      l [ l [a "foo"; Int.sexp_of_t t.foo  ];
          l [a "bar"; Float.sexp_of_t t.bar]; ];;
val sexp_of_t : t -> Sexp.t = <fun>
# sexp_of_t { foo = 3; bar = -5.5 };;
- : Sexp.t = ((foo 3) (bar -5.5))
```

This is somewhat tiresome to write, and it gets more so when you consider the parser, i.e., t_of_sexp, which is considerably more complex. Writing this kind of parsing and printing code by hand is mechanical and error prone, not to mention a drag.

Given how mechanical the code is, you could imagine writing a program that inspects the type definition and automatically generates the conversion code for you. As it turns out, there's a *syntax extension* called ppx_sexp_conv which does just that, creating the required functions for every type annotated with [@@deriving sexp]. To enable ppx_sexp_conv, we're going to enable ppx_jane, which is a larger collection of useful extensions that includes ppx_sexp_conv.

```
# #require "ppx_jane";;
```

We can use the extension as follows.

```
# type t = { foo: int; bar: float } [@@deriving sexp];;
type t = { foo : int; bar : float; }
val t_of_sexp : Sexp.t -> t = <fun>
val sexp_of_t : t -> Sexp.t = <fun>
# t_of_sexp (Sexp.of_string "((bar 35) (foo 3))");;
- : t = {foo = 3; bar = 35.}
```

The syntax extension can be used outside of type declarations as well. As discussed in Chapter 8 (Error Handling), [@@deriving sexp] can be attached to the declaration of an exception to improve the quality of errors printed by OCaml's top-level exception handler.

Here are two exception declarations, one with an annotation, and one without:

```
exception Ordinary_exn of string list;;
exception Exn_with_sexp of string list [@@deriving sexp];;
```

And here's the difference in what you see when you throw these exceptions.

```
# raise (Ordinary_exn ["1";"2";"3"]);;
Exception: Ordinary_exn(_).
# raise (Exn_with_sexp ["1";"2";"3"]);;
Exception: (//toplevel//.Exn_with_sexp (1 2 3))
```

ppx_sexp_conv also supports inline declarations that generate converters for anonymous types.

```
# [%sexp_of: int * string ];;
- : int * string -> Sexp.t = <fun>
# [%sexp_of: int * string ] (3, "foo");;
- : Sexp.t = (3 foo)
```

The syntax extensions bundled with Base and Core almost all have the same basic structure: they auto-generate code based on type definitions, implementing functionality that you could in theory have implemented by hand, but with far less programmer effort.

Syntax Extensions and PPX

OCaml doesn't directly support deriving s-expression converters from type definitions. Instead, it provides a mechanism called *PPX* which allows you to add to the compilation pipeline code for transforming OCaml programs at the syntactic level, via the -ppx compiler flag.

PPXs operate on OCaml's *abstract syntax tree*, or AST, which is a data type that represents the syntax of a well-formed OCaml program. Annotations like [%sexp_of: int] or [@@deriving sexp] are part of special extensions to the syntax, called *extension points*, which were added to the language to give a place to put information that would be consumed by syntax extensions like ppx_sexp_conv.

ppx_sexp_conv is part of a family of syntax extensions, including ppx_compare, described in Chapter 15 (Maps and Hash Tables), and ppx_fields, described in Chapter 6 (Records), that generate code based on type declarations.

Using these extensions from a dune file is as simple as adding this directive to a (library) or (executable) stanza to indicate that the files should be run through a preprocessor:

```
(executable
  (name hello)
  (preprocess (pps ppx_sexp_conv))
)
```

21.2   The Sexp Format

The textual representation of s-expressions is pretty straightforward. An s-expression is written down as a nested parenthetical expression, with whitespace-separated strings as the atoms. Quotes are used for atoms that contain parentheses or spaces themselves; backslash is the escape character; and semicolons are used to introduce single-line comments. Thus, the following file, example.scm:

```
((foo 3.3) ;; This is a comment
 (bar "this is () an \" atom"))
```

can be loaded as follows.

```
# Sexp.load_sexp "example.scm";;
- : Sexp.t = ((foo 3.3) (bar "this is () an \" atom"))
```

As you can see, the comment is not part of the loaded s-expression.

All in, the s-expression format supports three comment syntaxes:

; Comments out everything to the end of line
#|,|# Delimiters for commenting out a block
#; Comments out the first complete s-expression that follows

The following example shows all of these in action:

```
;; comment_heavy_example.scm
((this is included)
 ; (this is commented out
 (this stays)
 #; (all of this is commented
     out (even though it crosses lines.))
  (and #| block delimiters #| which can be nested |#
     will comment out
     an arbitrary multi-line block))) |#
  now we're done
  ))
```

Again, loading the file as an s-expression drops the comments:

```
# Sexp.load_sexp "comment_heavy.scm";;
- : Sexp.t = ((this is included) (this stays) (and now we're done))
```

If we introduce an error into our s-expression, by, say, creating a file
broken_example.scm which is example.scm, without the open-paren in front of bar,
we'll get a parse error:

```
# Sexp.load_sexp "example_broken.scm";;
Exception:
(Sexplib.Sexp.Parse_error
   ((err_msg "unexpected character: ')'") (text_line 4) (text_char 30)
     (global_offset 78) (buf_pos 78)))
```

21.3   Preserving Invariants

Modules and module interfaces are an important part of how OCaml code is structured
and designed. One of the key reasons we use module interfaces is to make it possible
to enforce invariants. In particular, by restricting how values of a given type can be
created and transformed, interfaces let you enforce various rules, including ensuring
that your data is well-formed.

When you add s-expression converters (or really any deserializer) to an API, you're
adding an alternate path for creating values, and if you're not careful, that alternate
path can violate the carefully maintained invariants of your code.

In the following, we'll show how this problem can crop up, and how to resolve it.
Let's consider a module Int_interval for representing closed integer intervals, similar
to the one described in Chapter 11 (Functors).

Here's the signature.

```
type t [@@deriving sexp]

(** [create lo hi] creates an interval from [lo] to [hi] inclusive,
    and is empty if [lo > hi]. *)
val create : int -> int -> t

val is_empty : t -> bool
val contains : t -> int -> bool
```

In addition to basic operations for creating and evaluating intervals, this interface also exposes s-expression converters. Note that the `[@@deriving sexp]` syntax works in a signature as well, but in this case, it just adds the signature for the conversion functions, not the implementation.

Here's the implementation of `Int_interval`.

```
open Core

(* for [Range (x,y)], we require that [y >= x] *)
type t =
  | Range of int * int
  | Empty
[@@deriving sexp]

let create x y = if x > y then Empty else Range (x, y)

let is_empty = function
  | Empty -> true
  | Range _ -> false

let contains i x =
  match i with
  | Empty -> false
  | Range (low, high) -> x >= low && x <= high
```

One critical invariant here is that `Range` is only used to represent non-empty intervals. A call to `create` with a lower bound above the upper bound will return an `Empty`.

Now, let's demonstrate the functionality with some tests, using the expect test framework described in Chapter 18.2 (Expect Tests). First, we'll write a test helper that takes an interval and a list of points, and prints out the result of checking for emptiness, and a classification of which points are inside and outside the interval.

```
let test_interval i points =
  let in_, out =
    List.partition_tf points ~f:(fun x -> Int_interval.contains i x)
  in
  let to_string l =
    List.map ~f:Int.to_string l |> String.concat ~sep:", "
  in
  print_endline
    (String.concat
       ~sep:"\n"
       [ (if Int_interval.is_empty i then "empty" else "non-empty")
       ; "in:  " ^ to_string in_
       ; "out: " ^ to_string out
       ])
```

We can run this test on a non-empty interval,

```
let%expect_test "ordinary interval" =
  test_interval (Int_interval.create 3 6) (List.range 1 10);
  [%expect
    {|
    non-empty
    in:  3, 4, 5, 6
    out: 1, 2, 7, 8, 9 |}]
```

And also on an empty one.

```
let%expect_test "empty interval" =
  test_interval (Int_interval.create 6 3) (List.range 1 10);
  [%expect {|
    empty
    in:
    out: 1, 2, 3, 4, 5, 6, 7, 8, 9 |}]
```

Note that the result of checking is_empty lines up with the test of what elements are contained and not contained in the interval.

Now, let's test out the s-expression converters, starting with sexp_of_t. This test lets you see that a flipped-bounds interval is represented by Empty.

```
let%expect_test "test to_sexp" =
  let t lo hi =
    let i = Int_interval.create lo hi in
    print_s [%sexp (i : Int_interval.t)]
  in
  t 3 6;
  [%expect {| (Range 3 6) |}];
  t 4 4;
  [%expect {| (Range 4 4) |}];
  t 6 3;
  [%expect {| Empty |}]
```

The next thing to check is the t_of_sexp converters, and here, we run into a problem. In particular, consider what would happen if we create an interval from the s-expression (Range 6 3). That's an s-expression that shouldn't ever be generated by the library, since intervals should never have swapped bounds. But there's nothing to stop us from generating that s-expression by hand.

```
let%expect_test "test (range 6 3)" =
  let i = Int_interval.t_of_sexp (Sexp.of_string "(Range 6 3)") in
  test_interval i (List.range 1 10);
  [%expect
    {|
    non-empty
    in:
    out: 1, 2, 3, 4, 5, 6, 7, 8, 9 |}]
```

You can see something bad has happened, since this interval is detected as non-empty, but doesn't appear to contain anything. The problem traces back to the fact that t_of_sexp doesn't check the same invariant that create does. We can fix this, by overriding the auto-generated s-expression converter with one that checks the invariant, in this case, by calling create.

```
let t_of_sexp sexp =
  match t_of_sexp sexp with
  | Empty -> Empty
  | Range (x, y) -> create x y
```

Overriding an existing function definition with a new one is perfectly acceptable in OCaml. Since t_of_sexp is defined with an ordinary let rather than a let rec, the call to the t_of_sexp goes to the derived version of the function, rather than being a recursive call.

Note that, rather than fixing up the invariant, we could have instead thrown an exception if the invariant was violated. In any case, the approach we took means that rerunning our test produces a more consistent and sensible result.

```
let%expect_test "test (range 6 3)" =
  let i = Int_interval.t_of_sexp (Sexp.of_string "(Range 6 3)") in
  test_interval i (List.range 1 10);
  [%expect
    {|
    empty
    in:
    out: 1, 2, 3, 4, 5, 6, 7, 8, 9 |}]
```

21.4   Getting Good Error Messages

There are two steps to deserializing a type from an s-expression: first, converting the bytes in a file to an s-expression; and the second, converting that s-expression into the type in question. One problem with this is that it can be hard to localize errors to the right place using this scheme. Consider the following example.

```
open Core

type t =
  { a : string
  ; b : int
  ; c : float option
  }
[@@deriving sexp]

let () =
  let t = Sexp.load_sexp "example.scm" |> t_of_sexp in
  printf "b is: %d\n%!" t.b
```

If you were to run this on a malformatted file, say, this one:

```
((a not-a-string)
 (b not-a-string)
 (c 1.0))
```

you'll get the following error. (Note that we set the OCAMLRUNPARAM environment variable to suppress the stack trace here.)

```
$ OCAMLRUNPARAM=b=0 dune exec -- ./read_foo.exe
Uncaught exception:

  (Of_sexp_error "int_of_sexp: (Failure int_of_string)"
   (invalid_sexp not-a-string))

[2]
```

If all you have is the error message and the string, it's not terribly informative. In particular, you know that the parsing errored out on the atom "not-an-integer," but you don't know which one! In a large file, this kind of bad error message can be pure misery.

But there's hope! We can make a small change to the code to improve the error message greatly:

```
open Core

type t =
  { a : string
  ; b : int
  ; c : float option
  }
[@@deriving sexp]

let () =
  let t = Sexp.load_sexp_conv_exn "example.scm" t_of_sexp in
  printf "b is: %d\n%!" t.b
```

If we run it again, we'll see a more informative error.

```
$ OCAMLRUNPARAM=b=0 dune exec -- ./read_foo.exe
Uncaught exception:

  (Of_sexp_error example.scm:2:4 "int_of_sexp: (Failure
    int_of_string)"
   (invalid_sexp not-an-integer))

[2]
```

Here, `example.scm:2:5` tells us that the error occurred in the file `"example.scm"` on line 2, character 5. This is a much better start for figuring out what went wrong. The ability to find the precise location of the error depends on the sexp converter reporting errors using the function `of_sexp_error`. This is already done by converters generated by `ppx_sexp_conv`, but you should make sure to do the same when you write custom converters.

21.5   Sexp-Conversion Directives

`ppx_sexp_conv` supports a collection of directives for modifying the default behavior of the auto-generated sexp converters. These directives allow you to customize the way in which types are represented as s-expressions without having to write a custom converter.

21.5.1   @sexp.opaque

The most commonly used directive is `[@sexp_opaque]`, whose purpose is to mark a given component of a type as being unconvertible. Anything marked with the `[@sexp.opaque]` attribute will be presented as the atom `<opaque>` by the to-sexp converter, and will trigger an exception from the from-sexp converter.

Note that the type of a component marked as opaque doesn't need to have a sexp converter defined. By default, if we define a type without a sexp converter and then try to use it as part of another type with a sexp converter, we'll error out:

```
# type no_converter = int * int;;
type no_converter = int * int
# type t = { a: no_converter; b: string } [@@deriving sexp];;
Line 1, characters 15-27:
Error: Unbound value no_converter_of_sexp
```

But with [@sexp.opaque], we can embed our opaque no_converter type within the other data structure without an error.

```
type t =
  { a: (no_converter [@sexp.opaque]);
    b: string
  } [@@deriving sexp];;
```

And if we now convert a value of this type to an s-expression, we'll see the contents of field a marked as opaque:

```
# sexp_of_t { a = (3,4); b = "foo" };;
- : Sexp.t = ((a <opaque>) (b foo))
```

Note that t_of_sexp is still generated, but will fail at runtime when called.

```
# t_of_sexp (Sexp.of_string "((a whatever) (b foo))");;
Exception:
(Of_sexp_error "opaque_of_sexp: cannot convert opaque values"
  (invalid_sexp whatever))
```

It might seem perverse to create a parser for a type containing a [@sexp.opaque] value, but it's not as useless as it seems. In particular, such a converter won't necessarily fail on all inputs. Consider a record containing a list of opaque values:

```
type t =
  { a: (no_converter [@sexp.opaque]) list;
    b: string
  } [@@deriving sexp];;
```

The t_of_sexp function can still succeed, as long as the list is empty.

```
# t_of_sexp (Sexp.of_string "((a ()) (b foo))");;
- : t = {a = []; b = "foo"}
```

Sometimes, though, one or other of the converters is useless, and you want to explicitly choose what to generate. You can do that by using [@@deriving sexp_of] or [@@deriving of_sexp] instead of [@@deriving sexp].

21.5.2   @sexp.list

Sometimes, sexp converters have more parentheses than one would ideally like. Consider the following variant type.

```
type compatible_versions =
  | Specific of string list
  | All
[@@deriving sexp];;
```

Here's what the concrete syntax looks like.

```
# sexp_of_compatible_versions
    (Specific ["3.12.0"; "3.12.1"; "3.13.0"]);;
- : Sexp.t = (Specific (3.12.0 3.12.1 3.13.0))
```

The set of parens around the list of versions is arguably excessive. We can drop those parens using the [@sexp.list] directive.

```
type compatible_versions =
  | Specific of string list [@sexp.list]
  | All [@@deriving sexp]
```

And here's the resulting lighter syntax.

```
# sexp_of_compatible_versions
    (Specific ["3.12.0"; "3.12.1"; "3.13.0"]);;
- : Sexp.t = (Specific 3.12.0 3.12.1 3.13.0)
```

21.5.3   @sexp.option

By default, optional values are represented either as () for None. Here's an example of a record type containing an option:

```
type t =
  { a: int option;
    b: string;
  } [@@deriving sexp]
```

And here's what the concrete syntax looks like.

```
# sexp_of_t { a = None; b = "hello" };;
- : Sexp.t = ((a ()) (b hello))
# sexp_of_t { a = Some 3; b = "hello" };;
- : Sexp.t = ((a (3)) (b hello))
```

This all works as you might expect, but in the context of a record, you might want a different behavior, which is to make the field itself optional. The [@sexp.option] directive gives you just that.

```
type t =
  { a: int option [@sexp.option];
    b: string;
  } [@@deriving sexp]
```

And here is the new syntax. Note that when the value of a is Some, it shows up in the s-expression unadorned, and when it's None, the entire record field is omitted.

```
# sexp_of_t { a = Some 3; b = "hello" };;
- : Sexp.t = ((a 3) (b hello))
# sexp_of_t { a = None; b = "hello" };;
- : Sexp.t = ((b hello))
```

21.5.4   Specifying Defaults

[@sexp.option] gives you a way of interpreting the s-expression for a record where some of the fields are left unspecified. The [@default] directive provides another.

Consider the following type, which represents the configuration of a very simple web server:

```
type http_server_config = {
  web_root: string;
  port: int;
  addr: string;
} [@@deriving sexp];;
```

One could imagine making some of these parameters optional; in particular, by default, we might want the web server to bind to port 80, and to listen as localhost. We can do this as follows:

```
type http_server_config = {
  web_root: string;
  port: int [@default 80];
  addr: string [@default "localhost"];
} [@@deriving sexp];;
```

Now, if we try to convert an s-expression that specifies only the web_root, we'll see that the other values are filled in with the desired defaults:

```
# let cfg =
    "((web_root /var/www/html))"
    |> Sexp.of_string
    |> http_server_config_of_sexp;;
val cfg : http_server_config =
  {web_root = "/var/www/html"; port = 80; addr = "localhost"}
```

If we convert the configuration back out to an s-expression, you'll notice that all of the fields are present, even though they're not strictly necessary:

```
# sexp_of_http_server_config cfg;;
- : Sexp.t = ((web_root /var/www/html) (port 80) (addr localhost))
```

We could make the generated s-expression also drop default values, by using the [@sexp_drop_default] directive:

```
type http_server_config = {
  web_root: string;
  port: int [@default 80] [@sexp_drop_default.equal];
  addr: string [@default "localhost"] [@sexp_drop_default.equal];
} [@@deriving sexp];;
```

And here's an example of it in action:

```
# let cfg =
    "((web_root /var/www/html))"
    |> Sexp.of_string
    |> http_server_config_of_sexp;;
val cfg : http_server_config =
  {web_root = "/var/www/html"; port = 80; addr = "localhost"}
# sexp_of_http_server_config cfg;;
- : Sexp.t = ((web_root /var/www/html))
```

As you can see, the fields that are at their default values are omitted from the generated s-expression. On the other hand, if we convert a config with non-default values, they will show up in the generated s-expression.

```
# sexp_of_http_server_config { cfg with port = 8080 };;
- : Sexp.t = ((web_root /var/www/html) (port 8080))
# sexp_of_http_server_config
  { cfg with port = 8080; addr = "192.168.0.1" };;
- : Sexp.t = ((web_root /var/www/html) (port 8080) (addr 192.168.0.1))
```

This can be very useful in designing config file formats that are both reasonably terse and easy to generate and maintain. It can also be useful for backwards compatibility: if you add a new field to your config record but make that field optional, then you should still be able to parse older versions of your config.

The exact attribute you use depends on the comparison functions available over the type that you wish to drop:

- [@sexp_drop_default.compare] if the type supports [%compare]
- [@sexp_drop_default.equal] if the type supports [%equal]
- [@sexp_drop_default.sexp] if you want to compare the sexp representations
- [@sexp_drop_default f] and give an explicit equality function

Most of the type definitions supplied with Base and Core provide the comparison and equality operations, so those are reasonable default attributes to use.

22 The OCaml Platform

So far in Part II, we've gone through a number of libraries and techniques you can use to build larger scale OCaml programs. We'll now wrap up this part by examining the tools you can use for editing, compiling, testing, documenting and publishing your own projects.

The OCaml community has developed a suite of modern tools to interface it with IDEs such as Visual Studio Code, and to generate API documentation and implement modern software engineering practices such as continuous integration (CI) and unit or fuzz testing. All you need to do is to specify your project metadata (for example, library dependencies and compiler versions), and the OCaml Platform tools that we'll describe next will do much of the heavy lifting.

Using the Opam Source-Based Package Manager

opam is the official package manager and metadata packaging format that is used in the OCaml community. We've been using it in earlier chapters to install OCaml libraries, and we're going to take a closer look at how to use opam within a full project next. You've almost certainly done this already at this point in the book, but in case you've skipped straight to this chapter make sure you first initialize opam's global state.

```
$ opam init
```

By default, opam doesn't require any special user permissions and stores all of the files it installs in ~/.opam, such as the current build of the OCaml compiler if you didn't have one pre-installed when you initialized opam.

You can maintain multiple development environments with different packages and compilers installed, each of which is called a "switch" – the default one can be found under ~/.opam/default. Run opam switch to see all the different sandboxed environments you have available:

```
$ opam switch
#  switch    compiler     description
   default   ocaml.4.13.1  default
```

22.1   A Hello World OCaml Project

Let's start by creating a sample OCaml project and navigating around it. Dune has a basic built-in command to initialize a project template that is suitable to get us started.

```
$ dune init proj hello
Success: initialized project component named hello
```

Dune will create a `hello/` directory and populate it with a skeleton OCaml project. This sample project has the basic metadata required for us to learn more about the opam package manager and the dune build tool that we've used earlier in the book.

22.1.1   Setting Up an Opam Local Switch

The next thing we need is a suitable environment for this project, with dune and any other library dependencies available. The best way to do this is to create a new opam sandbox, via the `opam switch create` command. If you specify a project directory argument to this command, then it creates a "local switch" that stores all the dependencies within that directory rather than under `~/.opam`. This is a convenient way to keep all your build dependencies and source code in one place on your filesystem.

Let's make a local switch for our hello world project now:

```
$ cd hello
$ opam switch create .
```

This invokes opam to install the project dependencies (in this case, just the OCaml compiler and dune as we didn't specify any more when initializing the project). All of the files from the local switch will be present under `_opam/` in the working directory. You can find the dune binary that was just compiled inside that directory, for example:

```
$ ./_opam/bin/dune --version
3.0.2
```

Since opam will install other binaries and libraries in the local switch as your project grows, you will need to add the switch to your command-line path. You can use opam env to add the right directories to your local shell path so that you can invoke the locally installed tools:

```
$ eval $(opam env)
```

If you prefer not to modify your shell configuration, then you can also invoke commands via opam exec to modify the path for the subcommand specified in the remainder of the command line.

```
$ opam exec -- dune build
```

This executes dune build with the opam environment variables added to the command invocation, so it will pick up the locally built dune from your project. The double dash in the command line is a common Unix convention that tells opam to stop parsing its own optional arguments for the remainder of the command, so that they don't interfere with the command that is being executed.

22.1.2   Choosing an OCaml Compiler Version

When creating a switch, opam analyses the project dependencies and selects the newest OCaml compiler that is compatible with them. Sometimes though, you will want to select a specific version of the OCaml compiler, perhaps to ensure reproducibility or to use a particular feature. You can use `opam switch list-available` to get a full list of all the compilers that are available.

```
ocaml-system              4.13.1          The OCaml compiler
                                          (system version, from outside
                                          of opam)
ocaml-base-compiler  4.13.1          Official release 4.13.1
ocaml-variants            4.13.1+options  Official release of OCaml 4.13.1
```

You'll find many more versions present than the snippet above, but notice that there are three different types of OCaml compiler packages present.

`ocaml-system` is the name opam uses for the pre-existing version of the OCaml compiler that was already installed on your machine. This compiler is always fast to install since nothing needs to be compiled for it. The only thing needed to create a system switch is to have the right version of OCaml already installed (e.g. via `apt` or Homebrew) and to pass the same version to the switch creation as an additional argument.

For example, if you have OCaml 4.13.1 installed, then running this command will use the system compiler:

```
$ opam switch create . 4.13.1
```

On the other hand, if you didn't have that system compiler installed, then the compiler will need to be built from scratch. The command above would select the `ocaml-base-compiler` package in this case, which contains the full OCaml compiler source code. It will take a little longer than `ocaml-system`, but you have much more flexibility about the choice of versions. The default operation of `opam switch create` is to calculate the latest supported compiler version from your project metadata and use that one for the local switch.

If you always want to locally install a particular compiler, then you can refine the package description:

```
$ opam switch create . ocaml-base-compiler.4.13.1
```

Sometimes, you will also need to add custom configuration options to the compiler, such as the `flambda` optimiser. There are two packages that handle this: `ocaml-variants` is a package that detects the presence of various `ocaml-option` packages to activate configuration flags. For example, to build a compiler with `flambda`, you would:

```
$ opam switch create . ocaml-variants.4.13.1+options
    ocaml-option-flambda
```

You can specify multiple `ocaml-option` packages to cover all the customization your project needs. See the full set of option packages by using:

```
$ opam search ocaml-option
```

22.1.3   Structure of an OCaml Project

Back in Chapter 5 (Files, Modules, and Programs), we looked at what a simple program with a couple of OCaml modules looks like. Let's now look at the set of files in our `hello/` application to examine a fuller project structure.

```
.
|-- dune-project
|-- hello.opam
|-- lib
|    |-- dune
|-- bin
|    |-- dune
|    `-- main.ml
`-- test
     |-- dune
     `-- hello.ml
```

Some observations about this structure:

- The `dune-project` file marks the root of the project, and is used for writing down some key metadata for the project (more on that later).
- The `hello.opam` file contains metadata for registering this software as an opam project. As we'll see, we won't need to edit this manually because we can generate the file via dune.
- There are three source directories, each with its own dune file specifying the build parameters for that part of the codebase. The trio of `lib`, `bin` and `test` makes good sense for a project that is primarily an executable, rather than a reusable library. In that case, you would might use these directories as follows:
  - The `lib` directory would contain the bulk of the source.
  - The `bin` directory would contain a thin wrapper on top of the code in `lib` which actually launches the executable.
  - The `test` directory has the bulk of the tests for `lib`, which, following the advice in Chapter 18.1.2 (Where Should Tests Go?), are in a separate directory from the source.

Now we'll talk about the different parts of this structure in more detail.

22.1.4   Defining Module Names

A matching pair of `ml` and `mli` files define an OCaml module, named after the file and capitalized. Module names are the only kind of name you refer to within OCaml code.

Let's create a `Msg` module in our skeleton project inside `lib/`.

```
$ echo 'let greeting = "Hello World"' > lib/msg.ml
$ echo 'val greeting : string' > lib/msg.mli
```

A valid OCaml module name cannot contain dashes or other special characters other than underscores. If you need to refresh your memory about how files and modules interact, refer back to Chapter 5 (Files, Modules, and Programs).

22.1.5   Defining Libraries as Collections of Modules

One or more OCaml modules can be gathered together into a *library*, providing a convenient way to package up multiple dependencies with a single name. A project usually puts the business logic of the application into a library rather than directly into an executable binary, since this makes writing tests and documentation easier in addition to improving reusability.

Libraries are defined by putting a dune file into a directory, such as the one generated for us in lib/dune:

```
(library
 (name hello))
```

Dune will treat all OCaml modules in that directory as being part of the hello library (this behavior can be overridden by a modules field for more advanced projects). By default, dune also exposes libraries as *wrapped* under a single OCaml module, and the name field determines the name of that module.

In our example project, msg.ml is defined in lib/dune which defines a hello library. Thus, users of our newly defined module can access it as Hello.Msg. You can read more about wrapping and module aliases in Chapter 26.4.4 (Wrapping Libraries with Module Aliases). Although our hello library only currently contains a single Msg module, it is common to have multiple modules per library in larger projects. Other modules within the hello library can simply refer to Msg.

You must refer to library names in a dune file when deciding what libraries to link in, and never individual module names. You can query the installed libraries in your current switch via ocamlfind list at your command prompt, after running opam install ocamlfind to install it if necessary:

```
$ ocamlfind list
afl-persistent        (version: 1.2)
alcotest              (version: 1.5.0)
alcotest.engine       (version: 1.5.0)
alcotest.stdlib_ext   (version: 1.5.0)
angstrom              (version: 0.15.0)
asn1-combinators      (version: 0.2.6)
...
```

If there's a public_name field present in the dune library definition, this determines the publicly exposed name for the library. The public library name is what you specify via the libraries field in other projects that use your project's libraries. Without a public name, the defined library is local to the current dune project only. The (libraries) field in the lib/dune file is empty since this is a trivial standalone library.

22.1.6   Writing Test Cases for a Library

Our next step is to define a test case in test/dune for our library. In Chapter 18 (Testing), we showed you how to embed tests within a library, using the inline test mechanism. In this section, we'll show you how to use dune's test stanza to create a test-only executable, which is useful when you're not using inline tests.

Let's start by writing a test as a simple assertion in `test/hello.ml`.

```
let () = assert (String.equal Hello.Msg.greeting "Hello World")
```

We can use the `test` dune stanza to build an executable binary that is run when you invoke dune `runtest` (along with any inline tests defined within libraries). We'll also add a dependency on our locally defined `hello` library so that we can access it. The `test/dune` file looks like this:

```
(test
 (libraries hello)
 (name hello))
```

Once you run the tests via dune `runtest`, you can find the built artifacts in `_build/default/test/` in your project checkout.

```
$ ls -la _build/default/test
total 992
drwxr-xr-x  7 avsm  staff     224 27 Feb 16:13 .
drwxr-xr-x  9 avsm  staff     288 27 Feb 15:23 ..
drwxr-xr-x  4 avsm  staff     128 27 Feb 15:23 .hello.eobjs
drwxr-xr-x  3 avsm  staff      96 27 Feb 16:12 .merlin-conf
-r-xr-xr-x  1 avsm  staff  495766 27 Feb 16:13 hello.exe
-r--r--r--  1 avsm  staff      64 27 Feb 16:13 hello.ml
-r--r--r--  1 avsm  staff      28 27 Feb 15:23 hello.mli
```

We deliberately defined two files called `hello.ml` in both `lib/` and `test/`. It's completely fine to define an executable `hello.exe` (in `test/`) alongside the OCaml library called `hello` (in `lib/`).

22.1.7   Building an Executable Program

Finally, we want to actually use our hello world from the command-line. This is defined in `bin/dune` in a very similar fashion to test cases.

```
(executable
 (public_name hello)
 (name main)
 (libraries hello)))
```

There has to be a `bin/main.ml` alongside the `bin/dune` file that represents the entry module for the executable. Only that module and the modules and libraries it depends on will be linked into the executable. Much like libraries, the `(name)` field here has to adhere to OCaml module naming conventions, and the `public_name` field represents the binary name that is installed onto the system and just needs to be a valid Unix or Windows filename.

Now try modifying `bin/main.ml` to refer to our `Hello.Msg` module:

```
let () = print_endline Hello.Msg.greeting
```

You can build and execute the command locally using dune `exec` and the local name of the executable. You can also find the built executable in `_build/default/bin/main.exe`.

```
$ dune build
$ dune exec -- bin/main.exe
Hello World
```

You can also refer to the public name of the executable if it's more convenient.

```
$ dune exec -- hello
Hello World
```

The dune exec and opam exec command we mentioned earlier in the chapter both nest, so you could append them to each other using the double-dash directive to separate them.

```
$ opam exec -- dune exec -- hello --args
```

This is quite a common thing to do when integrating with continuous integration systems that need systematic scripting of both opam and dune (a topic we'll come to shortly in this chapter).

22.2   Setting Up an Integrated Development Environment

Now that we've seen the basic structure of the OCaml project, it's time to setup an integrated development environment. An IDE is particularly useful for OCaml because it lets you leverage the information that's extracted by OCaml's rich type-system. A good IDE will provide you with the facilities to browse interface documentation, see inferred types for code, and to jump to the definitions of external modules.

22.2.1   Using Visual Studio Code

The recommended IDE for newcomers to OCaml is Visual Studio Code [1] using the OCaml Platform plugin [2]. The plugin uses the Language Server Protocol to communicate with your opam and dune environment. All you need to do is to install the OCaml LSP server via opam:

```
opam install ocaml-lsp-server
```

Once installed, the VSCode OCaml plugin will ask you which opam switch to use. Just the default one should be sufficient to get you going with building and browsing your interfaces.

What Is The Language Server Protocol?

The Language Server Protocol defines a communications standard between an editor or IDE and a language-specific server that provides features such as auto-completion, definition search, reference indexing and other facilities that require specialized support from language tooling. This allows a programming language toolchain to implement all this functionality just once, and then integrate cleanly into the multiplicity of

---

[1] https://code.visualstudio.com
[2] https://marketplace.visualstudio.com/items?itemName=ocamllabs.ocaml-platform

IDE environments available these days – and even go beyond conventional desktop environments to web-based notebooks such as Jupyter.

Since OCaml has a complete and mature LSP server, you'll find that an increasing number of IDEs will just support it out of the box once you install the ocaml-lsp-server. It integrates automatically with the various tools we've used in this book, such as detecting opam switches, invoking dune rules, and so on.

22.2.2   Browsing Interface Documentation

The OCaml LSP server understands how to interface with dune and examine the build artifacts (such as the typed `.cmt` interface files), so opening your local project in VS Code is sufficient to activate all the features. Try navigating over to `bin/main.ml`, where you will see the invocation to the `hello` library.

```
let () = print_endline Hello.Msg.greeting
```

First perform a build of the project to generate the type annotation files. Then hover your mouse over the `Hello.Msg.greeting` function – you should see some documentation pop up about the function and its arguments. This information comes from the *docstrings* written into the `msg.mli` interface file in the `hello` library.

Modify the `msg.mli` interface file to contain some signature documentation as follows:

```
(** This is a docstring, as it starts with "**", as opposed to normal
    comments that start with a single star.

    The top-most docstring of the module should contain a description
    of the module, what it does, how to use it, etc.

    The function-specific documentation located below the function
    signatures. *)

(** This is the docstring for the [greeting] function.

    A typical documentation for this function would be:

    Returns a greeting message.

    {4 Examples}

    {[ print_endline greeting ]} *)
val greeting : string
```

Documentation strings are parsed by the odoc[3] tool to generate HTML and PDF documentation from a collection of opam packages. If you intend your code to be used by anyone else (or indeed, by yourself a few months later) you should take the time to annotate your OCaml signature files with documentation. An easy way to preview the HTML documentation is to build it locally with dune:

---

[3] https://github.com/ocaml/odoc

```
$ opam install odoc
$ dune build @doc
```

This will leave the HTML files in _build/default/_doc/_html, which you can view normally with a web browser.

22.2.3   Autoformatting Your Source Code

As you develop more OCaml code, you'll find it convenient to have it formatted to a common style. The ocamlformat tool can help you do this easily from within VSCode.

```
$ echo 'version=0.20.1' > .ocamlformat
$ opam install ocamlformat.0.20.1
```

The .ocamlformat file controls the autoformatting options available, and fixes the version of the tool that is used. You can upgrade to a newer ocamlformat version whenever you want, but it is a manual process to avoid an upstream release auto-reformatting your project code without your intervention. You can examine the formatting options via ocamlformat --help – most of the time the defaults should be fine.

Once you've got ocamlformat configured, you can either format your project from within VSCode (shift-alt-F being the default), or by running:

```
$ dune build @fmt
```

This will generate a set of reformatted files in the build directory, which you can accept with dune promote as you did earlier in the testing chapter.

22.3   Publishing Your Code Online

With your IDE all set up you'll quickly develop useful OCaml code and want to share it with others. We'll now go through how to define opam packages, set up continuous integration and publish your code.

22.3.1   Defining Opam Packages

The only metadata file that is really *required* to participate in the open-source OCaml ecosystem is an opam file in your source tree. Each opam file defines a *package* – a collection of OCaml libraries and executable binaries or application data. Each opam package can define dependencies on other opam packages, and includes build and testing directions for your project. This is what's installed when you eventually publish the package and someone else types in opam install hello.

A collection of opam files can be stored in an *opam repository* to create a package database, with a central one for the OCaml ecosystem available at https://github.com/ocaml/opam-repository. The official (but not exclusive) tool used for manipulating opam files is the eponymous opam package manager[4] that we've been using throughout this book.

---

[4] https://opam.ocaml.org

How Do We Name OCaml Modules, Libraries and Packages?

Much of the time, the module, library, and package names are all the same. But there are reasons for these names to be distinct as well:

- Some libraries are exposed as multiple top-level modules, which means you need a different name for that collection of modules.
- Even when the library has a single top-level module, you might want the library name to be different from the module name to avoid name clashes at the library level.
- Package names might differ from library names if a package combines multiple libraries and/or binaries together.

It's important to understand the difference between modules, libraries and packages as you work on bigger projects. These can easily have thousands of modules, hundreds of libraries and dozens of opam packages in a single codebase.

22.3.2   Generating Project Metadata from Dune

The `hello.opam` file in our sample project is currently empty, but you don't need to write it by hand – instead, we can define our project metadata using the dune build system and have the opam file autogenerated for us. The root directory of an OCaml project built by dune has a `dune-project` file that defines the project metadata. In our example project, it starts with:

```
(lang dune 3.0)
```

The line above is the version of the syntax used in your build files, and *not* the actual version of the dune binary. One of the nicest features of dune is that it is forwards-compatible with older metadata. By defining the version of the dune language that you are currently using, *future* versions of dune will do their best to emulate the current behavior until you choose to upgrade your project.

The rest of the `dune-project` file defines other useful project metadata:

```
(name hello)
(documentation "https://username.github.io/hello/")
(source (github username/hello))
(license ISC)
(authors "Your name")
(maintainers "Your name")
(generate_opam_files true)
```

The fields in here all represent project metadata ranging from textual descriptions, to project URLs, to other opam package dependencies. Go ahead and edit the metadata above to reflect your own details, and then build the project:

```
$ dune build
```

The build command will update the `hello.opam` file in your source tree as well, keeping it in sync with your changes. The final part of the `dune-project` file contains dependency information for other packages your project depends on.

```
(package
 (name hello)
 (synopsis "A short description of the project")
 (description "A short description of the project")
 (depends
  (ocaml (>= 4.08.0))
  (alcotest :with-test)
  (odoc :with-doc)))
```

The (package) stanza here refers to opam packages, both for the name and for the dependency specifications. This is in contrast to the dune files which refer to ocamlfind libraries, since those represent the compilation units for OCaml code (whereas opam packages are broader collections of package data).

Notice that the dependency specification can also include version information. One of the key features of opam is that each repository contains multiple versions of the same package. The opam CLI contains a constraint solver that will find versions of all dependencies that are compatible with your current project. When you add a dependency, you can therefore specify lower and upper version bounds as required by your use of that package. The with-test and with-doc are further constraints that only add those dependencies for test and documentation generation respectively.

Once you've defined your opam and dune dependencies, you can run various lint commands to check that your metadata is consistent.

```
$ opam dune-lint
$ opam lint
```

The opam-dune-lint plugin will check that the ocamlfind libraries and opam packages in your dune files match up, and offer to fix them up if it spots a mismatch. opam lint runs additional checks on the opam files within your project.

22.3.3   Setting up Continuous Integration

Once you have your project metadata defined, it's a good time to begin hosting it online. Two of the most popular platforms for this are GitHub[5] and GitLab[6]. The remainder of this chapter will assume you are using GitHub for simplicity, although you are encouraged to check out the alternatives to find the best solution for your own needs.

When you create a GitHub repository and push your code to it, you can also add an OCaml GitHub Action that will install the OCaml Platform tools and run your code across various architectures and operating systems. You can find the full documentation online at the Set up OCaml[7] page on the GitHub marketplace. Configuring an action is as simple as adding a .github/workflows/test.yml file to your project that looks something like this:

```
name: Hello world workflow
on:
  pull_request:
```

---

[5] https://github.com
[6] https://gitlab.com
[7] https://github.com/marketplace/actions/set-up-ocaml

```
    push:
jobs:
  build:
    strategy:
      matrix:
        os:
          - macos-latest
          - ubuntu-latest
          - windows-latest
        ocaml-compiler:
          - 4.13.x
    runs-on: ${{ matrix.os }}
    steps:
      - name: Checkout code
        uses: actions/checkout@v2
      - name: Use OCaml ${{ matrix.ocaml-compiler }}
        uses: ocaml/setup-ocaml@v2
        with:
          ocaml-compiler: ${{ matrix.ocaml-compiler }}
      - run: opam install . --deps-only --with-test
      - run: opam exec -- dune build
      - run: opam exec -- dune runtest
```

This workflow file will run your project on OCaml installations on Windows, macOS and Linux, using the latest patch release of OCaml 4.13. Notice that it also runs the test cases you have defined earlier on all those different operating systems as well. You can do an awful lot of customization of these continuous integration workflows, so refer to the online documentation for more options.

22.3.4 Other Conventions

There are a few other files you may also want to add to a project to match common conventions:

- A `Makefile` contains targets for common actions such as `all`, `build`, `test` or `clean`. While you don't need this when using VSCode, some other operating system package managers might benefit from having one present.
- The `LICENSE` defines the terms under which your code is made available. Our example defaults to the permissive ISC license, and this is generally a safe default unless you have specific plans for your project.
- A `README.md` is a Markdown-formatted introduction to your library or application.
- A `.gitignore` file contains the patterns for generated files from the OCaml tools so that they can be ignored by the Git version control software. If you're not familiar with using Git, look over one of the tutorials one such as GitHub's git hello world[8].

---

[8] https://guides.github.com/activities/hello-world/

22.3.5   Releasing Your Code into the Opam Repository

Once your continuous integration is passing, you are all set to try to tag a release of your project and share it with other users! The OCaml Platform supplies a convenient tool called dune-release which automates much of this process for you.

```
$ opam install dune-release
```

The first thing you need to do is to create a CHANGES.md file in your project in Markdown format, which contains a header per version. This is typically a succinct summary of the changes between versions that can be read by users. For our first release, we might have:

```
## v1.0.0

- Initial public release of our glorious hello world
  project (@avsm)
- Added test cases for making sure we do in fact hello world.
```

Commit this file to your repository in the root. Before you proceed with a release, you need to make sure that all of your local changes have been pushed to the remote GitHub repository, and that your working tree is clean. You can do this by using git:

```
$ git clean -dxf
$ git diff
```

This will remove any untracked files from the local checkout (such as the _build directory) and check that tracked files are unmodified. We should now be ready to perform the release! First create a git tag to mark this release:

```
$ dune-release tag
```

This will parse your CHANGES.md file and figure out the latest version, and create a local git tag in your repository after prompting you. Once that succeeds, you can start the release process via:

```
$ dune-release
```

This will begin an interactive session where you will need to enter some GitHub authentication details (via creating a personal access token). Once that is completed, the tool will run all local tests, generate documentation and upload it to your GitHub pages branch for that project, and finally offer to open a pull request to the central opam-repository. Recall that the central opam package set is all just a normal git repository, and so your opam file will be added to that and your GitHub account will create a PR.

At this point, you can sit back and relax while the central opam repository test system runs your package through a battery of installations (including on exotic architectures you might not access to, such as S390X mainframes or 32-bit ARMv7). If there is a problem detected, some friendly maintainers from the OCaml community will comment on the pull request and guide you through how to address it. You can simply delete the git tag and re-run the release process until the package is merged. Once it is merged, you can navigate to the <ocaml.org> site and view it online in an hour or so. It will also be available in the central repository for other users to install.

Creating Lock Files for Your Projects

Before you publish a project, you might also want to create an opam lock file to include with the archive. A lock file records the exact versions of all the transitive opam dependencies at the time you generate it. All you need to do is to run:

```
$ opam lock
```

This generates a `pkgname.opam.locked` file which contains the same metadata as your original file, but with all the dependencies explicitly listed. Later on, if a user wants to reconstruct your exact opam environment (as opposed to the package solution they might calculate with a future opam repository), then they can pass an option during installation:

```
$ opam install pkgname --locked
$ opam switch create . --locked
```

Lock files are an optional but useful step to take when releasing your project to the Internet.

22.4   Learning More from Real Projects

There's a lot more customization that happens in any real project, and we can't cover every aspect in this book. The best way by far to learn more is to dive in and compile an already established project, and perhaps even contribute to it. There are thousands of libraries and executable projects released on the opam repository which you can find online at `https://ocaml.org`.

A selection of some include:

- `patdiff` is an OCaml implementation of the patience diff algorithm, and is a nice self-contained CLI project using Core. `https://github.com/janestreet/patdiff`
- The source code to this book is published as a self-contained monorepo with all the dependencies bundled together, for convenient compilation. `https://github.com/realworldocaml/book`
- Flow is a static typechecker for JavaScript written in OCaml that uses Base and works on macOS, Windows and Linux. It's a good example of a large, cross-platform CLI-driven tool. `https://github.com/facebook/flow`
- Octez is an OCaml implementation of a proof-of-stake blockchain called Tezos, which contains a comprehensive collection[9] of libraries such as interpreters for a stack language, and a shell that uses Lwt to provide networking, storage and cryptographic communications to the outside world. `https://gitlab.com/tezos/tezos`
- MirageOS is a library operating system written in OCaml, that can compile code to a

[9] `https://tezos.gitlab.io/shell/the_big_picture.html#packages`

variety of embedded and hypervisor targets. There are 100s of libraries all written using dune in a variety of ways available at `https://github.com/mirage`.

- You can find a number of standalone OCaml libraries for unicode, parsing and computer graphics and OS interaction over at `https://erratique.ch/software`.

Part III

The Compiler and Runtime System

Part III discusses OCaml's runtime system and compiler toolchain. It is remarkably simple when compared to some other language implementations (such as Java's or .NET's CLR). Reading this part will enable you to build very-high-performance systems, or to interface with C libraries. This is also where we talk about profiling and debugging techniques using tools such as GNU gdb.

23 Foreign Function Interface

This chapter includes contributions from Jeremy Yallop.

OCaml has several options available to interact with non-OCaml code. The compiler can link with external system libraries via C code and also can produce standalone native object files that can be embedded within other non-OCaml applications.

The mechanism by which code in one programming language can invoke routines in a different programming language is called a *foreign function interface*. This chapter will:

- Show how to call routines in C libraries directly from your OCaml code
- Teach you how to build higher-level abstractions in OCaml from the low-level C bindings
- Work through some full examples for binding a terminal interface and UNIX date/-time functions

The simplest foreign function interface in OCaml doesn't even require you to write any C code at all! The Ctypes library lets you define the C interface in pure OCaml, and the library then takes care of loading the C symbols and invoking the foreign function call.

Let's dive straight into a realistic example to show you how the library looks. We'll create a binding to the Ncurses terminal toolkit, as it's widely available on most systems and doesn't have any complex dependencies.

Installing the Ctypes Library

If you want to use Ctypes interactively, you'll also need to install the `libffi` library as a prerequisite to using Ctypes. It's a fairly popular library and should be available in your OS package manager. If you're using opam 2.1 or higher, it will prompt you to install it automatically when you install `ctypes-foreign`.

```
$ opam install ctypes ctypes-foreign
$ utop
# require "ctypes-foreign" ;;
```

You'll also need the Ncurses library for the first example. This comes preinstalled on many operating systems such as macOS, and Debian Linux provides it as the `libncurses5-dev` package.

23.1   Example: A Terminal Interface

Ncurses is a library to help build terminal-independent text interfaces in a reasonably efficient way. It's used in console mail clients like Mutt and Pine, and console web browsers such as Lynx.

The full C interface is quite large and is explained in the online documentation [1]. We'll just use the small excerpt, since we just want to demonstrate Ctypes in action:

```
typedef struct _win_st WINDOW;
typedef unsigned int chtype;

WINDOW *initscr   (void);
WINDOW *newwin    (int, int, int, int);
void    endwin    (void);
void    refresh   (void);
void    wrefresh  (WINDOW *);
void    addstr (const char *);
int     mvwaddch  (WINDOW *, int, int, const chtype);
void    mvwaddstr (WINDOW *, int, int, char *);
void    box (WINDOW *, chtype, chtype);
int     cbreak (void);
```

The Ncurses functions either operate on the current pseudoterminal or on a window that has been created via newwin. The WINDOW structure holds the internal library state and is considered abstract outside of Ncurses. Ncurses clients just need to store the pointer somewhere and pass it back to Ncurses library calls, which in turn dereference its contents.

Note that there are over 200 library calls in Ncurses, so we're only binding a select few for this example. The initscr and newwin create WINDOW pointers for the global and subwindows, respectively. The mvwaddrstr takes a window, x/y offsets, and a string and writes to the screen at that location. The terminal is only updated after refresh or wrefresh are called.

Ctypes provides an OCaml interface that lets you map these C functions to equivalent OCaml functions. The library takes care of converting OCaml function calls and arguments into the C calling convention, invoking the foreign call within the C library and finally returning the result as an OCaml value.

Let's begin by defining the basic values we need, starting with the WINDOW state pointer:

```
open Ctypes

type window = unit ptr

let window : window typ = ptr void
```

We don't know the internal representation of the window pointer, so we treat it as a C void pointer. We'll improve on this later on in the chapter, but it's good enough for now. The second statement defines an OCaml value that represents the WINDOW C pointer. This value is used later in the Ctypes function definitions:

---

[1] http://www.gnu.org/software/ncurses/

```
open Foreign

let initscr = foreign "initscr" (void @-> returning window)
```

That's all we need to invoke our first function call to `initscr` to initialize the terminal. The `foreign` function accepts two parameters:

- The C function call name, which is looked up using the `dlsym` POSIX function.
- A value that defines the complete set of C function arguments and its return type. The `@->` operator adds an argument to the C parameter list, and `returning` terminates the parameter list with the return type.

The remainder of the Ncurses binding simply expands on these definitions:

```
let newwin =
  foreign "newwin" (int @-> int @-> int @-> int @-> returning window)

let endwin = foreign "endwin" (void @-> returning void)
let refresh = foreign "refresh" (void @-> returning void)
let wrefresh = foreign "wrefresh" (window @-> returning void)
let addstr = foreign "addstr" (string @-> returning void)

let mvwaddch =
  foreign
    "mvwaddch"
    (window @-> int @-> int @-> char @-> returning void)

let mvwaddstr =
  foreign
    "mvwaddstr"
    (window @-> int @-> int @-> string @-> returning void)

let box = foreign "box" (window @-> char @-> char @-> returning void)
let cbreak = foreign "cbreak" (void @-> returning int)
```

These definitions are all straightforward mappings from the C declarations in the Ncurses header file. Note that the `string` and `int` values here are nothing to do with OCaml type declarations; instead, they are values that come from opening the `Ctypes` module at the top of the file.

Most of the parameters in the Ncurses example represent fairly simple scalar C types, except for `window` (a pointer to the library state) and `string`, which maps from OCaml strings that have a specific length onto C character buffers whose length is defined by a terminating null character that immediately follows the string data.

The module signature for `ncurses.mli` looks much like a normal OCaml signature. You can infer it directly from the `ncurses.ml` by running a command called `ocaml-print-intf`, which you can install with opam.

```
$ ocaml-print-intf ncurses.ml
type window = unit Ctypes.ptr
val window : window Ctypes.typ
val initscr : unit -> window
val newwin : int -> int -> int -> int -> window
val endwin : unit -> unit
val refresh : unit -> unit
```

```
val wrefresh : window -> unit
val addstr : string -> unit
val mvwaddch : window -> int -> int -> char -> unit
val mvwaddstr : window -> int -> int -> string -> unit
val box : window -> char -> char -> unit
val cbreak : unit -> int
```

The ocaml-print-intf tool examines the default signature inferred by the compiler for a module file and prints it out as human-readable output. You can copy this into a corresponding mli file and customize it to improve its safety for external callers by making some of its internals more abstract.

Here's the customized ncurses.mli interface that we can safely use from other libraries:

```
type window

val window : window Ctypes.typ
val initscr : unit -> window
val endwin : unit -> unit
val refresh : unit -> unit
val wrefresh : window -> unit
val newwin : int -> int -> int -> int -> window
val mvwaddch : window -> int -> int -> char -> unit
val addstr : string -> unit
val mvwaddstr : window -> int -> int -> string -> unit
val box : window -> char -> char -> unit
val cbreak : unit -> int
```

Note that the window type is now abstract in the signature, to ensure that window pointers can only be constructed via the Ncurses.initscr function. This prevents void pointers obtained from other sources from being mistakenly passed to an Ncurses library call.

Now compile a "hello world" terminal drawing program to tie this all together:

```
open Ncurses

let () =
  let main_window = initscr () in
  ignore (cbreak ());
  let small_window = newwin 10 10 5 5 in
  mvwaddstr main_window 1 2 "Hello";
  mvwaddstr small_window 2 2 "World";
  box small_window '\000' '\000';
  refresh ();
  Unix.sleep 1;
  wrefresh small_window;
  Unix.sleep 5;
  endwin ()
```

The hello executable is compiled by linking with the ctypes-foreign package. We also add in a (flags) directive to instruct the compiler to link in the system ncurses C library to the executable. If you do not specify the C library in the dune file, then the program may build successfully, but attempting to invoke the executable will fail as not all of the dependencies will be available.

```
(executable
  (name       hello)
  (libraries  ctypes-foreign)
  (flags      :standard -cclib -lncurses))
```

And now we can build it with Dune.

```
$ dune build hello.exe
```

Running `hello.exe` should now display a Hello World in your terminal!

Ctypes wouldn't be very useful if it were limited to only defining simple C types, of course. It provides full support for C pointer arithmetic, pointer conversions, and reading and writing through pointers, using OCaml functions as function pointers to C code, as well as struct and union definitions.

We'll go over some of these features in more detail for the remainder of the chapter by using some POSIX date functions as running examples.

Linking Modes: libffi and Stub Generation

The core of ctypes is a set of OCaml combinators for describing the structure of C types (numeric types, arrays, pointers, structs, unions and functions). You can then use these combinators to describe the types of the C functions that you want to call. There are two entirely distinct ways to actually link to the system libraries that contain the function definitions: *dynamic linking* and *stub generation*.

The `ctypes-foreign` package used in this chapter uses the low-level `libffi` library to dynamically open C libraries, search for the relevant symbols for the function call being invoked, and marshal the function parameters according to the operating system's application binary interface (ABI). While much of this happens behind-the-scenes and permits convenient interactive programming while developing bindings, it is not always the solution you want to use in production.

The `ctypes-cstubs` package provides an alternative mechanism to shift much of the linking work to be done once at build time, instead of doing it on every invocation of the function. It does this by taking the *same* OCaml binding descriptions, and generating intermediate C source files that contain the corresponding C/OCaml glue code. When these are compiled with a normal dune build, the generated C code is treated just as any handwritten code might be, and compiled against the system header files. This allows certain C values to be used that cannot be dynamically probed (e.g. preprocessor macro definitions), and can also catch definition errors if there is a C header mismatch at compile time.

C rarely makes life easier though. There are some definitions that cannot be entirely expressed as static C code (e.g. dynamic function pointers), and those require the use of `ctypes-foreign` (and `libffi`). Using ctypes does make it possible to share the majority of definitions across both linking modes, all while avoiding writing C code directly.

While we do not cover the details of C stub generation further in this chapter, you can read more about how to use this mode in the "Dealing with foreign libraries" chapter in the dune manual.

23.2   Basic Scalar C Types

First, let's look at how to define basic scalar C types. Every C type is represented by
an OCaml equivalent via the single type definition:

```
type 'a typ
```

Ctypes.typ is the type of values that represents C types to OCaml. There are two types
associated with each instance of typ:

- The C type used to store and pass values to the foreign library.
- The corresponding OCaml type. The 'a type parameter contains the OCaml type
    such that a value of type t typ is used to read and write OCaml values of type t.

There are various other uses of typ values within Ctypes, such as:

- Constructing function types for binding native functions
- Constructing pointers for reading and writing locations in C-managed storage
- Describing component fields of structures, unions, and arrays

Here are the definitions for most of the standard C99 scalar types, including some
platform-dependent ones:

```
val void       : unit typ
val char       : char typ
val schar      : int typ
val short      : int typ
val int        : int typ
val long       : long typ
val llong      : llong typ
val nativeint  : nativeint typ

val int8_t     : int typ
val int16_t    : int typ
val int32_t    : int32 typ
val int64_t    : int64 typ
val uchar      : uchar typ
val uint8_t    : uint8 typ
val uint16_t   : uint16 typ
val uint32_t   : uint32 typ
val uint64_t   : uint64 typ
val size_t     : size_t typ
val ushort     : ushort typ
val uint       : uint typ
val ulong      : ulong typ
val ullong     : ullong typ

val float      : float typ
val double     : float typ

val complex32  : Complex.t typ
val complex64  : Complex.t typ
```

These values are all of type 'a typ, where the value name (e.g., void) tells you
the C type and the 'a component (e.g., unit) is the OCaml representation of that C

type. Most of the mappings are straightforward, but some of them need a bit more explanation:

- Void values appear in OCaml as the unit type. Using void in an argument or result type specification produces an OCaml function that accepts or returns unit. Dereferencing a pointer to void is an error, as in C, and will raise the IncompleteType exception.
- The C size_t type is an alias for one of the unsigned integer types. The actual size and alignment requirements for size_t varies between platforms. Ctypes provides an OCaml size_t type that is aliased to the appropriate integer type.
- OCaml only supports double-precision floating-point numbers, and so the C float and double types both map onto the OCaml float type, and the C float complex and double complex types both map onto the OCaml double-precision Complex.t type.

23.3 Pointers and Arrays

Pointers are at the heart of C, so they are necessarily part of Ctypes, which provides support for pointer arithmetic, pointer conversions, reading and writing through pointers, and passing and returning pointers to and from functions.

We've already seen a simple use of pointers in the Ncurses example. Let's start a new example by binding the following POSIX functions:

```
time_t time(time_t *);
double difftime(time_t, time_t);
char *ctime(const time_t *timep);
```

The time function returns the current calendar time and is a simple start. The first step is to open some of the Ctypes modules:

Ctypes The Ctypes module provides functions for describing C types in OCaml.

PosixTypes The PosixTypes module includes some extra POSIX-specific types (such as time_t).

Foreign The Foreign module exposes the foreign function that makes it possible to invoke C functions.

With these opens in place, we can now create a binding to time directly from the toplevel.

```
# #require "ctypes-foreign";;
# #require "ctypes.top";;
# open Core;;
# open Ctypes;;
# open PosixTypes ;;
# open Foreign;;
# let time = foreign "time" (ptr time_t @-> returning time_t);;
val time : time_t Ctypes_static.ptr -> time_t = <fun>
```

The `foreign` function is the main link between OCaml and C. It takes two arguments: the name of the C function to bind, and a value describing the type of the bound function. In the `time` binding, the function type specifies one argument of type `ptr time_t` and a return type of `time_t`.

We can now call `time` immediately in the same toplevel. The argument is actually optional, so we'll just pass a null pointer that has been coerced into becoming a null pointer to `time_t`:

```
# let cur_time = time (from_voidp time_t null);;
val cur_time : time_t = <abstr>
```

Since we're going to call `time` a few times, let's create a wrapper function that passes the null pointer through:

```
# let time' () = time (from_voidp time_t null);;
val time' : unit -> time_t = <fun>
```

Since `time_t` is an abstract type, we can't actually do anything useful with it directly. We need to bind a second function to do anything useful with the return values from `time`. We'll move on to `difftime`; the second C function in our prototype list:

```
# let difftime = foreign "difftime" (time_t @-> time_t @-> returning
    double);;
val difftime : time_t -> time_t -> float = <fun>
```

Here's the resulting function `difftime` in action.

```
# let delta =
    let t1 = time' () in
    Unix.sleep 2;
    let t2 = time' () in
    difftime t2 t1;;
val delta : float = 2.
```

The binding to `difftime` above is sufficient to compare two `time_t` values.

23.3.1   Allocating Typed Memory for Pointers

Let's look at a slightly less trivial example where we pass a nonnull pointer to a function. Continuing with the theme from earlier, we'll bind to the `ctime` function, which converts a `time_t` value to a human-readable string:

```
# let ctime = foreign "ctime" (ptr time_t @-> returning string);;
val ctime : time_t Ctypes_static.ptr -> string = <fun>
```

The binding is continued in the toplevel to add to our growing collection. However, we can't just pass the result of `time` to `ctime`:

```
# ctime (time' ());;
Line 1, characters 7-17:
Error: This expression has type time_t but an expression was expected
    of type
        time_t Ctypes_static.ptr = (time_t, [ `C ]) pointer
```

This is because `ctime` needs a pointer to the `time_t` rather than passing it by value. We thus need to allocate some memory for the `time_t` and obtain its memory address:

```
# let t_ptr = allocate time_t (time' ());;
...
```

The `allocate` function takes the type of the memory to be allocated and the initial value and it returns a suitably typed pointer. We can now call `ctime` passing the pointer as an argument:

```
# ctime t_ptr;;
...
```

23.3.2   Using Views to Map Complex Values

While scalar types typically have a 1:1 representation, other C types require extra work to convert them into OCaml. Views create new C type descriptions that have special behavior when used to read or write C values.

We've already used one view in the definition of `ctime` earlier. The `string` view wraps the C type `char *` (written in OCaml as `ptr char`) and converts between the C and OCaml string representations each time the value is written or read.

Here is the type signature of the `Ctypes.view` function:

```
val view :
  read:('a -> 'b) ->
  write:('b -> 'a) ->
  'a typ -> 'b typ
```

Ctypes has some internal low-level conversion functions that map between an OCaml `string` and a C character buffer by copying the contents into the respective data structure. They have the following type signature:

```
val string_of_char_ptr : char ptr -> string
val char_ptr_of_string : string -> char ptr
```

Given these functions, the definition of the `Ctypes.string` value that uses views is quite simple:

```
let string =
  view (char ptr)
    ~read:string_of_char_ptr
    ~write:char_ptr_of_string
```

The type of this `string` function is a normal `typ` with no external sign of the use of the view function:

```
val string    : string typ
```

OCaml Strings Versus C Character Buffers

Although OCaml strings may look like C character buffers from an interface perspective, they're very different in terms of their memory representations.

OCaml strings are stored in the OCaml heap with a header that explicitly defines their length. C buffers are also fixed-length, but by convention, a C string is terminated by a null (a \0 byte) character. The C string functions calculate their length by scanning the buffer until the first null character is encountered.

This means that you need to be careful that OCaml strings that you pass to C functions don't contain any null values, since the first occurrence of a null character will be treated as the end of the C string. Ctypes also defaults to a *copying* interface for strings, which means that you shouldn't use them when you want the library to mutate the buffer in-place. In that situation, use the Ctypes `Bigarray` support to pass memory by reference instead.

23.4   Structs and Unions

The C constructs `struct` and `union` make it possible to build new types from existing types. Ctypes contains counterparts that work similarly.

23.4.1   Defining a Structure

Let's improve the timer function that we wrote earlier. The POSIX function `gettimeofday` retrieves the time with microsecond resolution. The signature of `gettimeofday` is as follows, including the structure definitions:

```
struct timeval {
  long tv_sec;
  long tv_usec;
};

int gettimeofday(struct timeval *, struct timezone *tv);
```

Using Ctypes, we can describe this type as follows in our toplevel, continuing on from the previous definitions:

```
# type timeval;;
type timeval
# let timeval : timeval structure typ = structure "timeval";;
val timeval : timeval structure typ =
  Ctypes_static.Struct
    {Ctypes_static.tag = "timeval";
     spec = Ctypes_static.Incomplete {Ctypes_static.isize = 0}; fields
     = []}
```

The first command defines a new OCaml type `timeval` that we'll use to instantiate the OCaml version of the struct. This is a *phantom type* that exists only to distinguish the underlying C type from other pointer types. The particular `timeval` structure now has a distinct type from other structures we define elsewhere, which helps to avoid getting them mixed up.

The second command calls `structure` to create a fresh structure type. At this point, the structure type is incomplete: we can add fields but cannot yet use it in `foreign` calls or use it to create values.

23.4.2   Adding Fields to Structures

The `timeval` structure definition still doesn't have any fields, so we need to add those next:

```
# let tv_sec  = field timeval "tv_sec" long;;
val tv_sec : (Signed.long, timeval structure) field =
  {Ctypes_static.ftype = Ctypes_static.Primitive
    Ctypes_primitive_types.Long;
   foffset = 0; fname = "tv_sec"}
# let tv_usec = field timeval "tv_usec" long;;
val tv_usec : (Signed.long, timeval structure) field =
  {Ctypes_static.ftype = Ctypes_static.Primitive
    Ctypes_primitive_types.Long;
   foffset = 8; fname = "tv_usec"}
# seal timeval;;
- : unit = ()
```

The `field` function appends a field to the structure, as shown with `tv_sec` and `tv_usec`. Structure fields are typed accessors that are associated with a particular structure, and they correspond to the labels in C.

Every field addition mutates the structure variable and records a new size (the exact value of which depends on the type of the field that was just added). Once we `seal` the structure, we will be able to create values using it, but adding fields to a sealed structure is an error.

23.4.3   Incomplete Structure Definitions

Since `gettimeofday` needs a `struct timezone` pointer for its second argument, we also need to define a second structure type:

```
# type timezone;;
type timezone
# let timezone : timezone structure typ = structure "timezone";;
val timezone : timezone structure typ =
  Ctypes_static.Struct
    {Ctypes_static.tag = "timezone";
     spec = Ctypes_static.Incomplete {Ctypes_static.isize = 0}; fields
     = []}
```

We don't ever need to create `struct timezone` values, so we can leave this struct as incomplete without adding any fields or sealing it. If you ever try to use it in a situation where its concrete size needs to be known, the library will raise an `IncompleteType` exception.

We're finally ready to bind to `gettimeofday` now:

```
# let gettimeofday = foreign "gettimeofday" ~check_errno:true
    (ptr timeval @-> ptr timezone @-> returning int);;
val gettimeofday :
  timeval structure Ctypes_static.ptr ->
  timezone structure Ctypes_static.ptr -> int = <fun>
```

There's one other new feature here: the `returning_checking_errno` function behaves like `returning`, except that it checks whether the bound C function modifies

the C error flag. Changes to `errno` are mapped into OCaml exceptions and raise a
`Unix.Unix_error` exception just as the standard library functions do.

As before, we can create a wrapper to make `gettimeofday` easier to use. The
functions `make`, `addr`, and `getf` create a structure value, retrieve the address of a
structure value, and retrieve the value of a field from a structure.

```
# let gettimeofday' () =
    let tv = make timeval in
    ignore (gettimeofday (addr tv) (from_voidp timezone null) : int);
    let secs = Signed.Long.to_int (getf tv tv_sec) in
    let usecs = Signed.Long.to_int (getf tv tv_usec) in
    Float.of_int secs +. Float.of_int usecs /. 1_000_000.0;;
val gettimeofday' : unit -> float = <fun>
```

And we can now call that function to get the current time.

```
# gettimeofday' ();;
- : float = 1650045389.278065
```

Recap: a Time-Printing Command

We built up a lot of bindings in the previous section, so let's recap them with a complete
example that ties it together with a command-line frontend:

```
open Core
open Ctypes
open PosixTypes
open Foreign

let time = foreign "time" (ptr time_t @-> returning time_t)

let difftime =
  foreign "difftime" (time_t @-> time_t @-> returning double)

let ctime = foreign "ctime" (ptr time_t @-> returning string)

type timeval

let timeval : timeval structure typ = structure "timeval"
let tv_sec = field timeval "tv_sec" long
let tv_usec = field timeval "tv_usec" long
let () = seal timeval

type timezone

let timezone : timezone structure typ = structure "timezone"

let gettimeofday =
  foreign
    "gettimeofday"
    ~check_errno:true
    (ptr timeval @-> ptr timezone @-> returning int)

let time' () = time (from_voidp time_t null)

let gettimeofday' () =
```

```
let tv = make timeval in
ignore (gettimeofday (addr tv) (from_voidp timezone null) : int);
let secs = Signed.Long.to_int (getf tv tv_sec) in
let usecs = Signed.Long.to_int (getf tv tv_usec) in
Float.of_int secs +. (Float.of_int usecs /. 1_000_000.)

let float_time () = printf "%f%!\n" (gettimeofday' ())

let ascii_time () =
  let t_ptr = allocate time_t (time' ()) in
  printf "%s%!" (ctime t_ptr)

let () =
  Command.basic
    ~summary:"Display the current time in various formats"
    (let%map_open.Command human =
        flag "-a" no_arg ~doc:" Human-readable output format"
      in
      if human then ascii_time else float_time)
  |> Command.run
```

This can be compiled and run in the usual way:

```
(executable
  (name      datetime)
  (preprocess (pps ppx_jane))
  (libraries core ctypes-foreign))
```

```
$ dune build datetime.exe
$ ./_build/default/datetime.exe
1633964258.014484
$ ./_build/default/datetime.exe -a
Mon Oct 11 15:57:38 2021
```

Why Do We Need to Use returning?

The alert reader may be curious about why all these function definitions have to be terminated by returning:

```
(* correct types *)
val time: ptr time_t @-> returning time_t
val difftime: time_t @-> time_t @-> returning double
```

The returning function may appear superfluous here. Why couldn't we simply give the types as follows?

```
(* incorrect types *)
val time: ptr time_t @-> time_t
val difftime: time_t @-> time_t @-> double
```

The reason involves higher types and two differences between the way that functions are treated in OCaml and C. Functions are first-class values in OCaml, but not in C. For example, in C it is possible to return a function pointer from a function, but not to return an actual function.

Secondly, OCaml functions are typically defined in a curried style. The signature of a two-argument function is written as follows:

```
val curried : int -> int -> int
```

but this really means:

```
val curried : int -> (int -> int)
```

and the arguments can be supplied one at a time to create a closure. In contrast, C functions receive their arguments all at once. The equivalent C function type is the following:

```
int uncurried_C(int, int);
```

and the arguments must always be supplied together:

```
uncurried_C(3, 4);
```

A C function that's written in curried style looks very different:

```
/* A function that accepts an int, and returns a function
   pointer that accepts a second int and returns an int. */
typedef int (function_t)(int);
function_t *curried_C(int);

/* supply both arguments */
curried_C(3)(4);

/* supply one argument at a time */
function_t *f = curried_C(3); f(4);
```

The OCaml type of uncurried_C when bound by Ctypes is int -> int -> int: a two-argument function. The OCaml type of curried_C when bound by ctypes is int -> (int -> int): a one-argument function that returns a one-argument function.

In OCaml, of course, these types are absolutely equivalent. Since the OCaml types are the same but the C semantics are quite different, we need some kind of marker to distinguish the cases. This is the purpose of returning in function definitions.

23.4.4   Defining Arrays

Arrays in C are contiguous blocks of the same type of value. Any of the basic types defined previously can be allocated as blocks via the Array module:

```
module Array : sig
  type 'a t = 'a array

  val get : 'a t -> int -> 'a
  val set : 'a t -> int -> 'a -> unit
  val of_list : 'a typ -> 'a list -> 'a t
  val to_list : 'a t -> 'a list
  val length : 'a t -> int
  val start : 'a t -> 'a ptr
  val from_ptr : 'a ptr -> int -> 'a t
  val make : 'a typ -> ?initial:'a -> int -> 'a t
end
```

The array functions are similar to those in the standard library Array module except that they operate on arrays stored using the flat C representation rather than the OCaml representation described in Chapter 24 (Memory Representation of Values).

As with standard OCaml arrays, the conversion between arrays and lists requires copying the values, which can be expensive for large data structures. Notice that you can also convert an array into a `ptr` pointer to the head of the underlying buffer, which can be useful if you need to pass the pointer and size arguments separately to a C function.

Unions in C are named structures that can be mapped onto the same underlying memory. They are also fully supported in Ctypes, but we won't go into more detail here.

Pointer Operators for Dereferencing and Arithmetic

Ctypes defines a number of operators that let you manipulate pointers and arrays just as you would in C. The Ctypes equivalents do have the benefit of being more strongly typed, of course.

- `!@` p will dereference the pointer p.
- p `<-@` v will write the value v to the address p.
- p `+@` n computes the address of the nth next element, if p points to an array element.
- p `-@` n computes the address of the nth previous element, if p points to an array element.

There are also other useful non-operator functions available (see the Ctypes documentation), such as pointer differencing and comparison.

23.5   Passing Functions to C

It's also straightforward to pass OCaml function values to C. The C standard library function qsort sorts arrays of elements using a comparison function passed in as a function pointer. The signature for qsort is:

```
void qsort(void *base, size_t nmemb, size_t size,
           int(*compar)(const void *, const void *));
```

C programmers often use `typedef` to make type definitions involving function pointers easier to read. Using a typedef, the type of qsort looks a little more palatable:

```
typedef int(compare_t)(const void *, const void *);

void qsort(void *base, size_t nmemb, size_t size, compare_t *);
```

This also happens to be a close mapping to the corresponding Ctypes definition. Since type descriptions are regular values, we can just use `let` in place of `typedef` and end up with working OCaml bindings to qsort:

```
# open Core open Ctypes open PosixTypes open Foreign open
    Ctypes_static;;
# let compare_t = ptr void @-> ptr void @-> returning int;;
```

```
val compare_t : (unit Ctypes_static.ptr -> unit Ctypes_static.ptr ->
    int) fn =
  Function (Pointer Void,
   Function (Pointer Void, Returns (Primitive
   Ctypes_primitive_types.Int)))
# let qsort =
    foreign "qsort"
      (ptr void @-> size_t @-> size_t @-> funptr compare_t
      @-> returning void);;
val qsort :
  unit Ctypes_static.ptr ->
  size_t ->
  size_t -> (unit Ctypes_static.ptr -> unit Ctypes_static.ptr -> int)
    -> unit =
  <fun>
```

We only use compare_t once (in the qsort definition), so you can choose to inline it in the OCaml code if you prefer. As the type shows, the resulting qsort value is a higher-order function, since the fourth argument is itself a function.

Arrays created using Ctypes have a richer runtime structure than C arrays, so we don't need to pass size information around. Furthermore, we can use OCaml polymorphism in place of the unsafe void ptr type.

23.5.1   Example: A Command-Line Quicksort

The following is a command-line tool that uses the qsort binding to sort all of the integers supplied on the standard input:

```
open Core
open Ctypes
open PosixTypes
open Foreign

let compare_t = ptr void @-> ptr void @-> returning int

let qsort =
  foreign
    "qsort"
    (ptr void
    @-> size_t
    @-> size_t
    @-> funptr compare_t
    @-> returning void)

let qsort' cmp arr =
  let open Unsigned.Size_t in
  let ty = CArray.element_type arr in
  let len = of_int (CArray.length arr) in
  let elsize = of_int (sizeof ty) in
  let start = to_voidp (CArray.start arr) in
  let compare l r = cmp !@(from_voidp ty l) !@(from_voidp ty r) in
  qsort start len elsize compare

let sort_stdin () =
```

```
    let array =
      In_channel.input_line_exn In_channel.stdin
      |> String.split ~on:' '
      |> List.map ~f:int_of_string
      |> CArray.of_list int
    in
    qsort' Int.compare array;
    CArray.to_list array
    |> List.map ~f:Int.to_string
    |> String.concat ~sep:" "
    |> print_endline

  let () =
    Command.basic_spec
      ~summary:"Sort integers on standard input"
      Command.Spec.empty
      sort_stdin
    |> Command.run
```

Compile it in the usual way with *dune* and test it against some input data, and also build the inferred interface so we can examine it more closely:

```
(executable
  (name      qsort)
  (libraries core ctypes-foreign))
```

```
$ echo 2 4 1 3 | dune exec ./qsort.exe
1 2 3 4
```

The inferred mli shows us the types of the raw qsort binding and also the qsort' wrapper function.

```
$ ocaml-print-intf qsort.ml
val compare_t :
  (unit Ctypes_static.ptr -> unit Ctypes_static.ptr -> int) Ctypes.fn
val qsort :
  unit Ctypes_static.ptr ->
  PosixTypes.size_t ->
  PosixTypes.size_t ->
  (unit Ctypes_static.ptr -> unit Ctypes_static.ptr -> int) -> unit
val qsort' : ('a -> 'a -> int) -> 'a Ctypes.CArray.t -> unit
val sort_stdin : unit -> unit
```

The qsort' wrapper function has a much more canonical OCaml interface than the raw binding. It accepts a comparator function and a Ctypes array, and returns unit.

Using qsort' to sort arrays is straightforward. Our example code reads the standard input as a list, converts it to a C array, passes it through qsort, and outputs the result to the standard output. Again, remember to not confuse the Ctypes.Array module with the Core.Array module: the former is in scope since we opened Ctypes at the start of the file.

Lifetime of Allocated Ctypes

Values allocated via Ctypes (i.e., using allocate, Array.make, and so on) will not be garbage-collected as long as they are reachable from OCaml values. The system memory they occupy is freed when they do become unreachable, via a finalizer function registered with the garbage collector (GC).

The definition of reachability for Ctypes values is a little different from conventional OCaml values, though. The allocation functions return an OCaml-managed pointer to the value, and as long as some derivative pointer is still reachable by the GC, the value won't be collected.

"Derivative" means a pointer that's computed from the original pointer via arithmetic, so a reachable reference to an array element or a structure field protects the whole object from collection.

A corollary of the preceding rule is that pointers written into the C heap don't have any effect on reachability. For example, if you have a C-managed array of pointers to structs, then you'll need some additional way of keeping the structs themselves around to protect them from collection. You could achieve this via a global array of values on the OCaml side that would keep them live until they're no longer needed.

Functions passed to C have similar considerations regarding lifetime. On the OCaml side, functions created at runtime may be collected when they become unreachable. As we've seen, OCaml functions passed to C are converted to function pointers, and function pointers written into the C heap have no effect on the reachability of the OCaml functions they reference. With qsort things are straightforward, since the comparison function is only used during the call to qsort itself. However, other C libraries may store function pointers in global variables or elsewhere, in which case you'll need to take care that the OCaml functions you pass to them aren't prematurely garbage-collected.

23.6   Learning More About C Bindings

The Ctypes distribution[2] contains a number of larger-scale examples, including:

- Bindings to the POSIX fts API, which demonstrates C callbacks more comprehensively
- A more complete Ncurses binding than the example we opened the chapter with
- A comprehensive test suite that covers the complete library, and can provide useful snippets for your own bindings

This chapter hasn't really needed you to understand the innards of OCaml at all. Ctypes does its best to make function bindings easy, but the rest of this part will also fill you in about interactions with OCaml memory layout in Chapter 24 (Memory Representation of Values) and automatic memory management in Chapter 25 (Understanding the Garbage Collector).

Ctypes gives OCaml programs access to the C representation of values, shielding you from the details of the OCaml value representation, and introduces an abstraction layer that hides the details of foreign calls. While this covers a wide variety of situations,

---

[2] http://github.com/ocamllabs/ocaml-ctypes

it's sometimes necessary to look behind the abstraction to obtain finer control over the details of the interaction between the two languages.

You can find more information about the C interface in several places:

- The standard OCaml foreign function interface allows you to glue OCaml and C together from the other side of the boundary, by writing C functions that operate on the OCaml representation of values. You can find details of the standard interface in the OCaml manual[3] and in the book *Developing Applications with Objective Caml*[4].
- Florent Monnier maintains an excellent online tutorial[5] that provides examples of how to call OCaml functions from C. This covers a wide variety of OCaml data types and also more complex callbacks between C and OCaml.

23.6.1   Struct Memory Layout

The C language gives implementations a certain amount of freedom in choosing how to lay out structs in memory. There may be padding between members and at the end of the struct, in order to satisfy the memory alignment requirements of the host platform. Ctypes uses platform-appropriate size and alignment information to replicate the struct layout process. OCaml and C will have consistent views about the layout of the struct as long as you declare the fields of a struct in the same order and with the same types as the C library you're binding to.

However, this approach can lead to difficulties when the fields of a struct aren't fully specified in the interface of a library. The interface may list the fields of a structure without specifying their order, or make certain fields available only on certain platforms, or insert undocumented fields into struct definitions for performance reasons. For example, the `struct timeval` definition used in this chapter accurately describes the layout of the struct on common platforms, but implementations on some more unusual architectures include additional padding members that will lead to strange behavior in the examples.

The Cstubs subpackage of Ctypes addresses this issue. Rather than simply assuming that struct definitions given by the user accurately reflect the actual definitions of structs used in C libraries, Cstubs generates code that uses the C library headers to discover the layout of the struct. The good news is that the code that you write doesn't need to change much. Cstubs provides alternative implementations of the `field` and `seal` functions that you've already used to describe `struct timeval`; instead of computing member offsets and sizes appropriate for the platform, these implementations obtain them directly from C.

The details of using Cstubs are available in the online documentation[6], along with instructions on integration with `autoconf` platform portability instructions.

---

[3] `https://ocaml.org/manual/intfc.html`
[4] `http://caml.inria.fr/pub/docs/oreilly-book/ocaml-ora-book.pdf`
[5] `http://decapode314.free.fr/ocaml/ocaml-wrapping-c.html`
[6] `https://ocamllabs.github.io/ocaml-ctypes`

24 Memory Representation of Values

The FFI interface we described in Chapter 23 (Foreign Function Interface) hides the precise details of how values are exchanged across C libraries and the OCaml runtime. There is a simple reason for this: using this interface directly is a delicate operation that requires understanding a few different moving parts before you can get it right. You first need to know the mapping between OCaml types and their runtime memory representation. You also need to ensure that your code is interfacing correctly with OCaml runtime's memory management.

However, knowledge of the OCaml internals is useful beyond just writing foreign function interfaces. As you build and maintain more complex OCaml applications, you'll need to interface with various external system tools that operate on compiled OCaml binaries. For example, profiling tools report output based on the runtime memory layout, and debuggers execute binaries without any knowledge of the static OCaml types. To use these tools effectively, you'll need to do some translation between the OCaml and C worlds.

Luckily, the OCaml toolchain is very predictable. The compiler minimizes the amount of optimization magic that it performs, and relies instead on its straightforward execution model for good performance. With some experience, you can know rather precisely where a block of performance-critical OCaml code is spending its time.

Why Do OCaml Types Disappear at Runtime?

The OCaml compiler runs through several phases during the compilation process. The first phase is syntax checking, during which source files are parsed into abstract syntax trees (ASTs). The next stage is a *type checking* pass over the AST. In a validly typed program, a function cannot be applied with an unexpected type. For example, the `print_endline` function must receive a single `string` argument, and an `int` will result in a type error.

Since OCaml verifies these properties at compile time, it doesn't need to keep track of as much information at runtime. Thus, later stages of the compiler can discard and simplify the type declarations to a much more minimal subset that's actually required to distinguish polymorphic values at runtime. This is a major performance win versus something like a Java or .NET method call, where the runtime must look up the concrete instance of the object and dispatch the method call. Those languages amortize some of the cost via "Just-in-Time" dynamic patching, but OCaml prefers runtime simplicity instead.

We'll explain this compilation pipeline in more detail in Chapter 26 (The Compiler Frontend: Parsing and Type Checking) and Chapter 27 (The Compiler Backend: Bytecode and Native code).

This chapter covers the precise mapping from OCaml types to runtime values and walks you through them via the toplevel. We'll cover how these values are managed by the runtime later on in Chapter 25 (Understanding the Garbage Collector).

24.1 OCaml Blocks and Values

A running OCaml program uses blocks of memory (i.e., contiguous sequences of words in RAM) to represent values such as tuples, records, closures, or arrays. An OCaml program implicitly allocates a block of memory when such a value is created:

```
# type t = { foo: int; bar: int };;
type t = { foo : int; bar : int; }
# let x = { foo = 13; bar = 14 };;
val x : t = {foo = 13; bar = 14}
```

The type declaration t doesn't take up any memory at runtime, but the subsequent let binding allocates a new block of memory with two words of available space. One word holds the foo field, and the other word holds the bar field. The OCaml compiler translates such an expression into an explicit allocation for the block from OCaml's runtime system.

OCaml uses a uniform memory representation in which every OCaml variable is stored as a *value*. An OCaml value is a single memory word that is either an immediate integer or a pointer to some other memory. The OCaml runtime tracks all values so that it can free them when they are no longer needed. It thus needs to be able to distinguish between integer and pointer values, since it scans pointers to find further values but doesn't follow integers that don't point to anything meaningful beyond their immediate value.

24.1.1 Distinguishing Integers and Pointers at Runtime

Wrapping primitive types (such as integers) inside another data structure that records extra metadata about the value is known as *boxing*. Values are boxed in order to make it easier for the garbage collector (GC) to do its job, but at the expense of an extra level of indirection to access the data within the boxed value.

OCaml values don't all have to be boxed at runtime. Instead, values use a single tag bit per word to distinguish integers and pointers at runtime. The value is an integer if the lowest bit of the block word is nonzero, and a pointer if the lowest bit of the block word is zero. Several OCaml types map onto this integer representation, including bool, int, the empty list, and unit. Some types, like variants, sometimes use this integer representation and sometimes don't. In particular, for variants, constant constructors, i.e., constructors with no arguments like None, are represented as integers, but constructors like Some that carry associated values are boxed.

This representation means that integers are unboxed runtime values in OCaml so that they can be stored directly without having to allocate a wrapper block. They can be passed directly to other function calls in registers and are generally the cheapest and fastest values to use in OCaml.

A value is treated as a memory pointer if its lowest bit is zero. A pointer value can still be stored unmodified despite this, since pointers are guaranteed to be word-aligned (with the bottom bits always being zero).

The only problem that remains with this memory representation is distinguishing between pointers to OCaml values (which should be followed by the GC) and pointers into the system heap to C values (which shouldn't be followed).

The mechanism for this is simple, since the runtime system keeps track of the heap blocks it has allocated for OCaml values. If the pointer is inside a heap chunk that is marked as being managed by the OCaml runtime, it is assumed to point to an OCaml value. If it points outside the OCaml runtime area, it is treated as an opaque C pointer to some other system resource.

Some History About OCaml's Word-Aligned Pointers

The alert reader may be wondering how OCaml can guarantee that all of its pointers are word-aligned. In the old days, when RISC chips such as Sparc, MIPS, and Alpha were commonplace, unaligned memory accesses were forbidden by the instruction set architecture and would result in a CPU exception that terminated the program. Thus, all pointers were historically rounded off to the architecture word size (usually 32 or 64 bits).

Modern CISC processors such as the Intel x86 do support unaligned memory accesses, but the chip still runs faster if accesses are word-aligned. OCaml therefore simply mandates that all pointers be word-aligned, which guarantees that the bottom few bits of any valid pointer will be zero. Setting the bottom bit to a nonzero value is a simple way to mark an integer, at the cost of losing that single bit of precision.

An even more alert reader will be wondering about the performance implications are for integer arithmetic using this tagged representation. Since the bottom bit is set, any operation on the integer has to shift the bottom bit right to recover the "native" value. The native code OCaml compiler generates efficient x86 assembly code in this case, taking advantage of modern processor instructions to hide the extra shifts where possible. Addition is a single LEA x86 instruction, subtraction can be two instructions, and multiplication is only a few more.

24.2   Blocks and Values

An OCaml *block* is the basic unit of allocation on the heap. A block consists of a one-word header (either 32 or 64 bits depending on the CPU architecture) followed by variable-length data that is either opaque bytes or an array of *fields*. The header has a multipurpose tag byte that defines whether to interpret the subsequent data as opaque bytes or OCaml fields.

The GC never inspects opaque bytes. If the tag indicates an array of OCaml fields are present, their contents are all treated as more valid OCaml values. The GC always inspects fields and follows them as part of the collection process described earlier.

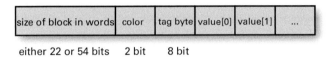

either 22 or 54 bits   2 bit   8 bit

The `size` field records the length of the block in memory words. This is 22 bits on 32-bit platforms, which is the reason OCaml strings are limited to 16 MB on that architecture. If you need bigger strings, either switch to a 64-bit host, or use the `Bigarray` module.

The 2-bit `color` field is used by the GC to keep track of its state during mark-and-sweep collection. We'll come back to this field in Chapter 25 (Understanding the Garbage Collector). This tag isn't exposed to OCaml source code in any case.

A block's tag byte is multipurpose, and indicates whether the data array represents opaque bytes or fields. If a block's tag is greater than or equal to `No_scan_tag` (251), then the block's data are all opaque bytes, and are not scanned by the collector. The most common such block is the `string` type, which we describe in more detail later in this chapter.

The exact representation of values inside a block depends on their static OCaml type. All OCaml types are distilled down into `values`, and summarized below.

- `int` or `char` are stored directly as a value, shifted left by 1 bit, with the least significant bit set to 1.
- `unit`, `[]`, `false` are all stored as OCaml int 0.
- `true` is stored as OCaml int 1.
- `Foo | Bar` variants are stored as ascending OCaml ints, starting from 0.
- `Foo | Bar of int` variants with parameters are boxed, while variants with no parameters are unboxed.
- Polymorphic variants with parameters are boxed with an extra header word to store the value, as compared to normal variants. Polymorphic variants with no parameters are unboxed.
- Floating-point numbers are stored as a block with a single field containing the double-precision float.
- Strings are word-aligned byte arrays with an explicit length.

- [1; 2; 3] lists are stored as 1::2::3::[] where [] is an int, and h::t a block with tag 0 and two parameters.
- Tuples, records, and arrays are stored as a C array of values. Arrays can be variable size, but tuples and records are fixed-size.
- Records or arrays that are all float use a special tag for unboxed arrays of floats, or records that only have float fields.

24.2.1   Integers, Characters, and Other Basic Types

Many basic types are efficiently stored as unboxed integers at runtime. The native int type is the most obvious, although it drops a single bit of precision due to the tag bit. Other atomic types such as unit and the empty list [] value are stored as constant integers. Boolean values have a value of 1 and 0 for true and false, respectively.

These basic types such as empty lists and unit are very efficient to use, since integers are never allocated on the heap. They can be passed directly in registers and not appear on the stack if you don't have too many parameters to your functions. Modern architectures such as x86_64 have a lot of spare registers to further improve the efficiency of using unboxed integers.

24.3   Tuples, Records, and Arrays

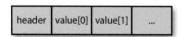

Tuples, records, and arrays are all represented identically at runtime as a block with tag 0. Tuples and records have constant sizes determined at compile time, whereas arrays can be of variable length. While arrays are restricted to containing a single type of element in the OCaml type system, this is not required by the memory representation.

You can check the difference between a block and a direct integer yourself using the Obj module, which exposes the internal representation of values to OCaml code:

```
# Obj.is_block (Obj.repr (1,2,3));;
- : bool = true
# Obj.is_block (Obj.repr 1);;
- : bool = false
```

The Obj.repr function retrieves the runtime representation of any OCaml value. Obj.is_block checks the bottom bit to determine if the value is a block header or an unboxed integer.

24.3.1 Floating-Point Numbers and Arrays

Floating-point numbers in OCaml are always stored as full, double-precision values. Individual floating-point values are stored as a block with a single field that contains the number. This block has the `Double_tag` set, which signals to the collector that the floating-point value is not to be scanned:

```
# Obj.tag (Obj.repr 1.0);;
- : int = 253
# Obj.double_tag;;
- : int = 253
```

Since each floating-point value is boxed in a separate memory block, it can be inefficient to handle large arrays of floats in comparison to unboxed integers. OCaml therefore special-cases records or arrays that contain *only* `float` types. These are stored in a block that contains the floats packed directly in the data section, with `Double_array_tag` set to signal to the collector that the contents are not OCaml values.

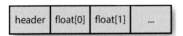

First, let's check that float arrays do in fact have a different tag number from normal floating-point values:

```
# Obj.double_tag;;
- : int = 253
# Obj.double_array_tag;;
- : int = 254
```

This tells us that float arrays have a tag value of 254. Now let's test some sample values using the `Obj.tag` function to check that the allocated block has the expected runtime tag, and also use `Obj.double_field` to retrieve a float from within the block:

```
# Obj.tag (Obj.repr [| 1.0; 2.0; 3.0 |]);;
- : int = 254
# Obj.tag (Obj.repr (1.0, 2.0, 3.0) );;
- : int = 0
# Obj.double_field (Obj.repr [| 1.1; 2.2; 3.3 |]) 1;;
- : float = 2.2
# Obj.double_field (Obj.repr 1.234) 0;;
- : float = 1.234
```

The first thing we tested was that a float array has the correct unboxed float array tag value (254). However, the next line tests a tuple of floating-point values instead, which are *not* optimized in the same way and have the normal tuple tag value (0).

Only records and arrays can have the float array optimization, and for records, every single field must be a float.

24.4   Variants and Lists

Basic variant types with no extra parameters for any of their branches are simply stored as an OCaml integer, starting with 0 for the first option and in ascending order:

```
# type t = Apple | Orange | Pear;;
type t = Apple | Orange | Pear
# ((Obj.magic (Obj.repr Apple)) : int);;
- : int = 0
# ((Obj.magic (Obj.repr Pear)) : int);;
- : int = 2
# Obj.is_block (Obj.repr Apple);;
- : bool = false
```

Obj.magic unsafely forces a type cast between any two OCaml types; in this example, the int type hint retrieves the runtime integer value. The Obj.is_block confirms that the value isn't a more complex block, but just an OCaml int.

Variants that have parameters are a little more complex. They are stored as blocks, with the value *tags* ascending from 0 (counting from leftmost variants with parameters). The parameters are stored as words in the block:

```
# type t = Apple | Orange of int | Pear of string | Kiwi;;
type t = Apple | Orange of int | Pear of string | Kiwi
# Obj.is_block (Obj.repr (Orange 1234));;
- : bool = true
# Obj.tag (Obj.repr (Orange 1234));;
- : int = 0
# Obj.tag (Obj.repr (Pear "xyz"));;
- : int = 1
# (Obj.magic (Obj.field (Obj.repr (Orange 1234)) 0) : int);;
- : int = 1234
# (Obj.magic (Obj.field (Obj.repr (Pear "xyz")) 0) : string);;
- : string = "xyz"
```

In the preceding example, the Apple and Kiwi values are still stored as normal OCaml integers with values 0 and 1, respectively. The Orange and Pear values both have parameters and are stored as blocks whose tags ascend from 0 (and so Pear has a tag of 1, as the use of Obj.tag verifies). Finally, the parameters are fields that contain OCaml values within the block, and Obj.field can be used to retrieve them.

Lists are stored with a representation that is exactly the same as if the list was written as a variant type with Nil and Cons. The empty list [] is an integer 0, and subsequent blocks have tag 0 and two parameters: a block with the current value, and a pointer to the rest of the list.

Obj Module Considered Harmful

Obj is an undocumented module that exposes the internals of the OCaml compiler and runtime. It is very useful for examining and understanding how your code will behave at runtime but should *never* be used for production code unless you understand the implications. The module bypasses the OCaml type system, making memory corruption and segmentation faults possible.

Some theorem provers such as Coq do output code that uses Obj internally, but the external module signatures never expose it. Unless you too have a machine proof of correctness to accompany your use of Obj, stay away from it except for debugging!

Due to this encoding, there is a limit around 240 variants with parameters that applies to each type definition, but the only limit on the number of variants without parameters is the size of the native integer (either 31 or 63 bits). This limit arises because of the size of the tag byte, and that some of the high-numbered tags are reserved.

24.5   Polymorphic Variants

Polymorphic variants are more flexible than normal variants when writing code but are slightly less efficient at runtime. This is because there isn't as much static compile-time information available to optimize their memory layout.

A polymorphic variant without any parameters is stored as an unboxed integer and so only takes up one word of memory, just like a normal variant. This integer value is determined by applying a hash function to the *name* of the variant. The hash function is exposed via the compiler-libs package that reveals some of the internals of the OCaml compiler:

```
# #require "ocaml-compiler-libs.common";;
# Btype.hash_variant "Foo";;
- : int = 3505894
# (Obj.magic (Obj.repr `Foo) : int);;
- : int = 3505894
```

The hash function is designed to give the same results on 32-bit and 64-bit architectures, so the memory representation is stable across different CPUs and host types.

Polymorphic variants use more memory space than normal variants when parameters are included in the data type constructors. Normal variants use the tag byte to encode the variant value and save the fields for the contents, but this single byte is insufficient to encode the hashed value for polymorphic variants. They must allocate a new block (with tag 0) and store the value in there instead. Polymorphic variants with constructors thus use one word of memory more than normal variant constructors.

Another inefficiency over normal variants is when a polymorphic variant constructor has more than one parameter. Normal variants hold parameters as a single flat block with multiple fields for each entry, but polymorphic variants must adopt a more flexible uniform memory representation, since they may be reused in a different context across compilation units. They allocate a tuple block for the parameters that is pointed to from the argument field of the variant. There are thus three additional words for such variants, along with an extra memory indirection due to the tuple.

The extra space usage is generally not significant in a typical application, and polymorphic variants offer a great deal more flexibility than normal variants. However, if you're writing code that demands high performance or must run within tight memory bounds, the runtime layout is at least very predictable. The OCaml compiler never switches memory representation due to optimization passes. This lets you predict the precise runtime layout by referring to these guidelines and your source code.

24.6   String Values

OCaml `strings` (and their mutable cousins, `bytes`) are standard OCaml blocks with the header size defining the size of the string in machine words. The `String_tag` (252) is higher than the `No_scan_tag`, indicating that the contents of the block are opaque to the collector. The block contents are the contents of the string, with padding bytes to align the block on a word boundary.

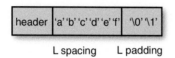

On a 32-bit machine, the padding is calculated based on the modulo of the string length and word size to ensure the result is word-aligned. A 64-bit machine extends the potential padding up to 7 bytes instead of 3. Given a string length modulo 4:

- 0 has padding 00 00 00 03
- 1 has padding 00 00 02
- 2 has padding 00 01
- 3 has padding 00

This string representation is a clever way to ensure that the contents are always zero-terminated by the padding word and to still compute its length efficiently without scanning the whole string. The following formula is used:

```
number_of_words_in_block * sizeof(word) - last_byte_of_block - 1
```

The guaranteed `NULL` termination comes in handy when passing a string to C, but is not relied upon to compute the length from OCaml code. OCaml strings can thus contain `NULL` bytes at any point within the string.

Care should be taken that any C library functions that receive these buffers can also cope with arbitrary bytes within the buffer contents and are not expecting C strings. For instance, the C `memcopy` or `memmove` standard library functions can operate on arbitrary data, but `strlen` or `strcpy` both require a `NULL`-terminated buffer, and neither has a mechanism for encoding a `NULL` value within its contents.

24.7   Custom Heap Blocks

OCaml supports *custom* heap blocks via a `Custom_tag` that lets the runtime perform user-defined operations over OCaml values. A custom block lives in the OCaml heap like an ordinary block and can be of whatever size the user desires. The `Custom_tag` (255) is higher than `No_scan_tag` and so isn't scanned by the GC.

The first word of the data within the custom block is a C pointer to a `struct` of custom operations. The custom block cannot have pointers to OCaml blocks and is opaque to the GC:

```
struct custom_operations {
  char *identifier;
  void (*finalize)(value v);
  int (*compare)(value v1, value v2);
  intnat (*hash)(value v);
  void (*serialize)(value v,
                    /*out*/ uintnat * wsize_32 /*size in bytes*/,
                    /*out*/ uintnat * wsize_64 /*size in bytes*/);
  uintnat (*deserialize)(void * dst);
  int (*compare_ext)(value v1, value v2);
};
```

The custom operations specify how the runtime should perform polymorphic comparison, hashing and binary marshaling. They also optionally contain a *finalizer* that the runtime calls just before the block is garbage-collected. This finalizer has nothing to do with ordinary OCaml finalizers (as created by `Gc.finalize` and explained in Chapter 25 (Understanding the Garbage Collector)). They are instead used to call C cleanup functions such as `free`.

24.7.1   Managing External Memory with Bigarray

A common use of custom blocks is to manage external system memory directly from within OCaml. The Bigarray interface was originally intended to exchange data with Fortran code, and maps a block of system memory as a multidimensional array that can be accessed from OCaml. Bigarray operations work directly on the external memory without requiring it to be copied into the OCaml heap (which is a potentially expensive operation for large arrays).

Bigarray sees a lot of use beyond just scientific computing, and several Core libraries use it for general-purpose I/O:

Iobuf   The `Iobuf` module maps I/O buffers as a one-dimensional array of bytes. It provides a sliding window interface that lets consumer processes read from the buffer while it's being filled by producers. This lets OCaml use I/O buffers that have been externally allocated by the operating system without any extra data copying.

Bigstring   The `Bigstring` module provides a `String`-like interface that uses `Bigarray` internally. The `Bigbuffer` collects these into extensible string buffers that can operate entirely on external system memory.

The Lacaml[1] library isn't part of Core but provides the recommended interfaces to the widely used BLAS and LAPACK mathematical Fortran libraries. These allow

---

[1] `http://mmottl.github.io/lacaml/`

developers to write high-performance numerical code for applications that require linear algebra. It supports large vectors and matrices, but with static typing safety of OCaml to make it easier to write safe algorithms.

25 Understanding the Garbage Collector

This chapter includes contributions from Stephen Weeks and Sadiq Jaffer.

We've described the runtime format of individual OCaml variables earlier, in Chapter 24 (Memory Representation of Values). When you execute your program, OCaml manages the lifecycle of these variables by regularly scanning allocated values and freeing them when they're no longer needed. This in turn means that your applications don't need to manually implement memory management, and it greatly reduces the likelihood of memory leaks creeping into your code.

The OCaml runtime is a C library that provides routines that can be called from running OCaml programs. The runtime manages a *heap*, which is a collection of memory regions that it obtains from the operating system. The runtime uses this memory to hold *heap blocks* that it fills up with OCaml values in response to allocation requests by the OCaml program.

25.1 Mark and Sweep Garbage Collection

When there isn't enough memory available to satisfy an allocation request from the pool of allocated heap blocks, the runtime system invokes the garbage collector (GC). An OCaml program can't explicitly free a value when it is done with it. Instead, the GC regularly determines which values are *live* and which values are *dead*, i.e., no longer in use. Dead values are collected and their memory made available for reuse by the application.

The GC doesn't keep constant track of values as they are allocated and used. Instead, it regularly scans them by starting from a set of *root* values that the application always has access to (such as the stack). The GC maintains a directed graph in which heap blocks are nodes, and there is an edge from heap block b1 to heap block b2 if some field of b1 is a pointer to b2.

All blocks reachable from the roots by following edges in the graph must be retained, and unreachable blocks can be reused by the application. The algorithm used by OCaml to perform this heap traversal is commonly known as *mark and sweep* garbage collection, and we'll explain it further now.

25.2   Generational Garbage Collection

The usual OCaml programming style involves allocating many small values that are used for a short period of time and then never accessed again. OCaml takes advantage of this fact to improve performance by using a *generational* GC.

A generational GC maintains separate memory regions to hold blocks based on how long the blocks have been live. OCaml's heap is split into two such regions:

- A small, fixed-size *minor heap* where most blocks are initially allocated
- A larger, variable-size *major heap* for blocks that have been live longer

A typical functional programming style means that young blocks tend to die young and old blocks tend to stay around for longer than young ones. This is often referred to as the *generational hypothesis*.

OCaml uses different memory layouts and garbage-collection algorithms for the major and minor heaps to account for this generational difference. We'll explain how they differ in more detail next.

The Gc Module and OCAMLRUNPARAM

OCaml provides several mechanisms to query and alter the behavior of the runtime system. The Gc module provides this functionality from within OCaml code, and we'll frequently refer to it in the rest of the chapter. As with several other standard library modules, Core alters the Gc interface from the standard OCaml library. We'll assume that you've opened Core in our explanations.

You can also control the behavior of OCaml programs by setting the OCAMLRUNPARAM environment variable before launching your application. This lets you set GC parameters without recompiling, for example to benchmark the effects of different settings. The format of OCAMLRUNPARAM is documented in the OCaml manuala.

a https://ocaml.org/manual/runtime.html

25.3   The Fast Minor Heap

The minor heap is where most of your short-lived values are held. It consists of one contiguous chunk of virtual memory containing a sequence of OCaml blocks. If there is space, allocating a new block is a fast, constant-time operation that requires just a couple of CPU instructions.

To garbage-collect the minor heap, OCaml uses *copying collection* to move all live blocks in the minor heap to the major heap. This takes work proportional to the number of live blocks in the minor heap, which is typically small according to the generational hypothesis. In general, the garbage collector *stops the world* (that is, halts the application) while it runs, which is why it's so important that it complete quickly to let the application resume running with minimal interruption.

25.3.1   Allocating on the Minor Heap

The minor heap is a contiguous chunk of virtual memory that is usually a few megabytes in size so that it can be scanned quickly.

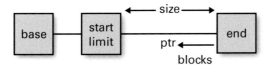

The runtime stores the boundaries of the minor heap in two pointers that delimit the start and end of the heap region (`caml_young_start` and `caml_young_end`, but we will drop the `caml_young` prefix for brevity). The base is the memory address returned by the system `malloc`, and `start` is aligned against the next nearest word boundary from base to make it easier to store OCaml values.

In a fresh minor heap, the `limit` equals the `start`, and the current `ptr` will equal the end. `ptr` decreases as blocks are allocated until it reaches `limit`, at which point a minor garbage collection is triggered.

Allocating a block in the minor heap just requires `ptr` to be decremented by the size of the block (including the header) and a check that it's not less than `limit`. If there isn't enough space left for the block without decrementing past `limit`, a minor garbage collection is triggered. This is a very fast check (with no branching) on most CPU architectures.

Understanding Allocation

You may wonder why `limit` is required at all, since it always seems to equal `start`. It's because the easiest way for the runtime to schedule a minor heap collection is by setting `limit` to equal end. The next allocation will never have enough space after this is done and will always trigger a garbage collection. There are various internal reasons for such early collections, such as handling pending UNIX signals, but they don't ordinarily matter for application code.

It is possible to write loops or recurse in a way that may take a long time to do an allocation - if at all. To ensure that UNIX signals and other internal bookkeeping that require interrupting the running OCaml program still happen the compiler introduces *poll points* into generated native code.

These poll points check `ptr` against `limit` and developers should expect them to be placed at the start of every function and the back edge of loops. The compiler includes a dataflow pass that removes all but the minimum set of points necessary to ensure these checks happen in a bounded amount of time.

Setting the Size of the Minor Heap

The default minor heap size in OCaml is normally 2 MB on 64-bit platforms, but this is increased to 8 MB if you use Core (which generally prefers default settings that improve performance, but at the cost of a bigger memory profile). This setting can be

overridden via the s=<words> argument to OCAMLRUNPARAM. You can change it after the
program has started by calling the Gc.set function:

```
# open Core;;
# let c = Gc.get ();;
val c : Gc.Control.t =
  {Core.Gc.Control.minor_heap_size = 262144; major_heap_increment =
     15;
   space_overhead = 120; verbose = 0; max_overhead = 500;
   stack_limit = 1048576; allocation_policy = 2; window_size = 1;
   custom_major_ratio = 44; custom_minor_ratio = 100;
   custom_minor_max_size = 8192}
# Gc.tune ~minor_heap_size:(262144 * 2) ();;
- : unit = ()
```

Changing the GC size dynamically will trigger an immediate minor heap collection. Note that Core increases the default minor heap size from the standard OCaml
installation quite significantly, and you'll want to reduce this if running in very memory-
constrained environments.

25.4   The Long-Lived Major Heap

The major heap is where the bulk of the longer-lived and larger values in your program
are stored. It consists of any number of noncontiguous chunks of virtual memory, each
containing live blocks interspersed with regions of free memory. The runtime system
maintains a free-list data structure that indexes all the free memory that it has allocated,
and uses it to satisfy allocation requests for OCaml blocks.

The major heap is typically much larger than the minor heap and can scale to
gigabytes in size. It is cleaned via a mark-and-sweep garbage collection algorithm that
operates in several phases:

- The *mark* phase scans the block graph and marks all live blocks by setting a bit in
  the tag of the block header (known as the *color* tag).
- The *sweep* phase sequentially scans the heap chunks and identifies dead blocks that
  weren't marked earlier.
- The *compact* phase relocates live blocks into a freshly allocated heap to eliminate
  gaps in the free list. This prevents the fragmentation of heap blocks in long-
  running programs and normally occurs much less frequently than the mark and
  sweep phases.

A major garbage collection must also stop the world to ensure that blocks can be
moved around without this being observed by the live application. The mark-and-sweep
phases run incrementally over slices of the heap to avoid pausing the application for
long periods of time, and also precede each slice with a fast minor collection. Only the
compaction phase touches all the memory in one go, and is a relatively rare operation.

25.4.1   Allocating on the Major Heap

The major heap consists of a singly linked list of contiguous memory chunks sorted in increasing order of virtual address. Each chunk is a single memory region allocated via *malloc(3)* and consists of a header and data area which contains OCaml heap chunks. A heap chunk header contains:

- The *malloc*ed virtual address of the memory region containing the chunk
- The size in bytes of the data area
- An allocation size in bytes used during heap compaction to merge small blocks to defragment the heap
- A link to the next heap chunk in the list
- A pointer to the start and end of the range of blocks that may contain unexamined fields and need to be scanned later. Only used after mark stack overflow.

Each chunk's data area starts on a page boundary, and its size is a multiple of the page size (4 KB). It contains a contiguous sequence of heap blocks that can be as small as one or two 4 KB pages, but are usually allocated in 1 MB chunks (or 512 KB on 32-bit architectures).

Controlling the Major Heap Increment

The Gc module uses the `major_heap_increment` value to control the major heap growth. This defines the number of words to add to the major heap per expansion and is the only memory allocation operation that the operating system observes from the OCaml runtime after initial startup (since the minor is fixed in size).

Allocating an OCaml value on the major heap first checks the free list of blocks for a suitable region to place it. If there isn't enough room on the free list, the runtime expands the major heap by allocating a fresh heap chunk that will be large enough. That chunk is then added to the free list, and the free list is checked again (and this time will definitely succeed).

Older versions of OCaml required setting a fixed number of bytes for the major heap increment. That was a value that was tricky to get right: too small of a value could lead to lots of smaller heap chunks spread across different regions of virtual memory that require more housekeeping in the OCaml runtime to keep track of them; too large of a value can waste memory for programs with small heaps.

You can use `Gc.tune` to set that value, but the values are a little counter-intuitive, for backwards-compatibility reasons. Values under 1000 are interpreted as percentages, and the default is 15%. Values 1000 and over are treated as a raw number of bytes. But most of the time, you won't set the value at all.

25.4.2   Memory Allocation Strategies

The major heap does its best to manage memory allocation as efficiently as possible and relies on heap compaction to ensure that memory stays contiguous and unfragmented.

The default allocation policy normally works fine for most applications, but it's worth bearing in mind that there are other options, too.

The free list of blocks is always checked first when allocating a new block in the major heap. The default free list search is called *best-fit allocation*, with alternatives *next-fit* and *first-fit* algorithms also available.

Best-Fit Allocation

The best-fit allocator is a combination of two strategies. The first, size-segregated free lists, is based on the observation that nearly all major heap allocations in OCaml are small (consider list elements and tuples which are only a couple of machine words). Best fit keeps separate free lists for sizes up to and including 16 words which gives a fast path for most allocations. Allocations for these sizes can be serviced from their segregated free lists or, if they are empty, from the next size with a space.

The second strategy, for larger allocations, is the use of a specialized data structure known as a *splay tree* for the free list. This is a type of search tree that adapts to recent access patterns. For our use this means that the most commonly requested allocation sizes are the quickest to access.

Small allocations, when there are no larger sizes available in the segregated free lists, and large allocations greater than sixteen words are serviced from the main free list. The free list is queried for the smallest block that is at least as large as the allocation requested.

Best-fit allocation is the default allocation mechanism. It represents a good trade-off between the allocation cost (in terms of CPU work) and heap fragmentation.

Next-Fit Allocation

Next-fit allocation keeps a pointer to the block in the free list that was most recently used to satisfy a request. When a new request comes in, the allocator searches from the next block to the end of the free list, and then from the beginning of the free list up to that block.

Next-fit allocation is quite a cheap allocation mechanism, since the same heap chunk can be reused across allocation requests until it runs out. This in turn means that there is good memory locality to use CPU caches better. The big downside of next-fit is that since most allocations are small, large blocks at the start of the free list become heavily fragmented.

First-Fit Allocation

If your program allocates values of many varied sizes, you may sometimes find that your free list becomes fragmented. In this situation, the GC is forced to perform an expensive compaction despite there being free chunks, since none of the chunks alone are big enough to satisfy the request.

First-fit allocation focuses on reducing memory fragmentation (and hence the number of compactions), but at the expense of slower memory allocation. Every allocation scans the free list from the beginning for a suitable free chunk, instead of reusing the most recent heap chunk as the next-fit allocator does.

For some workloads that need more real-time behavior under load, the reduction in the frequency of heap compaction will outweigh the extra allocation cost.

Controlling the Heap Allocation Policy

You can set the heap allocation policy by calling `Gc.tune`:

```
# Gc.tune ~allocation_policy:First_fit ();;
- : unit = ()
```

The same behavior can be controlled via an environment variable by setting `OCAMLRUNPARAM` to a=0 for next-fit, a=1 for first-fit, or a=2 for best-fit.

25.4.3   Marking and Scanning the Heap

The marking process can take a long time to run over the complete major heap and has to pause the main application while it's active. It therefore runs incrementally by marking the heap in *slices*. Each value in the heap has a 2-bit *color* field in its header that is used to store information about whether the value has been marked so that the GC can resume easily between slices.

- Blue: On the free list and not currently in use
- White (during marking): Not reached yet, but possibly reachable
- White (during sweeping): Unreachable and can be freed
- Black: Reachable, and its fields have been scanned

The color tags in the value headers store most of the state of the marking process, allowing it to be paused and resumed later. On allocation, all heap values are initially given the color white indicating they are possibly reachable but haven't been scanned yet. The GC and application alternate between marking a slice of the major heap and actually getting on with executing the program logic. The OCaml runtime calculates a sensible value for the size of each major heap slice based on the rate of allocation and available memory.

The marking process starts with a set of *root* values that are always live (such as the application stack and globals). These root values have their color set to black and are pushed on to a specialized data structure known as the *mark* stack. Marking proceeds by popping a value from the stack and examining its fields. Any fields containing white-colored blocks are changed to black and pushed onto the mark stack.

This process is repeated until the mark stack is empty and there are no further values to mark. There's one important edge case in this process, though. The mark stack can only grow to a certain size, after which the GC can no longer recurse into intermediate values since it has nowhere to store them while it follows their fields. This is known as mark stack *overflow* and a process called *pruning* begins. Pruning empties the mark stack entirely, summarizing the addresses of each block as start and end ranges in each heap chunk header.

Later in the marking process when the mark stack is empty it is replenished by *redarkening* the heap. This starts at the first heap chunk (by address) that has blocks needing redarkening (i.e were removed from the mark stack during a prune) and entries from the redarkening range are added to the mark stack until it is a quarter full. The emptying and replenishing cycle continues until there are no heap chunks with ranges left to redarken.

Controlling Major Heap Collections

You can trigger a single slice of the major GC via the `major_slice` call. This performs a minor collection first, and then a single slice. The size of the slice is normally automatically computed by the GC to an appropriate value and returns this value so that you can modify it in future calls if necessary:

```
# Gc.major_slice 0;;
- : int = 0
# Gc.full_major ();;
- : unit = ()
```

The `space_overhead` setting controls how aggressive the GC is about setting the slice size to a large size. This represents the proportion of memory used for live data that will be "wasted" because the GC doesn't immediately collect unreachable blocks. Core defaults this to `100` to reflect a typical system that isn't overly memory-constrained. Set this even higher if you have lots of memory, or lower to cause the GC to work harder and collect blocks faster at the expense of using more CPU time.

25.4.4   Heap Compaction

After a certain number of major GC cycles have completed, the heap may begin to be fragmented due to values being deallocated out of order from how they were allocated. This makes it harder for the GC to find a contiguous block of memory for fresh allocations, which in turn would require the heap to be grown unnecessarily.

The heap compaction cycle avoids this by relocating all the values in the major heap into a fresh heap that places them all contiguously in memory again. A naive implementation of the algorithm would require extra memory to store the new heap, but OCaml performs the compaction in place within the existing heap.

Controlling Frequency of Compactions

The `max_overhead` setting in the `Gc` module defines the connection between free memory and allocated memory after which compaction is activated.

A value of `0` triggers a compaction after every major garbage collection cycle, whereas the maximum value of `1000000` disables heap compaction completely. The default settings should be fine unless you have unusual allocation patterns that are causing a higher-than-usual rate of compactions:

```
# Gc.tune ~max_overhead:0 ();;
- : unit = ()
```

25.4.5   Intergenerational Pointers

One complexity of generational collection arises from the fact that minor heap sweeps are much more frequent than major heap collections. In order to know which blocks in the minor heap are live, the collector must track which minor-heap blocks are directly pointed to by major-heap blocks. Without this information, each minor collection would also require scanning the much larger major heap.

OCaml maintains a set of such *intergenerational pointers* to avoid this dependency between a major and minor heap collection. The compiler introduces a write barrier to update this so-called *remembered set* whenever a major-heap block is modified to point at a minor-heap block.

The Mutable Write Barrier

The write barrier can have profound implications for the structure of your code. It's one of the reasons using immutable data structures and allocating a fresh copy with changes can sometimes be faster than mutating a record in place.

The OCaml compiler keeps track of any mutable types and adds a call to the runtime caml_modify function before making the change. This checks the location of the target write and the value it's being changed to, and ensures that the remembered set is consistent. Although the write barrier is reasonably efficient, it can sometimes be slower than simply allocating a fresh value on the fast minor heap and doing some extra minor collections.

Let's see this for ourselves with a simple test program. You'll need to install the Core benchmarking suite via opam install core_bench before you compile this code:

```
open Core
open Core_bench

module Mutable = struct
  type t =
    { mutable iters : int
    ; mutable count : float
    }

  let rec test t =
    if t.iters = 0
    then ()
    else (
      t.iters <- t.iters - 1;
      t.count <- t.count +. 1.0;
      test t)
end

module Immutable = struct
  type t =
    { iters : int
    ; count : float
    }

  let rec test t =
    if t.iters = 0
```

```
      then ()
      else test { iters = t.iters - 1; count = t.count +. 1.0 }
  end

let () =
  let iters = 1_000_000 in
  let count = 0.0 in
  let tests =
    [ Bench.Test.create ~name:"mutable" (fun () ->
          Mutable.test { iters; count })
    ; Bench.Test.create ~name:"immutable" (fun () ->
          Immutable.test { iters; count })
    ]
  in
  Bench.make_command tests |> Command.run
```

This program defines a type t1 that is mutable and t2 that is immutable. The benchmark loop iterates over both fields and increments a counter. Compile and execute this with some extra options to show the amount of garbage collection occurring:

```
$ dune exec -- ./barrier_bench.exe -ascii alloc -quota 1
Estimated testing time 2s (2 benchmarks x 1s). Change using '-quota'.
```

Name	Time/Run	mWd/Run	mjWd/Run	Prom/Run	Percentage
mutable	5.06ms	2.00Mw	20.61w	20.61w	100.00%
immutable	3.95ms	5.00Mw	95.64w	95.64w	77.98%

There is a space/time trade-off here. The mutable version takes longer to complete than the immutable one but allocates many fewer minor-heap words than the immutable version. Minor allocation in OCaml is very fast, and so it is often better to use immutable data structures in preference to the more conventional mutable versions. On the other hand, if you only rarely mutate a value, it can be faster to take the write-barrier hit and not allocate at all.

The only way to know for sure is to benchmark your program under real-world scenarios using Core_bench and experiment with the trade-offs. The command-line benchmark binaries have a number of useful options that affect garbage collection behavior and the output format:

```
$ dune exec -- ./barrier_bench.exe -help
Benchmark for mutable, immutable

  barrier_bench.exe [COLUMN ...]

Columns that can be specified are:
    time       - Number of nano secs taken.
    cycles     - Number of CPU cycles (RDTSC) taken.
    alloc      - Allocation of major, minor and promoted words.
    gc         - Show major and minor collections per 1000 runs.
    percentage - Relative execution time as a percentage.
    speedup    - Relative execution cost as a speedup.
    samples    - Number of samples collected for profiling.
    ...
```

25.5   Attaching Finalizer Functions to Values

OCaml's automatic memory management guarantees that a value will eventually be freed when it's no longer in use, either via the GC sweeping it or the program terminating. It's sometimes useful to run extra code just before a value is freed by the GC, for example, to check that a file descriptor has been closed, or that a log message is recorded.

What Values Can Be Finalized?

Various values cannot have finalizers attached since they aren't heap-allocated. Some examples of values that are not heap-allocated are integers, constant constructors, Booleans, the empty array, the empty list, and the unit value. The exact list of what is heap-allocated or not is implementation-dependent, which is why Core provides the Heap_block module to explicitly check before attaching the finalizer.

Some constant values can be heap-allocated but never deallocated during the lifetime of the program, for example, a list of integer constants. Heap_block explicitly checks to see if the value is in the major or minor heap, and rejects most constant values. Compiler optimizations may also duplicate some immutable values such as floating-point values in arrays. These may be finalized while another duplicate copy is being used by the program.

Core provides a Heap_block module that dynamically checks if a given value is suitable for finalizing. Core keeps the functions for registering finalizers in the Core.Gc.Expert module. Finalizers can run at any time in any thread, so they can be pretty hard to reason about in multi-threaded contexts. Async, which we discussed in Chapter 17 (Concurrent Programming with Async), shadows the Gc module with its own module that contains a function, Gc.add_finalizer, which is concurrency-safe. In particular, finalizers are scheduled in their own Async job, and care is taken by Async to capture exceptions and raise them to the appropriate monitor for error-handling.

Let's explore this with a small example that finalizes values of different types, all of which are heap-allocated.

```
open Core
open Async

let attach_finalizer n v =
  match Heap_block.create v with
  | None -> printf "%20s: FAIL\n%!" n
  | Some hb ->
    let final _ = printf "%20s: OK\n%!" n in
    Gc.add_finalizer hb final

type t = { foo : bool }

let main () =
  attach_finalizer "allocated variant" (`Foo (Random.bool ()));
  attach_finalizer "allocated string" (Bytes.create 4);
  attach_finalizer "allocated record" { foo = (Random.bool ()) };
```

```
  Gc.compact ();
  return ()

let () =
  Command.async
    ~summary:"Testing finalizers"
    (Command.Param.return main)
  |> Command.run
```

Building and running this should show the following output:

```
$ dune exec -- ./finalizer.exe
    allocated record: OK
    allocated string: OK
    allocated variant: OK
```

The GC calls the finalization functions in the order of the deallocation. If several values become unreachable during the same GC cycle, the finalization functions will be called in the reverse order of the corresponding calls to add_finalizer. Each call to add_finalizer adds to the set of functions, which are run when the value becomes unreachable. You can have many finalizers all pointing to the same heap block if you wish.

After a garbage collection determines that a heap block b is unreachable, it removes from the set of finalizers all the functions associated with b, and serially applies each of those functions to b. Thus, every finalizer function attached to b will run at most once. However, program termination will not cause all the finalizers to be run before the runtime exits.

The finalizer can use all features of OCaml, including assignments that make the value reachable again and thus prevent it from being garbage-collected. It can also loop forever, which will cause other finalizers to be interleaved with it.

26   The Compiler Frontend: Parsing and Type Checking

Compiling source code into executable programs involves a fairly complex set of libraries, linkers, and assemblers. While Dune mostly hides this complexity from you, it's still useful to understand how these pieces work so that you can debug performance problems, or come up with solutions for unusual situations that aren't well handled by existing tools.

OCaml has a strong emphasis on static type safety and rejects source code that doesn't meet its requirements as early as possible. The compiler does this by running the source code through a series of checks and transformations. Each stage performs its job (e.g., type checking, optimization, or code generation) and discards some information from the previous stage. The final native code output is low-level assembly code that doesn't know anything about the OCaml modules or objects that the compiler started with.

In this chapter, we'll cover the following topics:

- An overview of the compiler codebase and the compilation pipeline, and what each stage represents
- Parsing, which goes from raw text to the abstract syntax tree
- PPX's, which further transform the AST
- Type-checking, including module resolution

The details of the remainder of the compilation process, which gets all the way to executable code comes next, in Chapter 27 (The Compiler Backend: Bytecode and Native code).

26.1   An Overview of the Toolchain

The OCaml tools accept textual source code as input, using the filename extensions .ml and .mli for modules and signatures, respectively. We explained the basics of the build process in Chapter 5 (Files, Modules, and Programs), so we'll assume you've built a few OCaml programs already by this point.

Each source file represents a *compilation unit* that is built separately. The compiler generates intermediate files with different filename extensions to use as it advances through the compilation stages. The linker takes a collection of compiled units and produces a standalone executable or library archive that can be reused by other applications.

The overall compilation pipeline looks like this:

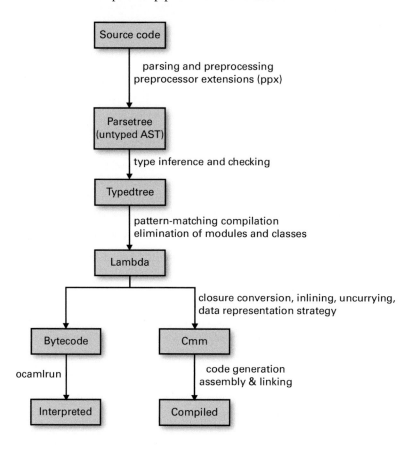

Notice that the pipeline branches toward the end. OCaml has multiple compiler backends that reuse the early stages of compilation but produce very different final outputs. The *bytecode* can be run by a portable interpreter and can even be transformed into JavaScript (via js_of_ocaml[1]) or C source code (via OCamlCC[2]). The *native code* compiler generates specialized executable binaries suitable for high-performance applications.

26.1.1   Obtaining the Compiler Source Code

Although it's not necessary to understand the examples, you may find it useful to have a copy of the OCaml source tree checked out while you read through this chapter. The source code is available from multiple places:

[1] http://ocsigen.org/js_of_ocaml
[2] https://github.com/ocaml-bytes/ocamlcc

- Stable releases as zip and tar archives from the OCaml download site [3]
- A Git repository with all the history and development branches included, browsable online at GitHub [4]

The source tree is split up into subdirectories. The core compiler consists of:

asmcomp/ Native-code compiler that converts OCaml into high performance native code executables.

bytecomp/ Bytecode compiler that converts OCaml into an interpreted executable format.

driver/ Command-line interfaces for the compiler tools.

file_formats/ Serializer and deserializers for on-disk files used by the compiler driver.

lambda/ The lambda conversion pass.

middle_end/ The clambda, closure and flambda passes.

parsing/ The OCaml lexer, parser, and libraries for manipulating them.

runtime/ The runtime library with the garbage collector.

typing/ The static type checking implementation and type definitions.

A number of tools and scripts are also built alongside the core compiler:

debugger/ The interactive bytecode debugger.

toplevel/ Interactive top-level console.

stdlib/ The compiler standard library, including the `Pervasives` module.

otherlibs/ Optional libraries such as the Unix and graphics modules.

tools/ Command-line utilities such as `ocamldep` that are installed with the compiler.

testsuite/ Regression tests for the core compiler.

We'll go through each of the compilation stages now and explain how they will be useful to you during day-to-day OCaml development.

26.2   Parsing Source Code

When a source file is passed to the OCaml compiler, its first task is to parse the text into a more structured abstract syntax tree (AST). The parsing logic is implemented in OCaml itself using the techniques described earlier in Chapter 20 (Parsing with OCamllex and Menhir). The lexer and parser rules can be found in the `parsing` directory in the source distribution.

26.2.1   Syntax Errors

The OCaml parser's goal is to output a well-formed AST data structure to the next phase of compilation, and so it fails on any source code that doesn't match basic syntactic

---

[3] http://ocaml.org/docs/install.html
[4] https://github.com/ocaml/ocaml

requirements. The compiler emits a *syntax error* in this situation, with a pointer to the filename and line and character number that's as close to the error as possible.

Here's an example syntax error that we obtain by performing a module assignment as a statement instead of as a `let` binding:

```
let () =
  module MyString = String;
  ()
```

The code results in a syntax error when compiled:

```
$ ocamlc -c broken_module.ml
File "broken_module.ml", line 2, characters 2-8:
2 |   module MyString = String;
      ^^^^^^
Error: Syntax error
[2]
```

The correct version of this source code creates the `MyString` module correctly via a local open, and compiles successfully:

```
let () =
  let module MyString = String in
  ()
```

The syntax error points to the line and character number of the first token that couldn't be parsed. In the broken example, the `module` keyword isn't a valid token at that point in parsing, so the error location information is correct.

26.2.2   Generating Documentation from Interfaces

Whitespace and source code comments are removed during parsing and aren't significant in determining the semantics of the program. However, other tools in the OCaml distribution can interpret comments for their own ends.

OCaml uses specially formatted comments in the source code to generate documentation bundles. These comments are combined with the function definitions and signatures, and output as structured documentation in a variety of formats. Tools such as odoc and ocamldoc can generate HTML pages, LaTeX and PDF documents, UNIX manual pages, and even module dependency graphs that can be viewed using Graphviz[5].

Here's a sample of some source code that's been annotated with docstring comments:

```
(** The first special comment of the file is the comment associated
    with the whole module. *)

(** Comment for exception My_exception. *)
exception My_exception of (int -> int) * int

(** Comment for type [weather]   *)
type weather =
  | Rain of int (** The comment for constructor Rain *)
```

[5] http://www.graphviz.org

```
  | Sun            (** The comment for constructor Sun *)

(** Find the current weather for a country
    @author Anil Madhavapeddy
    @param location The country to get the weather for.
*)
let what_is_the_weather_in location =
  match location with
  | `Cambridge  -> Rain 100
  | `New_york   -> Rain 20
  | `California -> Sun
```

The docstrings are distinguished by beginning with the double asterisk. There are formatting conventions for the contents of the comment to mark metadata. For instance, the @tag fields mark specific properties such as the author of that section of code.

There are two main tools used to manipulate docstring comments: the ocamldoc tool that is supplied with the compiler, and the odoc tool that is developed outside the compiler but is intended to be the long-term replacement. Try compiling the HTML documentation and UNIX man pages by running ocamldoc over the source file:

```
$ mkdir -p html man/man3
$ ocamldoc -html -d html doc.ml
$ ocamldoc -man -d man/man3 doc.ml
$ man -M man Doc
```

You should now have HTML files inside the html/ directory and also be able to view the UNIX manual pages held in man/man3. There are quite a few comment formats and options to control the output for the various backends. Refer to the OCaml manual[6] for the complete list.

You can also use odoc to generate complete snapshots of your project via integration with dune, as described earlier in Chapter 22.2.2 (Browsing Interface Documentation).

26.3   Preprocessing with ppx

One powerful feature in OCaml is a facility to extend the standard language via *extension points*. These represent placeholders in the OCaml syntax tree and are ignored by the standard compiler tooling, beyond being delimited and stored in the abstract syntax tree alongside the normal parsed source code. They are intended to be expanded by external tools that select extension nodes that can interpret them. The external tools can choose to generate further OCaml code by transforming the input syntax tree, thus forming the basis of an extensible preprocessor for the language.

There are two primary forms of extension points in OCaml: *attributes* and *extension nodes*. Let's first run through some examples of what they look like, and then see how to use them in your own code.

---

[6] https://ocaml.org/manual/native.html

26.3.1   Extension Attributes

Attributes supply additional information that is attached to a node in the OCaml syntax tree, and subsequently interpreted and expanded by external tools.

The basic form of an attribute is the [@ ...] syntax. The number of @ symbols defines which part of the syntax tree the attribute is bound to:

- a single [@ binds using a postfix notation to algebraic categories such as expressions or individual constructors in type definitions.
- a double [@@ binds to blocks of code, such as module definitions, type declarations or class fields.
- a triple [@@@ appears as a standalone entry in a module implementation or signature, and are not tied to any specific source code node.

The OCaml compiler has some useful builtin attributes that we can use to illustrate their use without requiring any external tools. Let's first look at the use of the standalone attribute @@@warning to toggle an OCaml compiler warning.

```
# module Abc = struct

  [@@@warning "+non-unit-statement"]
  let a = Sys.get_argv (); ()

  [@@@warning "-non-unit-statement"]
  let b = Sys.get_argv (); ()
  end;;
Line 4, characters 11-26:
Warning 10 [non-unit-statement]: this expression should have type
    unit.
module Abc : sig val a : unit val b : unit end
```

The warning in our example is taken from the compiler manual page [7]. This warning emits a message if the expression in a sequence doesn't have type unit. The @@@warning nodes in the module implementation cause the compiler to change its behavior within the scope of that structure only.

An annotation can also be more narrowly attached to a block of code. For example, a module implementation can be annotated with @@deprecated to indicate that it should not be used in new code:

```
# module Planets = struct
    let earth = true
    let pluto = true
  end [@@deprecated "Sorry, Pluto is no longer a planet. Use the
    Planets2016 module instead."];;
module Planets : sig val earth : bool val pluto : bool end
# module Planets2016 = struct
    let earth = true
    let pluto = false
  end;;
module Planets2016 : sig val earth : bool val pluto : bool end
```

---

[7] https://ocaml.org/manual/native.html

In this example, the `@@deprecated` annotation is only attached to the `Planets` module, and the human-readable argument string redirects developers to the newer code. Now if we try to use the value that has been marked as deprecated, the compiler will issue a warning.

```
# let is_pluto_a_planet = Planets.pluto;;
Line 1, characters 25-38:
Alert deprecated: module Planets
Sorry, Pluto is no longer a planet. Use the Planets2016 module
    instead.
val is_pluto_a_planet : bool = true
# let is_pluto_a_planet = Planets2016.pluto;;
val is_pluto_a_planet : bool = false
```

Finally, an attribute can also be attached to an individual expression. In the next example, the `@warn_on_literal_pattern` attribute indicates that the argument to the type constructor should not be pattern matched upon with a constant literal.

```
# type program_result =
  | Error of string [@warn_on_literal_pattern]
  | Exit_code of int;;
type program_result = Error of string | Exit_code of int
# let exit_with = function
  | Error "It blew up" -> 1
  | Exit_code code -> code
  | Error _ -> 100;;
Line 2, characters 11-23:
Warning 52 [fragile-literal-pattern]: Code should not depend on the
    actual values of
this constructor's arguments. They are only for information
and may change in future versions. (See manual section 11.5)
val exit_with : program_result -> int = <fun>
```

26.3.2   Commonly Used Extension Attributes

We have already used extension points in Chapter 21 (Data Serialization with S-Expressions) to generate boilerplate code for handling s-expressions. These are introduced by a third-party library using the `(preprocess)` directive in a dune file, for example:

```
(library
 (name hello_world)
 (libraries core)
 (preprocess (pps ppx_jane)))
```

This allows you to take advantage of a community of syntax augmentation. There are also a number of builtin attributes in the core OCaml compiler. Some are performance oriented and give directives to the compiler, whereas others will activate usage warnings. The full list is available in the attributes section[8] of the OCaml manual.

---

[8] https://ocaml.org/manual/attributes.html

26.3.3   Extension Nodes

While extension points are useful for annotating existing source code, we also need a mechanism to store generic placeholders within the OCaml AST for code generation. OCaml provides this facility via the *extension node* syntax.

The general syntax for an extension node is [%id expr], where id is an identifier for a particular extension node rewriter and expr is the payload for the rewriter to parse. An infix form is also available when the payload is of the same kind of syntax. For example let%foo bar = 1 is equivalent to [%foo let bar = 1].

We've already seen extension nodes in use via the Core syntax extensions earlier in the book, where they act as syntactic sugar for error handling (let%bind), for command-line parsing (let%map) or inline testing (let%expect_test). Extension nodes are introduced via dune rules in the same fashion as extension attributes, via the (preprocess) attribute.

26.4   Static Type Checking

After obtaining a valid abstract syntax tree, the compiler has to verify that the code obeys the rules of the OCaml type system. Code that is syntactically correct but misuses values is rejected with an explanation of the problem.

Although type checking is done in a single pass in OCaml, it actually consists of three distinct steps that happen simultaneously:

automatic type inference An algorithm that calculates types for a module without requiring manual type annotations

module system Combines software components with explicit knowledge of their type signatures

explicit subtyping Checks for objects and polymorphic variants

Automatic type inference lets you write succinct code for a particular task and have the compiler ensure that your use of variables is locally consistent.

Type inference doesn't scale to very large codebases that depend on separate compilation of files. A small change in one module may ripple through thousands of other files and libraries and require all of them to be recompiled. The module system solves this by providing the facility to combine and manipulate explicit type signatures for modules within a large project, and also to reuse them via functors and first-class modules.

Subtyping in OCaml objects is always an explicit operation (via the :> operator). This means that it doesn't complicate the core type inference engine and can be tested as a separate concern.

26.4.1   Displaying Inferred Types from the Compiler

We've already seen how you can explore type inference directly from the toplevel. It's also possible to generate type signatures for an entire file by asking the compiler to do the work for you. Create a file with a single type definition and value:

```
type t = Foo | Bar
let v = Foo
```

Now run the compiler with the -i flag to infer the type signature for that file. This runs the type checker but doesn't compile the code any further after displaying the interface to the standard output:

```
$ ocamlc -i typedef.ml
type t = Foo | Bar
val v : t
```

The output is the default signature for the module that represents the input file. It's often useful to redirect this output to an mli file to give you a starting signature to edit the external interface without having to type it all in by hand.

The compiler stores a compiled version of the interface as a cmi file. This interface is either obtained from compiling an mli signature file for a module, or by the inferred type if there is only an ml implementation present.

The compiler makes sure that your ml and mli files have compatible signatures. The type checker throws an immediate error if this isn't the case. For example, if you have this as your ml file:

```
type t = Foo
```

and this as your mli:

```
type t = Bar
```

then, when you try to build, you'll get this error:

```
$ ocamlc -c conflicting_interface.mli conflicting_interface.ml
File "conflicting_interface.ml", line 1:
Error: The implementation conflicting_interface.ml
       does not match the interface conflicting_interface.cmi:
       Type declarations do not match:
         type t = Foo
       is not included in
         type t = Bar
       Constructors number 1 have different names, Foo and Bar.
       File "conflicting_interface.mli", line 1, characters 0-12:
         Expected declaration
       File "conflicting_interface.ml", line 1, characters 0-12:
         Actual declaration
[2]
```

Which Comes First: The ml or the mli?

There are two schools of thought on which order OCaml code should be written in. It's very easy to begin writing code by starting with an ml file and using the type inference to guide you as you build up your functions. The `mli` file can then be generated as described, and the exported functions documented.

If you're writing code that spans multiple files, it's sometimes easier to start by writing all the `mli` signatures and checking that they type-check against one another. Once the signatures are in place, you can write the implementations with the confidence that they'll all glue together correctly, with no cyclic dependencies among the modules.

As with any such stylistic debate, you should experiment with which system works best for you. Everyone agrees on one thing though: no matter in what order you write them, production code should always explicitly define an `mli` file for every `ml` file in the project. It's also perfectly fine to have an `mli` file without a corresponding `ml` file if you're only declaring signatures (such as module types).

Signature files provide a place to write succinct documentation and to abstract internal details that shouldn't be exported. Maintaining separate signature files also speeds up incremental compilation in larger code bases, since recompiling a `mli` signature is much faster than a full compilation of the implementation to native code.

26.4.2   Type Inference

Type inference is the process of determining the appropriate types for expressions based on their use. It's a feature that's partially present in many other languages such as Haskell and Scala, but OCaml embeds it as a fundamental feature throughout the core language.

OCaml type inference is based on the Hindley-Milner algorithm, which is notable for its ability to infer the most general type for an expression without requiring any explicit type annotations. The algorithm can deduce multiple types for an expression and has the notion of a *principal type* that is the most general choice from the possible inferences. Manual type annotations can specialize the type explicitly, but the automatic inference selects the most general type unless told otherwise.

OCaml does have some language extensions that strain the limits of principal type inference, but by and large, most programs you write will never *require* annotations (although they sometimes help the compiler produce better error messages).

Adding Type Annotations to Find Errors

It's often said that the hardest part of writing OCaml code is getting past the type checker—but once the code does compile, it works correctly the first time! This is an exaggeration of course, but it can certainly feel true when moving from a dynamically typed language. The OCaml static type system protects you from certain classes of bugs such as memory errors and abstraction violations by rejecting your program at compilation time rather than by generating an error at runtime. Learning how to navigate the type checker's compile-time feedback is key to building robust libraries and applications that take full advantage of these static checks.

There are a couple of tricks to make it easier to quickly locate type errors in your code. The first is to introduce manual type annotations to narrow down the source of your error more accurately. These annotations shouldn't actually change your types and can be removed once your code is correct. However, they act as anchors to locate errors while you're still writing your code.

Manual type annotations are particularly useful if you use lots of polymorphic variants or objects. Type inference with row polymorphism can generate some very large signatures, and errors tend to propagate more widely than if you are using more explicitly typed variants or classes.

For instance, consider this broken example that expresses some simple algebraic operations over integers:

```
let rec algebra =
  function
  | `Add (x,y) -> (algebra x) + (algebra y)
  | `Sub (x,y) -> (algebra x) - (algebra y)
  | `Mul (x,y) -> (algebra x) * (algebra y)
  | `Num x     -> x

let _ =
  algebra (
    `Add (
      (`Num 0),
      (`Sub (
          (`Num 1),
          (`Mul (
              (`Nu 3),(`Num 2)
            ))
        ))
    ))
```

There's a single character typo in the code so that it uses `Nu` instead of `Num`. The resulting type error is impressive:

```
$ ocamlc -c broken_poly.ml
File "broken_poly.ml", lines 9-18, characters 10-6:
 9 | ..........(
10 |        `Add (
11 |          (`Num 0),
12 |          (`Sub (
13 |              (`Num 1),
14 |              (`Mul (
15 |                  (`Nu 3),(`Num 2)
16 |                ))
17 |            ))
18 |        ))
Error: This expression has type
         [> `Add of
              ([< `Add of 'a * 'a
                | `Mul of 'a * 'a
                | `Num of int
                | `Sub of 'a * 'a
                > `Num ]
               as 'a) *
              [> `Sub of 'a * [> `Mul of [> `Nu of int ] * [> `Num of
     int ] ]
                ] ]
```

```
        but an expression was expected of type
            [< `Add of 'a * 'a | `Mul of 'a * 'a | `Num of int | `Sub of
        'a * 'a
                > `Num ]
            as 'a
        The second variant type does not allow tag(s) `Nu
    [2]
```

The type error is perfectly accurate, but rather verbose and with a line number that doesn't point to the exact location of the incorrect variant name. The best the compiler can do is to point you in the general direction of the algebra function application.

This is because the type checker doesn't have enough information to match the inferred type of the algebra definition to its application a few lines down. It calculates types for both expressions separately, and when they don't match up, outputs the difference as best it can.

Let's see what happens with an explicit type annotation to help the compiler out:

```
type t = [
    | `Add of t * t
    | `Sub of t * t
    | `Mul of t * t
    | `Num of int
]

let rec algebra (x:t) =
    match x with
    | `Add (x,y) -> (algebra x) + (algebra y)
    | `Sub (x,y) -> (algebra x) - (algebra y)
    | `Mul (x,y) -> (algebra x) * (algebra y)
    | `Num x       -> x

let _ =
    algebra (
        `Add (
            (`Num 0),
            (`Sub (
                (`Num 1),
                (`Mul (
                    (`Nu 3),(`Num 2)
                ))
            ))
        ))
```

This code contains exactly the same error as before, but we've added a closed type definition of the polymorphic variants, and a type annotation to the algebra definition. The compiler error we get is much more useful now:

```
$ ocamlc -i broken_poly_with_annot.ml
File "broken_poly_with_annot.ml", line 22, characters 14-21:
22 |                 (`Nu 3),(`Num 2)
                     ^^^^^^^
Error: This expression has type [> `Nu of int ]
        but an expression was expected of type t
        The second variant type does not allow tag(s) `Nu
    [2]
```

This error points directly to the correct line number that contains the typo. Once you fix the problem, you can remove the manual annotations if you prefer more succinct code. You can also leave the annotations there, of course, to help with future refactoring and debugging.

Enforcing Principal Typing

The compiler also has a stricter *principal type checking* mode that is activated via the -principal flag. This warns about risky uses of type information to ensure that the type inference has one principal result. A type is considered risky if the success or failure of type inference depends on the order in which subexpressions are typed.

The principality check only affects a few language features:

- Polymorphic methods for objects
- Permuting the order of labeled arguments in a function from their type definition
- Discarding optional labeled arguments
- Generalized algebraic data types (GADTs) present from OCaml 4.0 onward
- Automatic disambiguation of record field and constructor names (since OCaml 4.1)

Here's an example of principality warnings when used with record disambiguation.

```
type s = { foo: int; bar: unit }
type t = { foo: int }

let f x =
  x.bar;
  x.foo
```

Inferring the signature with -principal will show you a new warning:

```
$ ocamlc -i -principal non_principal.ml
File "non_principal.ml", line 6, characters 4-7:
6 |    x.foo
       ^^^
Warning 18 [not-principal]: this type-based field disambiguation is
    not principal.
type s = { foo : int; bar : unit; }
type t = { foo : int; }
val f : s -> int
```

This example isn't principal, since the inferred type for x.foo is guided by the inferred type of x.bar, whereas principal typing requires that each subexpression's type can be calculated independently. If the x.bar use is removed from the definition of f, its argument would be of type t and not type s.

You can fix this either by permuting the order of the type declarations, or by adding an explicit type annotation:

```
type s = { foo: int; bar: unit }
type t = { foo: int }

let f (x:s) =
  x.bar;
  x.foo
```

There is now no ambiguity about the inferred types, since we've explicitly given the argument a type, and the order of inference of the subexpressions no longer matters.

```
$ ocamlc -i -principal principal.ml
type s = { foo : int; bar : unit; }
type t = { foo : int; }
val f : s -> int
```

The dune equivalent is to add the flag -principal to your build description.

```
(executable
  (name principal)
  (flags :standard -principal)
  (modules principal))

(executable
  (name non_principal)
  (flags :standard -principal)
  (modules non_principal))
```

The :standard directive will include all the default flags, and then -principal will be appended after those in the compiler build flags.

```
$ dune build principal.exe
$ dune build non_principal.exe
File "non_principal.ml", line 6, characters 4-7:
6 |    x.foo
       ^^^
Error (warning 18 [not-principal]): this type-based field
    disambiguation is not principal.
[1]
```

Ideally, all code should systematically use -principal. It reduces variance in type inference and enforces the notion of a single known type. However, there are drawbacks to this mode: type inference is slower, and the cmi files become larger. This is generally only a problem if you extensively use objects, which usually have larger type signatures to cover all their methods.

If compiling in principal mode works, it is guaranteed that the program will pass type checking in non-principal mode, too. Bear in mind that the cmi files generated in principal mode differ from the default mode. Try to ensure that you compile your whole project with it activated. Getting the files mixed up won't let you violate type safety, but it can result in the type checker failing unexpectedly very occasionally. In this case, just recompile with a clean source tree.

26.4.3   Modules and Separate Compilation

The OCaml module system enables smaller components to be reused effectively in large projects while still retaining all the benefits of static type safety. We covered the basics of using modules earlier in Chapter 5 (Files, Modules, and Programs). The module language that operates over these signatures also extends to functors and first-class modules, described in Chapter 11 (Functors) and Chapter 12 (First-Class Modules), respectively.

This section discusses how the compiler implements them in more detail. Modules are essential for larger projects that consist of many source files (also known as *compilation units*). It's impractical to recompile every single source file when changing just one or two files, and the module system minimizes such recompilation while still encouraging code reuse.

The Mapping Between Files and Modules

Individual compilation units provide a convenient way to break up a big module hierarchy into a collection of files. The relationship between files and modules can be explained directly in terms of the module system.

Create a file called `alice.ml` with the following contents:

```
let friends = [ Bob.name ]
```

and a corresponding signature file:

```
val friends : Bob.t list
```

These two files produce essentially the same result as the following code.

```
module Alice : sig
   val friends : Bob.t list
end = struct
   let friends = [ Bob.name ]
end
```

Defining a Module Search Path

In the preceding example, `Alice` also has a reference to another module `Bob`. For the overall type of `Alice` to be valid, the compiler also needs to check that the `Bob` module contains at least a `Bob.name` value and defines a `Bob.t` type.

The type checker resolves such module references into concrete structures and signatures in order to unify types across module boundaries. It does this by searching a list of directories for a compiled interface file matching that module's name. For example, it will look for `alice.cmi` and `bob.cmi` on the search path and use the first ones it encounters as the interfaces for `Alice` and `Bob`.

The module search path is set by adding `-I` flags to the compiler command line with the directory containing the `cmi` files as the argument. Manually specifying these flags gets complex when you have lots of libraries, and is the reason why tools like dune and `ocamlfind` exist. They both automate the process of turning third-party package names and build descriptions into command-line flags that are passed to the compiler command line.

By default, only the current directory and the OCaml standard library will be searched for `cmi` files. The `Stdlib` module from the standard library will also be opened by default in every compilation unit. The standard library location is obtained by running `ocamlc -where` and can be overridden by setting the `CAMLLIB` environment variable. Needless to say, don't override the default path unless you have a good reason to (such as setting up a cross-compilation environment).

Inspecting Compilation Units with ocamlobjinfo

For separate compilation to be sound, we need to ensure that all the cmi files used to type-check a module are the same across compilation runs. If they vary, this raises the possibility of two modules checking different type signatures for a common module with the same name. This in turn lets the program completely violate the static type system and can lead to memory corruption and crashes.

OCaml guards against this by recording a MD5 checksum in every cmi. Let's examine our earlier typedef.ml more closely:

```
$ ocamlc -c typedef.ml
$ ocamlobjinfo typedef.cmi
File typedef.cmi
Unit name: Typedef
Interfaces imported:
    cdd43318ee9dd1b187513a4341737717    Typedef
    9b04ecdc97e5102c1d342892ef7ad9a2    Pervasives
    79ae8c0eb753af6b441fe05456c7970b    CamlinternalFormatBasics
```

ocamlobjinfo examines the compiled interface and displays what other compilation units it depends on. In this case, we don't use any external modules other than Pervasives. Every module depends on Pervasives by default, unless you use the -nopervasives flag (this is an advanced use case, and you shouldn't normally need it).

The long alphanumeric identifier beside each module name is a hash calculated from all the types and values exported from that compilation unit. It's used during type-checking and linking to ensure that all of the compilation units have been compiled consistently against one another. A difference in the hashes means that a compilation unit with the same module name may have conflicting type signatures in different modules. The compiler will reject such programs with an error similar to this:

```
$ ocamlc -c foo.ml
File "foo.ml", line 1, characters 0-1:
Error: The files /home/build/bar.cmi
        and /usr/lib/ocaml/map.cmi make inconsistent assumptions
        over interface Map
```

This hash check is very conservative, but ensures that separate compilation remains type-safe all the way up to the final link phase. Your build system should ensure that you never see the preceding error messages, but if you do run into it, just clean out your intermediate files and recompile from scratch.

26.4.4   Wrapping Libraries with Module Aliases

The module-to-file mapping described so far rigidly enforces a 1:1 mapping between a top-level module and a file. It's often convenient to split larger modules into separate files to make editing easier, but still compile them all into a single OCaml module.

Dune provides a very convenient way of doing this for libraries via automatically generating a toplevel *module alias* file that places all the files in a given library as submodules within the toplevel module for that library. This is known as *wrapping* the library, and works as follows.

Let's define a simple library with two files a.ml and b.ml that each define a single value.

```
let v = "hello"
```

```
let w = 42
```

The dune file defines a library called hello that includes these two modules.

```
(library
  (name hello)
  (modules a b))
(executable
  (name test)
  (libraries hello)
  (modules test))
```

If we now build this library, we can look at how dune assembles the modules into a Hello library.

```
$ dune build
$ cat _build/default/hello.ml-gen
(** @canonical Hello.A *)
module A = Hello__A


(** @canonical Hello.B *)
module B = Hello__B
```

Dune has generated a hello.ml file which forms the toplevel module exposed by the library. It has also renamed the individual modules into internal mangled names such as Hello__A, and assigned those internal modules as aliases within the generated hello.ml file. This then allows a user of this library to access the values as Hello.A. For example, our test executable contains this:

```
let v = Hello.A.v
let w = Hello.B.w
```

One nice aspect about this module alias scheme is that a single toplevel module provides a central place to write documentation about how to use all the submodules exposed by the library. We can manually add a hello.ml and hello.mli to our library that does exactly this. First add the hello module to the dune file:

```
(library
  (name hello)
  (modules a b hello))
(executable
  (name test)
  (libraries hello)
  (modules test))
```

Then the hello.ml file contains the module aliases (and any other code you might want to add to the toplevel module).

```
module A = A
module B = B
```

Finally, the `hello.mli` interface file can reference all the submodules and include documentation strings:

```
(** Documentation for module A *)
module A : sig
  (** [v] is Hello *)
  val v : string
end

(** Documentation for module B *)
module B : sig
  (** [w] is 42 *)
  val w : int
end
```

If you want to disable this behavior of dune and deliberately include multiple toplevel modules, you can add (wrapped false) to your libraries stanza. However, this is discouraged in general due to the increased likelihood of linking clashes when you have a lot of library dependencies, since every module that is linked into an executable must have a unique name in OCaml.

26.4.5   Shorter Module Paths in Type Errors

Core uses the OCaml module system quite extensively to provide a complete replacement standard library. It collects these modules into a single Std module, which provides a single module that needs to be opened to import the replacement modules and functions.

There's one downside to this approach: type errors suddenly get much more verbose. We can see this if you run the vanilla OCaml toplevel (not utop).

```
$ ocaml
# List.map print_endline "";;
Error: This expression has type string but an expression was expected
    of type
          string list
```

This type error without Core has a straightforward type error. When we switch to Core, though, it gets more verbose:

```
$ ocaml
# open Core;;
# List.map ~f:print_endline "";;
Error: This expression has type string but an expression was expected
    of type
          'a Core.List.t = 'a list
```

The default List module in OCaml is overridden by Core.List. The compiler does its best to show the type equivalence, but at the cost of a more verbose error message.

The compiler can remedy this via a so-called short paths heuristic. This causes the compiler to search all the type aliases for the shortest module path and use that as the preferred output type. The option is activated by passing `-short-paths` to the compiler, and works on the toplevel, too.

```
$ ocaml -short-paths
# open Core;;
# List.map ~f:print_endline "foo";;
Error: This expression has type string but an expression was expected
     of type
          'a list
```

The `utop` enhanced toplevel activates short paths by default, which is why we have not had to do this before in our interactive examples. However, the compiler doesn't default to the short path heuristic, since there are some situations where the type aliasing information is useful to know, and it would be lost in the error if the shortest module path is always picked.

You'll need to choose for yourself if you prefer short paths or the default behavior in your own projects, and pass the `-short-paths` flag to the compiler if you need

26.5   The Typed Syntax Tree

When the type checking process has successfully completed, it is combined with the AST to form a *typed abstract syntax tree*. This contains precise location information for every token in the input file, and decorates each token with concrete type information.

The compiler can output this as compiled `cmt` and `cmti` files that contain the typed AST for the implementation and signatures of a compilation unit. This is activated by passing the `-bin-annot` flag to the compiler.

The `cmt` files are particularly useful for IDE tools to match up OCaml source code at a specific location to the inferred or external types. For example, the `merlin` and `ocaml-lsp-server` opam packages both use this information to provide you with tooltips and docstrings within your editor, as described earlier in Chapter 22.2.1 (Using Visual Studio Code).

26.5.1   Examining the Typed Syntax Tree Directly

The compiler has a couple of advanced flags that can dump the raw output of the internal AST representation. You can't depend on these flags to give the same output across compiler revisions, but they are a useful learning tool.

We'll use our toy `typedef.ml` again:

```
type t = Foo | Bar
let v = Foo
```

Let's first look at the untyped syntax tree that's generated from the parsing phase:

```
$ ocamlc -dparsetree typedef.ml 2>&1
[
  structure_item (typedef.ml[1,0+0]..[1,0+18])
    Pstr_type Rec
```

```
[
  type_declaration "t" (typedef.ml[1,0+5]..[1,0+6])
(typedef.ml[1,0+0]..[1,0+18])
      ptype_params =
        []
      ptype_cstrs =
        []
      ptype_kind =
        Ptype_variant
          [
            (typedef.ml[1,0+9]..[1,0+12])
              "Foo" (typedef.ml[1,0+9]..[1,0+12])
              []
              None
            (typedef.ml[1,0+13]..[1,0+18])
              "Bar" (typedef.ml[1,0+15]..[1,0+18])
              []
              None
          ]
      ptype_private = Public
      ptype_manifest =
        None
  ]
structure_item (typedef.ml[2,19+0]..[2,19+11])
  Pstr_value Nonrec
  [
    <def>
      pattern (typedef.ml[2,19+4]..[2,19+5])
        Ppat_var "v" (typedef.ml[2,19+4]..[2,19+5])
      expression (typedef.ml[2,19+8]..[2,19+11])
        Pexp_construct "Foo" (typedef.ml[2,19+8]..[2,19+11])
        None
  ]
]
```

This is rather a lot of output for a simple two-line program, but it shows just how much structure the OCaml parser generates even from a small source file.

Each portion of the AST is decorated with the precise location information (including the filename and character location of the token). This code hasn't been type checked yet, so the raw tokens are all included.

The typed AST that is normally output as a compiled cmt file can be displayed in a more developer-readable form via the -dtypedtree option:

```
$ ocamlc -dtypedtree typedef.ml 2>&1
[
  structure_item (typedef.ml[1,0+0]..typedef.ml[1,0+18])
    Tstr_type Rec
    [
      type_declaration t/81 (typedef.ml[1,0+0]..typedef.ml[1,0+18])
        ptype_params =
          []
        ptype_cstrs =
          []
        ptype_kind =
          Ttype_variant
```

```
                    [
                       (typedef.ml[1,0+9]..typedef.ml[1,0+12])
                          Foo/82
                          []
                          None
                       (typedef.ml[1,0+13]..typedef.ml[1,0+18])
                          Bar/83
                          []
                          None
                    ]
                ptype_private = Public
                ptype_manifest =
                    None
          ]
    structure_item (typedef.ml[2,19+0]..typedef.ml[2,19+11])
      Tstr_value Nonrec
      [
        <def>
          pattern (typedef.ml[2,19+4]..typedef.ml[2,19+5])
            Tpat_var "v/84"
          expression (typedef.ml[2,19+8]..typedef.ml[2,19+11])
            Texp_construct "Foo"
            []
      ]
  ]
```

The typed AST is more explicit than the untyped syntax tree. For instance, the type declaration has been given a unique name (t/1008), as has the v value (v/1011).

You'll rarely need to look at this raw output from the compiler unless you're building IDE tools, or are hacking on extensions to the core compiler itself. However, it's useful to know that this intermediate form exists before we delve further into the code generation process next, in Chapter 27 (The Compiler Backend: Bytecode and Native code).

There are several new integrated tools emerging that combine these typed AST files with common editors such as Emacs or Vim. The best of these is Merlin[9], which adds value and module autocompletion, displays inferred types and can build and display errors directly from within your editor. There are instructions available on its homepage for configuring Merlin with your favorite editor, or its bigger sibling ocaml-lsp-server is described earlier in Chapter 22.2.1 (Using Visual Studio Code).

[9] https://github.com/def-lkb/merlin

27 The Compiler Backend: Bytecode and Native code

Once OCaml has passed the type checking stage, it can stop emitting syntax and type errors and begin the process of compiling the well-formed modules into executable code.

In this chapter, we'll cover the following topics:

- The untyped intermediate lambda code where pattern matching is optimized
- The bytecode `ocamlc` compiler and `ocamlrun` interpreter
- The native code `ocamlopt` code generator, and debugging and profiling native code

27.1 The Untyped Lambda Form

The first code generation phase eliminates all the static type information into a simpler intermediate *lambda form*. The lambda form discards higher-level constructs such as modules and objects and replaces them with simpler values such as records and function pointers. Pattern matches are also analyzed and compiled into highly optimized automata.

The lambda form is the key stage that discards the OCaml type information and maps the source code to the runtime memory model described in Chapter 24 (Memory Representation of Values). This stage also performs some optimizations, most notably converting pattern-match statements into more optimized but low-level statements.

27.1.1 Pattern Matching Optimization

The compiler dumps the lambda form in an s-expression syntax if you add the `-dlambda` directive to the command line. Let's use this to learn more about how the OCaml pattern-matching engine works by building three different pattern matches and comparing their lambda forms.

Let's start by creating a straightforward exhaustive pattern match using four normal variants:

```
type t = | Alice | Bob | Charlie | David

let test v =
  match v with
  | Alice    -> 100
```

```
| Bob     -> 101
| Charlie -> 102
| David   -> 103
```

The lambda output for this code looks like this:

```
$ ocamlc -dlambda -c pattern_monomorphic_large.ml 2>&1
(setglobal Pattern_monomorphic_large!
  (let
    (test/86 =
      (function v/88 : int
        (switch* v/88
          case int 0: 100
          case int 1: 101
          case int 2: 102
          case int 3: 103)))
    (makeblock 0 test/86)))
```

It's not important to understand every detail of this internal form, and it is explicitly undocumented since it can change across compiler revisions. Despite these caveats, some interesting points emerge from reading it:

- There are no mentions of modules or types any more. Global values are created via `setglobal`, and OCaml values are constructed by `makeblock`. The blocks are the runtime values you should remember from Chapter 24 (Memory Representation of Values).
- The pattern match has turned into a switch case that jumps to the right case depending on the header tag of `v`. Recall that variants without parameters are stored in memory as integers in the order in which they appear. The pattern-matching engine knows this and has transformed the pattern into an efficient jump table.
- Values are addressed by a unique name that distinguishes shadowed values by appending a number (e.g., `v/1014`). The type safety checks in the earlier phase ensure that these low-level accesses never violate runtime memory safety, so this layer doesn't do any dynamic checks. Unwise use of unsafe features such as the `Obj.magic` module can still easily induce crashes at this level.

The compiler computes a jump table in order to handle all four cases. If we drop the number of variants to just two, then there's no need for the complexity of computing this table:

```
type t = | Alice | Bob

let test v =
  match v with
  | Alice   -> 100
  | Bob     -> 101
```

The lambda output for this code is now quite different:

```
$ ocamlc -dlambda -c pattern_monomorphic_small.ml 2>&1
(setglobal Pattern_monomorphic_small!
  (let (test/84 = (function v/86 : int (if v/86 101 100)))
    (makeblock 0 test/84)))
```

The compiler emits simpler conditional jumps rather than setting up a jump table, since it statically determines that the range of possible variants is small enough. Finally, let's consider code that's essentially the same as our first pattern match example, but with polymorphic variants instead of normal variants:

```
let test v =
  match v with
  | `Alice   -> 100
  | `Bob     -> 101
  | `Charlie -> 102
  | `David   -> 103
```

The lambda form for this also reflects the runtime representation of polymorphic variants:

```
$ ocamlc -dlambda -c pattern_polymorphic.ml 2>&1
(setglobal Pattern_polymorphic!
  (let
    (test/81 =
      (function v/83 : int
        (if (>= v/83 482771474) (if (>= v/83 884917024) 100 102)
          (if (>= v/83 3306965) 101 103)))))
    (makeblock 0 test/81)))
```

We mentioned in Chapter 7 (Variants) that pattern matching over polymorphic variants is slightly less efficient, and it should be clearer why this is the case now. Polymorphic variants have a runtime value that's calculated by hashing the variant name, and so the compiler can't use a jump table as it does for normal variants. Instead, it creates a decision tree that compares the hash values against the input variable in as few comparisons as possible.

Pattern matching is an important part of OCaml programming. You'll often encounter deeply nested pattern matches over complex data structures in real code. A good paper that describes the fundamental algorithms implemented in OCaml is "Optimizing pattern matching"[1] by Fabrice Le Fessant and Luc Maranget.

The paper describes the backtracking algorithm used in classical pattern matching compilation, and also several OCaml-specific optimizations, such as the use of exhaustiveness information and control flow optimizations via static exceptions. It's not essential that you understand all of this just to use pattern matching, of course, but it'll give you insight as to why pattern matching is such an efficient language construct in OCaml.

27.1.2   Benchmarking Pattern Matching

Let's benchmark these three pattern-matching techniques to quantify their runtime costs more accurately. The Core_bench module runs the tests thousands of times and also calculates statistical variance of the results. You'll need to opam install core_bench to get the library:

---

[1] http://dl.acm.org/citation.cfm?id=507641

```ocaml
open Core
open Core_bench

module Monomorphic = struct
  type t =
    | Alice
    | Bob
    | Charlie
    | David

  let bench () =
    let convert v =
      match v with
      | Alice -> 100
      | Bob -> 101
      | Charlie -> 102
      | David -> 103
    in
    List.iter
      ~f:(fun v -> ignore (convert v))
      [ Alice; Bob; Charlie; David ]
end

module Monomorphic_small = struct
  type t =
    | Alice
    | Bob

  let bench () =
    let convert v =
      match v with
      | Alice -> 100
      | Bob -> 101
    in
    List.iter
      ~f:(fun v -> ignore (convert v))
      [ Alice; Bob; Alice; Bob ]
end

module Polymorphic = struct
  type t =
    [ `Alice
    | `Bob
    | `Charlie
    | `David
    ]

  let bench () =
    let convert v =
      match v with
      | `Alice -> 100
      | `Bob -> 101
      | `Charlie -> 102
      | `David -> 103
    in
    List.iter
```

```
        ~f:(fun v -> ignore (convert v))
        [ `Alice; `Bob; `Alice; `Bob ]
  end

let benchmarks =
  [ "Monomorphic large pattern", Monomorphic.bench
  ; "Monomorphic small pattern", Monomorphic_small.bench
  ; "Polymorphic large pattern", Polymorphic.bench
  ]

let () =
  List.map benchmarks ~f:(fun (name, test) ->
      Bench.Test.create ~name test)
  |> Bench.make_command
  |> Command.run
```

Building and executing this example will run for around 30 seconds by default, and you'll see the results summarized in a neat table:

```
$ dune exec -- ./bench_patterns.exe -ascii -quota 0.25
Estimated testing time 750ms (3 benchmarks x 250ms). Change using
    '-quota'.

  Name                          Time/Run   Percentage
  ---------------------------   ---------- ------------
  Monomorphic large pattern      6.54ns      67.89%
  Monomorphic small pattern      9.63ns     100.00%
  Polymorphic large pattern      9.63ns      99.97%
```

These results confirm the performance hypothesis that we obtained earlier by inspecting the lambda code. The shortest running time comes from the small conditional pattern match, and polymorphic variant pattern matching is the slowest. There isn't a hugely significant difference in these examples, but you can use the same techniques to peer into the innards of your own source code and narrow down any performance hotspots.

The lambda form is primarily a stepping stone to the bytecode executable format that we'll cover next. It's often easier to look at the textual output from this stage than to wade through the native assembly code from compiled executables.

27.2   Generating Portable Bytecode

After the lambda form has been generated, we are very close to having executable code. The OCaml toolchain branches into two separate compilers at this point. We'll describe the bytecode compiler first, which consists of two pieces:

ocamlc Compiles files into a bytecode that is a close mapping to the lambda form
ocamlrun A portable interpreter that executes the bytecode

The big advantage of using bytecode is simplicity, portability, and compilation speed. The mapping from the lambda form to bytecode is straightforward, and this results in predictable (but slow) execution speed.

The bytecode interpreter implements a stack-based virtual machine. The OCaml stack and an associated accumulator store values that consist of:

long Values that correspond to an OCaml `int` type

block Values that contain the block header and a memory address with the data fields that contain further OCaml values indexed by an integer

code offset Values that are relative to the starting code address

The interpreter virtual machine only has seven registers in total: - program counter, - stack, exception and argument pointers, - accumulator, - environment and global data.

You can display the bytecode instructions in textual form via `-dinstr`. Try this on one of our earlier pattern-matching examples:

```
$ ocamlc -dinstr pattern_monomorphic_small.ml 2>&1
    branch L2
L1: acc 0
    branchifnot L3
    const 101
    return 1
L3: const 100
    return 1
L2: closure L1, 0
    push
    acc 0
    makeblock 1, 0
    pop 1
    setglobal Pattern_monomorphic_small!
```

The preceding bytecode has been simplified from the lambda form into a set of simple instructions that are executed serially by the interpreter.

There are around 140 instructions in total, but most are just minor variants of commonly encountered operations (e.g., function application at a specific arity). You can find full details online [2].

Where Did the Bytecode Instruction Set Come From?

The bytecode interpreter is much slower than compiled native code, but is still remarkably performant for an interpreter without a JIT compiler. Its efficiency can be traced back to Xavier Leroy's ground-breaking work in 1990, "The ZINC experiment: An Economical Implementation of the ML Language".a

This paper laid the theoretical basis for the implementation of an instruction set for a strictly evaluated functional language such as OCaml. The bytecode interpreter in modern OCaml is still based on the ZINC model. The native code compiler uses a different model since it uses CPU registers for function calls instead of always passing arguments on the stack, as the bytecode interpreter does.

Understanding the reasoning behind the different implementations of the bytecode interpreter and the native compiler is a very useful exercise for any budding language hacker.

a `http://hal.inria.fr/docs/00/07/00/49/PS/RT-0117.ps`

[2] `http://cadmium.x9c.fr/distrib/caml-instructions.pdf`

27.2.1   Compiling and Linking Bytecode

The ocamlc command compiles individual ml files into bytecode files that have a cmo extension. The compiled bytecode files are matched with the associated cmi interface, which contains the type signature exported to other compilation units.

A typical OCaml library consists of multiple source files, and hence multiple cmo files that all need to be passed as command-line arguments to use the library from other code. The compiler can combine these multiple files into a more convenient single archive file by using the -a flag. Bytecode archives are denoted by the cma extension.

The individual objects in the library are linked as regular cmo files in the order specified when the library file was built. If an object file within the library isn't referenced elsewhere in the program, then it isn't included in the final binary unless the -linkall flag forces its inclusion. This behavior is analogous to how C handles object files and archives (.o and .a, respectively).

The bytecode files are then linked together with the OCaml standard library to produce an executable program. The order in which .cmo arguments are presented on the command line defines the order in which compilation units are initialized at runtime. Remember that OCaml has no single main function like C, so this link order is more important than in C programs.

27.2.2   Executing Bytecode

The bytecode runtime comprises three parts: the bytecode interpreter, GC, and a set of C functions that implement the primitive operations. The bytecode contains instructions to call these C functions when required.

The OCaml linker produces bytecode that targets the standard OCaml runtime by default, and so needs to know about any C functions that are referenced from other libraries that aren't loaded by default.

Information about these extra libraries can be specified while linking a bytecode archive:

```
$ ocamlc -a -o mylib.cma a.cmo b.cmo -dllib -lmylib
```

The dllib flag embeds the arguments in the archive file. Any subsequent packages linking this archive will also include the extra C linking directive. This in turn lets the interpreter dynamically load the external library symbols when it executes the bytecode.

You can also generate a complete standalone executable that bundles the ocamlrun interpreter with the bytecode in a single binary. This is known as a *custom runtime* mode and is built as follows:

```
$ ocamlc -a -o mylib.cma -custom a.cmo b.cmo -cclib -lmylib
```

The custom mode is the most similar mode to native code compilation, as both generate standalone executables. There are quite a few other options available for compiling bytecode (notably with shared libraries or building custom runtimes). Full details can be found in the OCaml[3].

Dune can build a self-contained bytecode executable if you specify the byte_complete mode in the executable rule. For example, this dune file will generate a prog.bc.exe target:

```
(executable
  (name prog)
  (modules prog)
  (modes byte byte_complete))
```

27.2.3   Embedding OCaml Bytecode in C

A consequence of using the bytecode compiler is that the final link phase must be performed by ocamlc. However, you might sometimes want to embed your OCaml code inside an existing C application. OCaml also supports this mode of operation via the -output-obj directive.

This mode causes ocamlc to output an object file containing the bytecode for the OCaml part of the program, as well as a caml_startup function. All of the OCaml modules are linked into this object file as bytecode, just as they would be for an executable.

This object file can then be linked with C code using the standard C compiler, needing only the bytecode runtime library (which is installed as libcamlrun.a). Creating an executable just requires you to link the runtime library with the bytecode object file. Here's an example to show how it all fits together.

Create two OCaml source files that contain a single print line:

```
let () = print_endline "hello embedded world 1"
```

```
let () = print_endline "hello embedded world 2"
```

Next, create a C file to be your main entry point:

```
#include <stdio.h>
#include <caml/alloc.h>
#include <caml/mlvalues.h>
#include <caml/memory.h>
#include <caml/callback.h>

int
main (int argc, char **argv)
{
  printf("Before calling OCaml\n");
  fflush(stdout);
  caml_startup (argv);
  printf("After calling OCaml\n");
  return 0;
}
```

Now compile the OCaml files into a standalone object file:

[3] https://ocaml.org/manual/comp.html#s%3Acomp-options

```
$ rm -f embed_out.c
$ ocamlc -output-obj -o embed_out.o embed_me1.ml embed_me2.ml
```

After this point, you no longer need the OCaml compiler, as `embed_out.o` has all of the OCaml code compiled and linked into a single object file. Compile an output binary using `gcc` to test this out:

```
$ gcc -fPIC -Wall -I`ocamlc -where` -L`ocamlc -where` -ltermcap -lm
    -ldl \
  -o finalbc.native main.c embed_out.o -lcamlrun
$ ./finalbc.native
Before calling OCaml
hello embedded world 1
hello embedded world 2
After calling OCaml
```

You can inspect the commands that `ocamlc` is invoking by adding `-verbose` to the command line to help figure out the GCC command line if you get stuck. You can even obtain the C source code to the `-output-obj` result by specifying a `.c` output file extension instead of the `.o` we used earlier:

```
$ ocamlc -output-obj -o embed_out.c embed_me1.ml embed_me2.ml
```

Embedding OCaml code like this lets you write OCaml that interfaces with any environment that works with a C compiler. You can even cross back from the C code into OCaml by using the `Callback` module to register named entry points in the OCaml code. This is explained in detail in the interfacing with C[4] section of the OCaml manual.

27.3   Compiling Fast Native Code

The native code compiler is ultimately the tool that most production OCaml code goes through. It compiles the lambda form into fast native code executables, with cross-module inlining and additional optimization passes that the bytecode interpreter doesn't perform. Care is taken to ensure compatibility with the bytecode runtime, so the same code should run identically when compiled with either toolchain.

The `ocamlopt` command is the frontend to the native code compiler and has a very similar interface to `ocamlc`. It also accepts `ml` and `mli` files, but compiles them to:

- A `.o` file containing native object code
- A `.cmx` file containing extra information for linking and cross-module optimization
- A `.cmi` compiled interface file that is the same as the bytecode compiler

When the compiler links modules together into an executable, it uses the contents of the cmx files to perform cross-module inlining across compilation units. This can be a significant speedup for standard library functions that are frequently used outside of their module.

Collections of `.cmx` and `.o` files can also be linked into a `.cmxa` archive by passing

---

[4] https://ocaml.org/manual/intfc.html

the -a flag to the compiler. However, unlike the bytecode version, you must keep the individual cmx files in the compiler search path so that they are available for cross-module inlining. If you don't do this, the compilation will still succeed, but you will have missed out on an important optimization and have slower binaries.

27.3.1   Inspecting Assembly Output

The native code compiler generates assembly language that is then passed to the system assembler for compiling into object files. You can get ocamlopt to output the assembly by passing the -S flag to the compiler command line.

The assembly code is highly architecture-specific, so the following discussion assumes an Intel or AMD 64-bit platform. We've generated the example code using -inline 20 and -nodynlink since it's best to generate assembly code with the full optimizations that the compiler supports. Even though these optimizations make the code a bit harder to read, it will give you a more accurate picture of what executes on the CPU. Don't forget that you can use the lambda code from earlier to get a slightly higher-level picture of the code if you get lost in the more verbose assembly.

The Impact of Polymorphic Comparison

We warned you in Chapter 15 (Maps and Hash Tables) that using polymorphic comparison is both convenient and perilous. Let's look at precisely what the difference is at the assembly language level now.

First let's create a comparison function where we've explicitly annotated the types, so the compiler knows that only integers are being compared:

```
let cmp (a:int) (b:int) =
  if a > b then a else b
```

Now compile this into assembly and read the resulting compare_mono.S file.

```
$ ocamlopt -S compare_mono.ml
```

This file extension may be lowercase on some platforms such as Linux. If you've never seen assembly language before, then the contents may be rather scary. While you'll need to learn x86 assembly to fully understand it, we'll try to give you some basic instructions to spot patterns in this section. The excerpt of the implementation of the cmp function can be found below:

```
_camlCompare_mono__cmp_1008:
        .cfi_startproc
.L101:
        cmpq    %rbx, %rax
        jle     .L100
        ret
        .align  2
.L100:
        movq    %rbx, %rax
        ret
        .cfi_endproc
```

The _camlCompare_mono__cmp_1008 is an assembly label that has been computed from the module name (Compare_mono) and the function name (cmp_1008). The numeric suffix for the function name comes straight from the lambda form (which you can inspect using -dlambda, but in this case isn't necessary).

The arguments to cmp are passed in the %rbx and %rax registers, and compared using the jle "jump if less than or equal" instruction. This requires both the arguments to be immediate integers to work. Now let's see what happens if our OCaml code omits the type annotations and is a polymorphic comparison instead:

```
let cmp a b =
  if a > b then a else b
```

Compiling this code with -S results in a significantly more complex assembly output for the same function:

```
_camlCompare_poly__cmp_1008:
        .cfi_startproc
        subq    $24, %rsp
        .cfi_adjust_cfa_offset   24
.L101:
        movq    %rax, 8(%rsp)
        movq    %rbx, 0(%rsp)
        movq    %rax, %rdi
        movq    %rbx, %rsi
        leaq    _caml_greaterthan(%rip), %rax
        call    _caml_c_call
.L102:
        leaq    _caml_young_ptr(%rip), %r11
        movq    (%r11), %r15
        cmpq    $1, %rax
        je      .L100
        movq    8(%rsp), %rax
        addq    $24, %rsp
        .cfi_adjust_cfa_offset   -24
        ret
        .cfi_adjust_cfa_offset   24
        .align  2
.L100:
        movq    0(%rsp), %rax
        addq    $24, %rsp
        .cfi_adjust_cfa_offset   -24
        ret
        .cfi_adjust_cfa_offset   24
        .cfi_endproc
```

The .cfi directives are assembler hints that contain Call Frame Information that lets the debugger provide more sensible backtraces, and they have no effect on runtime performance. Notice that the rest of the implementation is no longer a simple register comparison. Instead, the arguments are pushed on the stack (the %rsp register), and a C function call is invoked by placing a pointer to caml_greaterthan in %rax and jumping to caml_c_call.

OCaml on x86_64 architectures caches the location of the minor heap in the %r15 register since it's so frequently referenced in OCaml functions. The minor heap pointer can also be changed by the C code that's being called (e.g., when it allocates OCaml values), and so %r15 is restored after returning from the caml_greaterthan call. Finally, the return value of the comparison is popped from the stack and returned.

Benchmarking Polymorphic Comparison

You don't have to fully understand the intricacies of assembly language to see that this polymorphic comparison is much heavier than the simple monomorphic integer comparison from earlier. Let's confirm this hypothesis again by writing a quick Core_bench test with both functions:

```
open Core
open Core_bench

let polymorphic_compare () =
  let cmp a b = Stdlib.(if a > b then a else b) in
  for i = 0 to 1000 do
    ignore(cmp 0 i)
  done

let monomorphic_compare () =
  let cmp (a:int) (b:int) = Stdlib.(if a > b then a else b) in
  for i = 0 to 1000 do
    ignore(cmp 0 i)
  done

let tests =
  [ "Polymorphic comparison", polymorphic_compare;
    "Monomorphic comparison", monomorphic_compare ]

let () =
  List.map tests ~f:(fun (name,test) -> Bench.Test.create ~name test)
  |> Bench.make_command
  |> Command.run
```

Running this shows quite a significant runtime difference between the two:

```
$ dune exec -- ./bench_poly_and_mono.exe -ascii -quota 1
Estimated testing time 2s (2 benchmarks x 1s). Change using '-quota'.
```

Name	Time/Run	Percentage
Polymorphic comparison	4_050.20ns	100.00%
Monomorphic comparison	471.75ns	11.65%

We see that the polymorphic comparison is close to 10 times slower! These results shouldn't be taken too seriously, as this is a very narrow test that, like all such microbenchmarks, isn't representative of more complex codebases. However, if you're building numerical code that runs many iterations in a tight inner loop, it's worth manually peering at the produced assembly code to see if you can hand-optimize it.

Accessing Stdlib Modules from Within Core

In the benchmark above comparing polymorphic and monomorphic comparison, you may have noticed that we prepended the comparison functions with Stdlib. This is because the Core module explicitly redefines the > and < and = operators to be specialized for operating over int types, as explained in Chapter 15.1.4 (The Polymorphic Comparator). You can always recover any of the OCaml standard library functions by accessing them through the Stdlib module, as we did in our benchmark.

27.3.2   Debugging Native Code Binaries

The native code compiler builds executables that can be debugged using conventional system debuggers such as GNU gdb. You need to compile your libraries with the -g option to add the debug information to the output, just as you need to with C compilers.

Extra debugging information is inserted into the output assembly when the library is compiled in debug mode. These include the CFI stubs you will have noticed in the profiling output earlier (.cfi_start_proc and .cfi_end_proc to delimit an OCaml function call, for example).

Understanding Name Mangling

So how do you refer to OCaml functions in an interactive debugger like gdb? The first thing you need to know is how OCaml function names compile down to symbol names in the compiled object files, a procedure generally called *name mangling*.

Each OCaml source file is compiled into a native object file that must export a unique set of symbols to comply with the C binary interface. This means that any OCaml values that may be used by another compilation unit need to be mapped onto a symbol name. This mapping has to account for OCaml language features such as nested modules, anonymous functions, and variable names that shadow one another.

The conversion follows some straightforward rules for named variables and functions:

- The symbol is prefixed by caml and the local module name, with dots replaced by underscores.
- This is followed by a double __ suffix and the variable name.
- The variable name is also suffixed by a _ and a number. This is the result of the lambda compilation, which replaces each variable name with a unique value within the module. You can determine this number by examining the -dlambda output from ocamlopt.

Anonymous functions are hard to predict without inspecting intermediate compiler output. If you need to debug them, it's usually easier to modify the source code to let-bind the anonymous function to a variable name.

Interactive Breakpoints with the GNU Debugger

Let's see name mangling in action with some interactive debugging using GNU gdb.

Let's write a mutually recursive function that selects alternating values from a list. This isn't tail-recursive, so our stack size will grow as we single-step through the execution:

```
open Core

let rec take =
  function
  |[] -> []
  |hd::tl -> hd :: (skip tl)
and skip =
  function
  |[] -> []
  |_::tl -> take tl

let () =
  take [1;2;3;4;5;6;7;8;9]
  |> List.map ~f:string_of_int
  |> String.concat ~sep:","
  |> print_endline
```

Compile and run this with debugging symbols. You should see the following output:

```
(executable
  (name       alternate_list)
  (libraries core))
```

```
$ dune build alternate_list.exe
$ ./_build/default/alternate_list.exe -ascii -quota 1
1,3,5,7,9
```

Now we can run this interactively within gdb:

```
$ gdb ./alternate_list.native
GNU gdb (GDB) 7.4.1-debian
Copyright (C) 2012 Free Software Foundation, Inc.
License GPLv3+: GNU GPL version 3 or later
    <http://gnu.org/licenses/gpl.html>
This is free software: you are free to change and redistribute it.
There is NO WARRANTY, to the extent permitted by law.  Type "show
    copying"
and "show warranty" for details.
This GDB was configured as "x86_64-linux-gnu".
For bug reporting instructions, please see:
<http://www.gnu.org/software/gdb/bugs/>...
Reading symbols from /home/avsm/alternate_list.native...done.
(gdb)
```

The gdb prompt lets you enter debug directives. Let's set the program to break just before the first call to take:

```
(gdb) break camlAlternate_list__take_69242
Breakpoint 1 at 0x5658d0: file alternate_list.ml, line 5.
```

We used the C symbol name by following the name mangling rules defined earlier. A convenient way to figure out the full name is by tab completion. Just type in a portion of the name and press the <tab> key to see a list of possible completions.

Once you've set the breakpoint, start the program executing:

```
(gdb) run
Starting program: /home/avsm/alternate_list.native
```

```
[Thread debugging using libthread_db enabled]
Using host libthread_db library
    "/lib/x86_64-linux-gnu/libthread_db.so.1".

Breakpoint 1, camlAlternate_list__take_69242 () at alternate_list.ml:5
4          function
```

The binary has run until the first take invocation and stopped, waiting for further instructions. GDB has lots of features, so let's continue the program and check the backtrace after a couple of recursions:

```
(gdb) cont
Continuing.

Breakpoint 1, camlAlternate_list__take_69242 () at alternate_list.ml:5
4          function
(gdb) cont
Continuing.

Breakpoint 1, camlAlternate_list__take_69242 () at alternate_list.ml:5
4          function
(gdb) bt
#0  camlAlternate_list__take_69242 () at alternate_list.ml:4
#1  0x00000000005658e7 in camlAlternate_list__take_69242 () at
    alternate_list.ml:6
#2  0x00000000005658e7 in camlAlternate_list__take_69242 () at
    alternate_list.ml:6
#3  0x00000000005659f7 in camlAlternate_list__entry () at
    alternate_list.ml:14
#4  0x0000000000560029 in caml_program ()
#5  0x000000000080984a in caml_start_program ()
#6  0x00000000008099a0 in ?? ()
#7  0x0000000000000000 in ?? ()
(gdb) clear camlAlternate_list__take_69242
Deleted breakpoint 1
(gdb) cont
Continuing.
1,3,5,7,9
[Inferior 1 (process 3546) exited normally]
```

The cont command resumes execution after a breakpoint has paused it, bt displays a stack backtrace, and clear deletes the breakpoint so the application can execute until completion. GDB has a host of other features we won't cover here, but you can view more guidelines via Mark Shinwell's talk on "Real-world debugging in OCaml." [5]

One very useful feature of OCaml native code is that C and OCaml share the same stack. This means that GDB backtraces can give you a combined view of what's going on in your program *and* runtime library. This includes any calls to C libraries or even callbacks into OCaml from the C layer if you're in an environment which embeds the OCaml runtime as a library.

---

[5] http://www.youtube.com/watch?v=NF2WpWnB-nk%3C

27.3.3   Profiling Native Code

The recording and analysis of where your application spends its execution time is known as *performance profiling*. OCaml native code binaries can be profiled just like any other C binary, by using the name mangling described earlier to map between OCaml variable names and the profiler output.

Most profiling tools benefit from having some instrumentation included in the binary. OCaml supports two such tools:

- GNU gprof, to measure execution time and call graphs
- The Perf[6] profiling framework in modern versions of Linux

Note that many other tools that operate on native binaries, such as Valgrind, will work just fine with OCaml as long as the program is linked with the -g flag to embed debugging symbols.

Gprof

gprof produces an execution profile of an OCaml program by recording a call graph of which functions call one another, and recording the time these calls take during the program execution.

Getting precise information out of gprof requires passing the -p flag to the native code compiler when compiling *and* linking the binary. This generates extra code that records profile information to a file called gmon.out when the program is executed. This profile information can then be examined using gprof.

Perf

Perf is a more modern alternative to gprof that doesn't require you to instrument the binary. Instead, it uses hardware counters and debug information within the binary to record information accurately.

Run Perf on a compiled binary to record information first. We'll use our write barrier benchmark from earlier, which measures memory allocation versus in-place modification:

```
$ perf record -g ./barrier_bench.native
Estimated testing time 20s (change using -quota SECS).

  Name        Time (ns)                  Time 95ci    Percentage
  ----        ---------                  ---------    ----------
  mutable     7_306_219    7_250_234-7_372_469            96.83
  immutable   7_545_126    7_537_837-7_551_193           100.00

[ perf record: Woken up 11 times to write data ]
[ perf record: Captured and wrote 2.722 MB perf.data (~118926
    samples) ]
perf record -g ./barrier.native
Estimated testing time 20s (change using -quota SECS).

  Name        Time (ns)                  Time 95ci    Percentage
```

---

[6] https://perf.wiki.kernel.org/

```
  ----        ---------       ---------     ----------
mutable     7_306_219     7_250_234-7_372_469         96.83
immutable   7_545_126     7_537_837-7_551_193        100.00
```

```
[ perf record: Woken up 11 times to write data ]
[ perf record: Captured and wrote 2.722 MB perf.data (~118926
    samples) ]
```

When this completes, you can interactively explore the results:

```
$ perf report -g
+   48.86%  barrier.native  barrier.native   [.]
      camlBarrier__test_immutable_69282
+   30.22%  barrier.native  barrier.native   [.]
      camlBarrier__test_mutable_69279
+   20.22%  barrier.native  barrier.native   [.] caml_modify
```

This trace broadly reflects the results of the benchmark itself. The mutable benchmark consists of the combination of the call to test_mutable and the caml_modify write barrier function in the runtime. This adds up to slightly over half the execution time of the application.

Perf has a growing collection of other commands that let you archive these runs and compare them against each other. You can read more on the home page[7].

Using the Frame Pointer to Get More Accurate Traces

Although Perf doesn't require adding in explicit probes to the binary, it does need to understand how to unwind function calls so that the kernel can accurately record the function backtrace for every event. Since Linux 3.9 the kernel has had support for using DWARF debug information to parse the program stack, which is emitted when the -g flag is passed to the OCaml compiler. For even more accurate stack parsing, we need the compiler to fall back to using the same conventions as C for function calls. On 64-bit Intel systems, this means that a special register known as the *frame pointer* is used to record function call history. Using the frame pointer in this fashion means a slowdown (typically around 3-5%) since it's no longer available for general-purpose use.

OCaml thus makes the frame pointer an optional feature that can be used to improve the resolution of Perf traces. opam provides a compiler switch that compiles OCaml with the frame pointer activated:

```
$ opam switch create 4.13+fp ocaml-variants.4.13.1+options
    ocaml-option-fp
```

Using the frame pointer changes the OCaml calling convention, but opam takes care of recompiling all your libraries with the new interface.

[7] http://perf.wiki.kernel.org

27.3.4   Embedding Native Code in C

The native code compiler normally links a complete executable, but can also output a standalone native object file just as the bytecode compiler can. This object file has no further dependencies on OCaml except for the runtime library.

The native code runtime is a different library from the bytecode one, and is installed as libasmrun.a in the OCaml standard library directory.

Try this custom linking by using the same source files from the bytecode embedding example earlier in this chapter:

```
$ ocamlopt -output-obj -o embed_native.o embed_me1.ml embed_me2.ml
$ gcc -Wall -I `ocamlc -where` -o final.native embed_native.o main.c \
    -L `ocamlc -where` -lasmrun -ltermcap -lm -ldl
$ ./final.native
Before calling OCaml
hello embedded world 1
hello embedded world 2
After calling OCaml
```

The embed_native.o is a standalone object file that has no further references to OCaml code beyond the runtime library, just as with the bytecode runtime. Do remember that the link order of the libraries is significant in modern GNU toolchains (especially as used in Ubuntu 11.10 and later) that resolve symbols from left to right in a single pass.

Activating the Debug Runtime

Despite your best efforts, it is easy to introduce a bug into some components, such as C bindings, that causes heap invariants to be violated. OCaml includes a libasmrund.a variant of the runtime library which is compiled with extra debugging checks that perform extra memory integrity checks during every garbage collection cycle. Running these extra checks will abort the program nearer the point of corruption and help isolate the bug in the C code.

To use the debug library, just link your program with the -runtime-variant d flag:

```
$ ocamlopt -runtime-variant d -verbose -o hello.native hello.ml
+ as   -o 'hello.o' '/tmp/build_cd0b96_dune/camlasmd3c336.s'
+ as   -o '/tmp/build_cd0b96_dune/camlstartup9d55d0.o'
    '/tmp/build_cd0b96_dune/camlstartup2b2cd3.s'
+ gcc -O2 -fno-strict-aliasing -fwrapv -pthread -Wall
    -Wdeclaration-after-statement -fno-common
    -fexcess-precision=standard -fno-tree-vrp -ffunction-sections
    -Wl,-E   -o 'hello.native'
    '-L/home/yminsky/.opam/rwo-4.13.1/lib/ocaml'
    '/tmp/build_cd0b96_dune/camlstartup9d55d0.o'
    '/home/yminsky/.opam/rwo-4.13.1/lib/ocaml/std_exit.o' 'hello.o'
    '/home/yminsky/.opam/rwo-4.13.1/lib/ocaml/stdlib.a'
    '/home/yminsky/.opam/rwo-4.13.1/lib/ocaml/libasmrund.a' -lm -ldl
$ ./hello.native
### OCaml runtime: debug mode ###
Initial minor heap size: 256k words
Initial major heap size: 992k bytes
```

```
Initial space overhead: 120%
Initial max overhead: 500%
Initial heap increment: 15%
Initial allocation policy: 2
Initial smoothing window: 1
Hello OCaml World!
```

27.4   Summarizing the File Extensions

We've seen how the compiler uses intermediate files to store various stages of the compilation toolchain. Here's a cheat sheet of all them in one place.

- .ml are source files for compilation unit module implementations.
- .mli are source files for compilation unit module interfaces. If missing, generated from the .ml file.
- .cmi are compiled module interface from a corresponding .mli source file.
- .cmo are compiled bytecode object file of the module implementation.
- .cma are a library of bytecode object files packed into a single file.
- .o are C source files that have been compiled into native object files by the system cc.
- .cmt are the typed abstract syntax tree for module implementations.
- .cmti are the typed abstract syntax tree for module interfaces.
- .annot are old-style annotation file for displaying typed, superseded by cmt files.

The native code compiler also generates some additional files.

- .o are compiled native object files of the module implementation.
- .cmx contains extra information for linking and cross-module optimization of the object file.
- .cmxa and .a are libraries of cmx and o units, stored in the cmxa and a files respectively. These files are always needed together.
- .S or .s are the assembly language output if –S is specified.

Index